Integrating Advanced Computer–Aided Design, Manufacturing, and Numerical Control:
Principles and Implementations

Xun Xu
University of Auckland, New Zealand

INFORMATION SCIENCE REFERENCE

Hershey · New York

Director of Editorial Content: Kristin Klinger
Director of Production: Jennifer Neidig
Managing Editor: Jamie Snavely
Assistant Managing Editor: Carole Coulson
Typesetter: Jeff Ash
Cover Design: Lisa Tosheff
Printed at: Yurchak Printing Inc.

Published in the United States of America by
         Information Science Reference (an imprint of IGI Global)
         701 E. Chocolate Avenue, Suite 200
         Hershey PA 17033
         Tel: 717-533-8845
         Fax: 717-533-8661
         E-mail: cust@igi-global.com
         Web site: http://www.igi-global.com/reference

and in the United Kingdom by
         Information Science Reference (an imprint of IGI Global)
         3 Henrietta Street
         Covent Garden
         London WC2E 8LU
         Tel: 44 20 7240 0856
         Fax: 44 20 7379 0609
         Web site: http://www.eurospanbookstore.com

Library of Congress Cataloging-in-Publication Data

Xu, Xun, 1959-
Integrating advanced computer-aided design, manufacturing, and numerical control : principles and implementations / by Xun Xu.

       p. cm.

Includes bibliographical references and index.
Summary: "This book presents basic principles of geometric modelling while featuring contemporary industrial case studies"--Provided by publisher.

ISBN 978-1-59904-714-0 (hardcover) -- ISBN 978-1-59904-716-4 (ebook)

1. Design, Industrial--Data processing. 2. Geometrical models--Data processing. 3. CAD/CAM systems. I. Title.
TS171.4.X86 2009
670.285--dc22
                              2008033938

British Cataloguing in Publication Data
A Cataloguing in Publication record for this book is available from the British Library.

Dedication

To my wife Wei Cui, my daughters Sylvia and Cecilia, and to our parents Zuxing Xu and Huaizhen Zhou, for their endless love, support and inspiration

Table of Contents

Section I:
Principles and Backgrounds

Chapter I
Geometric Modelling and Computer-Aided Design 1

Chapter II
CAD Data Exchange and CAD Standards 32

Section II:
Integration and Implementations

Chapter X
Integration of CAD/CAPP/CAM/CNC 231

Foreword

The late Dr. M. Eugene Merchant, then director of research planning of Cincinnati Milacron Inc., made an interesting Delphi-type technological forecast of the future of production engineering at the General Assembly of CIRP in 1971. Five years later, he made another report on the "Future Trends in Manufacturing – Towards the Year 2000" at the 1976 CIRP GA. He reported that between now (1976) and the then (2000), the overall future trend in manufacturing will be towards the implementation of the computer-integrated automatic factories. More than 30 years have since whisked past, most heartedly, manufacturing technology had progressed even faster than Dr. Merchant's prediction.

One of the forerunners of automated manufacturing is the CAD/CAM technology which had made its debut more than 30 years ago. Numerous research papers and books have since been written on the topic. As new technologies constantly emerge and efficient IT tools, and faster and affordable computing facilities become more pervasive, the demand for updating the development of this field is clear. The author of this book has put together a comprehensive perspective of computer-aided design, manufacturing and numerical control, addressing their retrospective developments, present state-of-the-art review and future trends and directions.

Design, in particular, underpins all manufacturing activities at an early stage of a product development process. The design stage is well known to have the capability of locking in most of the subsequent costs, and any changes made will prove to be unwise and expensive. Concurrent engineering has provided a solution to this problem to some extent, but not a panacea. The intricacy and interactions of all the related activities, such as business needs, time-to-market requirement, ecological aspects of manufacturing, and so forth, would need to be thoroughly understood. This book has elucidated many connected aspects of automated manufacturing such as CAD, CNC, CAD/CAM, CAPP, STEP, PDM, PLM, expert systems, evolutionary computing techniques, and so forth, in a single volume. In particular, the theoretical and practical aspects of these technologies, which may be integrated effectively, have been addressed. It provides an invaluable updated text and reference for senior students, researchers, and practitioners. I am delighted that the author has generously shared years of his own research expertise, as well as those of the others with such a fine effort.

I congratulate the author on having produced this splendid new book.

A. Y. C. Nee, DEng, PhD
National University of Singapore
Fellow of Institution of Engineers, Singapore
Fellow of Society of Manufacturing Engineers (SME), USA
Fellow of International Academy for Production Engineering Research (CIRP)
Regional Editor for International Journal of Advanced Manufacturing Technology
Regional Editor for International Journal of Machine Tools and Manufacture
Associate Editor for Journal of Manufacturing Systems
Associate Editor for Journal of Manufacturing Processes

A.Y.C. Nee is a professor of manufacturing engineering, Department of Mechanical Engineering, National University of Singapore (NUS) since 1989. He received his PhD and DEng from Manchester and UMIST respectively. His research interest is in computer applications to tool, die, fixture design and planning, distributed manufacturing systems, virtual and augmented reality applications in manufacturing. He is a Fellow of CIRP and a fellow of the Society of Manufacturing Engineers (USA), both elected in 1990. He had held appointments as head of the Department of Mechanical Engineering, Dean of Faculty of Engineering, co-director of Singapore-MIT Alliance (SMA), and currently, he is the director of Research Administration of NUS. He has over 200 refereed journal publications and 8 authored and edited books. Currently, he is regional editor of the International Journal of Advanced Manufacturing Technology *and the* International Journal of Machine Tools and Manufacture. *He is also editorial board member of some 20 refereed journals in the areas of manufacturing and precision engineering.*

Preface

Since the very first computer (Electronic Numerical Integrator And Computer, ENIAC for short) was conceived, designed, and built in 1946 at the University of Pennsylvania's Moore School of Electrical Engineering, its impact on almost all walks of our lives has been readily recognisable. Computers have certainly been responsible for the modern manufacturing industry that exists today. Indeed, applications of computers have been found in the entire spectrum of the product development process, ranging from conceptual design to product realization and even recycling.

Nowadays, regardless of company size, every manufacturing organization needs a well thought-out, long-term strategy in investing computer-related technologies, solutions, and systems. Selecting vendors and defining the scope of each business system from a plethora of rapidly changing options is incredibly difficult. Claims and testimonials are hard to evaluate against your business requirements. Previous generations of computer-based systems have had clean boundaries between system types as well as data formats, such as computer-aided design, process planning and manufacturing (CAD/CAPP/CAM), computer numerical control (CNC), product data management (PDM), and product lifecycle management (PLM) systems; whereas boundaries between today's products and product development processes are fuzzy. Some vendors offer a full suite of products covering "all" needs, nicely linked together, while others focus on a specific business need and provide a "best-of-breed" system, leaving it to customers to debate the benefits of each. Most users, even those choosing a product suite, will need to interface or integrate with multiple systems. Each organization and the systems to be interfaced and integrated have unique requirements and necessitate comparing those needs to the organization's long-term interconnection strategy.

COMPUTER AIDED TECHNOLOGIES

One of the areas that computers were first used to assist in engineering process is design, hence the birth of computer-aided design technology. Three-dimensional (3-D) computer-aided design models led to the development of new branches of technologies such as computational graphics and geometric modelling. These technologies are needed to serve as the underlying principles for a complete and unambiguous internal representation of any product. The wire-frame and surface-based models were first developed. A need for solid modelling then arose with the development of application programs such as numerical control (NC) verification codes and automatic mesh generation for finite element analysis (FEA). The research work on solid modelling technology commenced in the mid-1970s, and a decade later the technology was seen to be utilized by a number of CAD systems that are advanced enough to represent most of the common geometric entities, thanks to the underpinning solid modelling kernels such as ACIS®, Parasolid®, and Granite®. Most of these systems use a boundary representation (B-rep) scheme to represent 3-D information. It is also noticeable that computer hardware advancements have been in company with the development of geometric modelling techniques and CAD systems. The hierarchy of CAD hardware resources has progressed from large-scale computers to workstations and PCs. This trend was not accompanied by a reduction in functionality, owing to the rapid advancement of computer hardware.

Two critical advancements in the domain of computer-aided design are *parametric* and *feature-based design* (FBD) technology. Parametric design is a method of linking dimensions and variables to geometry in such a way that when the values change, the part changes as well – hence the dimension-driven capability. Designing with pre-defined features can reduce the number of input commands substantially. The most valuable attribute however, is the fact that the features can be used to capture the designer's intent as well as to convey other engineering connotations.

These days, users can easily be "spoiled" by a large number of choices of CAD systems offering targeted competitive solutions. While this may not be a bad thing, the data compatibility, or lack of it, has proven to be more than a nuisance. Companies are more and more involved in manufacturing various parts of their end-products using different subcontractors, many of whom are often geographically diverse as well as operationally heterogeneous. The rise of such globalization has created an acute need for sharing and exchanging information among vendors involved in multi-disciplinary projects. Accurate data transmission is of paramount importance. Thus, a mechanism for good data transfer is needed. Direct data translators provide a direct solution, which entails translating the modelling data stored in a product database directly from one CAD system format to another, usually in one step. A more viable option however, is the use of a common translator, which converts a proprietary CAD data format into a neutral data format and vice versa. This neutral data format may be of an international or industry accepted data format or a proprietary data format. Among these standards is STEP (Standard for the Exchange of Product model data), the only international standard that is soon becoming the norm of product data exchange.

Representation of a product's geometry and topology is just the beginning of any product development process. Manufacturing is often one of many subsequent activities. When computers are used to assist process planning and manufacturing activities (i.e. CAPP and CAM), multiple benefits can be derived. CAPP relies on the produce model data provided by a CAD system to perform precise and consistent process planning for manufacturing. The key research issue herein stems from the differing product descriptions used, (i.e. CAD is usually geometry-based whereas CAPP is manufacture-oriented (Zhou, Qiu, Hua, Wang & Ruan, 2007). It is a common practice to use design features in a CAD model and manufacturing features in a CAPP and/or CAM system. Design features are stereotypical shapes related to a part's function, its design intent, or the model construction methodology, whereas manufacturing features are stereotypical shapes that can be made by typical manufacturing operations (Shen & Shah, 1994). A feature, be it a design feature or a manufacturing feature, can be represented as a collection of faces or a solid. Careful examination about which representation scheme suits the jobs of process planning and manufacturing best, suggests that the volumetric scheme has more advantages over the surface scheme (Xu, 2001).

The differences between design features and machining features, and the need for "deriving" one from the other, have led to a new field of research: feature recognition. Specifically, the goal is to bridge the gap between a CAD database and a CAPP system by automatically recognizing features of a part from the data stored in the CAD system. Based on the recognized features, then one has to drive the CAPP system which produces process plans for manufacturing the part. It is important to acknowledge that the task of recognizing manufacturing features still remains with the usage of a feature-based design (FBD) tool. The reason is obvious; design features would be used in a FBD system and manufacturing features are needed for process planning. Difficulties in developing a generic feature recognition system arise from both presentational challenges of specifying the analysis required, and from computational challenges (Corney, Hayes, Sundararajan & Wright, 2005). When features come to interact with one another, recognizing and interpreting them can be even more difficult. Feature interactions tend to violate feature validity one way or another, which in turn may affect the semantics of a feature, ranging from slight changes in actual parameter values, to some substantial alterations to both geometry and topology, or even complete suppression of its contribution to the model shape. More importantly, feature interactions also impact on process planning and manufacturing.

Let there be no doubt that features are a common thread in any CAD, CAPP, CAM, or CNC system. They are often used to interface or integrate CAD, CAPP, CAM, and CNC. However, confusion often exists between integrated and interfaced feature technologies. One difference between interfacing and integration is that interfacing can be achieved at the result level, while integration must be addressed at the task level. In order to achieve an integrated environment and to make sure the features formed can be directly related to machining processes, machining information needs to be considered, such as roughing and finishing operations, as well as the cutting tools that may be used. In a feature-based design system, feature mapping from design to manufacturing can be an option.

The process plan for a part is usually further processed in a CAM system/module to obtain a set of machine control data (MCD), which is then used to drive a CNC machine tool. Numerical controllers were developed in the late 1940s and early 1950s by John T. Parsons in collaboration with the MIT Servomechanisms Laboratory. The first CNC systems still used NC-style hardware where the computer was used for the tool compensation calculations and sometimes for editing. Today's CNC machines have advanced to a point of little resemblance to their predecessors. With the increased automation of manufacturing processes using CNC machining, considerable improvements in consistency and quality have been achieved.

The MCD codes (or G-codes) used on a CNC machine contain mostly sequential machining commands that are structured in blocks of data. An alternative to G-codes when it comes to manually programming a CNC machine is the Automatic Programming Tool (APT). APT can describe some simple parts without using a 3-D modelling system or a graphics user interface. For complicated parts however, one has to use some of the contemporary tools (e.g. CAD/CAM systems). These systems can work with a design model, which is augmented with manufacturing information such as machining features and machining parameters, to arrive at a process plan.

In the recent past, manufacturing companies have been facing increasingly frequent and unpredictable market changes. As such, there is a recognised need for CNC machine tools to be further advanced so that they become more open, adaptable, interoperable, distributable, reconfigurable, and modular. Issues related to both hardware and software need more attention. More research seems to have been directed toward software improvement rather than hardware improvement. A noticeable advancement has been the development, publication, and implementations of a new international standard for CNC data models, (i.e. STEP AP238 or ISO 14649, both collectively known as STEP-NC). Unlike G-codes, STEP-NC contains higher-level information such as machining features.

FROM "POINT SOLUTIONS" TO A "COMPLETE SOLUTION"

Technologies developed for CAD, CAPP, CAM, and CNC are by and large localized within each of their domains, forming so-called individual "automation islands". Though there has been some success in bringing CAD, CAPP, and CAM under the same roof, there has been a lack of a universal platform on which data conversion across the board can be kept to a minimum. In fact, the gap between CAD/CAPP/CAM and CNC is even larger.

The STEP standard was initially designed to offer a neutral data exchange method in replacement of IGES. However, the standard is much more than a neutral data format that translates geometrical data between CAD systems. The ultimate goal of STEP is to provide a complete computer-interpretable product data format, so that users can integrate business and technical data to support the whole product life cycle: design, analysis, manufacturing, sales, and customer services. Currently, most of the commercial CAD systems can output STEP AP203 and/or STEP AP214 files via STEP translators. By implementing STEP AP203 and STEP AP214 within CAD systems, data exchange barriers are only partially upheaved in a heterogeneous design environment. This is because both APs only document pure geometric information, leaving high-level data such as features behind. Furthermore, data exchange problems between CAD/CAPP/CAM and CNC systems still remain unsolved. This is because on the output side of a CAM system, the 50-year-old international standard ISO 6983 (i.e. G-code) still dominates the control systems of most CNC machines. Outdated, yet still widely used, ISO 6983 has become an impediment for the contemporary collaborative manufacturing environment (Xu & He, 2004).

In order to achieve a complete integration of CAD, CAPP, CAM, and CNC, a suite of STEP Application Protocols may be used. When STEP AP224 is used to bridge CAD with CAPP, information more than just geometry and topology can be shared. This information includes machining feature information; dimensional and geometric tolerances; material properties and process properties; and even administrative information. STEP AP240 can support macro process planning by connecting CAPP with CAM. This is because AP240 defines such a high-level process plan for a machined part, and contains data about manufacture of a single piece or assembly of single piece parts. It serves as an interface for capturing technical data out of the upstream application protocols, and issuing work instructions for the tasks required to manufacture a part and the information required to support NC programming of processes specified in the process plan.

After macro process planning comes the micro process planning, which acts as a link between CAM and CNC. This can be done via STEP-NC. STEP-NC defines the process information for a specific class of machine tools. It describes the task of removing volumes defined as AP224 machining features in a sequential order, with specific tolerances, and with tools that meet all engineering and design requirements. In essence, STEP-NC describes "tasks", while G-code describes "methods" for CNC machines. The task-based NC programs can be made portable across different machine tools. Modifications at the shop-floor can also be saved and transferred back to the planning department that enables a better exchange and preservation of experience and knowledge.

Different STEP Data Access Interfaces (SDAI) may be used for implementing a STEP-compliant environment. Thus integrated product data can be easily managed by making complex engineering applications available across data implementations. Use of STEP-NC in replacement of G-code also promises a new generation of CNCs that are open, adaptable, and distributed. Alongside STEP-NC, the function block technology offers a complementary solution. Function blocks are based on an explicit event driven model and can provide for data flow and finite state automata-based control. Based on previous research, function blocks can be used as the enabler to encapsulate process plans, integrate with a third-party dynamic scheduling system, monitor process plans during execution, and control machining jobs under normal and abnormal conditions. They are suitable for machine-level monitoring, shop-floor execution control and CNC control (Wang & Shen, 2003).

EXTENDING INTEGRATION IN VERTICAL AND HORIZONTAL DIMENSIONS

Integration does not stop at CAD/CAPP/CAM/CNC, since the business of product development and manufacturing goes beyond activities such as design, process planning, and machining. Extension of an integrated CAD/CAPP/CAM/CNC system may occur in both vertical and horizontal dimensions.

Vertical integration may be backward or forward in the spectrum of a product development process. An example of forward vertical integration can be inspection as it is a logic step after CNC machining. With inspections, Closed-Loop Machining (CLM) can be realized to maximize the efficiency of a machining process by exercizing a tight control in a manufacturing system. Probing is defined in STEP-NC for inspection operations, and the dimensional inspection data model is specified in ISO 10303 AP219. Hence, it has become possible to consolidate machining and inspection operations in one single program.

Likewise, businesses have increasingly moved to outsourcing many functions, leading to the need for horizontal integration. Companies that have been practicing CAD/CAPP/CAM/CNC integration have now realized that there is a need to operate in a much broader scope with wider boundaries. This leads to the increased implementation of PDM and PLM systems. PDM systems integrate and manage all applications, information, and processes that define a product, from design to manufacture, and to end-user support. PLM brings PDM into an even broader paradigm in that all the information pertaining to the lifecycle of a product is actively managed. Unlike PDM, PLM is much more than a technology or software product. PLM is a strategic business approach that empowers the business.

Extensions of CAD/CAPP/CAM/CNC integration, be it vertical or horizontal, have a common request for an environment in which manufacturing businesses should operate. Today, companies often have operations distributed around the world, and production facilities and designers are often in different locations. Such globalization means that companies should be able to design anywhere, build anywhere, and maintain anywhere at any time. Manufacturing engineers need to employ collaborative tools during planning to help improve production processes, plant designs and tooling, and to allow earlier impact on product designs. For all of this to happen in an orderly manner, an effective collaborative environment is a must. STEP and XML combined with the latest multi-tiered network technology can provide such a solution.

EMBRACING THE TECHNOLOGIES

While computers have proven to be instrumental in the advancement of modern product design and manufacturing processes, the role that various technologies have played can never be over-estimated. In the recent years, there has been a wealth of technologies being used in CAD/CAPP/CAM/CNC. Among them are the knowledge-based (expert) system, artificial neural network, genetic algorithm, agent-based technology, fuzzy logic, Petri Nets, and ant colony optimisation.

An expert system is a computer system that has a well-organized body of knowledge in a bounded domain, and is able to simulate the problem solving skill of a human expert in a particular field. Artificial neural networks, or simply neural networks, are techniques that simulate the human neuron function, using the weights distributed among their neurons to perform implicit inference. Neural networks have been used to assist both automatic feature recognition and process planning. Genetic algorithms mimic the process of natural evolution by combining the survival of the fittest among solution structures with a structured, yet randomized, information exchange. The agent-based technology utilizes agents as intelligent entities capable of independently regulating, reasoning and decision-making to carry out actions and to achieve a specific goal or a set of goals. Agent-based approaches enable functionality for distributed product design and manufacturing (i.e. modularity, reconfigurability, scalability, upgradeability and robustness). Other technologies such as fuzzy logic, Petri Nets, and ant colony optimisation methods have also been used. There is, however, a consensus that systems developed using a combination of two or more such technologies fare better than otherwise.

ORGANIZATION OF THE BOOK

The book is organized into two sections and altogether 17 chapters. Section I, titled "Principles and Backgrounds", contains Chapters I-IX; and Section 2, named "Integration and Implementations", contains Chapters X-XVII. A brief description of each of the chapters follows:

Chapter I, "Geometric Modelling and Computer-Aided Design" reviews various geometric modelling approaches, such as wire-frame, surface, and solid modelling techniques. Basic computational geometric methods for defining simple entities such as curves, surfaces, and solids are given. Concepts of parametric, variational and feature-based design in a CAD system are explained.

Chapter II "CAD Data Exchange and CAD Standards" discusses the data interoperability issues, such as the different types of data translation and conversion methods. The common data exchange protocols are explained together with some examples. These data exchange protocols include DXF, IGES, PDES, and STEP standards.

Chapter III, "Computer-Aided Process PLannning and Manufacturing" presents the basic concepts of, and steps taken by, a computer-aided process planning and manufacturing system. Two principal approaches of CAPP are discussed. They are manual experience-based planning method and computer-aided process method.

Chapter IV, "Feature Technology" gives an overall view of feature technology. Features are defined and classified according to design and manufacturing applications. Issues about surface and volume features are discussed and different feature-based methodologies are presented.

Chapter V, "Feature Recognition" discusses some of the basic issues and methodologies concerning feature recognition. Feature recognition systems are divided into two different types: feature detection and feature generation. Issues regarding concavity and convexity of a geometric entity, optimal interpretation of machineable volumes and the necessity of considering raw workpieces are all discussed at a length.

Chapter VI, "Feature Interactions" analyses the feature-feature interaction problems, which have a strong bearing on process planning. Feature interactions may be studied on the basis of surface information and volumetric information of a part. Either way, identification of interacting entities is the key to an effective way of dealing with feature interactions.

Chapter VII, "Integrated Feature Technology" addresses feature technologies from the integration point of view. When features are recognized, the related machining operations and cutting tools are considered. For a feature-based system, mapping design features to machining features can be an effective method.

Chapter VIII, "CNC Machine Tools" presents an overview of CNC machine tools and their designations of axis and motion. The tooling for CNC machine tools is also discussed.

Chapter IX, "Program CNCs" provides a detailed account of the basics of CNC programming. The emphasis is on the G-codes and APT. To programme using G-codes, both compensation and interpolation are the key issues.

Chapter X, "Integration of CAD/CAPP/CAM/CNC" begins with a general description of traditional CAD/CAPP/CAM/CNC integration models. This is followed by an industry case study showcasing how a proprietary CAD/CAM system can be used to achieve centralized integration.

Chapter XI, "Integration Based on STEP Standards" presents a scenario whereby CAD, CAPP, CAM, and CNC are fully integrated. The underlying mechanisms are those enabled by the STEP standard, or rather its suite of Application Protocols. Function blocks also contribute to building such an integrated environment.

Chapter XII, "Function Block-Enabled Integration" introduces the function block architecture that has been implemented in two types of integration. The first brings together CAD, CAPP, and CAM and the second connects CAM with CNC.

Chapter XIII, "Development of An Integrated, Adaptable CNC System" discusses topics related to the task-level and method-level information in machine control data, and the methodology of converting the task-level data to the method-level data.

Chapter XIV, "Integrating CAD/CAPP/CAM/CNC with Inspections" discusses the extension of CAD, CAPP, CAM, and CNC to include inspections. The objective is to maximize the efficiency of a machining process by maintaining a tight control in a manufacturing system.

Chapter XV, "Internet-Based Integration" describes the methods of developing an Internet-enabled, integrated CAD, CAPP, CAM, and CNC system to support collaborative product development. The main goal is to provide a team environment enabling a group of designers and engineers to collaboratively develop a product in real time.

Chapter XVI, "From CAD/CAPP/CAM/CNC To PDM, PLM, and Beyond" presents an even broader scope and wider boundary in which CAD, CAPP, CAM, and CNC systems need to operate, (i.e. PDM and PLM). PDM systems integrate and manage all applications, information, and processes about a product. PLM brings PDM into an even broader scope in that all the information pertaining to the lifecycle of a product is actively managed.

Chapter XVII, "Key Enabling Technologies" discusses some key enabling technologies in the field of design and manufacturing. These are knowledge-based systems, artificial neural network, genetic algorithm, and agent-based technology. Also briefly mentioned are the fuzzy logic, Petri Nets, and ant colony optimisation methods.

WHO AND HOW TO READ THIS BOOK

This book has three groups of people as its potential audience, (i) senior undergraduate students and postgraduate students conducting research in the areas of CAD, CAPP, CAM, CNC, and their integration; (ii) researchers at universities and other institutions working in these fields; and (iii) practitioners in the R&D departments of an organization working in these fields. This book differs from other books that also have CAD, CAPP, CAM, and CNC as the focus in two aspects. First of all, integration is an essential theme of the book. Secondly, STEP is used as a common data model for many integration implementations.

The book can be used as an advanced reference for a course taught at the postgraduate level. It can also be used as a source of modern computer-aided technologies and contemporary applications in the areas of CAD, CAPP, CAM, CNC, and beyond, since some 300 hundreds publications have been cited and listed in the reference lists of all chapters, in particular Chapter XVII.

As the book title suggests, the book commences with presentations of some of the basic principles (in Section I) and ends with integration implementations as well as implementation approaches (in Section II). For readers who need a "crash course" or revision on topics of CAD, CAPP, CAM, and CNC, in addition to integration issues, both sections of the book can be found useful. Those who are well informed about these topics and only have an interest in integration issues can start with Section II, for instance Chapter X, or even better start with Chapter VII which discusses the integration issues based on feature concepts. Those who are conversant with CAD and CAM technologies but less acquainted with topics in CNC may skip the first 7 chapters.

As mentioned above, this book can also be used as an introduction to STEP data models, their principles, and implementations. Should this be of a reader's interest, the following chapters may be considered for study, (a) Chapter II to read for some introduction to STEP and its use in exchanging CAD data; (b) Chapter XI to read for a grand idea of STEP-in, STEP-out and STEP-throughout as in an integration implementation; (c) Chapter XIV to see how a STEP-based integration between machining and inspection may be achieved; and (d) Chapter XV to see how an Internet-based integration may be realized using STEP.

REFERENCES

Corney, J., Hayes, C., Sundararajan, V., & Wright, P. (2005) The CAD/CAM Interface: A 25-year retrospective, *Transactions of ASME, Journal of Computing and Information Science in Engineering, 5*, 188-196.

Shen, Y., & Shah, J. J. (1994). Feature recognition by volume decomposition using half-space partitioning. *Advances in Design Automation, ASME, 1*, 575-583.

Wang, L., & Shen, W. (2003). *DPP:* An agent-based approach for distributed process planning. *Journal of Intelligent Manufacturing, 14*(5), 429-439.

Xu, X. (2001). Feature Recognition Methodologies and Beyond. *Australian Journal of Mechanical Engineering, ME25*(1), 1-20.

Xu, X., & He, Q. (2004). Striving for a total integration of CAD, CAPP, CAM and CNC. *Robotics and Computer Integrated Manufacturing, 20*, 101-109.

Zhou, X., Qiu, Y., Hua, G., Wang, H., & Ruan, X. (2007) A feasible approach to the integration of CAD and CAPP. *Computer-adied Design, 39*, 324-338.

Acknowledgment

This book bears years of my teaching and research at the University of Auckland, New Zealand. In particular, I am indebted to two groups of people whose research vigour and output constitute the bulk of the chapters. First of all, I feel fortunate to be able to draw upon a wealth of knowledge and expertise from a number of international collaborators. Although it is impossible to mention all of them, I would like to thank Professor Sri Hinduja at the University of Manchester (then UMIST) for leading me into the intriguing world of CAD/CAPP/CAM through my PhD program, Professor Stephen Newman at the University of Bath for introducing me into the new era of CAD/CAPP/CAM, i.e. STEP-NC, Mr. Fredrick Proctor, Dr. Thomas Kramer and Mr. John Michaloski at the National Institute of Standards and Technology (NIST) for hosting my research leave at NIST and giving me a much needed early education of STEP, Dr. Lihiu Wang at the National Research Council of Canada for his induction of Function Block technology, Professor Kevin Rong at the Worchester Polytechnic University for sharing his knowledge in the area of process planning and fixture design, and Professor Andrew Nee at the National University of Singapore for kindly supplying the Forward of this book. Another group of people are my research students; without their dedicated work in my research group, this book would not be a reality. To only name a few, these students are Tony Liu, Jin Mao, Hongqiang Wang, Mohamad Bin Minhat, Fiona Zhao, Albert Yang, Yanyan Wang, Lankesh Madduma, Salah Habeeb, Renaud Gardes, Michel Wagner, Hugo Bouyer, Sébastien Armando, Mathieu Bravo, Adrien Moller, Christian Mose, Iñigo Lazcanotegoi Larrarte, Tobias Dipper, Alireza Mokhtar and of course many more.

Directly and indirectly, I benefited immensely from my interactions with a large number of industries, research institutions and universities around the world, such as Boeing, Airbus, Sandvik, STEP Tools Inc., Fisher&Paykel, International Organisation of Standards (ISO), Standards Australia, China National Engineering Research Centre for High-end CNC, Japan National Institute of Advanced Industrial Science and Technology, ISW University of Stuttgart, RWTH Aachen University, Loughborough University, University of Vigo, Shandong University, Shenyang Ligong University, Shenyang Jianzhu University, Southeast University, Huazhong University of Science and Technology, Xi'an Jiaotong University and Pohang University of Science and Technology.

Special gratitude goes towards the reviewers of this book whose comments and suggestions at various stages of this book project were very helpful in reshaping the final version of the text. I am also indebted to Rebecca Beistline as well as the others at IGI Global. I appreciate their patience and understanding during the preparation of the manuscript.

Xun Xu
Unviversity of Auckland, New Zealand

About the Author

Xun Xu has been working in the Department of Mechanical Engineering, The University of Auckland since 1996 after obtaining a PhD from the University of Manchester, then UMIST. Dr. Xu is currently an associate professor of manufacturing systems and leads the "Intelligent and Interoperable Manufacturing Systems" research group. Dr. Xu was a guest researcher at the U.S. National Institute of Standards and Technology (NIST), and a senior research fellow at the Japan National Institute of Advanced Industrial Science and Technology (AIST). He has broad research interests – from CAD/CAPP/CAM/CNC to product lifecycle assessment and management, and from 3D digitisation of artefacts to re-modelling and visualisation, although his recent research work has been around STEP-compliant design and manufacturing, in particular STEP-NC. Dr. Xu has over 100 research publications, and is now serving in a number of editorial boards for international journals and has guest-edited three special journal issues. Dr. Xu also consults extensively in industry and has very close ties with industries both in New Zealand and overseas.

Section I
Principles and Backgrounds

Chapter I
Geometric Modelling and Computer–Aided Design

ABSTRACT

One of the key activities in any product design process is to develop a geometric model of the product from the conceptual ideas, which can then be augmented with further engineering information pertaining to the application area. For example, the geometric model of a design may be developed to include material and manufacturing information that can later be used in computer-aided process planning and manufacturing (CAPP/CAM) activities. A geometric model is also a must for any engineering analysis, such as finite elopement analysis (FEA). In mathematic terms, geometric modelling is concerned with defining geometric objects using computational geometry, which is often, represented through computer software or rather a geometric modelling kernel. Geometry may be defined with the help of a wire-frame model, surface model, or solid model. Geometric modelling has now become an integral part of any computer-aided design (CAD) system. In this chapter, various geometric modelling approaches, such as wire-frame, surface, and solid modelling will be discussed. Basic computational geometric methods for defining simple entities such as curves, surfaces, and solids are given. Concepts of parametric, variational, history-based, and history-free CAD systems are explained. These topics are discussed in this opening chapter because (a) CAD was the very first computer-aided technologies developed and (b) its related techniques and methods have been pervasive in the other related subjects like computer-aided manufacturing. This chapter only discusses CAD systems from the application point of view; CAD data formats and data exchange issues are covered in the second chapter.

INTRODUCTION TO GEOMETRIC MODELLING

The geometric information about an object essentially includes types of surfaces, edges and their dimensions and tolerances. Prior to the availability of commercial CAD systems, this information was represented on blueprints by a draftsperson, hence in a two-dimensional (2D) form. This form of representation has three acute problems. First of all, it is hard to comprehend complex geometry through a 2D form of description. This is particularly true with assemblies that have many components, e.g. an engine assembly. Secondly, the design information in this form is difficult to be archived for a longer period of time and it is cumbersome to search for. Thirdly, it is considered unfit for the modern manufacturing industry in which data management is mostly in the electronic format. As manufacturing rapidly enters into the digital era, the emphasis is on paperless and total integration. That is, the means is being sought for the geometric information to be directly transferred from a CAD database to a CAPP/CAM database (sometimes bi-directional data flow is also required) to enable subsequent manufacture of the part. This way, product development and manufacturing lead time can be significantly shortened. In order to meet the above discussed needs, an accurate, efficient and effective representation of the complete information about a design becomes a prerequisite for many subsequent applications. The remaining of the chapter provides a detailed account of various geometric modelling approaches and the ways today's CAD systems use these modelling approaches.

GEOMETRIC MODELLING APPROACHES

The development of geometric modelling is coupled with three departments of sciences and technologies. They are computer graphics techniques, three-dimensional (3D) geometric representation schemes and computer hardware advances. The research started in the 1960's. The basic geometric modelling approaches used in today's CAD/CAM systems are wire-frame, surface and solid modelling. In the following sections, a basic account of these approaches to geometric modelling is presented.

Wire-Frame Modelling

In the historical roadmap of geometric modelling, wire-frame is the first developed and is also the most basic method of geometric modelling techniques. The techniques were initially developed particularly for computer version of a 3D object. The basic entities in a wire-frame model may include points, lines, arcs and circles, conics, and other type of curves. Figure 1.1 shows the wire-frame representation of a part.

Wire-frame representation may be regarded as an extension into a third dimension of the techniques used for 2D drafting. The construction techniques used for the definition of wire-frame geometry are again broadly similar to those for 2D drafting. Therefore, the wire-frame scheme is relatively straightforward to use, and is the most economical of the 3D schemes in terms of computing time and memory requirements. This is why wire-frame was also well matched for the early models of computer hardware that was probably just capable enough to handle wire-frame representations. The scheme was found, and is till, particularly useful in certain applications involving visualisation of the motion of simple

Figure 1.1. Wire-frame representation

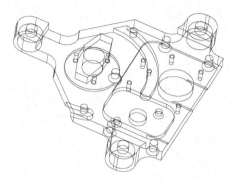

shapes (for example in animating the movement of a mechanism). It however, exhibits a number of serious deficiencies when used to model more complex engineering artefacts (Singh, 1996). These include:

- Ambiguity in representation and possible nonsense objects (Figure 1.2);
- Deficiencies in pictorial representation;
- Limited ability to calculate mechanical properties and geometric intersections;
- Limited value as a basis for manufacture or analysis.

Wire-Frame Entities

Vertices (points) and edges (lines) are the main entities in a wire-frame model. When these entities are represented in a computer, a data structure is used so that management of these entities (e.g. modify, save and load) is made easier. Normally, wire-frame entities are divided into two categorise: analytic and synthetic entities. The choice of a curve in a CAD system depends on the effectiveness of a curve in terms of manipulating complex geometries such as blends, trims and intersections.

Analytic Entities

Analytic entities include points, straight lines, arcs, circles, ellipses, parabolas, and hyperbolas. The properties of these entities and the techniques for manipulating them have been well studied and the math behind them is generally easy to understand. Likewise, the methods for representing these entities in a computer are also relatively straight-forward. Different CAD systems may provide a different set of methods. For example, a straight line may be defined by two 3D vertices, or by an existing line that may be parallel or perpendicular to the line being defined. The latter method suits the modelling option of defining a line with an imbedded reference to an existing one, or simply to support a "copy&paste" option for line creation.

Figure 1.2. Ambiguous wire-frame models

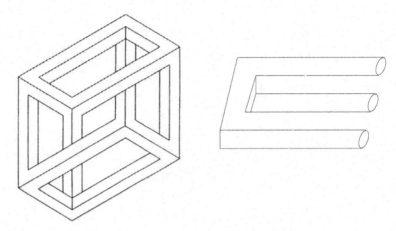

The representation schemes of curves in a CAD system dictate the ways that thousands of curves or lines (including straight lines, a special case of curves) are stored and manipulated. It is important to represent them effectively and efficiently so that the computation effort and storage requirement are minimized. Mathematically, there are two ways of describing a curve, using nonparametric and parametric equations. Both methods may be equally valid to represent a curve. The difficulty of solving a particular problem may be much greater with one method than the other.

Nonparametric Representation of a Curve

In the case of a 2D straight line for example, its nonparametric representation can be defined as $y = x + 1$. This equation defines the x and y coordinates of each point without the assistance of extra parameters. Thus, it is called the nonparametric equation of a line. The same line however may be described by defining the coordinates of each point using equation,

$$L = [x, y]^T = [x = t, y = t + 1]^T \qquad (1.1)$$

where T represents transpose.

In this equation, the coordinates of each point are defined with the help of an "extra" parameter t, hence the name parametric equation. This form of representation is further discussed in the next section.

Nonparametric equations of curves can be further divided into explicit and implicit nonparametric equations. The explicit nonparametric representation of a general 3D curve takes the form of,

$$L = [x, y, z]^T = [x, f(x), g(x)]^T \qquad (1.2)$$

where L is the position vector of the point L in the 3D space.

This equation enables us to obtain the y and z-coordinates of the points on a curve by direct substitution of values of x. This suits well for displaying purposes on a computer as a series of points or straight-line segments are normally used.

The implicit nonparametric representation of a general 3D curve takes the form of,

$$\begin{cases} F(x,y,z) = 0 \\ G(x,y,z) = 0 \end{cases} \tag{1.3}$$

Equation (1.3) expresses the relationship between the coordinates x and y, x and z of each point in the 3D space. Therefore, the relationship between y and z is implicit. This equation, however, must be solved analytically to obtain the explicit form. Whereas it is possible to solve it, accurate data cannot always be guaranteed. This limits its use in CAD systems.

Parametric Representation of a Curve

Parametric representation of a curve, on the other hand, has properties well suited for its use in CAD systems. In the parametric form, each point on a curve is expressed as a function of a parameter t by equations, $x = X(t)$, $y = Y(t)$, and $z = Z(t)$. Equations in this form are also known as parametric or freedom equations for x, y, and z. The value of the parameter t can be either bounded by the minimum (t_{min}) and maximum (t_{max}) range or the normalized range between 0 and 1. The parametric equation for a 3D curve takes the form of,

$$L(t) = [x, y, z]^T = [X(t), Y(t), Z(t)]^T, \quad t_{min} < t < t_{max} \tag{1.4}$$

where $L(t)$ is the point vector and t is the parameter of the equation.

Synthetic Entities

A major part of synthetic entities are synthetic curves. These are more genetic curves that can take virtually any shape in order to meet geometric design requirements of a mechanical part and/or various engineering applications. Take car body as an example. The curves of a car body are usually designed to increase aerodynamic performances as well as to meet the aesthetic requirements. They could take any shape that is required. Other examples include the fuselage, wings, and propeller blades of an aircraft, whose shapes may be purely based on aerodynamic and fluid flow simulations. A third category of products such as the casing for a computer mouse and electrical shaver would be defined mainly on the basis of ergonomics and aesthetic appearance. Some of the common synthetic curves used in the major CAD systems are, Hermite cubic spline, Bézier curves, B-spline curves, Rational B-splines, and Nonuniform rational B-splines.

The main idea of the Hermite cubic spline is that a curve is divided into segments. Each segment is approximated by an expression, namely a parametric cubic function. The general form of a cubic function can be written as,

$$r = V(t) = a_0 + a_1 t + a_2 t^2 + a_3 t^3 \tag{1.5}$$

where the point vector r of the cubic curve is defined by the parametric equation $V(t)$. The segment defined by the equation has highest-degree polynomial t^3. The parameter t is traditionally bounded by the parameter interval $(0 < t < 1)$. The Hermite form of a cubic spline is determined by defining positions and tangent vectors at the actual data points. Therefore, the Hermite curve is based on the interpolation techniques.

Bézier curves on the contrary, are based on approximation techniques that produce curves that do not necessarily pass through all the given data points except the first and the last control points. A Bézier curve does not require first-order derivative; the shape of the curve is controlled by the control points. For $n + 1$ control points, the Bézier curve is defined by a polynomial of degree n as follows,

$$V(t) = \sum_{i=0}^{n} V_i B_{i,n}(t) \qquad\qquad (1.6)$$

where $V(t)$ *is* the position vector of a point on the curve segment and $B_{i,n}$ are the Bernstein polynomials, which serve as the blending or basis function for the Bézier curve.

B-spline is considered a generalization of the Bézier curve. Local control is a specific feature of B-spline curves, which allows changing of a local control point to only affect part of the curve. With Hermite and Bézier curves however, changing one control point (or slope) affects the whole curve. This may cause some inconvenience for designers when they only wish to modify a curve locally.

Rational B-splines (RBSs) are generalizations of B-splines. More specifically, an RBS has an added parameter (also called weight) associated with each control point to control the behaviour of the curve. An RBS can be used to define a variety of curves and surfaces. The most widely used class of RBS is the nonuniform rational B-spline (NURBS). The NURBS is used on a scale that it has almost become a de facto industrial standard. Using a NURBS, a designer can model free-form surfaces by defining a mesh of control points.

Surface Modelling

As the name implies, a surface design model mainly consists of a set of faces. When wire-frame is used to represent a face, only the boundary of a face can be precisely represented, not the actual geometric property of the face itself. For faces such as a plane and cylindrical surface, this may not present a problem. For other more general type of surfaces however, this does create problems. An obvious question one would ask is, "what are the geometric properties of a certain area on the surface represented?"

A surface model scheme may involve representing the model by mathematically specifying all of the surfaces of a component. The representation generally involves a series of geometric entities, each surface forming a single entity. These are often constructed from surface edges and curves on the surface, alongside the geometric properties of the surface. Therefore, surface representations are often mixed with, or developed from, wire-frame representations. Many of the ambiguities of wire-frame models can be overcome by using the surface representation scheme.

In general, real parts are represented using surface geometry by an assembly of surface 'patches (or quilts)' (Figure 1.3). A complete car body, for example, may require several hundred patches. Surface modelling has made great inroads in the branches of engineering such as automobile or mould and die manufacture, where extensive use has traditionally been made of physical models of complex forms. In the automotive industry for example, full-size clay models of body shapes are used for styling purposes, and subsequently to

Figure 1.3. Surface models of a spray gun with (left) and without (right) surface boundaries shown

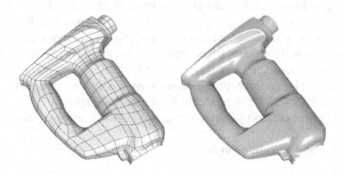

provide master models to define the vehicle form. Surface modelling has allowed the shape of these models to be captured and used for engineering models and for the preparation of instructions to manufacture, for example the dies for sheet metal work. A surface model of an object can be used to determine the cutter path of a machining operation, whereas a wire-frame usually cannot. In such surface modelling systems, a user may input the vertices and edges of a workpiece in a manner that outlines or bounds one face at a time. Surface modelling systems also offer better graphic interaction, although the models are more difficult to create than wire-frame models.

Surface representations are not, however, without their drawbacks. In general they require more skill in construction and use. Models of any complexity are difficult to interpret unless viewed with hidden surfaces removed. As in the case of wire-frame representations, there is also nothing inherent in the surface-modelling scheme to prevent nonsense or erroneous models. There is no indication of which side of a surface is the "solid" side. In other words, the representation of an object is simply in terms of a collection of surfaces with no higher-level information about the solid object. A perfectly constructed surface modelling system may not guarantee that the user has designed a realizable object; that is, the collection of surfaces may not define a valid physical part.

Surfaces Used in a Geometric Model

For argument sake, we define a surface as an unbounded, geometric description of a face. In other words, surface is a pure geometric entity and face carries both geometric and topologic information (e.g. boundaries are connectivity). This point will be better illustrated when solid modelling techniques are discussed latter in this chapter.

Plane Surface

A plane surface is a surface that can be defined by three non-coincident points or its variation. It is the most basic surface in the engineering design. There are of course other ways of defining a plane, e.g. a point and a vector that represents the surface normal.

Ruled Surface

In geometry, a surface is ruled if through every point of it there can be found a straight line that lies on the surface. Apparently, planes, cylinders and cones are all specialised ruled surfaces. In terms of construction, a ruled (lofted) surface can be defined as an interpolation between two straight lines through a determined trajectory be it linear or non linear. The faces of a thread for example are of this type of surface. It is worth noting that this type of surface is favoured by machine tool operators when it comes to manufacturing it. This is to do with the ability with which a machining operation is capable of generating a surface using simple form of cutters often containing straight-line cutting edges.

Bézier Surface and B-Spline Surface

Bézier and B-spline surfaces are both synthetic surfaces. Like synthetic curves, a synthetic surface approximates the given input data, often in form of an array of given points in *3D* space. Bézier and B-spline surfaces are general surfaces that permit twists and kinks. The difference between them, also similar to the case of curves, is that local control is possible for a B-spline surface but not for a Bézier surface. These surfaces can be of any degree, but bicubic Bézier and B-spline generally provide enough degrees of freedom and accuracy of representation for most applications, such as automobile body design.

Analytic Surface Representations

Like a general analytic curve, general analytic surface can also be defined by either an implicit or an explicit equation.

Implicit Equation

$$F(x, y, z) = 0 \tag{1.7}$$

Its geometric meaning is that the locus of the points that satisfy the above constraint equation defines the surface.

Explicit Equation

$$V = [x, y, z]^T = [x, y, f(x, y)]^T \tag{1.8}$$

where V is the position vector of a variable point on the surface. In this equation, the variable point coordinates x, y, z are directly defined. The z coordinates of the position vector of the variable points are defined by x and y through function $f(x, y)$, as shown in Figure 1.4.

Parametric Equation

The above equations illustrate that the points on a surface have two degrees of freedom that are directly controlled by the x and y coordinates. There are no extra parameters in these equations. Therefore, this type of surface representation is called nonparametric representation. The fact that the surface can be controlled by x and y coordinates, also means

Figure 1.4. Explicit equation in surface representation

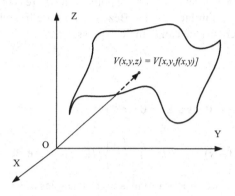

that two parameters (e.g. *s* and *t*) can always be found as the controlling parameters as the *x* and *y* coordinates do. Understandably, the equations that utilize this type of parameter are called parametric equations and can be expressed as follows,

$$V(s, t) = [x, y, z]^T = [X(s, t), Y(s, t), Z(s, t)]^T, \quad s_{min} < s < s_{max}, t_{min} < t < t_{max} \quad (1.9)$$

where *X, Y,* and *Z* are the functions of the two parameters, *s* and *t*.

Synthetic Surface Representations

Hermite Bicubic Surface

As discussed before, synthetic curves are dealt with as curve segments in a single parameter (e.g. *s*) domain. Likewise, synthetic surfaces are defined in patches, each corresponding to a rectangular domain in the *s - t* space. Hermite Bicubic Surface is one of the common types of synthetic surfaces used in CAD systems.

   In mathematic terms, a Hermite Bicubic surface can be described using the following cubic parametric equation,

$$r = V(s,t)$$

$$= \sum_{i=0}^{3} \sum_{j=0}^{3} a_{ij} s^i t^j, \qquad 0 \le s \le 1, \quad 0 \le t \le 1 \qquad (1.10)$$

Note that this is a 16-term, third-power series. Like Hermite bicubic curves, a Hermite surface also requires the values of the tangent vectors at the corners of the surface.

Bézier Surface Patches

Mathematically, the only difference between a Hermite surface patch and a Bézier surface patch is that different basis functions[1] are used. As with the Bézier curve, the Bernstein basis function is used for the Bézier surface patch. Generally, the most common use of

Bézier surfaces is as nets of bi-cubic patches. The geometry of a single bi-cubic patch is thus completely defined by a set of 16 control points. These are typically linked up to form a B-spline surface in the similar way that Bézier curves are linked up to form a B-spline curve. The cubic Bézier surface can then be expressed as,

$$r = V(s,t)$$

$$= \sum_{i=0}^{3} \sum_{j=0}^{3} a_{ij} b_i^3(s) b_j^3(t), \qquad 0 \le s \le 1, \qquad 0 \le t \le 1 \tag{1.11}$$

where, $b_i^3(s) = \binom{3}{i} s^i (1-s)^{3-i}$, $b_j^3(t) = \binom{3}{i} t^j (1-t)^{3-j}$ are Bernstein polynomials.

Bézier patch meshes are superior to meshes of triangles as a representation of smooth surfaces, since they are much more compact, easier to manipulate, and have much better continuity properties. In addition, other common parametric surfaces such as spheres and cylinders can be well approximated by relatively small numbers of cubic Bézier patches. However, Bézier patch meshes are difficult to render directly. Another problem with Bézier patches is that calculating their intersections with lines is difficult, making them awkward for pure ray tracing or other direct geometric techniques which do not use subdivision or successive approximation techniques. They are also difficult to combine directly with perspective projection algorithms.

Uniform Cubic B-Spline Surfaces

Using a corresponding basis function, uniform cubic B-Spline surface can be formed and has a net of control points that define the surface, none of which interpolate the patch, as in the case of the B-spline curve. Likewise, an advantage of B-spline surface is that it supports local control of the surface.

Surface Manipulation

Various surface manipulation techniques are employed in CAD systems. The simplest and most widely used method is to display a surface by a mesh of curves. This is usually called *a mesh* in the CAD software. By holding one parameter constant at a time, a mesh of curves can be generated to represent the surface. Shading of a surface is an effective way of rendering a design model and is available in many CAD systems.

Segmentation and trimming is a way of representing part of a surface with localised interests. Some surfaces can present computational difficulties when split and partitioned. Similar to segmentation and trimming, intersection is another useful function where curves can be defined as a result of intersection.

Sometimes, projection is required by projecting an entity onto a plane or surface. When a curve or surface is projected, the point projections are performed repeatedly. This function is often used in determining shadows of entities. As with the curve transformation, one can translate, rotate, mirror and scale a surface in most CAD systems. To transform a surface, the control points of the surface are evaluated and then transformed to new positions and/or orientations. The new surface is then created according to the newly transformed control points.

Solid Modelling

The geometric representations discussed thus far are essentially partial models, i.e. the three-dimensional representation of edges and/or surfaces. The solid form of an object needs to be inferred from these models and it is not possible the complete solid form of an object can always be obtained from a wire-frame or surface model. Although for many engineering purposes wire-frame and surface models are satisfactory, the increasing application of computers in engineering analysis, or generation of various engineering information, means that representation of an object should be as complete as possible. For this reason, solid model representations have been developed and become a predominate form of design representation. Figure 1.5 shows the two renderings of a solid model initially described as in Figure 1.1.

A solid model is an "informationally complete" representation and in the words of Requicha (1980, 1982), "permits (at least in principle) *any* well-defined geometric property of any represented solid to be calculated automatically". The more complete the representation, the smaller the requirement for human transcription between models, and thus the smaller the risk of errors in transcription. In a simpler term, "solid form" of information about a 3D object is the type of information that can uniquely define two spaces, one denoting the interior of the object and the other denoting the outside of the object. Because of the "completeness" of the information contained in a solid model, it is relatively straightforward for a computer to render a line image with hidden lines removed as seen in Figure 1.5 (a) as well as a real-life, shaded view as seen in Figure 1.5 (b).

The wire-frame and surface modelling approaches, as mentioned earlier, have limited engineering applications. Solid modelling has now found wide applications that cut across functional boundaries, such as the use of solid models with finite-element analysis and fluid flow analysis in the conceptual design of products, numerical control (NC) part programming for computer-aided manufacturing, and generation of computer-aided process plans. Furthermore, solid models can be easily used to evaluate the size, shape, and weight of products early during the conceptual design phase. In a solid modelling system, objects are often defined directly by primitive shapes called building blocks or solid primitives, instead of the surfaces, edges and vertices used in wire-frame and surface modelling.

There are a number of representation schemes for solid modelling, such as boundary representation (B-rep), constructive solid geometry (CSG), destructive solid geometry

Figure 1.5. Rendering the solid model of a part

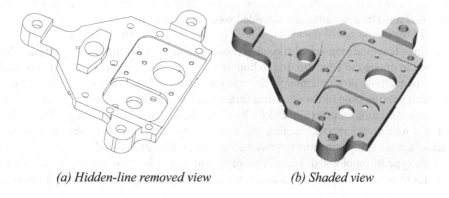

(a) *Hidden-line removed view*   (b) *Shaded view*

(DSG), sweep representation, parameterized primitive instancing, cell decomposition, spatial occupancy (voxel), and analytical solid modelling.

B-rep and CSG are the most widely used representation schemes. For different applications, one may be more suitable than the other. For example, B-rep is more suitable for representing complex designs, whereas with CSG, models are easy to create and are usually used in representing relatively simple objects. In some modellers, a hybrid scheme employing both B-rep and CSG is used. These representation schemes are discussed in more details in the following sections.

Boundary Representation

Boundary representation is a method for representing shapes using the limits, or rather boundaries as the name suggests. A solid is represented as a collection of connected surface elements and the boundary between solid (inside the object) and non-solid (outside the object). The method was initially developed in the early 1970s.

In order to represent a solid object by its surfaces, the orientation of each surface needs to be defined to show the inside or outside of the object. By convention, the inside is the material and the outside is the void space. The direction of the face normal is usually used as the orientation of the face, and the face that carries the orientation information is called orientable surface. This surface normal is usually defined to be always pointing away from the solid. Since a solid is bounded by orientable surfaces, one can define a solid by a set of faces. A face is generally bounded by edges which are bounded by vertices (with the exception of spheres and circles). Although any complex solid can be represented by faces, the system of equations known as Euler's equations (to be further discussed later in this section) is used to ensure the validity of a B-rep model, which is to ensure that a real object is formed, bounded or closed. For example, three planes will not form a solid object. Similarly, a face will not be bounded by two straight lines.

However, boundary representation has now been extended to allow special, non-solid model types called non-manifold models (Lee, 1999). An important sub-class of non-manifold models are sheet objects which are used to represent thin-plate objects and to integrate surface modelling into a solid modelling environment.

Basic Entities and the Connectivity of B-rep

Boundary representation models contain two pieces of critical information, geometry and topology. The main geometric items are: faces, edges and vertices. A face is a bounded portion of a surface; an edge is a bounded piece of a curve (or line) and a vertex lies at a point. Other elements are the shell (a set of connected faces), the loop (a circuit of edges bounding a face) and loop-edge links (also known as winged-edge links or half-edges) which are used to create the edge circuits to bound a face. Equally important in a B-rep model is the connectivity present amongst the topological items (e.g. faces, edges and vertices). The most popular type of the data structure for defining such connectivity is Baumgart's winged-edge data structure (Figure 1.6). Note that the structure is drastically different from that of a wire-frame model, because the winged-edge data structure uses edges to keep track of almost everything and to traverse various entities in the model.

This type of topological data structure is also useful (or "computer-friendly") when it comes to representing data in a computer program. Take a simple cube as an example

Figure 1.6. Winged-edge data structure

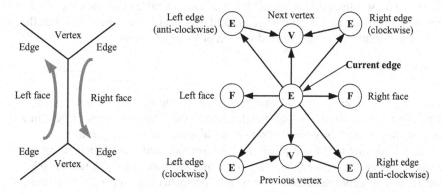

as shown in Figure 1.7. There are 6 faces, each containing a loop of 4 edges. Each edge is bounded by 2 vertices. Every edge is shared by two faces and every vertex is shared by three edges. The edges in a loop are stored in a particular sequence, one after the other, in the database so that the normal of the face (pointing away from the object) is defined using the right-hand rule (e.g. n_1, n_2, n_3 ...) as shown in Figure 1.7 (a). Figure 1.7 (b) illustrates the connections between the faces, edges and vertices. This structure will also be mirrored in a CAD system by a computer program.

Validation of a B-rep Model

Euler's law states that a polyhedron is topologically valid (or a sane solid) if the following equation is satisfied,

$$F-E+V=2 \qquad\qquad (1.12)$$

Figure 1.7. The winged-edge data structure for a cube

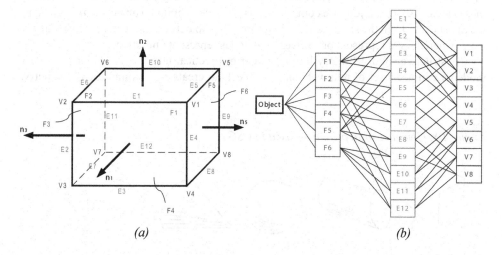

which means that for a polyhedron to be valid, the number of faces (F), edges (E), and vertices (V) must satisfy this equation. For example, a simple cube consists of 6 faces, 12 edges, and 8 vertices, making the object a valid one. In order to cope with solids that have passageways or holes, the generalized version of Euler's law can be used,

$$F-E+V-L = 2(B-G) \qquad (1.13)$$

where F, E, V, L, B, and G are the numbers of faces, edges, vertices, inner loops, bodies, and genera (such as torus, through-hole), respectively. These laws are critical in a CAD system as they govern the construction syntax of a solid modelling kernel.

While B-rep provides a complete set of information and it is explicit, using operators such as "make vertex, make face, kill vertex, and kill face" can be a tedious job to construct a reasonably complex solid. A useful advancement in this regard is the formation and definition of geometric (or form) features. Features in this respect can be defined as logical units that relate to a group of sub-elements (e.g. faces and edged) of the shape. Features are the basis of many other developments, allowing high-level "geometric reasoning" about the shape for comparison, process-planning, manufacturing, etc. Modern CAD systems all have features as the "interface" between the designer and the complicated B-rep modelling kernel. Chapters IV, V and VI discuss the different aspects of a feature.

Constructive Solid Geometry

Constructive solid geometry allows a modeller to create a complex surface or object by using Boolean operators to combine objects. The common Boolean operators include set-theoretic intersection ($\cap$), set-theoretic union ($\cup$), and difference (-). The simplest solid objects used for representation are called primitives. An object is constructed from primitives by means of allowable Boolean operations. Typically they are the objects of simple shape: cuboids, cylinders, spheres, cones, tedious (Figure 1.8).

The allowable primitives vary with different software packages. A primitive can typically be described by a procedure which accepts some number of parameters. For example, a sphere may be described by the coordinates of its centre point, along with a radius value. These primitives can be combined into compound objects using Boolean operations. When these elementary operations are combined, it is possible to build up objects with high complexity starting from the simple ones. Therefore, CSG objects can be represented by binary trees, where leaves represent primitives, and nodes represent operations.

Constructive solid geometry has a number of practical uses. It is popular because a modeller can use a set of relatively simple objects to create very complicated geometry.

Figure 1.8. Common solid primitives used in CSG

Figure 1.9. Different ways of constructing the same part using CSG

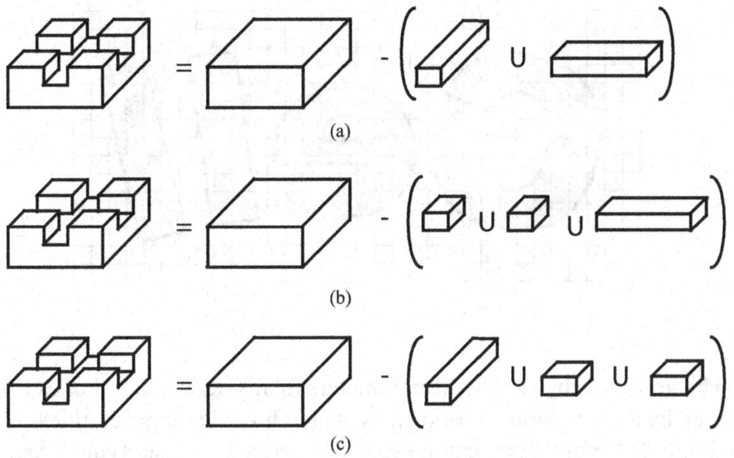

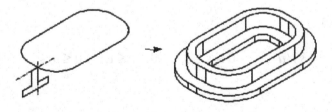

(a)

(b)

(c)

When CSG is procedural or parametric, the user can revise his complex geometry by changing the position of the objects or by changing the Boolean operation(s) used to combine those objects. However, there are some disadvantages, too. For example, CSG is slow in displaying objects. It is usually converted internally into a B-rep model for displaying. This is why many systems are built using both B-rep and CSG. Another problem with CSG is its non-uniqueness in representing an object. Figure 1.9 shows a simple component which can be constructed in three different ways.

Other Types of Representations

Sweep representation defines a solid in terms of volumes swept out by two- or three-dimensional laminae as they move along a curve, which is usually called a path or trajectory. The path types can take virtually any shape, but usually non-self-intersecting. Figure 1.10 shows an inverted "T" cross section sweeping along a closed path to give solid geometry.

The primitive instancing technique is based on a concept that considers an object that has the same topology as a potential primitive (also called generic primitive) but different geometry. Through a set of parameters that govern the topology of the object, different

Figure 1.10. A swept solid

Figure 1.11. Simple regular grid decomposition

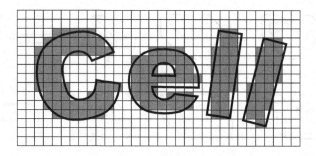

objects can be generated by setting the parameters to different values. For example, a gear can be defined by a set of parameters such as, its pitch-circle diameter, thickness, number of teeth and etc. Different gears can be easily generated by specifying a specific set of parameters. Many CAD systems utilise this type of construction method to provide tables of family parts, e.g. standardised nuts and bolts.

A solid can also be represented by a collection of smaller, often regular volumes or cells that are mutually contiguous and do not interpenetrate. This method is called cell decomposition. The cells may be any shape and do not have to be identical. Use of identical, cuboid cells can simplify the representation and in many cases it is sufficient. Figure 1.11 shows how an array of simple Regular Grids is used to represent a 2D geometry. Each cell is either "empty (white)" if the shape covers less than 50% of the cell, or "full (black)" if the shape covers more than 50% of the cell.

Analytical Solid Modelling

Similar to representing a curve by one-dimensional parametric space with one parameter (e.g. t) and a surface by two-dimensional parametric space with two parameters (e.g. s and t), a solid object can also be represented by three-dimensional parametric space with three parameters (e.g. s, t and u). This method is called analytical solid modelling. The solid thus created is called a parametric solid or a hyperpatch because it is similar to a surface patch in surface representation. The variable point of the solid is given by,

$$V(s, t, u) = [x, y, z] = [x(s, t, u), y(s, t, u), z(s, t, u)],$$
$$s_{min} \leq s \leq s_{max}, \ t_{min} \leq t \leq t_{max}, \ u_{min} \leq u \leq u_{max} \tag{1.14}$$

A general solid can be represented by the following polynomial,

$$r = V(s, t, u)$$
$$= \sum_{i=0}^{3} \sum_{j=0}^{3} \sum_{k=0}^{3} c_{ijk} s^i t^j u^k, \qquad 0 \leq s \leq 1, \qquad 0 \leq t \leq 1, \qquad 0 \leq u \leq 1 \tag{1.15}$$

COMPUTER-AIDED DESIGN

Although development of computer-aided design systems started as early as the 1960's, its progress was severely hampered by the capability of the computers at that time. A decade later, CAD development and implementations began to enter the commercial market. Initially, with 2D in the 1970s, it was typically limited to producing drawings similar to hand-drafted drawings. Advances in programming and computer hardware, notably solid modelling in the 1980s, allowed more versatile applications of computers in design activities. Key products were the solid modelling packages. Among them are Romulus™ (ShapeData) and Uni-Solid (Unigraphics®) based on PADL-2 and the release of the surface modeller Catia® (Dassault Systems); all were released in 1981. Autodesk® was founded 1982 and its product, AutoCAD® soon became one of the most successful 2D CAD systems. The next milestone was the release of Pro/Engineer® (Pro/E® for short) in 1988, which heralded greater usage of feature-based modelling methods and parametric linking of the parameters of features. Also of importance to the development of CAD was the development of B-rep solid modelling kernels (engines for manipulating geometrically and topologically consistent 3D objects) such as Parasolid® (ShapeData) and ACIS® (Spatial Technology Inc.) at the end of the 1980s and beginning of the 1990s. This led to the release of many affordable, mid-range packages such as SolidWorks® in 1995, SolidEdge® (Intergraph™) in 1996, and IronCAD® in 1998. Today, CAD has become one of the main tools for product design and development.

The bulk of the development in commercial CAD systems has been in modelling the form of products (i.e. in providing techniques to assist in the representation of form using conventional drawings or new modelling techniques). The driving force behind CAD has been the desire to improve the productivity of the designer by automating the more repetitive and tedious aspects of design, and also to improve the precision of the design models. New techniques have been developed in an attempt to overcome perceived limitations in conventional practice - particularly in dealing with complexity - for example designs as complex as automobile bodies, or as intricate as integrated circuits. Computer-aided design therefore enables the designer to tackle a task more quickly and accurately, or in a way that could not be achieved by other means.

In principle, CAD could be applied throughout the design process, but in practice its impact on the early stages, where very imprecise representations such as sketches are used extensively, has been limited. It must also be stressed that at present CAD does little in helping a designer in a more creative and intuitive way such as generation of possible design solutions, or in those aspects that involve complex reasoning about the design - for example in assessing, by visual examination of drawings, whether a component may be (easily) made, or whether it matches the specifications. These aspects are, however, the subjects of considerable current research. In practising concurrent engineering, there is a pressing need for CAD systems to interface or integrate design with all the down-stream activities, e.g. manufacturing and marketing.

CAD System Architecture

So far, CAD systems have been described in very general terms. More specifically, they can be thought of as comprising (Figure 1.12),

Figure 1.12. The architecture of a computer-aided design system

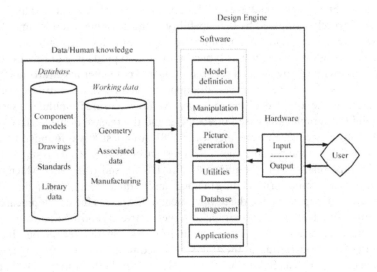

- **hardware:** the computer and associated peripheral equipment;
- **software:** the computer program(s) running on the hardware;
- **data:** the data structure created and manipulated by the software; and
- **human knowledge and activities**.

Today most CAD workstations are Windows®-based PCs; some run on hardware running with one of the UNIX operating systems and a few with Linux. Some others such as NX™ provide multiplatform support including Windows®, LINUX, UNIX and Mac OSX.

Generally no special hardware is required with the exception of perhaps a high-end OpenGL®-based graphics card. However, for complex product design, machines with high speed CPUs and large amount of RAM are recommended. The human-machine interface is generally via a computer mouse but can also be via a pen and a digitizing graphics tablet. Manipulation of the view of a model on the screen is also sometimes done with the use of a SpaceMouse/SpaceBall. Some systems also support stereoscopic glasses for viewing 3D models.

CAD in its Infancy

The original version of CAD is believed to be Computer-aided Drafting tools because in the early days CAD was really a replacement for a traditional drafting board. Computer-aided drafting is mainly concerned with representing the geometry, displaying and manipulating the model, and annotating it to show dimensions, material and other data. The representation itself is, in general, identical to that found on a drafting board. Perhaps the milestone of such a system is the Sketchpad (aka Robot Draftsman), a revolutionary computer program written by Ivan Sutherland in 1963 in the course of his PhD thesis (Sutherland, 1963).

Because the component geometry could be defined precisely and constructed at full size, the risk of error in creation and interrogation of a computer-based drawing is much lower than for the manual equivalent. In addition to lines and curves, drawings also contain other elements that give information, such as dimensions, surface conditions, materials and tolerances of a design.

However, these systems present little robustness and flexibility in terms of coping with design changes. The early CAD tools are primarily based on building geometry with specific dimensions and creating geometry with specific initial relationships to existing geometry. When a line is drawn for example, it cannot be changed except redrawing it. That is, neither its position nor its length can be changed by changing the values associated with it. At the preliminary design stage, design engineers are often not sure what configurations will satisfy the design requirements. This leads to various modifications in product configurations and inevitably leads to changes in the geometric models and dimensions. It is therefore important for any CAD systems to have the functionalities to support such modifications.

To overcome this inflexibility of the early generation CAD systems, many new approaches have been developed since. Three of the popular ones are feature-based design, parametric and variational design.

Feature-Based Design

Most of the contemporary CAD/CAM systems, such as Pro/Engineer®, Catia® and NX™, adopt a feature-based design approach. This is an approach by which both B-rep and CSG methods are used for model construction. While B-rep is usually the underlying geometric representation scheme, CSG is used as the front-end of the software. Instead of simple solid primitives, form features are used for modelling purposes. By definition, features are viewed upon as information sets that refer to aspects of form or other attributes of a part, in such a way that these sets can be used in reasoning about design (and maybe performance and manufacture) of the part or the assemblies they constitute. Further discussions on feature-based technologies can be found in Chapter IV.

A product model can be built by using features; this is known as design by features or feature-based design. One can start either with a more or less complete geometric model and define form features on it, or start from scratch by combining form features from a standard library. Designing with pre-defined form features can reduce the number of input commands substantially. This is especially advantageous in re-design. The parametric representation of features provides a powerful way to change features with respect to their dimensions. Features can serve as functional elements for designers. However, it is worth noting that design features often differ from the features used in "downstream" application features, e.g. manufacturing features.

Parametric Design

Parametric design is a method of linking dimensions and variables to geometry in such a way that when the values change, the part changes as well – hence the dimension-driven capability. Take a part shown in Figure 1.13 as an example. The dimensions are given

Figure 1.13. Dimensions shown as values and parameters

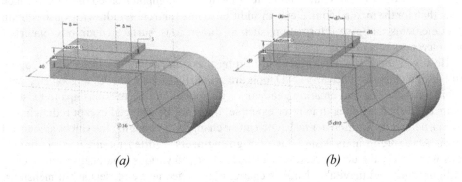

(a) (b)

in two forms for the 2D sketch based on which the solid part is created, true value form (Figure 1.13(a)) and parameter form (Figure 1.13(b)). This implies that the CAD system treats all dimensions as variables that can be changed any time and almost anywhere, be it in the modelling mode or drawing mode. The geometry is of course governed by these dimensions in the parameter form.

Being variables, dimensions can be obtained by means of parametric relations and equations. Take the same part shown in Figure 1.13 as an example. One can establish a relationship between dimensions "*d6*" and "*d7*" as "*d6 = d7*". This way, three pieces of design intents are assumed,

- If *d7* changes, *d6* changes to the same value;
- *d7* is a "strong" dimension in the sense that it can be changed any time and also governs *d6*;
- *d6* is a "derived" dimension in that direct modification to it is not possible.

A parametrically defined model can also perform design modifications and creation of a family of parts in remarkably quick time compared with the redrawing required by a traditional CAD. In recent years, almost all CAD systems have adopted this approach. More conveniently, parametric modification can be accomplished with a spreadsheet, script, as well as by manually changing dimension text in the digital model and/or its associated drawings.

Variational Design

Variational design is a design methodology that utilizes fundamental graph theory and robust constraint-solving techniques to provide constraint-driven capability. As this definition indicates, parametric design and variational design have much in common. In practice, terms "parametric" and "variational" have been used almost interchangeably in technical and particularly commercial contexts. From the viewpoint of the end user, the two types of systems are similar to the extent that it is not always straightforward to determine from the outside which type of system one is using (Shah & Mäntylä, 1995). In fact, variational design may be considered as a superset of parametric design. Therefore, it is more general than parametric design. This book does not wish to make clear distinctions between these two types of design schemes. This said, in variational design constraints are typical types of modelling means and they are often modelled as relations between various geometric entities and dimensions.

Depending on different CAD systems, different types of relations can be defined, e.g. equality, constraint, conditional and simultaneous equations. Table 1.2 lists the constraints with the corresponding graphical symbols found in the Pro/Engineer® system. Equality relations set a parameter on the left side of an equation equal to an expression on the right. A relation that limits the permissible values for a dimension is a constraint relation. A conditional relation is used to assign values to variables only when specific criteria are satisfied. Simultaneous equations use the value from one relation to obtain the results for another relation.

Table 1.2. Pro/E® constraints

Constraint	Symbol
Midpoint	M
Same points	o
Horizontal entities	H
Vertical entities	V
Point on entity	-O- - -
Tangent entities	T
Perpendicular entities	⊥
Parallel lines	$//_1$
Equal radii	R with an index in subscript
Line segments with equal lengths	L with an index in subscript
Symmetry	→←| Entities are lined up horizontally or vertically	▬ ▬ ▌
Collinear	▬
Alignment	Symbol for the appropriate alignment type.
Use Edge/Offset Edge	▬▬ O

Figure 1.14. Constraints in sketches

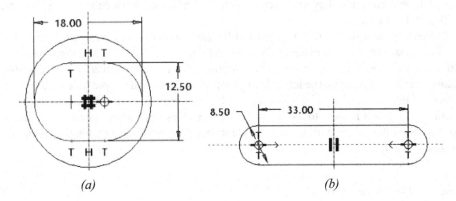

(a)   (b)

Figure 1.14 shows some of the constraints in a sketch. In Figure 1.14 (a), two sets of collinear constraints applied to the centre lines; two horizontal lines are constrained; and the two arcs join the two horizontal lines through the four tangent points. Also note that the sketch symmetry is implied through the two dimensions (18.00 and 12.50). Alternatively, symmetry can be defined explicitly as shown in Figure 1.14(b).

In essence, relations use operators and functions in equations to control dimensions or parameters. Table 1.3 gives some examples of relations.

The following is an example of a conditional statement which could be used with the part given in Figure 1.15:

IF *d1* > *d2*
    length = 12.1
ENDIF
IF *d1* <= *d2*
    length = 23.2
ENDIF

Table 1.3. Examples of relations used in a variational design system

Relations	Type of relation	Evaluation
$d0$ = 34.8	Equality	Assigns $d0$ equal to 34.8
$d1$ <= 26.5	Constraint	Constrains $d1$ to less than or equal 26.5
$d3$ = d2 + 52.1 $d4$ = d3 * 3.4	Simultaneous	Assigns $d3$ equal to $d2$ plus 52.1 Assigns $d4$ equal to $d3$ times 3.4
IF $d5$ = 243.8 *diameter* = 23.4 ENDIF	Conditional	Assigns value 23.4 to *diameter* when $d5$ is equal to 243.8
IF $d6$ < abs($d5$) *diameter* = 23.4 ENDIF	Conditional relation including a mathematical function	Assigns value 23.4 to *diameter* when $d6$ is less than the absolute value of $d5$

Figure 1.15. An example to show a conditional statement

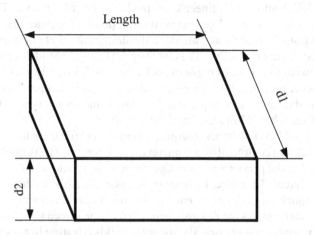

As shown in the model in Figure 1.15, *d1* is greater than *d2*. Therefore the dimension "*length*" takes a value of 12.1. Another way to create a relation for the previous example would be to use an "ELSE" statement, and it can be written as,

IF *d1 > d2*
    length = 12.1
ELSE
    length = 23.2
ENDIF

In addition, nested IF-ENDIF and IF-ELSE-ENDIF structures may also be used. Using the previous example, if the design intent was for the dimension "*length*" to have the value 32.5 when *d1* is greater than *d2* plus 10. The following relations could be entered to obtain this result,

IF *d1 > d2*
    IF *d1 > d2* + 10
        length = 32.5
    ELSE
        length = 12.1
    ENDIF
ELSE
    length = 23.2
ENDIF

History-Based and History-Free CAD

In addition to geometry, CAD systems may also capture the history of, or the procedural data about, the creation of the design model. When this type of data is also captured and modelled together with the geometric information of a design, it may be called a history-based approach to CAD (Gordon, 2006). In fact, many of the contemporary CAD systems such as Catia®, NX™ and Pro/Engineer®, adopted this type of approach. The alternative to this approach is to only record geometric information in a manner that is as loose as possible, so that fast and flexible alterations to the design model at any point in time and the design process are made possible. The OneSpace™ Designer Modelling software from CoCreate™ Software Inc., is an example of such a system. Such software may provide the robustness in model revisions by letting users directly "push and pull" models to make changes any time during the design process. For clarity, the former type of CAD systems can be called "history-based" and the latter "history-free".

In a history-based CAD system, subsequent geometry is built upon the previous one(s). All geometries are often controlled by parameters, which comprise constraints and relationships as discussed in the previous section. Constraints and relationships are often used to define the design intent. Therefore, it seems to be easier for a history-based CAD system to capture an original user's design intent because the software remembers and enforces relationships between objects the designer generated on the screen (Gordon, 2006).

As the design process progresses, the software builds a feature history tree (or otherwise known as model tree), which tracks all relationships, parameters and dependency, and stores the order in which features are created. The tree effectively serves as a part "recipe". Changing a step or replaying the recipe forces associations in the tree to ripple through the model and "regenerate" a new part. During the process of building a part, the user can roll back to "re-visit" a feature created at an early stage. History-based models may exhibit some intelligent natures. For instance, a designer might specify that a hole be created in the centre of a square-shaped pocket. He locates it half-way from both sides of the pocket. So no matter what size the pocket may be changed to, once the history recipe gets replayed, the hole always gets its desired position, i.e. the centre of the pocket.

Whereas such a model can be handy in accommodating design changes with some of the design intent preserved, the process of designing it can be a non-travail task. This can be compared to building a house of cards. In this analogy, the "cards" would be modelling features that are interrelated in the history tree. When an original designer predicts all possible future changes and designs the model with them in mind, it is not a problem to later rearrange a card or pull one out to modify the model. This means that the designer has a lot of front-thinking to do. So much so, foreseeing all possible changes is not always an easy task. With insufficient design foresight, pulling a card would affect relationships to such a point where the model is no longer stable and may fail to regenerate.

Another point to note about a history-based CAD system is that the data structure (or rather the historical data in the structure) is primarily proprietary. When a history-based system imports a foreign model, the design may need to be re-built to have the type of history desired. When a history-based system exports a model to a foreign model, the model tree information is often stripped off, turning the history-based model into a history-free model, hence losing the design intent data.

In a history-free CAD system, an operator builds all components, parts, and assemblies in one common workspace. Multiple parts and assemblies can be loaded at the same time and a single command may allow users to arrange parts in a subassembly or move subassemblies within a top-level assembly. Some history-free systems have users constructing models from fully rendered 3D shapes by dragging and dropping them from libraries. In other systems, designers sketch and extrude 2D profiles, similar to history-based CAD software. Because designers build models in a way resembling how they would mould physical structures in the real world, history-free CAD systems are often compared to working with lumps of "digital clay".

After operators create geometry, they can modify any feature locally, e.g. adding a fillet or changing the size. When a feature is removed, the model is supposed to "heal" itself. Consider again the pocket-hole example above. In a history-based model, the hole will be dependent on the pocket from which constraints such as the hole centring dimensions, are made. The hole will be the "child" of the pocket; removing the pocket also removes the hole. In a history-based model on the other hand, one would expect the model to keep the hole even if the pocket is removed. This is where the healing action is needed. Instead of a history tree, history-free systems use an assembly-structure browser that displays a list of parts and assemblies the designer has built. When a new part is created, its default location is at the top level of the browser. To place a part in an assembly, a user drags the part's position in the browser to a different location.

The difference between the two approaches boils down to how and what type of design intent is defined. Design intent can be captured in a history-tree recipe using relationships and constraints as in a history-based system. However, this type of intent is pre-determined and very often rigid. If design intent is defined as having a final product be exactly as a designer intended, the necessity for a system to respond to all the unexpected changes that should happen throughout the discovery process of new product development may be the ultimate intent of the designer.

History-based systems usually fare better for the type of products involving large families of similar parts in which, say, only sizes or lengths change (entailing predicted and simpler form of design intent). History-free systems on the other hand, are said to best fit in well in R&D environments and the conceptual stage of design. History-based systems have been prevalent in the marketplace because they let users modify designs in a highly predictable way. 70, 80, or even 90% of a new product is simply reused components. Take as an example a company developing an engine block. Once a valve is modelled for instance, users can tweak sketches or parameters and generate a new valve with ease. For companies committing and documenting a design, a system with built-in design intent that has logic about how modifications are propagated, makes subsequent reuse fast, efficient, and reliable (Gordon, 2006).

An important strength that a history-free system possesses lies in the early stages of design. Designers can capture and present design ideas to clients on-the-spot because they do not have to think about the process of modelling. Instead, they can focus solely on the designs they are trying to create. Designers can, for instance, quickly generate 100 ideas and throw away 95 of them without investing a lot of time in modelling. History-free modellers are effective and economic when multiple design systems are used. This is because a history-based model, when exported to a different format, will almost always have the history data stripped off. Currently, the gray area between the two is larger than in the past. That is because history-based systems are increasingly adding local direct-editing operations. The author believes that the future of CAD systems will have a well-balanced structure with historical data about the design and sufficient robustness in making design alterations.

Adding Intelligence to CAD

When geometric constraints are coupled with engineering equations, computer-aided design presents a much broader range of benefits. This type of modelling technique is sometimes called functional modelling or behavioural modelling, where geometry, engineering equations, and other designer's intent are all regarded as constraints. These constraints can be arbitrarily coupled and solved simultaneously if needed to arrive at a design configuration that satisfies all the design criteria specified by the engineer. This type of CAD functions can optimize and in some cases automate model creation. This is done by embedding design knowledge into, or capturing designer's intent in, the geometric model, generally in the form of "features" (Allada, 2001). This design knowledge consists of specifications and goals which provide the basis for generating first feasible and then optimum models meeting design requirements. The modelling tools leverage the standard model attributes (mass, surface area etc.) and combine them with inference engines to drive a design model. Additionally, external user defined applications can be linked to the solid modeller to drive the optimization process. To this end, functional modelling can be considered a type of artificial intelligence applied to solid modelling which animates an experienced designer's thinking pattern and reasoning behaviour by way of constraint-based method to generate a design space of feasible solutions. Some applications have taken this to a higher level and implemented knowledge-based engineering (KBE) solutions which allow automatic feature creation as part of a total product design process (McMahon & Browne, 1998).

Many CAD systems have started to provide this type of high-level modelling capabilities during the detailed, embodiment and even conceptual design stage. In the conceptual design stage, stored design knowledge, in the form of customized templates containing rules and formulae, could be combined with objective driven specifications to quickly produce an initial realization of the new concept. This facilitates more concepts being considered comprehensively, thus allowing more innovation and better design decisions to be made. In the Pro/E® system, this is carried out by using the so-called User Defined Analysis (UDA) features to capture designer's intent and/or formulate the design specifications (PTC, 2006). Figure 1.16 shows the design of a lampshade at its concept design stage, when the proper geometry of the shade is being sought to achieve a set of design specifications or goals. Such goals may entail that "a circular area defined by r and R be lighted with a uniform reflection". The UDA features defined may include the location of the light bulb (h and H); location and geometry of the shade (note that the lamp shade can also take form of any free form surfaces). The uniform reflection of light by the shade is another UDA feature which makes use of other UFD features along with some physics formulae.

CAD is now so extensively applied that in many manufacturing companies all design work is done using CAD systems. Despite this considerable success, there is widespread view that CAD is not yet adequate as an aid to the designer in generating a design. CAD is considered to concentrate rather too heavily on providing means of representing the final form of the design, whereas designers also need a continual stream of advice and information to assist in decision-making.

The tasks of CAD systems of the future are, therefore, to represent a wider variety of a design's properties, in terms that are familiar to engineers, and to handle those aspects of engineering practice that influence the design. The way in which it is hoped to achieve this is to bring ideas and techniques from artificial intelligence and information systems into design systems, and also to search for higher-level methods for modelling design rep-

Figure 1.16. Concept design of a lamp shade. ©2005 Elsevier Limited, used with permission.

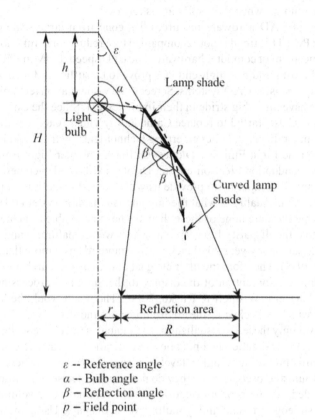

ε -- Reference angle
α -- Bulb angle
β -- Reflection angle
p -- Field point

resentations. Functional design, or behavioural modelling, is moving in the right direction. Implementation techniques are however rather clumsy and narrowly-scoped.

There are a number of strands of research into intelligent CAD systems, such as application of artificial intelligence and neural network in a CAD system and design for any applications (DFX) (Colombo, Mosca & Sartori, 2007, Feijo, Gomes, Scheer & Bento, 2001, Gallas & Brown, 2008, Hao, Zhao & Li, 2001, Osman, Abdel-Aal, Elkenany & Salem, 2001, Shu, Hao & Wang, 2002). The future of CAD is believed to be integrated with other activities in both horizontal and vertical dimensions.

COMPUTER HARDWARE FOR CAD

Computer hardware advancements have been essential for the development of geometric modelling techniques and CAD systems. In some way CAD hardware development has been pushed by the developments in CAD software rather than vice versa. Long term software development has counted on continuing increases in computing power to the point where developers plan their software development based on what computing power will be available in the future, when their software is released.

The hierarchy of CAD hardware resources has gone from large-scale computers to workstations and PCs. This trend is not accompanied by a reduction in functionality thanks to the rapid advancement of computer hardware. The CPU speed, ROM and RAM size, and graphics cards of most middle to high-end PCs prove to be sufficient for running some of today's most comprehensive CAD systems. Screens and visualization technologies used in the CAD systems have made big stride in their improvement. Since the early 2004, Liquid Crystal Displays (LCDs) started to replace Cathode Ray Tubes (CRTs) as the technology of choice for computer displays. Other emerging technologies such as Field Emission Displays (FEDs), Organic Light Emitting Diodes (OLEDs), Polymer Light Emitting Diodes (PLEDs), Surface-conduction Electron-emitter Display (SED) and even newer generation Plasma displays are all competing to provide us with the best visualisation platform possible. The upper limit of quality is what the human visualisation system (HVS) is able to receive, a goal which to date none of these displays have been able to achieve. In fact, it has been stated that the disparity between that which we see naturally and that what we see on a computer screen, by year 2000 technology standards, is a more than a factor of 1 million (Hopper, 1999). Therefore the ultimate goal of displays research and development is to match the information output of the display to the input and processing capacity of the human visual system (Wisnieff & Ritsko, 2000). The result would be looking into a computer screen which is as clear as the environment around you.

It is not however only these 2D visualization technologies which are seeking to improve CAD rendering. 3D visualization technologies and so called volumetric displays are also progressing towards providing a higher level of visual information. These types of displays are termed autostereoscopic since they do not require the use of additional eyewear. They can be divided into four main categories, swept volume, static volume, holograms and holographic stereograms, and highly multiview 3D displays. Using the swept volume technique, a volume filling image can be produced by projecting images or slices of an

Figure 1.17. The Perspecta Spatial swept volume 3D display by Actuality Systems

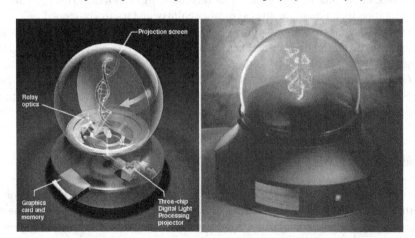

object onto a rapidly rotating or oscillating 2D surface as in Actuality Systems, Inc. (2007) Perspecta Spatial 3D display shown in Figure 1.17. This system generates ten inch diameter volume filling imagery with full 360 degree field of view. To create the volume filling image the display projects a series of 198 2D slices onto a diffuser screen rotating above 900rpm, resulting in a refresh rate of 30Hz. Normally the rotating surface is a plane as in the Perspecta Dome. However, a helical surface that translates points through the volume is also possible.

Another interesting technique used to create 3D imagery does not require any moving parts. One type of static volume display generates 3D imagery using glass doped with rare earth ions and coaxes these ions within the volume into emitting light at a point when excited by dual intersecting infrared laser beams.

It could be that a combination of technologies in the future may provide the answer. For example, an OLED or PLED screen display which can either remain stationary or rotate based on the visualization requirements maybe the favoured option for CAD designers and FEA analysts as well as computer game enthusiasts.

CONCLUSION

Geometric modelling, in particular three-dimensional geometric modelling is the back-bone of any contemporary CAD system. In wire-frame representations, the component geometry is represented largely as a collection of curves. In surface representations, the component geometry is represented as a collection of surfaces, often attached to a wire-frame. In solid modelling, a component is often represented either as a set-theoretic combination of geometric primitives (as in CSG), or as a collection of faces, edges and vertices (as in B-rep) defining the boundary of the form. A successful scheme for representing solids in a CAD system should be: (i) complete and unambiguous; (ii) appropriate for the world of engineering objects; and (iii) practical to use with existing computers. We have seen that the wire-frame and surface schemes fall down on, at least, the first of these conditions. Many methods have been proposed for solid modelling, two have been particularly successful, and have come to dominate the development of most CAD systems, i.e. B-rep and SCG.

Geometric modelling paved the road for contemporary CAD systems. While there is little to doubt about its mathematic background and theories, other technological advancements are also needed. These advancements take two forms, those concerning hardware and those concerning software. One such an example is the functional/behavioural modelling approach to effectively capture designer's intent in a CAD system. These types of CAD systems have extended the capabilities of solid modellers by enabling design models to be optimized for attributes such as geometry and functional properties. The supporting technologies are parametric and variational modelling methods. Constraints and relationships are the vehicles for carrying design intent. History-based architecture combined with sufficient robustness seems to be the future of the CAD hierarchy.

It is envisaged that as more and more smart modelling functionality becomes available in design systems, the duration of the design process will be shortened and quality of the design itself will be increased. While design intent is the main focus in our discussions, consideration of any other application-related intent alongside the design intent would make CAD systems more capable. This will lead to an easy realization of the concept of "design for manufacturing", "design for environment", "design for assembly", to name a few as the instances of DFXs.

REFERENCES

Actuality Systems, Inc. (2007). Retrieved January 30, 2008, from http://www.actuality-systems.com/index.html (accessed on July 28, 2007).

Allada, V. (2001). Feature-Based Design in Integrated Manufacturing. In C. Leondes (Ed.), *Computer-Aided Design Engineering, and Manufacturing Systems Techniques and Applications vol. 5 The Design of Manufacturing Systems*, (pp. 2-13). CRC Press, Boca Raton.

Colombo, G., Mosca, A., & Sartori, F. (2007). Towards the design of intelligent CAD systems: An ontological approach. *Advanced Engineering Informatics, 21*(2), 153-168.

Feijó, B., Gomes, P.C.R., Scheer, S., & Bento, J. (2001). Online algorithms supporting emergence in distributed CAD systems. Advances in Engineering Software, *32*(10-11), 779-787.

Gallas, B. D., & Brown, D. G. (2008). Reader studies for validation of CAD systems. *Neural Networks, 21*(2-3), 387-397.

Gordon, L. (2006, November 22). Comparing 3-D CAD modellers. *Machine Design.* Retrieved January 30, 2008, from http://machinedesign.com/ContentItem/57411/Comparing3DCADmodelers.aspx

Hopper, R., Owens, C., & Croll, M. (1999, February 28). Achieving full media interoperability using information systems and indexing schemes. *IEE Colloquium (Digest), 56*, 49-55.

Hao, Y.-T., Zhao, W.-D., & Li, Q.-Y. (2001). Pattern knowledge and artificial neural network based framework for intelligent cad system. *Journal of Computer-Aided Design and Computer Graphics, 13*(9), 834-839.

Lee, K. (1999). *Principles of CAD/CAM/CAE systems*. Rolland, USA: Addison Wesley Longman, Inc.

Osman, T. A., Abdel-Aal, U. M., Elkenany, A. H., & Salem, F. B. (2001). Development of intelligent CAD for the design of mechanical systems. *Journal of Engineering and Applied Science, 48*(5), 937-953.

PTC. (2006). Behavioural Modelling Extension. Parametric Technology Inc. USA. Retrieved April 14, 2005, from http://www.kxcad.net/proe/bemod/example__analyzing_the_reflectivity_of_a_lamp_sh.htm

Requicha, A. A. G. (1980). Representations for rigid solids: theory, methods, and systems. *ACM Computing Surveys, 12*(4), 437-464.

Requicha, A. A. G., & Voelcker, H. B. (1982). Solid modelling: a historical summary and contemporary assessment. *IEEE Computer Graphics and Applications, 2*(2), 9-24.

Shah, J. J., & Mäntylä, M. (1995). *Parametric and feature-based CAD/CAM – concept, techniques and applications*. New York, USA: John Wiley & Sons, Inc.

Shu, Q.-L., Hao, Y.-P., & Wang, D.-J. (2002). Implementation of an integrated CAD-DFA system based on assemblability evaluation. *Journal of Northeastern University, 23*(4), 387-390.

Singh, N. (1996). *Systems Approach to Computer-Integrated Design and Manufacturing*. New York, USA: John Wiley & Sons, Inc.

Sutherland, I. E. (1963). SketchPad: A man-machine graphical system. *AFIPS Conference Proceedings, 23*, 323-328.

Wisnieff, R. L., & Ritsko, J. J. (2000). Electronic displays for information technology, *IBM Journal of Research and Development, 44*(3), 409-422.

Xu, X., & Hinduja, S. (1998). Recognition of Rough Machining Features in 2½D Components. *Computer-Aided Design, 30*(7), 503-516.

Xu, X. W., & Galloway, R. (2005). Using Behavioral Modeling Technology to Capture Designer's Intent. *Computers in Human Behavior, 21*(2), 395-405.

Chapter II
CAD Data Exchange and CAD Standards

ABSTRACT

Today, more companies than ever before are involved in manufacturing various parts of their end products using different subcontractors, many of whom are often geographically diverse. The rise of such global efforts has created the need for sharing information among vendors involved in multi-disciplinary projects. Transfer of data is necessary so that, for example, one organization can be developing a CAD model, while another performs analysis work on the same model; at the same time a third organization is responsible for manufacturing the product. Data transfer fills the need to satisfy each of these functions in a specific way. Accurate transmission is of paramount importance. Thus, a mechanism for good data transfer is needed.

The CAD interoperability issue - using one CAD system in-house, yet needing to deliver designs to, or receive designs from, another system, poses a challenge to industries such as automotive, aerospace, shipbuilding, heavy equipment, and high-tech original equipment manufacturers and their suppliers. It is worth studying the issue and determining how engineering model data is delivered today to manufacturers and suppliers, how CAD conversion, geometric translation, and/or feature-based CAD interoperability are handled, at what expense, and under whose authority.

This chapter explores the various ways to make this vital transfer possible. The attention will be directed towards data exchange and standards for 3-D CAD systems. Since CAD data formats have a lot to do with CAD kernels that govern the data structure and therefore the data formats, some popular CAD kernels are discussed. The data interoperability section covers different types of data translations and conversions. The use of neutral or standardized data exchange protocols is one of the natural methods for data exchange and sharing. This topic is covered at the end of this chapter.

ISSUES AT HAND

Computers and information technology have been introduced into industry in an ad hoc manner to initially relieve particular bottlenecks in industrial processes. There are no need to think of the effect on the overall enterprise and the issue of integration. Any attempts to deal with data exchanges were also in an ad hoc manner (Bloor & Owen, 2003). As computers are used more and more in all walks of an organisation, in particular the product development process, data exchange and sharing has now risen to the top of the agenda for many businesses. These days, industrial cases related to CAD data conversion are not hard to come by. Consider large automobile manufacturer such as General Motor (GM®). The factory has facilities in 30 states of the U.S. and 33 countries. Parts for a car may come from within as well as outside the US. These parts are designed and manufactured according to the specifications prescribed by GM®. The companies that design these parts may not use the same CAD system, hence the necessity of data conversion. There is also a need for data sharing among the different parties of the design team. Pushing for a single CAD system across the supply chain will not sell. This is because any company may have other businesses which may lead to the choice of a different CAD system that suits a variety of applications. Companies that have more diverse businesses may end up maintaining two or more than two CAD or CAD/CAM systems. In this case, data incompatibility even exists in the company itself.

When it comes to working with other organizations, the format of design data that is exchanged tends to depend on its origin. Design data from customers and partners is more likely to be delivered in native CAD formats. Design data from suppliers is most likely to be received in neutral formats. This partially shows an increased level of awareness of data exchangeability among the suppliers. Design data from other internal engineering groups is largely delivered in native CAD formats as opposed to neutral formats.

It is worth noting that transferring data between various CAD systems must embrace the complete product description stored in its database. This includes the geometric data, metadata (non-graphic data), design intent data, and application data. Both *geometric data* and design intent data have been addressed in Chapter I. *Metadata* is the information (e.g. time stamps and the owner of the data) about a particular data (e.g. geometric data). This data is used to facilitate the understanding, use and management of core CAD data. *Application data* consists of any information related to the final manufacture and application of the design, e.g. tooling, NC tool paths, tolerancing, process planning, and bill of material. The types of data also depend on different stages of the product lifecycle during which the data is used. At some instances, data can be used in part or fully whereas in others it can be used with combination of different types. For example, while at the design stage more importance is given to the requirements of the customer, therefore geometric and design data are more relevant. Less emphasis is given to the metadata. Metadata can be critical when interacting with different systems and multiple users.

CAD KERNELS

CAD data formats are governed by the (solid) modelling kernels that the CAD systems were built upon. This is true with both history-based and history-free CAD systems as discussed in Chapter I. A modelling kernel is a collection of classes and components comprised of mathematical functions that perform specific modelling tasks. A modelling kernel may support solid modelling, generalized cellular modelling and freeform surface/sheet modelling. It may contain functions such as model creation and editing (e.g. Boolean modelling operators), feature modelling support, advanced surfacing, thickening and hollowing, blending and filleting and sheet modelling. Most of the kernels also provide graphical and rendering support, including hidden-line, wire-frame and drafting, as well as tessellation functionality and a suite of model data inquiries. The CAD graphic user interface (GUI) interfaces with the kernel's functions through so-called application user interface. Take Parasolid® modelling kernel as an example, which provides 3D digital representation capabilities for NX™, Solid Edge, Femap and Teamcenter solutions. The 3D-based application interacts with Parasolid® through one of its three interfaces as shown in Figure 2.1: Parasolid® Kernel (PK) interface, Kernel Interface (KI) and Downward Interface (DI).

PK and KI sit "on top" of the modeller (side-by-side), and are the means by which the application constructs models and manipulates objects, as well as controls the functioning of the modeller. In particular, the PK interfaces help the programmer access the modelling capabilities in the kernel. They are standard libraries of modelling functions. The programmer calls these modelling functions in their programs. The DI consists of three parts: graphical output, foreign geometry and frustum. It lies "beneath" the modeller, and is called by the modeller when there is a need for performing data-intensive or system type operations.

Frustum is a set of functions, which must be written by the application programmer. The kernel calls them when data are to be saved or retrieved. Transferring data through the frustum usually involves writing to, or reading from, a file or several files. The format and location of the files are determined at the time of writing the frustum functions. Graphical Output (GO) is another set of functions to be written by the application programmer. When a call is made to the PK rendering functions, the graphical data generate output through the GO interface. The graphical data are then passed to a 3D rendering package such as OpenGL®. Foreign Geometry provides functionality for the development of customised geometrical types such as in-house curves and surfaces. These are used together with the standard geometrical types for modelling within the Parasolid® modeller.

Figure 2.1. Kernel working diagram

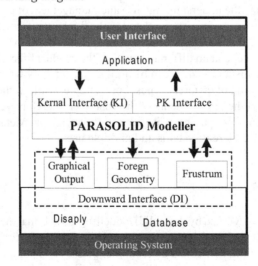

Over the years, various kernels have been developed and adopted by different CAD systems (Table 2.1). Some are proprietary; others use popular ones through licensing, e.g. ACIS® by Spatial Technology Corporation, and Parasolid® by UGS.

DATA INTEROPERABILITY

Inconsistencies occur when differing solid modelling kernels are used. Consequences of these inconsistencies can mean anomalies in data. Experiences gained by some Parasolid® customers showed that up to 20% of models imported from a different kernel contain errors that have to be mixed (CAD-User, 2000).

Different Types of Data Translation/Conversion

Different companies handle CAD conversions in different ways. When a product model received follows the neutral data exchanging formats such as STEP (Standard for Exchange of Product data model) (ISO 10303-1, 1994) and IGES (Initial Graphic Exchange Standard) (IGES, 1998), the company may opt to "re-establish" or re-create the features based on the received data model. This exercise is called "re-mastering" a model. Re-mastering is necessary because currently STEP and IGES can only describe a model's pure geometric and topological data (dummy data model, much similar to the models from a history-free CAD system) minus all other product-related data such as design features and tolerances. Alternatively, the company may just leave it as it is since it can be a costly exercise to

Table 2.1. CAD systems and their solid modelling kernels

CAD application	ACIS®	Parasolid®	Proprietary
ADINA®		*	
AutoCAD®	*		
CADKEY®	*		
Catia®			*
I-DEAS®			*
IronCAD®	*		
IX Design™	*		
Mechanical Desktop®	*		
MicroStation®		*	
Pro/Engineer®			*
SolidEdge®		*	
SolidWorks®		*	
ThinkDesign®			*
NX™		*	
VX CAD/CAM™		*	

re-master the model. When a vendor proprietary data model (often containing feature information) is received, companies may chose to re-master or send the data to other companies for re-mastering.

There have been different technique-oriented approaches being explored by different companies and software developers. Use of dual solid modelling kernels is one option. Use of so-called direct data translators is another. Some research has been carried out with an effort to enrich the neutral file formats (such as STEP) with feature information as well as other product data such as tolerances.

Dual Kernel CAD Systems

This is a rather unique type of CAD system with two differing kernels built into one system. The most popular example is IronCAD®, formally an ACIS®-only system, has now been twinned with Parasolid® to become the first dual-kernel system. IronCAD® uses both kernels simultaneously, switching back and forth when needed. The principal benefit is obviously the ability to work on models developed under either kernel, even to the extent of combining data from either kernel into a single model. Interestingly enough, this dual kernel system has been developed with a different mind. The switch from one kernel to the other in IronCAD® only happens when problems are encountered in one - say, complex bends - that can only be handled by the other. The nanosecond switch is usually invisible to the user. Another dual-kernel CAD system is CAXA™ (again, Parasolid® and ACIS®). CAXA™ is a product design and collaborative data management system. It is to become the PLM market leader in China as well as a major provider of PLM technologies worldwide.

This option is efficient when ACIS® and Parasolid® are the data formats involved. It has though proven to be extremely difficult to build such a system. Furthermore, there are numerous numbers of CAD kernels and CAD data formats in the market. This approach only partially solves the problems.

Direct Data Translators

Direct data translators (Figure 2.2) provide a direct solution which entails translating the modelling data stored in a product database directly from one CAD system format to another, usually in one step. There usually exists a neutral database in a direct data translator. The structure of the neutral database must be general, governed by the minimum required definitions of any of the modelling data types, and be independent of any vendor format.

A good example for direct data translation is CADporter from Elysium™ (Dean, 2005). CADporter is not CAD software for making models, but rather a CAD file reader. This product can read several different formats of CAD files from various vendors. Figure 2.3 shows an interaction between CAD vendors with Elysium™ operated from within Solid-Works®. As depicted, it is a two-way transfer between the CAD systems. With this type of integration, a CAD system can import a Pro/E® part and rewrite it to another vendor format such as Catia® or AutoCAD® DWG format.

However, as the CAD model gets more complicated the chances that the translation breaks down increase. When this happens, the model needs to be simplified or re-modelled. The remaining part of this section discusses some of the above-listed product data exchange formats.

Figure 2.2. Direct translators

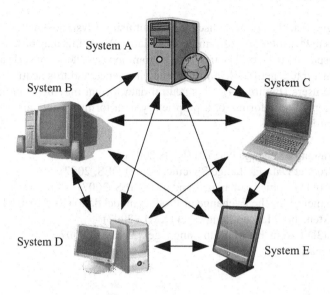

Figure 2.3. Two-way data transfer using Elysium™

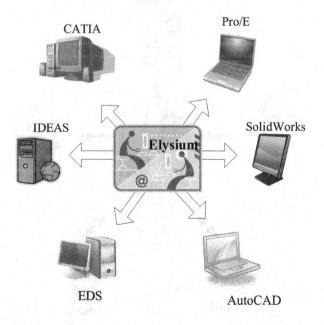

Common/Neutral Translators

One would argue that the solution discussed about using Elysium™ as the intermediate data "buffer" is in fact some sort of common translator. While this may be true, Elysium™ data is not transparent to users. The true type of common translator converts a proprietary CAD data format into a neutral data format and vice versa, and this neutral data is made available to the users (Figure 2.4). This neutral data format may be of an international or industry accepted data format or a proprietary data format. There are a few popular industry standards such as,

- DXF (Drawing eXchange Format) (DXF, 2007)
- PDES (Product Data Exchange Specification) (PDES, 2007)
- IGES (Initial Graphic Exchange Standard) (IGES, 2007)
- STEP (Standard for the Exchange of Product model data) (ISO 10303-1, 1994)
- XML (Extensible Markup Language) (XML, 2007)
- 3DXML (3D Extensible Markup Language) (3DXML, 2007)
- Other formats

DXF

DXF is the AutoCAD®'s CAD data file format, developed by Autodesk® as their solution for enabling data interoperability between AutoCAD® and other programs. DXF was originally introduced in December 1982 as part of AutoCAD® 1.0, and was intended to

Figure 2.4. Neutral translators

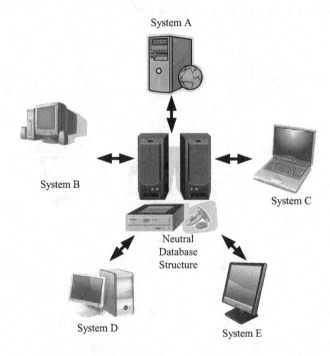

System A

System B

System C

Neutral
Database
Structure

System D

System E

provide an exact representation of the data in the AutoCAD® native file format, DWG (Drawing), whose specifications have never been published. This format has been the very first of the data transfer formats used in CAD. DXF is primarily a 2D-based data format. Versions of AutoCAD® Release 10 (October 1988) and up support both ASCII and binary forms of DXF. Earlier versions could only support the ASCII form. Nowadays, almost all significant commercial application software developers, including all of Autodesk®'s competitors, choose to support DWG as the format for AutoCAD® data interoperability, using libraries from the Open Design Alliance — a non-profit industry consortium which has reverse-engineered the DWG file format.

As AutoCAD® becomes more powerful and supports more complex object types, DXF has become less useful. This is because certain object types, including ACIS® solids and regions, cannot be easily documented using DXF files. Other object types, including AutoCAD® 2006's dynamic blocks, and all of the objects specific to the vertical-market versions of AutoCAD®, are partially documented, but not at a sufficient level to allow other developers to support them.

DXF File Structure

The DXF format is a tagged data representation of all the information contained in an AutoCAD® drawing file. Tagged data means that each data element in the file is preceded by an integer number that is called a group code. A group code's value indicates what type of data element follows. This value also indicates the meaning of a data element for a given object (or record) type.

ASCII versions of DXF can be read with a text-editor. The basic organization of a DXF file is as follows:

HEADER section – General information about the drawing. Each parameter has a variable name and an associated value.

CLASSES section – Holds the information for application-defined classes whose instances appear in the BLOCKS, ENTITIES, and OBJECTS sections of the database. Generally it does not provide sufficient information to allow interoperability with other programs.

TABLES section – This section contains definitions of named items. It contains the following tabulated data:

    Application ID (APPID)
    Block Record (BLOCK_RECORD)
    Dimension Style (DIMSTYPE)
    Layer (LAYER)
    Linetype (LTYPE)
    Text style (STYLE)
    User Coordinate System (UCS)
    View (VIEW)
    Viewport configuration (VPORT)

BLOCKS section – Contains Block Definition entities describing the entities comprising each Block in the drawing.

ENTITIES section – Contains the drawing entities, including any Block References.
OBJECTS section – Contains the data that apply to nongraphical objects, used by
AutoLISP™ and ObjectARX® applications.
THUMBNAILIMAGE section – Contains the preview image for the DXF file.
END OF FILE

IGES

This method of translation originated around the late 1970's. It is still one of the viable methods of transferring CAD data. The file format defined by this Specification treats the product definition as a file of entities. Each entity is represented in an application-independent format, to and from which the native representation of a specific CAD/CAM system can be mapped. The entity representations provided in this Specification include forms common to the CAD/CAM systems currently available and forms which support the system technologies currently emerging.

Entities are categorized as geometry and non-geometry. Geometry entities represent the definition of a physical shape. They include points, curves, surfaces, solids and relations. Relations are collections of similarly structured entities. Non-geometry entities typically serve to enrich the model by providing (a) a viewing perspective in which a planar drawing may be composed and (b) providing annotation and dimensioning appropriate to the drawing. Non-geometry entities further serve to provide specific attributes or characteristics for individual or groups of entities. The definitions of these groupings may reside in another file. Typical non-geometry entities for drawing definitions, annotations and dimensioning are the view, drawing, general note, witness line and leader. Typical non-geometry entities for attributes and groupings are the property and associated entities.

An IGES file consists of 5 sections, Start, Global, Directory Entry, Parameter Data, and Terminate. It may include any number of entities of any type as required to represent a product. Each entity occurrence consists of a directory entry and a parameter data entry. The directory entry provides an index and includes descriptive attributes about the data. The parameter data provides the specific entity definition. The directory data are organized in the fixed fields and are consistent across all entities to provide simple access to the frequently used descriptive data. The parameter data are entity-specific and are variable in length and format. The directory data and parameter data for all entities in a file are organized into separate sections, with pointers providing bi-directional links between the directory entry and parameter data for each entity.

IGES provides for groupings whose definitions will be found in a file other than the one in which they are used. Attributes for the geometric entity are defined in the directory segment; the corresponding data itself is defined in the parameter segment. The directory entry and the parameter portion contain all the information about the entity with linkages between the two segments. The connection between attributes and data segment is made with bi-directional pointers. Similar numerical identifiers are assigned for various finite element analyst entities and their post-processing entities.

IGES can also transfer both 2D and 3D finite elements for an FEA type of analysis. While IGES is a popular method of data transfer, it lacks a means of transferring solid objects. This leads to users spending more time to build the solid object on the receiving end. Although open-ended in terms of adding more entities, they are not standardized to be acceptable across all CAD systems. For more information, the readers are referred to the book by Bloor and Owen (2003).

PDES

PDES was designed to completely define a product for all applications over its expected life cycle. Product data include geometry, topology, tolerances, relationships, attributes, and features necessary to completely define a part or assembly of parts for the purpose of design, analysis, manufacture, test, inspection and product support.

The initial work carried out under the Product Definition Data Interface (PDDI) study was done by the McDonnell Aircraft Company on behalf of the U.S. Airforce. Parallel work in this area by CAM-I was carried out in support of this organization's Process Planning systems. PDES is designed to be informationally complete for all downstream applications and to be directly interpretable by these applications. The main types of data which are used in PDES to describe a product include,

- Administrative and Control data
- Geometry such as points, curves and surfaces
- Topology such as vertices, loops and faces
- Tolerances
- Form Features
- Attributes such as surface finish
- Material Properties
- Part Assemblies

It is clear from the above list that PDES provides the information required for both design and manufacturing. The following example shows how PDES describes a hole in the B-Rep format.

```
Hole:    FLS1, FLS2
FLS1:    FACE (LLS1,LLS2,SLS1)
FLS2:    FACE (LLS2,SLS2)
SLS1:    CYLINDRICAL SURFACE (RAD1,AXIS2 PLACEMENT (CENT PT, DIREC-
TION) P2 TSD0)
LLS1:    ELS1
LLS2:    ELS2
ELS1:    EDGE (VTX1,VTX1,CLS1)
ELS2:    EDGE (VTX2,VTX2,CLS2)
CLS1:    CIRCLE (RAD1,AXIS2 PLACEMENT (CENT PT, DIRECTION) P1 TSD1)
CLS2:    CIRCLE (RAD1,AXIS2 PLACEMENT (CENT PT, DIRECTION) P2 TSD1)
RAD1: 0.500
P1:  1.000,1.500,0.000
P2:  1.000,1.500,-0.500
```

Where,
FLSn -- Face Logical Structure *n*
SLSn -- Surface Logical Structure *n*

CLSn -- Curve Logical Structure *n*
TSDn -- Three Space Direction *n*
Pn --   Point *n*
LLSn -- Loop Logical Structure *n*
ELSn -- Edge Logical Structure *n*
VTXn -- Vertex *n*
RADn -- Radius *n*

When a program reads a PDES file, its counters are set to count the entries in each entity section as well as the total number of entities. For the above hole, the following parameters can be established:

- There is one entity of type *hole* therefore drawing code is given by Counter Value H1;
- Hole diameter = 2 × Hole Radius = 2 × 0.500 = 1.000;
- Depth o f hole -- Z distance between two points, P1 and P2 : 0.000 - (-0.500) = 0.500
- Centre Point: P1 (1.000, 1.500, 0.000)

PDES can be viewed as an expansion of IGES where organizational and technological data have been added. In fact, the later PDES contains IGES.

STEP

The development of PDES under the guidance of the IGES organization and in close collaboration with the International Organization for Standardisation, led to the birth of STEP (ISO 10303, 1994). As a result, STEP continues most of the work in PDES. STEP is developed by the Sub-committee 4 (SC4) of ISO Technical Committee 184 (TC 184) Industrial automation systems and integration (http://www.tc184-sc4.org).

STEP is intended to support data exchange, data sharing and data archiving. For data exchange, STEP defines the form of the product data that is to be transferred between a pair of applications. Each application holds its own copy of the product data in its own preferred form. The data conforming to STEP is transitory and defined only for the purpose of exchange. STEP supports data sharing by providing access of and operation on a single copy of the same product data by more than one application, potentially simultaneously. STEP is also suitable to support the interface to the archive. As in product data sharing, the architectural elements of STEP may be used to support the development of the archived product data itself. Archiving requires that the data conforming to STEP for exchange purposes is kept for use at some other time. This subsequent use may be through either product data exchange or product data sharing (Kemmerer, 1999).

Another primary concept contributing to the STEP architecture is that the content of the standard is to be completely driven by industrial requirements. This, in combination with the concept that the re-use of data specifications is the basis for standards, led to develop-ing two distinct types of data specifications. The first type - reusable, context-independent specifications - are the building blocks of the standard. The second type - application-con-text-dependent specifications (application protocols). This combination enables avoiding unnecessary duplication of data specifications between application protocols.

Components of STEP

The architectural components of STEP are reflected in the decomposition of the standard into several series of parts. Each part series contains one or more types of ISO 10303 parts. Figure 2.5 provides an overview of the structure of the STEP documentation.

• Description Methods

The first major architectural component is the description method series. Description methods are common mechanisms for specifying the data constructs of STEP. They include the formal data specification language developed for STEP, known as EXPRESS (ISO 10303-11, 1994). EXPRESS is similar to programming languages such as PASCAL. Within a SCHEMA, various data types can be defined together with structural constraints and algorithmic rules. A main feature of EXPRESS is the possibility to formally validate a population of data types, i.e. to check for all the structural and algorithmic rules. Other description methods include a graphical form of EXPRESS (EXPRESS-G) (ISO 10303-11, 1994), a form for instantiating EXPRESS models, and a mapping language for EXPRESS. EXPRESS-G, as a formal graphical notation for the display of data specifications defined in the EXPRESS language, supports only a subset of the EXPRESS language. EXPRESS-G is represented by graphic symbols forming a diagram. There are three main types of notations,

(a) Definition symbols denote simple data types, named data types, constructed data types and schema declaration;
(b) Relationship symbols are different types of lines describing relationships which exist among the definitions; and
(c) Supplementary text is used to further define a data entity or relationship, e.g. an aggregation data type, constraints and rules.

Description methods are standardized in the ISO 10303-10 series of parts. Various uses of the EXPRESS language are described in further detail in Chapter XI.

Figure 2.5. STEP document architecture

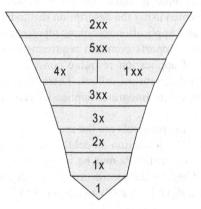

| 1: Overview/Introduction |
| 1x: Description Methods |
| 2x: Implementation Methods |
| 3x: Conformance Testing |
| 4x: Integrated Generic Resources |
| 1xx: Integrated Application Resources |
| 2xx: Application Protocols |
| 3xx: Abstract test suites |
| 5xx: Application Interpreted Constructs |

- Implementation Methods

The second major architectural component of STEP is the implementation method series. Implementation methods are standard implementation techniques for the information structures specified by the only STEP data specifications intended for implementation, application protocols. Each STEP implementation method defines the way in which the data constructs specified using STEP description methods are mapped to that implementation method. This series includes the physical file exchange structure (ISO 10303-21, 1994), the standard data access interface (ISO 10303-22, 1998), and its language bindings (ISO 10303-23, 2000, ISO 10303-24, 2001, ISO 10303-27, 2000, ISO 10303-28, 2007). Chapter XI discusses some of these implementation methods in further detail.

- Conformance Testing

The third major architectural component of STEP is in support of conformance testing. Conformance testing is covered by two series of 10303 parts: conformance testing methodology and framework, and abstract test suites.

The conformance testing methodology and framework series provide an explicit framework for conformance and other types of testing as an integral part of the standard. This methodology describes how testing of implementations of various STEP parts is accomplished. The fact that the framework and methodology for conformance testing is standardized reflects the importance of testing and testability within STEP. Conformance testing methods are standardized in the ISO 10303-30 series of parts.

An abstract test suite contains the set of abstract test cases necessary for conformance testing of an implementation of a STEP application protocol. Each abstract test case specifies input data to be provided to the implementation under test, along with information on how to assess the capabilities of the implementation. Abstract test suites enable the development of good processors and encourage expectations of trouble-free exchange.

- Data Specifications

The final major component of the STEP architecture is the data specifications. There are four part series of data specifications in the STEP documentation structure, though conceptually there are three primary types of data specifications: integrated resources, application protocols, and application interpreted constructs. All of the data specifications are documented using the description methods.

Integrated application resources represent concepts related to a particular application context that supports common requirements of many other product data applications. Examples of application resource constructs include drawing sheet revision, drawing revision, and dimension callout. These constructs may be used by any application that includes drawings. Integrated application resources are standardized in the ISO 10303-100 series of parts.

Application protocols are the implementable data specifications of STEP. APs include an EXPRESS information model that satisfies the specific product data needs of a given application context. APs may be implemented using one or more of the implementation methods. They are the central component of the STEP architecture, and the STEP architecture is designed primarily to support and facilitate developing APs.

Many of the components of an application protocol are intended to document the application domain in application-specific terminology. This facilitates the review of the application protocol by domain experts. The application interpreted model (AIM) is the component of the AP that is the normative, implementable information model in EXPRESS. Conformance classes are defined subsets of the AIM that may be used as a basis for conformance testing of implementations. Application protocols are standardized in the ISO 10303-200 series of parts.

Application interpreted constructs (AICs) are data specifications that satisfy a specific product data need that arises in more than one application context. An application interpreted construct specifies the data structures and semantics that are used to exchange product data common to two or more application protocols. Application protocols with similar information requirements are compared semantically to determine functional equivalence that, if present, leads to specifying that functional equivalence within a standardized AIC. This AIC would then be used by both application protocols and available for future APs to use as well. STEP has a requirement for interoperability between processors that share common information requirements. A necessary condition for satisfying this requirement is a common data specification. Application interpreted constructs provide this capability. Application interpreted constructs are standardized in the ISO 10303-500 series of parts.

STEP Methodology

The STEP methodology supports developing APs and the resources required by those APs. A principal feature of the STEP architecture is the layering of data specifications. Of primary interest are the context-independent integrated resources and the context-dependant application protocols. There are three classes of information models specified within these two types of specifications. The first class of information model is a collection of standardized EXPRESS schemas that are contained in the integrated resources. Each integrated resource schema is a representation of a specific subject area within the domain of product data. The integrated resources are abstract, conceptual structures of information that are generic with respect to various types of products and different stages of the product lifecycle. The process of ensuring that STEP integrated resources form a cohesive whole is called resource integration.

The second and third classes of information models are contained in application protocols: the application reference model (ARM) and the application interpreted model. An ARM captures the information requirements for an application context that has a scope bounded by a specific set of product types and product-lifecycle stages. ARMs are presented informatively in one of two graphical modelling languages (IDEF1X or EXPRESS-G) as well as normatively in text. An AIM is an EXPRESS schema that selects the applicable constructs from the integrated resources as baseline conceptual elements. An AIM may augment the baseline constructs with additional constraints and relationships specified by entities containing local rules, refined data types, global rules, and specialized textual definitions.

The two primary principles of the STEP methodology are resource integration and application interpretation. Resource integration brings together like elements -- information models. The result of the STEP integration process is a single information model, documented in multiple schemas in multiple standards. Application interpretation brings together unlike elements -- the information requirements of an application context and an information model. The result of the interpretation process is a single information model – an AIM (Kemmerer, 1999).

A STEP File

In STEP instead of using numerals, text is used in identifying the entity. For example "Cartesian_ point" is used as the identifier for points. These definitions are all given by the respective EXPRESS schema. The STEP file is generated conforming to the rules and format in the EXPRESS Schema. Unlike C or C++, EXPRESS is more like a formatted design language. Geometric objects are defined in terms of ENTITIES. An example of EXPRESS file is listed below,

```
SCHEMA TEST_SCHEMA;
    ENTITY CARTESIAN_POINT;
        x_coordinate: REAL;
        y_coordinate: REAL;
        z_coordinate: REAL;
    END_ENTITY;
END_SCHEMA;
```

When the CAD model is compiled with EXPRESS compiler and the data structure populated, a STEP file, whose format is defined in STEP Part 21 (ISO 10303-21, 1994), can be produced as shown below,

```
ISO-10303-21;
HEADER;
FILE_DESCRIPTION(("), '1');
FILE_NAME('CARTESIAN-POINT',
    '2007-07-10T09:19:11-04:00',
    ("),
    ("),
    'STEP INTERFACE',
    'STEP DESIGN SYSTEM',
    ");
FILE_SCHEMA(('TEST_SCHEMA'));
ENDSEC;
DATA;
#1=CARTESIAN_POINT(10.0,20.0,30.0);
#2=CARTESIAN_POINT(5.0,10.0,15.0);
#3=CARTESIAN_POINT(30.0,10.0,6.0);
ENDSEC;
END-ISO-10303-21;
```

Current Status of STEP

The current status of STEP standards development has been on four fronts. First of all, STEP AP 203, the most widely used AP in STEP application protocols, has been worked on for a number of years to produce its second edition. In this edition, construction history and geometric and dimensional tolerancing are for the first time included, providing foundation for additional future capabilities. Secondly, there has been some extensive development work undertaken to provide an effective tool for STEP data to be communicated via the Internet. This is evidenced by publication of STEP Part 25 in 2005. Part 25 describes the implementation method from EXPRESS to XMI. Also being worked on is STEP Part 28 Edition 2, which specifies the implementation methods for XML representations of EX-PRESS schemas and data. Thirdly, STEP has been extended to reach many other fields in addition to design. This is particularly true with manufacturing. Between 2004 and 2007, five such APs have been published. They are,

- STEP AP 215: Ship arrangement
- STEP AP 218: Ship structures
- STEP AP 224 ed3: Mechanical product definition for process planning using machining features
- STEP AP 238: Application interpreted model for computerized numerical controllers
- STEP AP 240: Process plans for machined products

In support of product life cycle management, PDM Implementers Forum (2002) and ISO 10303-239 (2005) have been published.

An Industry Case Study

One of the most significant STEP implementation program is AeroSTEP - the use of STEP in the digital pre-assembly of commercial aircraft engines. The basis of the AeroSTEP project lies in the commercial relationships between an aircraft manufacturer (Boeing) and its engine suppliers (General Electric, Pratt & Whitney, and Rolls-Royce). In the past, the only method to check the fit between an aircraft engine and the airframe was to construct a full-size physical mock-up. These mock-ups are used to check the various interfaces between the airframe, the engine, and the aircraft systems. As the use of advanced CAD technology for both engine and airframe design became standard practice, the need to create these physical mock-ups became an increasingly critical bottleneck in the design process.

The Boeing 777 is the first airliner designed completely using CAD. Similarly, the various engines that are fitted to the 777 are also designed using CAD. This created the opportunity to compare and analyse the designs of the airframe and the engines based on the respective CAD models, and to eliminate the need for a physical mock-up. This use of CAD models is referred to as "digital pre-assembly" (DPA). However, complex data translation was needed to accomplish this requirement, since Boeing and its three major engine suppliers use three different 3D CAD systems: Catia® (Dassault Systemes), CADDS5® (ComputerVision) and Unigraphics® (EDS). Previous attempts to exchange data between these systems using IGES, SET or direct translators had not delivered the necessary completeness or accuracy of exchange, hence a trial of STEP's capabilities in comparison to previous methods.

The basis of the AeroSTEP project is the use of one of the STEP application protocols – AP203 "Configuration controlled design" – to exchange data between Boeing and its engine suppliers in the context of digital pre-assembly (Figure 2.6).

The results of these trial exchanges were very promising, showing real improvement over the previous data exchange methods attempted. An interesting set of issues arose from the exchange of configuration management data. The ability to exchange such information is unique to STEP among CAD/CAM exchange standards. The analysis carried out of the configuration management data in the various companies revealed a number of significant differences in understanding terms such as "part", "version", and "assembly". STEP was therefore playing an unexpected role – as a neutral language forming the basis for alignment of working practices and terminology.

The success of the AeroSTEP project is now judged from the fact that complete, production implementations of AP203 were used for digital pre-assembly exchanges, and that elimination of physical mock-ups are now in the history-book. The shared benefits to the aircraft manufacturer and the engine suppliers from the effective use of STEP include, improved data integrity; reduction of cycle time; greatly reduced effort in data exchange; improved quality; and savings in configuration management (Fowler, 1995).

Apart from AP203, Boeing has also implemented AP210 (ISO 10303-210, 2001). This application protocol covers representation of the design of electronic assemblies, their interconnections and packaging, printed wiring assemblies (PWA) and printed wiring boards (Smith, 2002). This has enabled PWA designs to be moved directly between CAD systems, hence allowing CAD end-users to design PWAs on the CAD system of their choice. This supports the philosophy of "best of class".

DISCUSSIONS

This section compares different data exchanging methods and discusses some alternative ways of translating design data. Product data quality is also discussed in this section.

Figure 2.6. AeroSTEP project scenario

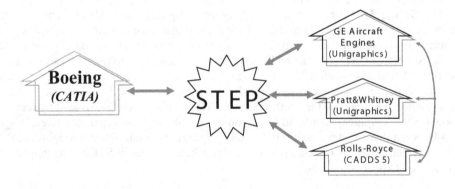

Comparing Data Exchange Methods

Based on the discussions in the previous sections, a matrix as shown in Table 2.2 is developed to describe the user-friendliness of different types of data translation methods.

It appears that use of common file formats is the most advantageous. However, it still is not a complete solution for an integrated system. The majority of the industry does not know the cost spent on the data exchanging of a feature-based model. This means that the dollar value spent on data translation is hidden and not actually seen as a cost that can be easily avoided or cut down.

There are a few intermediate approaches to data exchange. Instead of translating or re-creating all inbound design data into the CAD format that matches your internal tools, one may use engineering visualization tools to assemble the design data that exists in different CAD formats in order to perform all the necessary engineering activities. This practice should at least reduce engineering time and costs. As an intermediate step as you migrate to using a single data management tool to associate designs in different formats to one another, one can use spreadsheets to track the associations manually.

Some industry norm approaches are more effective. Instead of managing design data in multiple data management tools, each of which is specific to one CAD application, organisations can centralize their applications in order to reduce IT support costs and consolidate design data in a single repository. Original equipment manufacturers (OEMs), as opposed to suppliers and contract manufacturers, can use outsourced experts to translate and re-create design data between formats. This allows those manufacturers to focus on internal engineering efficiencies.

The best in class approach is to use the central data management tool to associate designs existing in different CAD formats that represent the same part or assembly. This increases design reuse as users realize that the designs already exist in the format required, reducing effort spent in re-creating or translating the design or, even worse, creating a new design.

Data Quality

Product data quality can be addressed intrinsically and extrinsically. The intrinsic aspect of product data quality refers to the fundamental issues of product data modelling. The

Table 2.2. Data translation matrix

Data Translation Method	User Friendly	Practical	Efficiency
Use of software with the same kernels	****	*	****
Applications that operates on dual kernels	**	**	****
Use of common file formats	****	***	***
Use of a direct data translator	***	**	**

* -- *Indicating the level of the category.*

Automotive Industry Action Group (AIAG) defines product data quality in the following way (Contero & Vila, 2005):

Quality Product Model Data is constructed accurately, completely representing the geometric model (math data), and accurately and completely representing all additional information in a way that can be shared and used by multiple users and managed with a minimum effort.

There are a host of product data quality standards. The most widely used seems to be VDA 4955 (Verband der Automobilindustrie, 2002) and its equivalent ODG11CQ9504 "ODETTE CAD/CAM Quality Assurance Method" ODETTE standard. VDA 4955 provides quality criteria for both geometrical and organizational aspects of CAD/CAM data. With the objective of unifying the emergent national recommendations related to product data quality, the "Strategic Automotive Product Data Standards Industry Group (SASIG)", established in 1995, has been working on developing an international recommendation (SASIG-PDQ) for product data quality in the automotive industry. This standard is a joint one between ISO and PAS (ISO/PAS 26183, 2006). ISO/PAS 26183 defines product data quality as a measure of the accuracy and appropriateness of product data, combined with the timeliness with which those data are provided to all the people who need them. Interested readers can find extra information from the article by Contero, Company, Vila and Aleixos (2005).

Design data, when converted from one type to the other, may also suffer from quality problems. This is the extrinsic aspect of product data quality. These problems are often related to topological errors, i.e., aggregate errors, such as zero-volume parts, duplicate or missing parts, inconsistent surface orientation, etc., and geometric errors, i.e., numerical imprecision errors, such as cracks or overlaps of geometry (Barequet & Duncan, 1998). These defects in the model can cause problems in finite element meshing, Stereolithography output, and NC tool-path generation routines. The software and algorithms that attempt to solve these problems are called (automatic) geometry (model) healing or repairing. Interested readers are referred to the work done by Barequet (1997), Chong, Kumar, & Lee (2007), Nooruddin, & Turk (2003), and Yau, Kuo, & Yeh (2003). It can be concluded that the development of STEP is the best solution to solve the extrinsic problems (Vergeest & Horváth, 2001) that appear during the data exchange process.

CONCLUSION

Due to the globalised manufacturing and business environment, data compatibility in the design domain has become an issue that companies cannot afford to ignore. CAD kernels all have their own proprietary data formats, presenting a challenging case for manufacturers to collaborate, in particular exchange their design work. There are two main types of data translation methods: direct data translation and neutral data translation. The latter is about standardising product data and its usage, and this method seems to hold the key to the ultimate solution of data compatibility in an integrated system. Among the various data exchange standard/protocols that can be used for neutral data translation, STEP stands out as the only international standard and is being used more and more widely in industry. The data formats used in STEP contain not only the information during the design stage of a product, but also that required for the entire product life cycle. No other currently available formats can emulate the same kind of capability. By using STEP, any products that support the standard can easily interconnect and flexibility in choice of components can be gained, allowing users to choose the best or the least expensive product without any commitments to proprietary products. The Aero STEP project is one of the successful industrial implementations of STEP. It has been made clear that STEP data exchange of solid model data was both feasible and desirable.

REFERENCES

Barequet, G. (1997). Using geometric hashing to repair CAD objects. *IEEE Computational Science & Engineering, 4*(4), 22-28

Barequet, G., & Duncan, C. A. (1998). RSVP: A geometric toolkit for controlled repair of solid models. *IEEE Transactions on Visualization And Computer Graphics, 4*(2), 162-177

Bloor, S., & Owen, J. (2003). *Product Data Exchange*. UK: Taylor & Francis.

CAD User. (2000). Healing the wounds of data conversion. *AEC Magazine, 13*(03).

Chong, C. S., Kumar, A. S., & Lee, H. P. (2007). Automatic mesh-healing technique for model repair and finite element model generation. *Finite Elements in Analysis and Design, 43*(15), 1109-1119.

Contero, M., Company, P., Vila, C., & Aleixos, N. (2002). Product Data Quality and Collaborative Engineering, *IEEE Computer Graphics and Applications, 22*(3), 32-42.

Contero, M., & Vila, C. (2005). Collaborative Engineering, in *Advances in Electronic Business (Volume one)*, by Li, E., & Du, T. C. (Ed.). Hershey, PA: Idea Group Inc (IGI).

Dassault Systemes. (2007). *3DXML (3D Extensible Markup Language)*. France: Dassault Systemes. Retrieved July 28, 2007, from http://www.3ds.com.

Dean, A. (2005 December). Elysium™ CAD doctor 5.2. *MCAD Magazine*, EDA Publications. Retrieved July 28, 2007, from http://www.mcadonline.com/index.php?option=com_content&task=view&id=179&Itemid=1)

DXF (Drawing eXchange Format) Specifications. (2007). Autodesk®, Inc., 111 McInnis Parkway, San Rafael, CA 94903 USA. Retrieved July 28, 2007, from http://usa.autodesk.com/adsk/servlet/item?siteID=123112&id=8446698)

Fowler, J. (1995). *STEP for Data Management - Exchange and Sharing*. Great Britain: Technology Appraisals.

IGES (Initial Graphics Exchange Specification). (1980). *ASME Y14.26M*. National Bureau of Standards, USA.

ISO 10303-1. (1994). *Industrial automation systems and integration -- Product data representation and exchange -- Part 1: Overview and fundamental principles*. Geneva, Switzerland: International Organisation for Standardisation (ISO).

ISO 10303-11. (1994). *Industrial automation systems and integration – Product data representation and exchange – Part 11: Description methods: The EXPRESS language reference manual.* Geneva, Switzerland: International Organisation for Standardisation (ISO).

ISO 10303-21. (1994). *Industrial automation systems and integration – Product data representation and exchange – Part 21: Implementation methods: Clear text encoding of the exchange structure.* Geneva, Switzerland: International Organisation for Standardisation (ISO).

ISO 10303-210. (2001). *Industrial automation systems and integration -- Product data representation and exchange -- Part 210: Application protocol: Electronic assembly, interconnection, and packaging design.* Geneva, Switzerland: International Organisation for Standardisation (ISO).

ISO 10303-22. (1998). *Industrial automation systems and integration – Product data representation and exchange – Part 22: Implementation methods: Standard data access interface.* Geneva, Switzerland: International Organisation for Standardisation (ISO).

ISO 10303-23. (2000). *Industrial automation systems and integration – Product data representation and exchange – Part 23: C++ language binding to the standard data access interface.* Geneva, Switzerland: International Organisation for Standardisation (ISO).

ISO 10303-239. (2005). *Industrial automation systems and integration -- Product data representation and exchange -- Part 239: Application protocol: Product life cycle support.* Geneva, Switzerland: International Organisation for Standardisation (ISO).

ISO 10303-24. (2001). *Industrial automation systems and integration – Product data representation and exchange – Part 24: C language binding of standard data access interface.* Geneva, Switzerland: International Organisation for Standardisation (ISO).

ISO 10303-27. (2000). *Industrial automation systems and integration – Product data representation and exchange – Part 27: Java programming language binding to the standard data access interface with Internet/Intranet extensions.* Geneva, Switzerland: International Organisation for Standardisation (ISO).

ISO 10303-28. (2007). *Industrial automation systems and integration – Product data representation and exchange – Part 28: XML representations of EXPRESS schemas and data, using XML schemas.* Geneva, Switzerland: International Organisation for Standardisation (ISO).

ISO/PAS 26183. (2006). *SASIG Product data quality guidelines for the global automotive industry.* Geneva, Switzerland: International Organisation for Standardisation (ISO).

Kemmerer, S. J. (Eds.) (1999). *STEP – Grand experience.* Gaithersburg US: Department of Commerce, U.S.

Nooruddin, F., & Turk, G. (2003). Simplification and repair of polygonal models using volumetric techniques. *IEEE Transactions on Visualization and Computer Graphics, 9*(2), 191-205.

PDES (Product Data Exchange Specification). (2007). 5300 International Blvd. N. Charleston, SC 29418. USA.: PDES, Inc. Retrieved July 28, 2007, from http://pdesinc.aticorp.org/

PDM Implementers Forum. (2002). *Usage Guide for the STEP PDM Schema*, V1.2, Release 4.3. January 2002

Smith, G. L. (2002). Utilisation of STEP AP 210 at the Boeing Company. *Computer-Aided Design, 34*, 1055-1062.

Verband der Automobilindustrie. (2002). *DVA Recommendation 4955/3: Scope and Quality of CAD/CAM Data*, German Assoc. Automotive Industry (VDA), Frankfurt, Germany.

Vergeest , J. S. M., & Horváth, I. (2001). Where Interoperability Ends. *Proceedings of the 2001 Computers and Information in Engineering Conference (DETC'01)* (Paper No. CIE-21233). New York: ASME.

XML (Extensible Markup Language). (2007). *Wide Wide Web Consortium*. MIT/CSAIL, USA. Retrieved July 28, 2007, from www.w3.org

Yau, H. T., Kuo, C. C., & Yeh, C. H. (2003). Extension of surface reconstruction algorithm to the global stitching and repairing of STL models. *Computer-Aided Design, 35*, 477-486.

Chapter III
Computer–Aided Process Planning and Manufacturing

ABSTRACT

Products and their components are designed to perform certain functions. Design specifications ensure the functionality aspects. The task in manufacturing is then to produce the components that meet the design specifications. The components are in turn assembled into the final products. When computers are used to assist the process planning and manufacturing activities, multiple benefits can be had. The related technologies are known as computer-aided process planning and computer-aided manufacturing. Often, they are not separable and are therefore discussed in tandem in this chapter. It should be emphasized that process planning is not only for metal-cutting processes. We need process planning for many other manufacturing processes such as casting, forging, sheet metal forming, compositesz and ceramic fabrication. In this chapter, the basic steps of developing a process plan are explained. There are two approaches to carrying out process planning tasks—manual experience-based method and computer-aided process planning method. The focus is on two computer-aided process planning methods, the variant approach, and generative approach. These discussions on process planning have been limited to machining processes. The topic of computer-aided manufacturing, on the other hand, is discussed with a more general point of view. A fictitious CAM plant is presented and some of the key aspects of CAM in a manufacturing system are discussed. A more specific version of CAM (i.e. computer numerical control) will be covered in Chapters VIII and IX.

COMPUTER-AIDED PROCESS PLANNING

Traditionally, process planning tasks are undertaken by manufacturing process experts. These experts use their experience and knowledge to generate instructions for the manufacture of the products based on the design specifications and the available installations and operators. Different process planner may come up with different plans when facing the same problem, leading to inconsistency in process planning and manufacturing. Consistent and correct planning requires knowledge of manufacturing process and experience (Park 2003, Vidal, Alberti, Ciurana & Casadesus, 2005). This has led to the development of computer-aided process planning and manufacturing systems.

The idea of developing process plans using computers was first conceived in the mid-1960's. The first CAPP system was developed in 1976 under sponsorship of Computer-Aided Manufacturing International (CAM-I) (Cay & Chassapis, 1997). Since then, there has been a great deal of research carried out in the area, which has been documented in a number of articles (Alting & Zhang, 989, Cay & Chassapis, 1997, Marri, Gunasekaran & Grieve, 1998, Shen, Hao, Yoon & Norrie, 2006, Zhang & Xie, 2007).

Process planning acts as a bridge between design and manufacturing by translating design specifications into manufacturing process details. Therefore, process planning refers to a set of instructions that are used to make a component or a part so that the design specifications are met, or as it is defined by the Society of Manufacturing Engineering (SME) -- "process planning is the systematic determination of the methods by which a product is to be manufactured economically and competitively". The question is what information is required and what activities are involved in transforming a raw part into a finished component, starting with the selection of raw material and ending with completion of the part. The answer to this question essentially defines the information and set of activities required to develop a process plan.

Basic Steps in Developing a Process Plan

The development of a process plan involves a number of activities (Singh, 1996):

- Analysis of part requirements.
- Selection of raw workpiece/material.
- Determination of manufacturing operations and their sequences.
- Selection of machine tools.
- Selection of tools, work-holding devices and inspection equipment.
- Determination of machining conditions (cutting speed, feed and depth of cut) and manufacturing times (setup time, processing time and lead time).

Figure 3.1 illustrates these activities. Note that these activities are not to be considered in a strict linear sequence. They are often intertwined and inter-dependent. Iterations often occur during the entire process planning cycle.

Analysis of Part Requirements

At the engineering design level, the part requirements are expressed through and as the part features, dimensions and tolerance specifications. These, in turn, dictate the processing

Figure 3.1. Activities in a process planning system

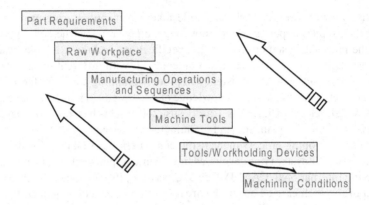

requirements. The analysis of the finished part requirements is therefore the first step in process planning. First, the design or geometric features of the parts are analysed. Examples of these features are plane, cylinder, cone, step, edge and fillet. Then, these common features have to be translated into manufacturing features, or machining features as in this case. Examples of machining features are slots, pockets, grooves and holes. This translation process is often known as feature recognition/conversion. For instance, consider the part designed by/within a conventional CAD package as shown in Figure 3.2. The results of feature recognition should provide a set of machining features such as the holes, slot and pocket. It is these machining features that can be utilised by a process planning system. After feature conversion, dimensional and tolerance analyses are performed to provide more information for manufacturing purposes.

Selection of Raw Workpiece

Selection of raw workpiece is an important element of process planning. It involves such attributes as shape, size (dimensions and weight) and material. For example, a raw part may be in the shape of a rod, slab, billet or just a rough forging; each has a preferred machining

Figure 3.2. Features for machining operations

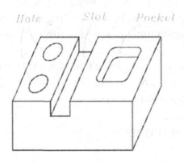

operation. From the view-point of dimensional accuracy as well as economics of manufacturing, it is essential to determine the required overall size of the raw part. The weight and material of the raw part are often dictated by the functional requirements of the part.

Determination of Manufacturing Operations and Their Sequences

The next logical step in process planning is to determine the appropriate types of processing operations and their sequence to transform the features, dimensions and tolerances of a part from the raw workpiece to the finished state. There may be several ways to produce a given design. Sometimes constraints such as accessibility and setup may require that some features be machined before or after others. Furthermore, the type of machine tools and cutting tools available as well as the batch sizes may also influence the process sequence. For example, a process plan that is optimal on a three- or four-axis machine may not be optimal on a five-axis machine because of the greater flexibility of higher-axis machines. Similarly, the tools that are available and the tools that can be loaded onto a particular machine might change the sequence, too. The common criteria for evaluating these alternatives include the quality and quantity of the product produced and the efficiency of machining.

Surface roughness and tolerance requirements also influence the operation sequence. For example, a part requiring a hole with low tolerance and surface roughness requirements would probably only require a simple drilling operation. The same part with much finer surface finish and tighter tolerance requirements would probably require first a drilling operation and then a boring operation to obtain the desired surface roughness and the tolerance on the hole.

Sometimes operations are dependent on one another. For example, consider Figure 3.3(a), in which the operations on the part are inter-dependent. The holes must be drilled before milling the inclined surface because a hole cannot be drilled accurately on an inclined surface. However, if the inclined surface has to be finished before drilling, an end mill should be used to obtain a flat surface perpendicular to the axis of the drill before drilling the hole (e.g. the hole to the right), in which case an extra operation is required.

Cutting forces and rigidity of the workpiece also influence the operation sequence. For example, consider the part shown in Figure 3.3(b). Hole 1 may be required to be drilled before machining the slot. If the hole is machined after finishing the slot, the workpiece may bend. Machining of Holes 2 and 3 may depend on their tolerance requirements. If these two holes have a concentricity requirement, it is desirable to drill them in one operation from either side. The slot may not be allowed to cut first as the concentricity requirement may be hard to maintain if one of the holes is re-entered. These simple examples demonstrate that the part features' geometry, dimensions, tolerances, accessibility and setup constraints are some of the many factors that dictate the processing requirements and their sequences.

Selection of Machine Tools

The next step in process planning after the selection of manufacturing operations and their sequence is to select the machine tool(s) on which these operations can be performed. A large number of factors influence the selection of a machine tool. They are,

Figure 3.3. Machining sequence of features

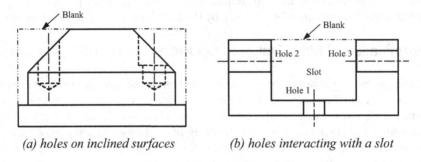

(a) holes on inclined surfaces   *(b) holes interacting with a slot*

- Workpiece-related attributes such as the material, kinds of features to be made, dimensions of the workpiece, its dimensional tolerances and raw material form;
- Machine tool-related attributes such as process capability, size, mode of operation (e.g. manual, semiautomatic, automatic and numerically controlled), the type of operation (e.g. turning, milling and grinding), tooling capabilities (e.g. size and type of the tool magazine) and automatic tool-changing capabilities. Chapter VIII gives a detailed account of different types of machine tools.
- Production volume-related information such as the production quantity and order frequency.

On the whole, there are three basic criteria for evaluating the suitability of a machine tool to accomplish an operation. They are unit cost of production, manufacturing lead-time and quality. There are many analytical methods proposed. These methods do not always yield a satisfied result because of the large number of factors involved. Instead, an expert system that embodies some of the qualitative and quantitative knowledge of machine tools, cutting tools and operations, is often regarded as a useful solution in process planning. It can suggest alternative machine tools and cutting tools for the various operations on the part. The user can then build alternative process plans using this information.

Selection of Cutters, Workholding Devices and Inspection Equipment

A combination of machine tool(s) and cutting tool(s) is required to generate a feature on a workpiece. The selection of machine tools, cutting tools, workholding devices and inspection equipment is based primarily on part features. For example, if a tight tolerance and smooth surface finish are required, a high-precision machine tool and cutting tool may have to be employed. Furthermore, cutting tool specifications such as rakes, clearances, cutting edge and nose radius are all to be determined accordingly. A detailed discussion on tooling on CNC machine tools is given in Chapter VIII.

Work-holding devices are used to locate and hold the workpiece securely during machining operations. These devices include clamps (e.g. chuck, faceplate and collets), jigs and fixtures. The shapes, dimensions, accuracy, production rate and variety of parts essentially determine the types of work-holding devices required. For example, a four-jaw chuck can accommodate prismatic parts; faceplates are used for clamping irregularly shaped workpiece; and collets are used to hold round bars only (and only those within a certain range of diameters). Jigs are designed to have various reference surfaces and points for accurate alignment of parts and tools. Fixtures are, however, designed for specific shapes and dimensions of parts (Rong & Zhu, 1999).

Inspection equipment is necessary to ensure the dimensional accuracy, tolerances and surface finish on the features. The major categories include on-line and off-line inspection equipment. Chapter XIV presents a model of on-line (on-machine) inspection. In the case of off-line inspection, co-ordinate measurement machines (CMMs) are often used.

Determining Machining Conditions and Manufacturing Times

Having specified the workpiece material, machine tool(s) and cutting tool(s), the question is what can be controlled to reduce cost and increase production rate. The controllable variables for machining operations (e.g. milling operations) are primarily cutting speed *(v)*, feed *(f)* and depth/width of cut *(a_p and/or a_e)*. Jointly, v, f, a_p and a_e are referred to as machining conditions. There are a number of models for determining the optimal machining conditions. The most commonly used models are the *minimum cost model* and *maximum product rate model*.

Minimum Cost Model

In a minimum cost model, the objective is to determine the machining conditions so that a minimum cost can be achieved. The average cost per piece to produce a workpiece consists of the following components (Singh, 1996),

C_u = non-productive cost per piece
   + machining time cost per piece
   + tool changing cost per piece
   + tooling cost per piece

or,

$$Cu = c_o t_l + c_o t_c + c_o t_d (t_{ac}/T) + c_t (t_{ac}/T) \qquad (3.1)$$

The tool life equation as a function of cutting speed *(v)* is expressed as

$$vT^n = C \qquad (3.2)$$

where

c_o = cost rate including labour and overhead cost rates (\$/*min*)
c_t = tool cost per cutting edge, which depends on the type of tool used
C = constant in the tool life equation, $vT^n = C$
v = cutting speed in meters/minute
f = feed-rate (*mm/rev*)
d = depth of cut (*mm*)

n = exponent in the tool life equation

t_l = non-productive time consisting of loading and unloading the part and other idle time (*min*)

t_c = machining time per piece (*min*/piece)

t_d = time to change a cutting edge (*min*)

t_{ac} = actual cutting time per piece, which is approximately equal to t_c, (*min*/piece)

T = tool life (*min*)

Consider a single-pass turning operation. If L, D and f are the length of cut (*mm*), diameter of the workpiece (*mm*), and feed-rate (*mm/rev*), respectively, then the cutting time per piece for a single-pass operation is,

$$t_c \approx t_{ac} = \frac{\pi L D}{1000 v f} \tag{3.3}$$

Upon substituting these values as well as the tool life equation in the cost per piece equation, the cost per component C_u can be expressed as a function of v (assuming that the feed-rate and depth of cut are normally fixed to their allowable values),

$$C_u = f(v) \tag{3.4}$$

Thus, the minimum unit cost cutting speed can be sought, so can the optimal tool life for the minimum unit cost.

Maximum Production Rate Model

In a maximum production rate model, the cost issue is overlooked. The objective is to obtain a maximum production rate, or in other words, a minimum production time. The production time per piece can be expressed as follows (Singh, 1996),

T_u = non-productive time per piece (t_l)
    + machining time per piece (t_c)
    + tool changing time per piece (t_t)

or,

$$T_u = t_l + t_c + t_d(t_{ac}/T) \tag{3.5}$$

Similarly, the optimal cutting speed that ensures maximum production rate and the corresponding tool life can be obtained.

Manufacturing Lead Time

Assuming that the lot size is Q units, then the average lead-time (T_l) to process these units is,

$$T_l = t_s + T_u \times Q \tag{3.6}$$

where t_s -- major setup time.

Once again, the above-mentioned six steps are not always performed sequentially; they are inter-connected. For instance, determining manufacturing operations, selecting machine tools and cutting tools are often inter-related tasks, any one of which cannot be performed in isolation from the others.

Principal Process Planning Approaches

The principal approaches to process planning are the *manual experience-based method* and *computer-aided process planning method.*

Manual Experience-Based Planning Method

The manual experience-based process planning method is still widely used. The basic steps involved are essentially the same as described above. The biggest problem with this approach is that it is time-consuming and the plans developed over a period of time may not be consistent.

The feasibility of process planning is dependent on many upstream factors such as the design and availability of machine tools. Also, a process plan has a great influence on many downstream manufacturing activities such as scheduling and machine tool allocation. Therefore, to develop a proper process plan (not to mention an optimal one), process planners must have sufficient knowledge and experience. It may take a relatively long time and is usually costly to develop the skill of a successful planner. Computer-aided process planning has been developed to overcome these problems to a certain extent.

Computer-Aided Process Planning Method

Why computer-aided process planning? As mentioned earlier, the primary purpose of process planning is to translate the design requirements into manufacturing process details. This suggests a feed forward system in which design information is processed by the process planning system to generate manufacturing process details. Unfortunately, this is not what is expected in a concurrent engineering environment, whose goal is to optimise the system performance in a global context. Therefore, there is a necessity of integrating the process planning system into the inter-organisational flow. For example, if changes are made to a design, one must be able to fall back on a module of CAPP to quickly re-generate the cost estimates for these design changes. Similarly, if there is a breakdown of a machine(s) on the shop-floor, the process planning system must be able to generate alternative process plans so that the most economical solution for the situation can be adopted. Chapter VII gives a detailed account of such an integrated environment. In such a setting of a multitude of interactions among various functions of an organisation and dynamic changes that take place in these sub-functional areas, the use of computers in process planning necomes essential (Singh, 1996).

By comparison with manual experience-based process planning, the use of computers in process planning also helps to achieve the following:

- Systematically producing accurate and consistent process plans;
- Reducing the cost and lead-time of process planning;
- Reducing the skill requirements of a process planner;
- Increasing productivity of a process planner;
- Being able to interface and integrate with application programs such as cost and manufacturing lead-time estimation and work standards.

Two major methods are used in CAPP. They are the *variant* method and *generative* method.

Variant CAPP Method

In the variant process planning approach, a process plan for a new part is created by recalling, identifying and retrieving an existing plan for a similar part and making necessary modifications for the new part (Figure 3.4). Quite often, process plans are developed for families of parts. Such parts are called *master parts*. The similarities in design attributes and manufacturing methods are exploited for the purpose of formation of part families.

A number of methods have been developed for part family formation. Among them, GT (Group Technology) is the most commonly used. Figure 3.5 shows different rotational parts that can be machined on the same lathe. A change of parts in this family would only require a new part program to generate a new contour. A tool change in this case probably

Figure 3.4. The variant CAPP approach

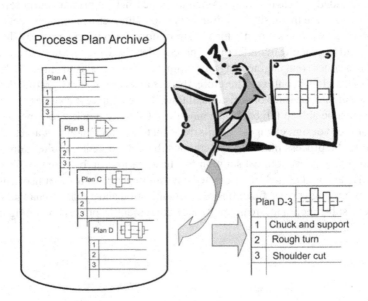

Figure 3.5. Rotational part family requiring similar turning operations

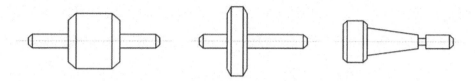

Figure 3.6. Similar cubical parts requiring similar milling operations

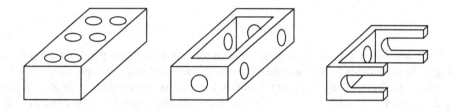

would not be necessary. Figure 3.6 shows cubical parts that are not very similar any more; however, they also form a production family as they can be made on the same multi-axis machining centre, requiring the same tools.

Figures 3.7 and 3.8 show two part families for electrodes that are used in an EDM (Electrical Discharging Machining) process. Note the difference and similarity between these two part families. Both families of parts have the same base. The parts in family A however, have side-faces that are not vertical, whereas those in family B are.

Thus, the variant process planning approach can be realised as a four-step process,

- define the coding scheme;
- group the parts into part families;
- develop a standard process plan; and
- retrieve and modify the standard plan.

Figure 3.7. Electrode part family A

Figure 3.8. Electrode part family B

There are different types of coding methods for classification of parts in Group Technology. These methods present a systematic process of establishing an alphanumeric value for parts on the basis of selected part features. Classification is then done through grouping of parts according to code values. Generally speaking, the following code structures are used,

- **Hierarchical:** The interpretation of each symbol depends of the value of the preceding symbols
- **Chain:** The interpretation of each symbol in the sequence is fixed
- **Hybrid:** Use of combination of the hierarchical and chain-type structures

Figure 3.9. Monocode structure

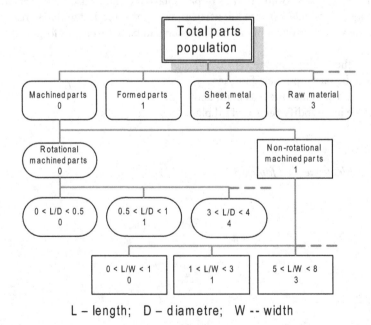

Figure 3.10. Polycode structure

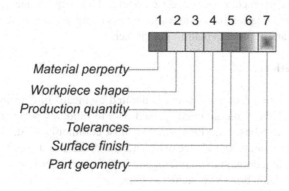

The hierarchical code structure (called a Monocode) (Figure 3.9), divides all parts of the total population into distinct subgroups of about equal size. The number of digits in the code is determined by the number of levels in the tree. The advantage of the hierarchical structure is that a few code numbers can represent a large amount of information. The singular disadvantage is the complexity associated with defining all the branches.

The chain structure, called a polycode, is created from a code table or matrix like the example shown in Figure 3.10. The type of part feature and digit position is defined by the left vertical columns. The numerical value placed in the digit position is determined by the feature descriptions across each row. The major advantages of polycodes are that they are compact and easy to use and develop. The primary disadvantage is that, for comparable code size, a polycode lacks the detail present in a hierarchical structure. A hybrid code captures the best features of the hierarchical and polycode structures.

Although variant process planning is quite similar to manual experience-based planning, its information management capabilities are much superior because of the use of computers. Advantages of the variant process planning approach include,

- Efficient processing and evaluation of complicated activities and decisions, thus reducing the time and labour requirements;
- Standardised procedures by structuring manufacturing knowledge of the process planners to company's needs;
- Lower development and hardware costs and shorter development times. This is especially important for small and medium-sized companies whose product variety is not high.

The obvious disadvantages of the variant process planning approach are,

- Maintaining consistency in editing is difficult;
- Adequately accommodating various combinations of material, geometry, size, precision, quality, alternative processing sequences and machine loading, is difficult;

- The quality of the final process plan generated depends to a large extent on the knowledge and experience of the process planners. This dependence on the process planners makes automation impossible and is considered as one of the major short-comings of the variant process planning approach.

Generative CAPP Method

In the generative approach, process plans are generated by means of decision logic, formulas, technology algorithms and geometry-based data to uniquely perform processing decisions. The knowledge-based CAPP system is most commonly used. It refers to a computer program that can store knowledge of a particular domain and use that knowledge to solve problems from that domain in an intelligent way. In such a system, computers are used to simulate the decision process of a human expert.

There are two major problems to be solved: *knowledge representation* and *inference mechanism*. The knowledge representation is a scheme by which a real-world problem can be represented in such a way that the computer can manipulate the information. For example, in defining a part, the presence of a hole may be sought for. Given that there is a hole, we then define the attributes of the hole, such as the type of hole, the length and the diameter. The reason for this is that the computer is not capable of reading the design from blueprints or databases as humans are. The inference mechanism is the way in which the computer finds a solution. One approach is based on IF-THEN structured knowledge. For example, IF there is a hole, THEN a drill may be used. When more technical information is considered, a rule for finish-machining a hole may be written as,

"finishing_operation for a hole:
(IT (8, 9))
(Ra (0.8, 1.6))
(Roundness (0.003, 0.010))
(Cylindricity (0.003, 0.008))
(Straightness (0.0008, 0.0012))"

which read, "if the tolerance grade of the hole is between $IT8$ and $IT9$, surface finish between $R_a0.8$ and $R_a1.6$, roundness between 0.003 and 0.01, cylindricity between 0.0003 and 0.008, and straightness between 0.0008 and 0.0012, then a finishing cut is needed proceeding a rough cut.

Through this type of knowledge, the computer can infer what operations are needed. Once the operations are known, it is easy to calculate other details and the process plan can be developed. Other aspects of a knowledge-based system include the interface, which contains the user interface, the interface with the CAD database and the inquiry facility that explains why a decision is made.

Decision tables provide a convenient way to facilitate a knowledge-based CAPP system. The elements of a decision table are conditions, actions and rules. They are organised in the form of an allocation matrix as shown in Table 3.1, where the conditions state the goals we want to achieve and the actions state the operations we have to perform. The rules, formed by entry values according to the experience of experts, establish the relationship between conditions and actions. Entries can be either Boolean-type values (true, false and do not care) or continuous values. The decision-making mechanism works as follows: for a particular set of condition entries, look for its corresponding rule, and from that rule determine the actions. Table 3.2 illustrates a decision table for the selection of lathes or grinding machines for jobs involving turning or grinding operations (Singh, 1996). Given the condition that the lot size of the job is 70 units; diameter is relatively small; the surface roughness desired is 30 μm; and the tolerance range required is $\pm$ 0.005 *mm*, it is easy to see from the table that rule 3 matches this situation. The action, therefore, is obviously turret lathe; that is, the operation is performed on a turret lathe. Chapter XVII presents a host of technologies that have been developed and employed in the development of various CAPP systems.

COMPUTER-AIDED MANUFACTURING

Much like in the design and process planning domains, computers are also intimately involved in various manufacturing activities. Computer-aided manufacturing can be understood from both a general point of view and a narrow point of view. In a general sense, computer-aided manufacturing refers to any computer applications to manufacturing problems, i.e.

- machine control
- machine monitoring
- simulation of manufacturing process
- plant communication
- mechanical testing
- electrical testing
- facilities and environmental control

However, in a manufacturing plant where mechanical and electrical equipment is produced, computer-aided manufacturing is often narrowly known as computer numerically controlled (CNC) machining. In this case, it is perhaps appropriate to re-term CAM as *Computer-aided machining*. The following section provides a broad view of CAM, leaving computer-aided machining (i.e. computer numerical control) to be explained in Chapters VIII, IX, XII, XIII.

Table 3.1. Format of a decision table

	Rule 1	Rule 2	...
Conditions	Entry	Entry	...
...	...	...	...
...	...	...	...
Actions	Entry	Entry	...
...	...	...	...
...	...	...	...

Table 3.2. Decision Table for the Selection of a Machine(s) for Turning Operation

Conditions*	Rule 1	Rule 2	Rule 3	Rule 4
LS ≤ 10	X			
LS ≥ 50		X	X	
LS ≥ 4000				X
Relatively large diameters				
Relatively small diameters	X	X	X	X
SF in the range 40-60 (*Ra*).	X			
SF in the range 16-32 (*Ra*)		X	X	X
±0.008 ≤ Tol ≤ ±0.013 *mm*	X			
±0.003 ≤ Tol ≤ ±0.008 *mm*			X	
±0.001 ≤ Tol ≤ ±0.003 *mm*	X	X		X
Actions				
Engine lathe	X	1		
Turret lathe			X	
Automatic screw machine				X
Centreless grinding machine		2		

*LS -- lot size; SF -- surface finish (μm); Tol -- tolerance.

Computer Applications in a Manufacturing Plant

In a modern day manufacturing plant, many of the computer applications are implemented and combined in a comprehensive and systematic way, e.g. there are computer applications in engineering, plant maintenance, and plant control. These computer applications are easily seen throughout the movement of a part through the plant, where it is manufactured from raw material, machined, measured, and finally assembled into a product.

The parts or the raw material arrive at the receiving inspection station by truck. The operator identifies the shipment to the computer. From the main computer information about the number of parts ordered and their quality control procedure and possibly the control program for the automatic test equipment is sent to the receiving inspection department. The number of parts tested is determined with the help of statistical methods which also take into consideration the vendor's historical quality performance record. The automatic test equipment measures the parts and sends the quality test together with information on number of parts accepted and rejected to the main computer. Here the vendor performance file is updated and, if necessary, new orders are issued to the vendor to replace defective or missing parts. In the next step, the parts are automatically stored in a warehouse, where a storage bin is selected according to such criteria as shortest travel distance, number of transactions for this type of part, and safety provisions. Critical parts may be stored in different isles to avoid part shortages during the possible breakdown of a stacker crane (Rembold, Blume & Dillmann, 1985).

When the central computer schedules the part for manufacturing, it releases the part and sends retrieval information to the computer in the warehouse. It, in turn, orders the part to be brought to the pickup area, and a computer-dispatched forklift truck carries the part to the machine tool. The machining instruction and machining sequence for the part have been determined automatically by the central computer and are known to the plant computer. The plant computer sends the NC program for the part to the corresponding machine tool and the part is machined under computer control of the machine tool. Operating data from the machine tool and quality data from the part are returned to the plant computer, evaluated and condensed, and sent back to the central computer. From the operating data of the machine tools and the attendant's identification number, the central computer can calculate the payroll. The part proceeds under computer control from one machine tool to another until it is again automatically stored in a finished part buffer. The inventory of this buffer is known to the central computer (Rembold, Blume & Dillmann, 1985).

When all parts for the product are completed and stored, the central computer schedules the assembly. The plant computer releases all the parts needed at the assembly station. They are brought to the individual stations by a conveyor system under computer control. The progress of the assembly is checked automatically at various quality control stations. When the product arrives at these stations, it is identified by a scanner and the computer retrieves its test program and controls the test run. Test data are channelled to the central computer. The finished product is tested again and brought to the finished-goods warehouse. Here it can be grouped together under computer control with other products that are to be shipped to the same destination (Rembold, Blume & Dillmann, 1985).

In this plant the computer performs scheduling, order release, machine control, machine status reporting, material movement control, warehouse control, attendance reporting, payroll calculation, maintenance scheduling, and other tasks. The conception of possible additional computer applications is, however, left to the reader's imagination.

Key Aspects of CAM in a Manufacturing System

Computers have been extensively used for detailed planning and the legitimate control of manufacturing systems. These planning and control activities for a manufacturing system are listed in Figure 3.11. Material-requirements planning (MRP), capacity planning, facility planning, inventory control, and tool management are planning and control activities for physical resources. Production scheduling is the planning and control of manufacturing resources over time. The manufacturing information/knowledge control comprises the information communication and manufacturing database management. The remaining text of this section briefly discusses these planning and control activities.

Material-requirements planning works as an initiator for the manufacturing system. When management determines the master production-schedule requirements (the MRP process unit integrates this information with the existing plant-capacity status and generates purchase orders, work orders, and schedule notices), based on the raw material required (bill of material (BOM)) and subassembly sequences determined by the engineering designer, and the inventory status reported from the storage warehouse manager, work orders and scheduling notices are sent to the shop-floor control manager to prepare for production.

Capacity planning comprises the information that is required to accomplish the production goal, such as identifying the number of machines, persons, material-handling resources, tooling, and so on. The availability of shifts per work day, the work days per

Figure 3.11. Planning/control activities of the manufacturing system

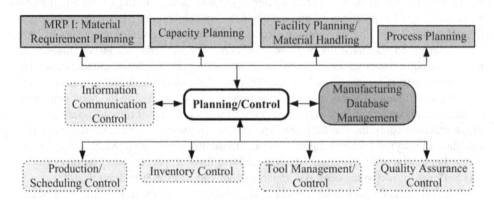

week, overtime, subcontracting, and machine/tool/material-handling device requirements are fed back to the MRP control unit, which adjusts the work orders, purchase orders, and schedule notices.

Facility and material-handling device planning are planning activities for selecting and arranging the physical layout of the manufacturing facilities, the material-handling devices, and the storage space. For several decades, group technology has gained increasing acceptance in this area. For small-to-medium production, GT cellular layout can reduce the part routing time and reduce part fixturing during transfer from machine to machine.

Inventory control deals with the control of (economic) inventory levels and the reorder point for any raw material, semi-finished, and finished parts. Also, the control of work in process (WIP) is another key element of this area. The philosophy of just-in-time (JIT) is a prevailing trend for reducing the WIP as well as the inventory. An ideal inventory-control mechanism guarantees no delays of the material supply.

Tool management is a vital activity that is frequently neglected by manufacturing engineers. It deals with tracking of tool location, cutting elapsed time, and times for re-conditioning, and so on. Minimizing tool breakage is another critical task of this control module.

Scheduling deals with the dispatching of job orders. Several rules such as FIFO (first in, first out), SPT (shortest-processing-time), and LIFO (last in, first out) are commonly used to schedule activities at workstations. The mean flow time, make span, machine utilization, and due-date constraints are measures of performance for the manufacturing system.

Quality control is the process that ensures the final acceptability of a product. Quality control deals with activities ranging from inspection and related procedures to sampling procedures used in manufacturing.

Manufacturing information management deals with the flow and allocation of information concerning manufacturing resources and functions. Included here are resources such as workers, machines, materials, tooling, and so on. This information is necessary for virtually all other manufacturing functions. Computer databases for managing manufacturing information can save storage space and standardize the information format, which is the major step for computer-integrated manufacturing.

Information and *communication* is especially important for large and computer-integrated manufacturing systems. Several different types of electronic communication protocol are available for different considerations. Manufacturing Applications Protocol (MAP) is an electronic hierarchical manufacturing-control protocol gaining rapid acceptance. Hierarchical control is suitable for many manufacturing systems, both manual and computer-controlled.

Manufacturing Control

Manufacturing control encompasses a large variety of activities in a factory environment (Figure 3.12). At the factory level of operations, control usually refers to the coordination of a variety of activities to ensure profitable operation. Materials management and capacity planning are principal control functions at this level. At the less-aggregate centres of a manufacturing facility, such as a production centre, the major focus of control is on the

Figure 3.12. Manufacturing-system control loop

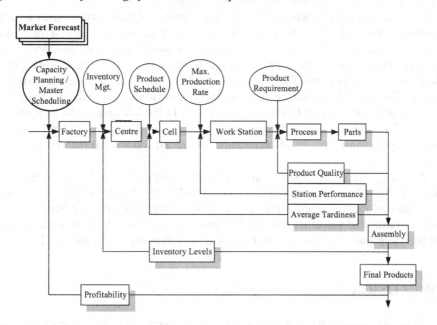

coordination of activities to maximize cell utilization and minimize inventory levels. At the cell level, control becomes involved with the scheduling of individual parts onto machines. Scheduling is a major component of cell control, although many other activities are part of cell control. When manufacturing engineers talk about control, this is the type of control that is normally addressed.

Two traditional control levels also exist below the cell. At the cell level, a given fixed time to produce a part is usually taken as a given to produce a schedule. However, a variety of speeds, feeds, tooling, tool paths, and so on, can be used for material processing. The selection and application of these variables form the primary focus of the workstation controller. Below the workstation resides the basic manufacturing process, which is the basis for all production. At the process level, motors, switches, feedback devices, and so on, must be controlled in order to attain the desired machine kinematics required to produce a part.

The impact of layout dictates many characteristics of a manufacturing system. Each layout brings certain advantages and disadvantages to the production floor. The control of these systems (cells) can also be quite different. For instance, in a product layout where a single product is to be produced, a significant amount of planning and analysis must be performed before the system becomes operational. A line balance must be conducted to assign operations to the processing machines in order to distribute operations as equally among the machines as is possible. Once the system is set up, the control is relatively easy because the only thing that needs to be controlled is the input station. Parts flow through the system at the rate of the slowest processing station.

The advent of today's modern flexible manufacturing systems has brought a wealth of control problems to the manufacturing engineer. In years past, many transfer lines operated automatically. However, these systems were product layout systems, and control from adjacent machine to adjacent machine was all that was necessary to control the entire system. Today's flexible manufacturing systems allow for a large selection of parts to be produced, and part transfer can be quite random. The sequence of operations and control of the required queues must be taken into account. In the job shop of the past, the machinist performed many of the scheduling activities required of today's control computer. Transferring the informal control to computer-controlled systems has proved to be a very difficult problem.

Controlling a programmable machining system has proved to be an exceptionally difficult problem for a variety of reasons. One problem that has been encountered in the development of these systems is protocol and interfacing. The time required to connect computer-controlled machines and the data that are transmitted to these machine tools, have been less than satisfactory. This point will be elaborated on in Chapter XI.

CONCLUSION

Feature-based approach has been adopted by many process planning systems, due to its ability to facilitate the representation of various types of part data in a meaningful form needed to drive the automated process planning. There are a number of key steps in the development of a process plan. It is important to note that these activities are inter-connected. Therefore, iterations are common activities in process planning.

Of the two types of CAPP approaches, the variant approach continues to be used by some manufacturing companies. The trend though is to strive for a generative approach. Expert systems are generally perceived to be useful in process planning and scheduling. It allows the capturing of knowledge from experts, and is able to simulate the problem solving skill of a human expert in a particular field. The benefits of expert systems are the accurate decision, time gains, improved quality and more efficient use of resources.

When computer-aided manufacturing is used in a broader sense, it refers to any manufacturing activities that have been assisted by use of computers, e.g. machine control, machine monitoring, simulation of manufacturing process, plant communication, mechanical testing, electrical testing and facilities and environmental control. When computer-aided manufacturing is used in a narrow sense, it refers to NC machining, and this will be discussed in the latter chapters.

REFERENCES

Alting, L., & Zhang, H. (1989). Computer aided process planning: the state-of-the-art survey. *International Journal of Production Research, 27*(4), 553-585.

Cay, F., & Chassapis, C. (1997). An IT view on perspectives of computer aided process planning research. *Computers in Industry, 34*(3), 307-337.

Chen, T-C., Wysk, R. A., & Wang, H-P. (1998). *Computer-aided manufacturing.* Prentice Hall. New York, USA.

Marri, H. B., Gunasekaran, A., & Grieve, R. J. (1998). Computer-aided process planning: A state of art. *International Journal of Advanced Manufacturing Technology, 14*(4), 261-268.

Park, S. C. (2003). Knowledge capturing methodology in process planning. *Computer-Aided Design, 35*(12), 1109-1117.

Rembold, U., Blume, C., & Dillmann, R. (1985). *Computer-Integrated Manufacturing Technology and Systems.* Marcel Dekker Inc.

Rong, Y., & Zhu, Y. (1999). *Computer-aided fixture design*, CRC Press: Carlisle, USA.

Shen, W., Hao, Q., Yoon, H. J., & Norrie, D. H. (2006). Applications of agent-based systems in intelligent manufacturing: An updated review. *Advanced Engineering Informatics, 20*(4), 415-431.

Singh, N. (1996). *Systems Approach to Computer-Integrated Design and Manufacturing.* New York, USA: John Wiley & Sons, Inc.

Vidal, A., Alberti, M., Ciurana, J., & Casadesus, M. (2005). A decision support system for optimising the selection of parameters when planning milling operations. *International Journal of Machine Tools and Manufacture*, *45*(2), 201-210.

Zhang, W. J., & Xie, S. Q. (2007). Agent technology for collaborative process planning: A review. *International Journal of Advanced Manufacturing Technology*, *32*(3-4), 315-325.

Chapter IV
Feature Technology

ABSTRACT

Throughout the course of the development of CAD, CAPP, and CAM systems, unambiguous representation of a design's geometry and topology remain an essential part of the task. Since the mid-1990's, the technology has matured enough to enable such a representation. While geometry and topology provides a basic description of a design part, direct use of it for creation of the part and other applications, can be cumbersome. Take creation of a simple plane with four straight edges as an example. For a B-rep model to fully define the plane, four points are to be created first to be used as four vertices. They are used to define four edges, which are connected one after another to form a closed loop. Finally, a flat surface is fitted onto the loop to form the plane. When a cube is to be designed, the above process needs to be repeated five more times for the other five faces though some of the vertices and edges may be re-used. In addition, the directions of the solid have to be defined through each face. Clearly, this is not a trivial task. Users would find it helpful if the creation of geometry and topology is hidden behind them and only some meaningful parameters of the solid are provided. In the case of a simple cube, length, width, and depth would be the parameters. Hence, the concept of features (i.e. cube or block in the above example) emerged, as did the associated technologies. The same applies for other domains, such as manufacturing and engineering analysis. This chapter aims to give a succinct introduction to various feature technologies such as feature defintions, feature taxonomy, feature representation schemes, and feature-based methodologies. Several important issues are highlighted. These include the application-dependent nature of features, and surface features versus volumetric features.

FEATURE DEFINITION

Features can be thought of as 'engineering primitives' suited for some engineering tasks. They originate in the reasoning processes used in various design, analysis and manufacturing activities, and are therefore often strongly associated with particular application domains. This explains why there are many different definitions for features. According to Shah and Mäntylä (1995), a feature should have,

- a physical constituent of a part;
- a generic shape that can be mapped to;
- engineering significance; and
- predictable properties.

In the context of CAD/CAPP/CAM, several more specific definitions have been suggested. One of such examples is,

A feature is referred to as a distinctive or characteristic part of a workpiece, defining a geometrical shape, which is either specific for a machining process or can be used for fixturing and/or measuring purposes (Erve & Kals, 1986).

Of particular relevance in this chapter are the machining features, which are normally related to machining methods or machining operations. Thus, a machining feature can be defined as

A portion of the workpiece generated by a certain mode of metal cutting. (Choi, Barash & Anderson, 1984), or

Feature information can be considered to be about volumes of material to be removed (Anderson, 1990).

A component with four machining features is shown in Figure 4.1, where the slot may require an end mill, the holes may require drilling operations and the pocket may require a slotting cutter or a slotting cutter and an end mill.

When dealing with features, there is a further complication: viewpoint dependence. That is, depending on the application domain, one could have different views towards the same, or combination of, feature(s) on a part. When a part is designed by features, the resulting model is not usually in a form convenient for other applications such as manufacturing process planning. Indeed, design features are stereotypical shapes related to a part's function, its design intent, or the model construction methodology, whereas manufacturing features are stereotypical shapes that can be made by typical manufacturing operations (Shen & Shah, 1994). To this context, design features may also be called function features. Table 4.1 illustrates a part whose different geometrical entities may be of interest for different applications.

Shah and Mäntylä (1995) distinguish between various types of features by using a sub-classification of features such as form features, tolerance features, assembly features, functional features and material features. Form features, tolerance features and assembly features are all closely related to the geometry of a part, and are therefore called geometric features.

Figure 4.1. A component with four machining features. ©2001, Engineers Australia used with permission.

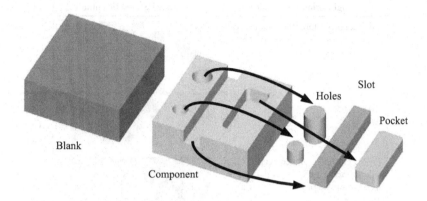

The same part may also be viewed differently, i.e. application's own "way of looking at an object" or definition of the object, with features relevant for that application. There can be, for example, a design, finite-element, machining, moulding and assembly view of a part. Figure 4.2 shows multiple views of a part. In a generic modelling mode, the three protrusions are the features; in the finite-element view, the stiffeners are the features; and in the machining view, the slots are the features.

Features can be used in reasoning about the design, performance or manufacture of the part or assemblies that they constitute. Feature technology, therefore, is also expected to be able to provide for a better approach to integrate design and applications such as engineering analysis, process planning, machining, and inspection.

In the feature-based design approach, the designer chooses pre-defined parametric volumes from a feature library to build a part. The set of solid primitives in the feature library has explicit shapes underlying several form features which convey engineering functionality. For example, the part as shown in Figure 4.2 may be constructed by three primitives, a protrusion and two cuts (Figure 4.3). The two cuts convey a special type of machining operation, i.e. slotting. This approach is also called design by features and is further discussed in a later section in this chapter.

FEATURE TAXONOMY

Features are usually classified into different categories to enable designers to access the feature data and manufacturing engineers to generate process plans for a group of features which have some common geometric, topological or other properties. Such categories/classes are normally further divided into sub-classes such that classes and sub-classes form a hierarchy. This classification structure is known as feature *taxonomy*. Since the taxonomy of features is often of a hierarchical nature, the attributes of a class are inherited by its sub-classes. The method of classifying features is largely dependent on the feature representation schemes and the application domains of the feature data.

Table 4.1. Domain specific features

Engineering significance	Interested geometric entities
Rib Design Feature (the middle section) used for structural support	
Profile Group Tolerance Feature (all side surfaces of the bigger pocket) used to apply a profile tolerance all-around the pocket	
Pocket Machining Feature (all surfaces inside the bigger pocket) required to define the surfaces which in turn defines the volume to be removed	
Multiple Measuring Features (planes and fillets inside the bigger pocket) necessary to perform inspections using a CMM for example	

There have been a number of feature taxonomy schemes suggested (Butterfield, Green & Stoker, 1985, Pratt, 1988, Mäntylä, Opas & Puhakka, 1989, Gindy, 1989, Wong & Wong, 1998). In general, features can be classified based on product category (be it a sheet metal, composite panel, machined part or injection modelling part), intended application of a feature (be it design, finite element analysis, process planning or inspection), or feature shape (be it prismatic, rotational, flat or uniform cross section).

Figure 4.2. Multiple views of a part

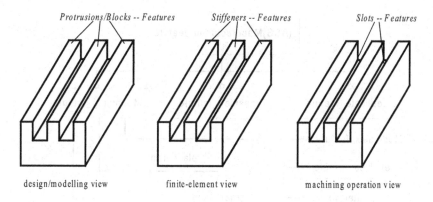

design/modelling view   finite-element view   machining operation view

Figure 4.3. Features related to machining operations

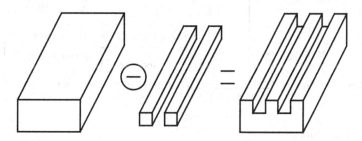

Clearly, features have been subject to numerous definitions and classifications over the years. The situation remained until the International Organisation for Standardization published AP224 as part of ISO 10303 STEP for the definition of product data for mechanical product definition for process planning using machining features (ISO 10303-224, 2001, Amaitik & Kiliç, 2007). Defined at the top level is the manufacturing_feature which contains the information necessary to identify shapes that represent volumes of material to be removed from a part by machining or resulted from machining. A Manufacturing_feature is defined as a Machining_feature, a Replicate_feature, or a Transition_feature. Figure 4.4 shows a simplified EXPRESS-G diagram of the STEP manufacturing feature taxonomy.

A Replicate_feature is defined by a basis shape and the arrangement of identical copies of that base shape. Each base shape is a Machining_feature oriented to the first defined position of a pattern. The patterns describe how to replicate that feature for different placements on the part. A Replicate_feature can be of a Circular_pattern, a General_pattern or a Rectangular_pattern. A Transition_feature defines a transition area between two surfaces. It can be a Chamfer, an Edge_round or a Fillet.

A Machining_feature identifies a volume of material that is to be removed to obtain the final part geometry from the initial stock. A Machining_feature may be one of the following,

Figure 4.4. Simplified manufacturing feature taxonomy in STEP

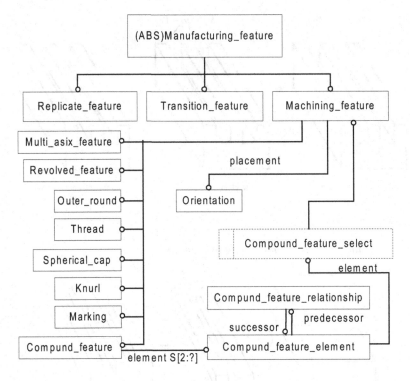

- Multi_axis_feature
- Revolved_feature
- Outer_round
- Spherical_cap
- Thread
- Knurl
- Marking
- Compound_feature

The remaining of this section briefly discusses the above eight machining features.

Multi_axis_feature is a type of milling feature; it may not be turned on a lathe. There are eleven types of Multi_axis_features,

- Boss (Circular_boss, General_boss, Rectangular_boss)
- General_removal_volume
- Hole (Counterbore_hole, Countersunk_hole, Round_ hole)
- Rounded_end
- Planar_face
- Pocket (Cutout, General_pocket, Recess, Rectangular_closed_pocket, Rectangular_open_pocket)
- Profile_feature (General_outside_profile, Shape_profile)

- Protrusion
- Rib_top
- Slot
- Step

Revolved_feature is the result of sweeping a planar shape by one complete revolution about an axis. The planar shape needs to be finite in length, coplanar with the axis of revolution, and should not intersect the axis of revolution. The axis of revolution shall be the same as the Z-axis of the feature. The Revolved_feature may be either an outer shape of a part or a volume removal, depending on the material direction. A Revolved_feature can be a General_revolution, Groove, Revolved_flat, or Revolved_round. Figure 4.5 shows a Groove feature generated by an open profile.

Outer_round is an outline or other significant shape that is swept through a complete revolution about an axis. An Outer_round can be an Outer_diameter or an Outer_diameter_to_shoulder. Like a revolved feature, the axis of revolution should be the same as the Z-axis of the feature. Figure 4.6 shows two Outer_diameter features, one with a constant diameter around the axis of rotation, and the other tapered.

Spherical_cap is a portion of sphere attached, often tangential, to an existing feature (often cylinder). Thread is defined as a ridge of uniform section on the form of a helix on the external or internal surface of a cylinder. A Thread can be a Catalogue_thread or a Defined_thread. Unlike other features, a thread feature has a suite of parameters associated with it, namely applied_shape, fit_class, form, inner_or_outer_thread, major_diameter, number_of_threads, partial_profile, qualifier, and thread_hand. Knurl is a scoring pattern made by a series of small ridges or beads on a surface. There are Catalogue_knurl and Turned_knurl features defined in this category. Marking is one or more text characters on a surface of a part and it can be a Defined_marking or a Catalogue_marking. Compound_feature is a union of various Machining_features. The placement of a Compound_feature is relative to either the part, another Compound_feature, or a Replicate_feature which uses a Compound_feature as the base feature. Features which are elements of a Compound_feature have placement defined relative to the Compound_feature placement (Figure 4.4). Figure

Figure 4.5. A Grove feature

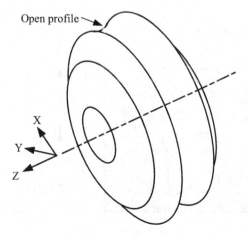

Open profile

X
Y
Z

Figure 4.6. Two Outer_diameter features

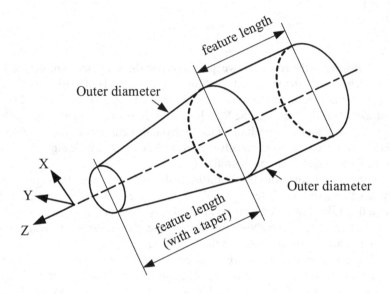

4.7 shows an example of a Compound_feature consisting of one Counterbore_hole feature and one Countersunk_hole feature.

It is worth noting that the standard does not explicitly distinguish turning features from milling features. If it had, all eight machining features minus Multi_axis_features would have been classified as turning features as they are conventionally perceived to be. However, the contemporary multi-functional machining centres (e.g. 5-axis machining centres), can theoretically cut any shapes, be it rotational or prismatic.

Figure 4.7. A Compound_feature

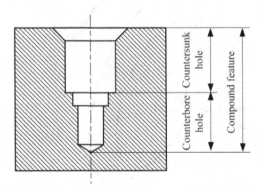

Figure 4.8. Surface and volumetric feature representations

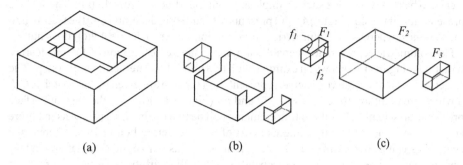

(a)   (b)   (c)

FEATURE REPRESENTATION SCHEMES

Regardless the type of features, it is fair to state that there are only two feature representation schemes, *surface* and *volume* representation scheme. They represent surface features and volume features respectively. Surface features are form features represented by a number of faces (and possibly edges and vertices) that characterise a feature. They do not form a closed volume. In a B-rep model, features can be represented in either of these two schemes, whereas in a CSG model, features are always represented as volumes. Figure 4.8 shows a component together with the two types of feature representations, surface scheme (Figure 4.8(b)) and volume scheme (Figure 4.8(c)). Clearly, the manufacturing features defined in ISO 10303-224 are mostly surface features.

The representation of a part in terms of features is known as the feature model of the part, and the associated database is known as the feature data model. Features are represented in a feature model so that the relations between/among features can be kept. When using the B-Rep scheme in a feature model, features can be connected through individual faces, edges or vertices, and interference between features (i.e. feature interaction, which is an important operation in some applications) becomes relatively easy to detect.

SURFACE FEATURES VS. VOLUMETRIC FEATURES

Careful examination about which representation scheme suits machining feature modelling systems best, suggests that the volumetric scheme has more advantages over the surface scheme (Xu, 2001, Xu & Hinduja, 1997). With the volumetric feature representation, it is easier to extend feature concepts to general machining volumes that are associated with particular machining operations. As feature volume can define precisely the stock to be machined, the machining cost and time can be easily determined. In Figure 4.8(c), volumetric features F_1, F_2 and F_3 are in essence the machining volumes for the part shown in Figure 4.8(a), if the blank is assumed to be the minimum enclosing box (MEB) of the part. The presence of a feature volume also makes it possible to represent other machining information such as tool approach and withdrawal directions. The normal to face f_1 of feature F_1 in Figure 4.8 represents the tool approach/withdrawal direction for machining feature F_1. Face f_2 can also serve the same purpose if feature F_2 is removed first. With a volumetric approach, it becomes easier to manipulate, decompose and merge a feature into volumes of material to be removed. One such example is a compound slot (Figure 4.9(a)). The surface representation of the slot (Figure 4.9(b)) presents difficulties in decomposing the feature into basic volumes, whereas the volumetric representation scheme (Figure 4.9(c)) does not.

The volumetric representation enables a more complete description of feature-feature interactions. Figure 4.10 shows an example with two blind slots interacting with a step. The interacting elements in the volumetric representation scheme are given by face patches (*p1, p2*) which are common to features *F1, F2* and *F3* (Figure 4.10(b)). In the case of surface representation scheme, the interacting elements will be two open wires, (w_1, w_2 as in Figure 10(c)). These open wires only designate part of the interacting boundaries, whereas the face patches can also tell the area of interaction as well as define the complete boundary of the interacting area. In fact, the incapability of handling arbitrary feature interactions by a system using surface representation scheme has been due to the inherent limitations of the pattern-matching nature of the surface representation scheme. Volumetric feature representation also makes it possible to detect certain feature interactions which would be otherwise difficult, if not impossible, for a surface representation scheme. This usually happens to those interacting features with boundary faces of un-equal heights. One of such examples is a closed pocket with an island whose height is different from that of the pocket boundary face(s) (Figure 4.11(a)). When these kinds of features are represented in volumes as seen in Figures 4.11(b) and (c), it leads to two features interacting to each other. A detailed account on feature interactions is given in Chapter VI. Furthermore, the two possible interpretations depend on the ways feature volumes are constructed. This is somehow to say that constructing feature volumes is also an indispensable part of feature recognition. This issue is essentially an "integration" issue which will also be discussed in detail in Chapter VII.

The intermediate shape of a workpiece can be obtained by using Boolean operations between volumetric features and the workpiece. The intermediate specification of a workpiece may include information relating to the current workpiece geometry, dimensions, and tolerances, relationships with the blank, stock material, component, previous and next intermediate workpieces, and features. This information is important not only for related manufacturing activities such as process selection, cutting condition determination and

Figure 4.9. A compound slot represented as surface and volume features

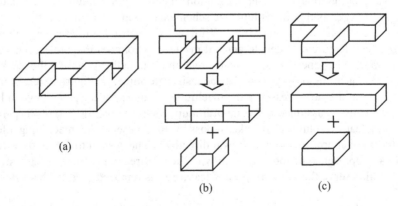

Figure 4.10. Surface and volumetric feature interactions

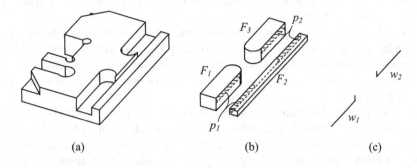

(a)   (b)   (c)

NC code generation, but also for manual/computerised fixture selection/design, and quality inspection. Using volumetric scheme, feature modelling operations for a FBD system are much simpler to implement. In fact, most FBD systems adopt the volumetric feature representation scheme. Detailed discussions on FBD are given in the next section. The obvious disadvantage of using a volumetric representation scheme is the additional complexity but this cannot be regarded as a serious objection since current solid modellers are powerful enough to handle a large number of complex components.

When the volumetric representation scheme is adopted by defining machining features as volumes to be machined, three propositions may have to be observed.

- Features should not be distinctively classified as depressions and protrusions because they do not all represent the volumes to be removed. Two such examples are an island

Figure 4.11. Feature interactions and protrusion features

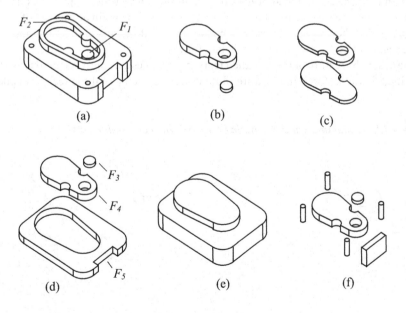

(a)   (b)   (c)

(d)   (e)   (f)

(F_1) in a pocket (F_2) which is in turn on top of a face as shown in Figure 4.11(a). In this case, it is the surrounding material that constitutes machining features, F_3, F_4 and F_5 (Figure 4.11(d)).

- To say that a machining feature is the actual material to be removed, a feature has to be an independent volume with no portion of it overlapping with another (machining) feature, i.e. there should be nil intersection between any pair of machining features. Machining features illustrated in Figure 4.12(b) are not valid but those in Figures 4.12(c) and (d) are.

- To guarantee valid machining volumes from a design part, the initial state of the workpiece, i.e. the blank, has to be taken into consideration. The importance of considering the blank is illustrated in Figure 4.13 (Xu, 2001). By assuming the blank to be a billet, most systems would recognise two volumetric features as shown in Figure 4.13(a). However, if this part were to be machined from a casting/forging as shown in Figure 4.13(b), the system would recognise two brick-shaped volumes and a hole. Furthermore, if the part were to be machined from a blank with a pre-cast hole as shown in Figure 4.13(c), the system would recognise another different set of features. Take the component shown in Figure 4.11(a) and its blank shown in Figure 4.11(e) as another example. A valid set of feature volumes should be as shown in Figure 4.11(f). Note that feature F_5 does not count in this instance.

FEATURE-BASED METHODOLOGIES

Feature-based methodologies can be grouped into two strands: feature recognition and design by feature. The feature recognition approach examines the topology and geometry of a part and matches them with the appropriate definition of predefined and domain-specific features. This way, a model of lower-level entities (e.g. faces, lines, points, etc.) is converted into a model of higher-level entities (e.g. holes, grooves, pockets, etc.). Many research works have been published in the field of feature recognition and various approaches have been adopted. These will be discussed in detail in Chapter V. The main advantage of these approaches is that they do not impose any constraints on designers and the method may be independent of CAD systems and CAD data formats.

The design by feature or the so-called feature-based design approach builds a part from predefined features stored in a feature library. The geometry of these features is defined

Figure 4.12. Invalid and valid machining features for a cross-shaped slot

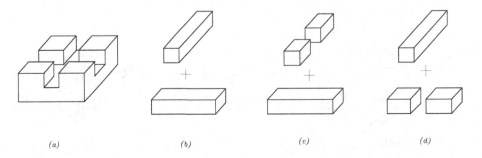

(a)   (b)   (c)   (d)

Figure 4.13. Machining features recognised with/without consideration of a blank. ©2001, Engineers Australia used with permission.

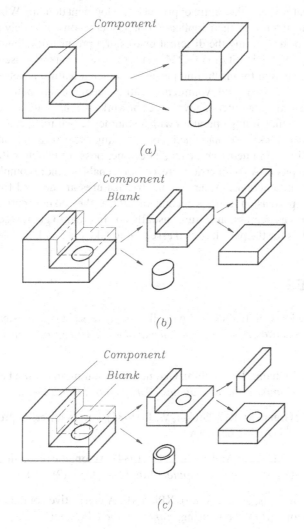

but their dimensions are left as variables to be instantiated when the feature is used in the modelling process. This process is, in principle, identical to the primitive instancing scheme (or CSG). Since the features are closely related to the applications concerned, all the essential geometry and technological information can be included in the model. Two distinct methodologies for design by feature approach are commonly used: destruction by machining features; and synthesis by design features. In destruction by machining features method, one starts with an initial design model of the raw stock from which a part is to be machined. The design model is generated by subtracting depression features corresponding to the material to be removed by machining operations from the stock. In synthesis by design features method, a design model can be built by adding protrusion features and subtracting depression features.

CONCLUSION

The concept of features is at the centre of product development domain. While their definitions may take varying forms, their application-dependent nature is widely appreciated, so is their potential of integrating the different phases of a product development cycle. The feature taxonomy defined in ISO 10303-224 seems to provide a standardised guideline that is comprehensive enough for machining purposes. When a feature is defined as a collection of surfaces or a closed solid, volumetric feature seems to fare better for machining applications. There are a number of advantages of working with volumetric features. It is easier to associate a machining operation with a volumetric feature. Feature volumes can define precisely the stock to be machined, thus enabling the determination of machining cost and time. With a volumetric approach, it becomes possible to obtain the intermediate shapes of the workpiece. A volumetric representation enables a more complete description of feature-feature interactions. When volumetric features are derived from the surface features on a part, protrusion features become invalid, as they do not contribute directly to volumetric features as depression features usually do. In order to guarantee the validity of the feature volumes for the part, it is also essential to take the blank into consideration.

REFERENCES

Amaitik, S. M., & Kiliç, S. E. (2007). An intelligent process planning system for prismatic parts using STEP features. *International Journal of Advanced Manufacturing Technology, 31*, 978–993.

Anderson, D. C., & Chang, T. C. (1990). Geometric reasoning in feature based design and process planning. *Computers and Graphics (Pergamon), 14*(2), 225-235.

Butterfield, W. R., Green, M. K, & Stoker, W. J. (1985). Part features for process planning. *CAM-I C-85-PPP-03.* Arlington, USA.

Choi, B. K., Barash, M. M., & Anderson, D. C. (1984). Automatic recognition of machined surfaces from a 3-D solid model. *Computer-Aided Design, 16*(2), 81-86.

van't Erve, A. H., & Kals, H. J. J. (1986). XPLANE. A generative computer aided process planning system for part manufacturing, *Annals of the CIRP, 35*(1), 325-329.

Gindy, N. N. (1989). A hierarchical structure for form features. *International Journal of Production Research, 27*(12), 2089-2103.

ISO 10303-224. (2001). *Industrial Automation Systems and Integration—Product Data Representation and Exchange—Part 224: Application Protocol: Mechanical Product Definition for Process Plans Using Machining Features,* Geneva, Switzerland: International Organisation for Standardisation (ISO).

Mäntylä, M., Opas, J., & Puhakka, J. (1989). Generative process planning of prismatic parts by feature relaxation. In *Proceddings of 15th ASME Design Automation Conference, 9*(1), 49-60.

Pratt, M. J. (1988). Synthesis of an optimal approach to form feature modelling. In *Proceddings of 1988 ASME International Computers in Engineering Conference and Exhibition, 1*, 263-274.

Shah, J. J., & Mäntylä, M. (1995). *Parametric and feature-based CAD/CAM – concepts, techniques and applications.* New York, USA: John Wiley & Sons, Inc.

Shen, Y., & Shah, J. J. (1994). Feature recognition by volume decomposition using half-space partitioning. *Advances in Design Automation, ASME, 1*, 575-583.

Wong, T. N., & Wong, K. W. (1998). Feature-based design by volumetric machining features. *International Journal of Production Research, 36*(10), 2839-2862.

Xu, X., & Hinduja, S. (1997). Determination of finishing features in 21/2D components. *Proceedings of IMechE, Journal of Engineering Manufacture, 211*(Part B), 125-142.

Xu, X. (2001). Feature Recognition Methodologies and Beyond. *Australian Journal of Mechanical Engineering, ME25*(1), 1-20.

Chapter V
Feature Recognition

ABSTRACT

Conventional CAD models only provide pure geometry and topology for mechanical designs such as vertices, edges, faces, simple primitives, and the relationship among them. Feature recognition is then required to interpret this low-level part information into high-level and domain-specific features such as machining features.

Over the years, CAD has been undergoing fundamental changes toward the direction of feature-based design or design by features. Commercial implementations of FBD technique became available in the late 1980's. One of the main benefits of adopting feature-based approach is the fact that features can convey and encapsulate designers' intents in a natural way. In other words, the initial design can be synthesized quickly from the high-level entities and their relations, which a conventional CAD modeller is incapable of doing. However, such a feature-based design system, though capable of generating feature models as its end result, lacks the necessary link to a CAPP system, simply because the design features do not always carry the manufacturing information which is essential for process planning activities. This type of domain-dependent nature has been elaborated on in the previous chapter.

In essence, feature recognition has become the first task of a CAPP system. It serves as an automatic and intelligent interpreter to link CAD with CAM, regardless of the CAD output being a pure geometric model or a feature model from a FBD system. To be specific, the goal of feature recognition systems is to bridge the gap between a CAD database and a CAPP system by automatically recognizing features of a part from the data stored in the CAD system, and based on the recognized features, to drive the CAPP system which produces process plans for manufacturing the part. Human interpretation of translating CAD data into technological information required by a CAPP system is thus minimized if not eliminated.

It soon became evident that feature recognition, for parts with multiple and interacting feature interpretations, requires extensive geometric reasoning and is often computationally expensive. Hence, generating features from a design part can be a computational bottleneck within an integrated product development system. This chapter discusses some basic concepts and methodologies concerning feature recognition. Feature recognition methods have been divided into two groups, feature detection and feature generation. Different methods in each of the two groups have been presented and analyzed. As a central issue, concavity and convexity of a geometric entity are discussed as they are often used to detect features. Also discussed are issues related to optimal interpretation of machining volumes (as machining features) and consideration of stock in the process of feature recognition. This chapter makes no attempt to provide a comprehensive coverage of the existing feature recognition methods. Interested readers are referred to the book by Shah and Mäntylä (1995) and the article by Vosniakos (1998).

BASIC CONCEPTS OF FEATURE RECOGNITION

The input of an automatic feature recognition system is often a conventional description of the geometry of a part, i.e. a geometric model. The output is a list of recognised instances of features with necessary technological parameters and their proper organisation. A distinction may be made between several phases: *feature identification, parameter determination, feature extraction,* and *feature organisation* (Figure 5.1) (Xu, 2001). In the identification phase, features are identified from/within a geometric model. In the parameter determination phase, the parameters of the features, i.e. geometrical parameters such as the diameter and depth of a hole, and technical parameters such as tool approaching directions, are computed from the geometric model. In the extraction phase, the features are removed from the geometric model to form a stand-alone feature entity. And finally, in the organisation phase, the features are named and arranged in a particular structure, e.g. a graph tree. The concept of feature recognition is sometimes narrowed to only mean feature identification -- the first phase mentioned above. The reason for this is that feature identification is easily the most difficult task among the four.

CLASSIFICATION OF FEATURE RECOGNITION SYSTEMS

Many attempts have been made to classify feature recognition systems. One of the most common ways is to classify them based upon the actual techniques used by the systems. Some of these techniques are known as, *syntactic pattern recognition approach, geometric decomposition approach, expert system rule/logic approach* and *graph-based approach.*

In the manufacturing domain, feature recognition approaches can also be classified based on the machining natures of the features (Singh & Qi, 1992), for example, approaches for recognising rotational (turning) features and approaches for recognising non-rotational (milling) features.

Shah and Mäntylä (1995) classified feature recognition techniques into four groups, those recognising features (a) from boundary models, (b) by volume decomposition, (c) from CSG models and (d) from 2D drawings. In a nutshell, some systems recognise features by detecting

Figure 5.1. Feature recognition process

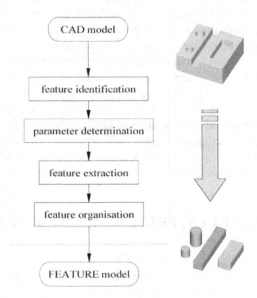

them from the geometric model with help of a completely pre-defined feature library. The capability of such a feature recogniser is therefore limited to the robustness of the feature database that has been pre-defined. Other systems recognise features by generating them using various techniques. Rules are normally built into systems to assist feature identification, but they are by no means complete feature libraries as mentioned above. For this reason, the author distinguishes feature recognition techniques between *feature detection* as in the former case and *feature generation* as in the later case, and discussions below are organised accordingly.

Feature Detection

Algorithms used for feature detection normally vary with the different feature representation schemes adopted in the feature libraries. Nevertheless, specific tasks in feature detection may include the following (although it is not necessary to have all of them included in a system),

- re-constituting (re-constructing) the geometric model topologically and/or geometrically;
- searching the database to match topologic/geometric patterns with those in the feature library;
- extracting detected feature(s) from the database;

- completing the feature geometric model;
- analysing and/or re-constructing features.

It is noted that most feature detection techniques are based on the depression-oriented approach, and they largely depend upon the different feature representation schemes employed. There are a number of feature detection techniques developed. They are, (a) *graph-based method*; (b) *syntax-based method*; (c) *rule-based method* and (d) *techniques for recognising features from CSG models*.

In many of the above feature detection algorithms, recognised features are not always closed volumes. To obtain a volumetric feature, which is more desirable, new face(s) may have to be added to close the feature volume (Figure 5.2). This post-processing technique is also referred to as *volume construction* or *entity growing*. Some methods use *edge extension* (Falcudieno & Giannini, 1989, Shah, 1991), and others use *face extension* (Dong & Wozny, 1991, Sakurai & Gossard, 1990).

Graph-Based Method

Graph-based methods became popular in the 1980's due to the well-established techniques of graph algorithms that can be readily adapted to feature-based modelling. When dealing with a boundary representation of a component, faces can be considered as nodes of the graph and face-face relationships form the arc/links of the graph. Take the notch feature in Figures 5.2 and 5.3 as an example. Faces 1, 2 and 3 form the notch feature, which is originated from a corner where faces 4, 5 and 6 meet. The diagraph as shown in Figure 5.3 (b) is called "face adjacency graph (FAG)". It illustrates the neighbourhood relationships of the faces concerned. The feature recognition methods utilising the graph-based techniques usually have two steps. First of all, the component model is represented in a FAG. Then, parsers are developed to decompose this FAG into pre-defined FAGs that correspond to various features. Pattern matching is eventually carried out to identify the features from the component. This type of graph-based feature recognition method is purely based on topologic information. To take into account some geometric information, FAG can be augmented or attributed with information such as the type of face, edge and vertex. This leads to an improved graph-based method named "attributed face adjacency graph (AFAG)". Figure 5.3(c) shows the AFAG in which "x" denotes a convex connecting

Figure 5.2. Closure faces added to make a feature volume

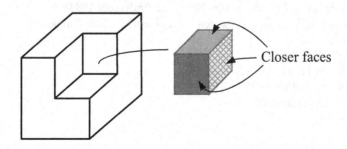

Closer faces

Figure 5.3. FAG and AFAG diagrams for a feature

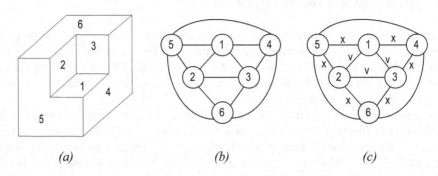

(a)   (b)   (c)

edge and "v" denotes a concave connecting edge. In this case, the three faces that give rise to the notch feature can be identified by separating a set of nodes (faces) from the graph that are connected by concave edges.

Early graph-based methods lack robustness when dealing with interactive features. Gao and Shah (1998) defined their feature hints using an Extended Attributed Adjacency graph, generated by graph decomposition and completed by adding virtual links, corresponding to entities lost by interactions. Verma and Rajotia (2004) reported in their paper a new edge classification scheme to extend the graph-based algorithms to handle parts with curved faces. A method of representing a feature, called a feature vector, is developed. The feature vector generation heuristic results in a recognition system with polynomial time complexity for any arbitrary attributed adjacency graph. The feature vector can be generated automatically from a B-Rep modeller. This helps in building incrementally a feature library as per the requirements of the specific domain. The modified attributed adjacency (MAA) scheme (Ibrahim & Mc-Cormack 2005) was used to define the part which allows more information to be stored in the part representation (graph or matrix), and this allows multiple interpretations to be solved.

Syntax-Based Method

Syntax-based methods are deeply rooted in classical pattern recognition techniques. The only difference is that these appropriate techniques have been extended from catering for 2D situations to 3D situations. Feature syntax can be expressed in terms of either edges or faces, and it is based on their local characteristics. In order to recognise some common types of holes, three different types of syntactic elements can be defined (Table 5.1). Figure 5.4 shows some of the syntactic elements for holes (Choi, Barash & Anderson, 1984).

With these syntactic elements, the general concept of a hole can be described as,

<hole> ::= HSS {HES}* HBS,
where,   <HES> ::= HES1 | HES2,
         <HBS> ::= HBS1 | HBS2 | HBS3,
         {X}* -- repetition of X,
         | -- "or".

Table 5.1. Syntactic elements for holes and their possible instances

Syntactic elements for holes	Possible surfaces
HSS – Hole-Starting-Surface	A planar surface with an internal circular loop
HES – Hole-Element-Surface	Cylindrical/conical surface bound by two circular edges
HBS – Hole-Bottom-Surface	Planar circle, cone, HSS

Figure 5.4 Syntactic elements for holes. ©1984 Elsevier Science Ltd. Used with permission.

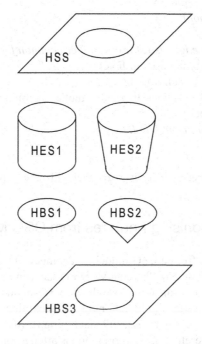

More specific types of holes can then be easily defined as,

<straight hole> ::= HSS HES1 HBS1,
<countersink hole> ::= HSS HES2 HES1 HBS2.

Rule-Based Method

Rule-based feature recognition methods borrowed those of expert system's concepts[1]. For different features, rules can be written for detecting directly the underlining features. Templates are normally defined first for both general and specific features. Then rules are constructed for each of the feature template. For example,

//recognise a 2.5D pocket//
If ((a face has an internal loop made up of a number of edges) +
    (all faces sharing these edges also share another common face))
Then (there exists a pocket)
End If

   More often than not, both geometric and topological conditions are tested. Therefore, rule-based methods can detect features that graph-based and syntax-based methods cannot. It is also easy to construct and alter rules when necessary. The above rule can be modified to detect a (close) pocket and (blind or through) hole,

//recognise a 2.5D pocket or hole//
If (a face has an internal loop)
   If (the loop has one edge)
      If (the face sharing the edge also shares another common face)
          Then (there exists a blind circular hole)
      Else(there exists a through circular hole)
   Else if (all faces sharing these edges also share another common face)
          Then (there exists a pocket)
   Else (there exists a general through hole)
End If

   Rule-based method has been widely used together with other types of methods for feature recognition.

Techniques for Recognising Features from CSG Models

When recognising features from a CSG model, re-arrangement and re-interpretation are usually the two steps to follow. The fact that a CSG model can be expressed in more than one way makes it possible to re-arrange it, so that it corresponds to the expression of the desired machining features. Often modifications of the machining features are needed. This is because CSG primitives are not necessarily machining feature volumes, and they often overlap with each other. Therefore, re-interpretation is often a non-dispensable step. Non-uniqueness of CSG representation scheme can impose difficulties for recognising features. An effective feature recognition method must consider all possible ways of representing a model in terms of CSG primitives. As the CSG tress gets complicated, computation can be extremely expensive, and sometimes impractical. This is one of the main reasons that there have been limited attempts in recognising features from a CSG model.

Feature Generation

Feature generation differs from feature detection in that there is not a complete, pre-defined feature library or feature template to be consulted with and/or matched to when features are being recognised. Therefore, feature generation approaches have to take into consideration more manufacturing information such as the types of machine tools and cutting tools to be used. Features that are generated are also more technologically oriented, and hence their actual output forms are often of different variety. Some systems output machining volumes or machining regions rather than distinctly form features. Some directly generate NC tool paths or NC code. Special techniques or tools are usually introduced and performed upon the geometric model to help generate features.

Feature generation techniques can be classified here into two categories: *technique-based approach* and *direct model interrogation approach*. Technique-based approaches include (a) *cell decomposition*; (b) *section techniques*; (c) *convex-hull algorithm* and (d) *backward growing*. Direct model interrogation approaches differ from technique-based approaches in that the geometric model of a part remains intact while the feature generation process is carried out. *Geometric reasoning* and *volume decomposition* belong to this methodology. Note that geometric reasoning techniques have been popular, but most of them can only detect surface features.

Convex-Hull Algorithm

The convex-hull approach is one of the pioneering works aimed at generating volumetric features (Woo, 1982). The difference between the object and its convex hull was computed recursively, until a null set was obtained, i.e. until the object equalled its convex hull. The object could then be represented as a sequence of convex volumes with alternating signs, starting with the initial convex hull (Woo, 1982). Such an expression is referred to as an *Alternating Sum of Volumes* (ASV) expression. To suit various manufacturing operations such as machining and welding, an ASV expression may be algebraically manipulated into a disjunctive normal form. The most serious problem of ASV decomposition is its non-convergence. This was later solved by using the method of *Alternative Sum of Volumes with Partitioning* (ASVP) (Kim, 1992, Kim, Pariente & Wang, 1997, Praiente & Kim, 1996). To obtain form features, ASVP volumes are converted into feature entities by various combinations between the volumes.

Both ASV and ASVP decompositions are entirely based on the component's geometry. Consequently, the decomposition may not always be useful, as it can result in a removal volume (an odd-shaped feature) that does not correspond to any machining operation. A post-processing module is therefore needed to generate manufacturing features. The ASV/ASVP-based feature recognition system is best suited for polyhedral parts and features. Extending the system to handle arbitrary curved surfaces does not appear to be a promising goal, because of the complexity this would introduce to the convex hull operation.

Cell-Decomposition

This method slices the total material to be removed (the difference between the component and its stock) into layers which were treated as machining volumes for a machine tool such as a mill. This algorithm recognises a limited set of machining features. Decomposition can also be performed using a lattice of planes parallel to the major axes to produce spatially enumerated cells of the component and stock. Each cell is then classified as either a stock cell, a part cell or a semi-part cell. The method was well suited for generating rough cuts. This is because the part is discretized into cells of a definite shape (usually cubical), which results in tool paths that are only approximate representations of the boundaries.

Volume Decomposition

Volume decomposition is carried out in two major stages. The primitive (parameterizable) volumes are first recognised and extracted by methods such as surface extension. Then, relationships between adjacent cross sections are determined when the volume is decomposed into disjoint "super-delta volumes". They may further be decomposed based on tool accessibility. A library of generic delta volumes was created. This set of generic delta volumes is required to meet some criteria to guarantee that any machining volume could be decomposed into a set of generic delta volumes.

Woo and Sakurai (2002) defined "maximal features (volumes)" as the volume that can be removed from the workpiece by one machining operation (Figure 5.5). Maximal features are obtained by decomposing the delta volume (the difference between the raw stock and the final part), and are intermediate features. This is because feature interpretation has to be performed based on the maximal features. Since Vol1 > Vol2, method1 is opted. This issue is further discussed in a later section of this chapter. Volume decomposition methodologies have difficulties in dealing with compound features and feature interactions.

Backward Growing

The backward growing approach reverses the machining/removal process by growing properly machined volume/feature back to other machined face(s) (Figure 5.6). Basic cavity features were generated, and compound and protrusion features were decomposed into basic ones by adding surrounding materials. During the growing procedure, manufacturing parameters, such as types of basic elementary machined shapes, tool approach directions,

Figure 5.5. Method of maximal machining features

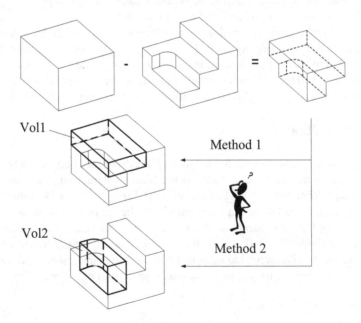

Figure 5.6. Backward growing method

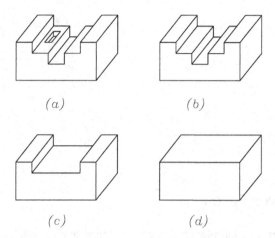

(a)

(b)

(c)

(d)

precedence between recognised features, refined features, and intermediate workpiece specifications/shapes may also be determined.

Entity Growing

Entity growing methods have been developed to generate volumetric features from surface features that have already been recognised. There are a number of methods developed. The edges of a face, other than the face that belongs to the surface feature, are extended to generate volume(s) through creating new edges and vertices (Figure 5.7). Feature volumes may also be created by adding half spaces corresponding to feature faces.

SOME ISSUES ON FEATURE RECOGNITION

Considerable progress has been made on feature recognition in the last three decades. However, features that are recognised by most of the systems are still limited to simple features. Although each methodology has its own drawbacks, there are a number of common issues at the centre of feature recognition, such as those regarding concave and convex properties of a geometric entity, optimal (combination of) machining volumes, consideration of the geometry of the raw material (blank) and integrating feature recognition with process planning.

Concavity/Convexity of a Geometric Entity

Concavity and convexity of an edge has been addressed and utilised by many researchers. Kyprianou (1980) gave a basic definition of a concave edge, and used it to classify edges in his feature recognition approach. Its significance was soon recognised by many other researchers. Given below is a more complete account of the concavity/convexity of different types of geometric entities such as faces, edges and vertices.

Figure 5.7. Entity growing using face extensions

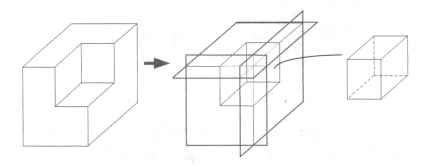

Concave/Convex Faces

For an analytic surface, i.e. planar, conical, spherical and toroidal, a face is said to be concave if the basic primitive (cone, sphere, and torus) which defines it, is hollow. Due to its surface nature, a planar surface is classified as neutral. Figure 5.8 shows several examples. Faces f_1, f_2 and f_4 are neutral; faces f_3 and f_{13} are convex; and faces f_5, f_9 and f_{11} are concave.

Figure 5.8. "Stairs" of concavity/convexity

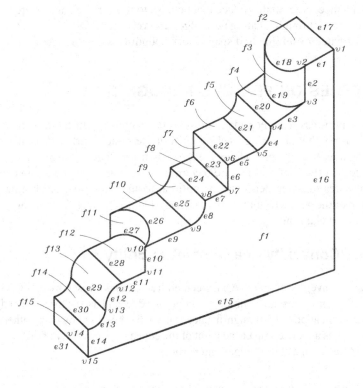

Concave/Convex Edges

In a sane solid, an edge is always shared by two faces. To determine if an edge is concave, consider a point on the edge and the reference plane passing through this point (Figure 5.9). The normal (*n*) of the plane follows the tangent (*t*) to the edge at this point. Contained in this plane are two intersection curves, one for each face. The tangents to these curves at this point are given by t_1 and t_2. Within the plane, a *bending direction* (*B*) is defined as the sum of the two tangents i.e. $B = t_1 + t_2$. This bending direction solely depends upon the geometry of the two faces. Next, the direction of the *solid normal* (*N*) is determined, which is defined as the sum of the normals to the two faces at this point, i.e. $N = n_1 + n_2$. A solid normal always points away from the solid. An edge is convex if *N* and *B* are in opposite directions, as in Figure 5.9. Otherwise, the edge is concave.

An edge is said to be *smooth* if $n_1 = n_2$ or $t_1 = -t_2$. A smooth edge can be further classified as being either *smooth concave, smooth convex* or *smooth neutral*. The first type occurs when two faces which share the edge are concave, or one of them is concave and the other neutral. A smooth convex edge occurs when the two faces are convex, or one of them is convex and the other neutral. The third type occurs when one face is concave and the other convex. Table 5.2 classifies some of the edges shown in Figure 5.8.

Concave/Convex Co-Edges

In a B-Rep model, faces are represented by a closing sequence of edges, or loops. The winged-edge data structure is a classical case. The edges that make up a loop are sometimes called "co-edges" (Figure 5.10). Since an edge is always common to two faces in a sane solid, every edge (i.e. the-edge) has two copies of co-edges (i.e. co-edge 1 and co-edge 2), each belonging to one of the faces that share the (original) edge. A co-edge can be classified as being either concave or convex. This can be determined by examining the nature of

Figure 5.9. Edge concavity/convexity

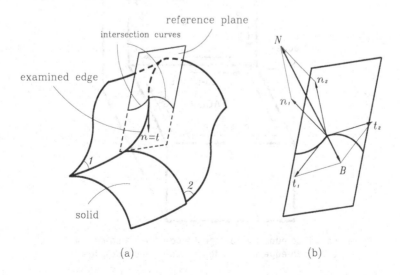

(a)   (b)

Table 5.2. Examples of different types of edges

Edge type	Examples in Figure 5.8
Concave	*e19, e23, e27*
Convex	*e1, e3, e4, e5, e18, e20, e22, e24, e26, e30*
Smooth concave	*e21, e25*
Smooth convex	*e2, e28*
Smooth neutral	*e29*

the parent edge and the nature of the face in which the other co-edge lies, i.e. partner face. Various combinations are summarised in Table 5.3. For example, a co-edge is concave if its parent edge is convex and the partner face is concave. In Figure 5.8, edge e_{18} and e_{27} are convex edges for faces f_2 and f_{12} respectively, while e_{19} and e_{26} are concave edges for faces f_4 and f_{10} respectively. A straight co-edge is said to be neutral.

Concave/Convex Vertices

The concavity/convexity of a vertex is defined with reference to the face on which it lies, or is studied. The definition given here is made on the assumption that a vertex be common to three edges, which is the most common situation. A vertex is said to be concave

Figure 5.10. Loops and co-edges in a winged-edge data structure

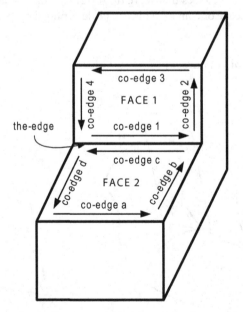

Loop1: co-edge 1 > co-edge 2 > co-edge 3 > co-edge 4
Loop2: co-edge a > co-edge b > co-edge c > co-edge d

Table 5.3. Co-edge concavity/convexity

Co-edge	Parent edge	Partner face
concave	concave	convex
	convex	concave
convex	convex	convex
	concave	concave

(or convex) if the third edge (the edge that does not lie in the face) is concave or smooth concave (or convex). In Figure 5.8, vertices v_3, v_5, v_7, v_9, v_{11} and v_{13} are concave vertices in face f_1, whereas vertices v_2, v_4, v_6, v_8, v_{10}, v_{12}, and v_{14} are convex vertices in face f_2.

Concave/Convex Face Outer Boundaries

The outer boundary (loop) of a face can also be classified as convex or concave. If the outer boundary of the face also defines the convex hull of the face, the outer boundary is said to be convex. Otherwise it is concave. In a concave outer boundary, one or more co-edges of the loop lie within the convex hull. In Figure 5.8, the outer boundaries of faces f_1, f_4 and f_{10} are concave, but the remaining faces have convex outer boundaries. More examples are shown in Figure 5.11, in which edges that make the outer boundary concave are thickened.

The above definitions can be easily used for detecting features. A concave entity, be it a face, edge or vertex, implies the existence of a surface feature as well as a feature interaction, i.e. it provides clues to feature existence and feature interaction. To be more specific, given a face, a feature exists if there is at least one concave edge lying on it. In Figure 5.12 for example, edges *e1* and *e2* provide clues that face *f1* belongs to a feature. Similarly, edges *e4* and *e5* suggest that face *f3* belongs to a feature. Given a cylindrical, spherical or toroidal face, a feature exists if the face is concave. In Figure 5.12 for example, faces *f2* and *f4* are concave and provide clues to the existence of a feature.

The concavity and convexity definitions can also be used to detect the base of a 2.5D feature. For a face to be the base of a feature, all the concave edges lying on the side faces must touch it. Consider for example the pocket in Figure 5.13 consisting of faces f_1 to f_5. If face f_2 is assumed to be the base surface, faces f_1, f_3 and f_5 become the side surfaces. The second condition is not satisfied because concave edges e_3, e_4 and e_5 do not touch face f_2. Hence f_2 cannot be the base face. Feature interactions may also be detected through concavity and convexity types. This is to be discussed in Chapter VI.

Optimal Interpretation of Machinable Volumes

Whilst most feature recognition systems address the problem at the geometrical and topological level, some tackle the problem from a more technological point-of-view. The basic concept is to determine an optimal combination of machinable volumes by the cut-and-collect method performed on the whole of the stock material (Figure 5.14). Seed or elementary volumes are obtained through methods such as sectioning or otherwise known as cell-decomposition. Optimal ways of combining these volumes into a set of

Figure 5.11. Convex/concave shapes

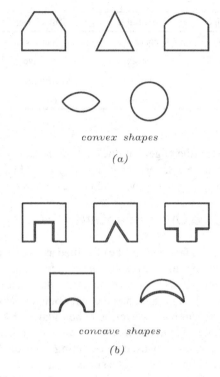

convex shapes

(a)

concave shapes

(b)

Figure 5.12. Feature existence clues

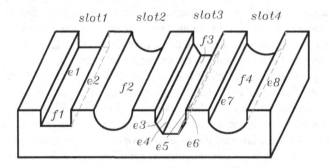

machining features are sought based on certain criteria, i.e. minimising the total sum of volume machining costs, tool and fixture utilisation costs. The tool life equation can also be used to compute the cost per unit volume. The observation has been that for each seed volume, the lowest cost per unit volume will occur when the maximum number of them are attached to it, or more succinctly when the seed volume is extended until there are no further volumes that can be cut together with the current compound volume. The major advantage of the procedure lies in the fact that it is not necessary to evaluate the costs of all possible volume alternatives. Manufacturing tolerances may also be used as criteria

Figure 5.13. Features and feature bases

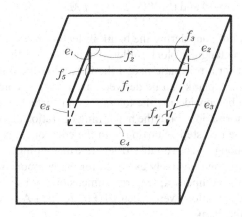

Figure 5.14. Interpreting machining volumes

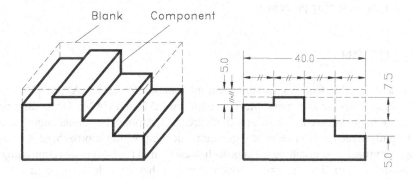

(Tseng & Joshi, 1994, Kang, Han & Moon, 2003, Kim, Wang & Rho, 2001, Shah, Yan & Zhang, 1998, Xu & Hinduja, 1997).

Consideration of Blanks

Volumetric features recognised by some systems may be erroneous with regard to their shape or non-existent. This is because the blank (or raw workpiece) is not (properly) considered. The component together with the blank, and their relative positions, may determine the shape and characteristics of a feature. The importance of considering the blank is illustrated in Figure 4.13 in Chapter IV.

Among the volume feature recognition approaches, blanks are often used to derive the stock material, i.e. the total material to be removed, from which a decomposition/sectioning method is used to decompose the material into machinable volumes -- machining features. This way, feature recognition can be defined as a process with its input being a *part* (component) and WP_0 (its blank), and its output being a feature model *FM* of the part and WP_0. The feature model is set of features,

$FM = \{M_1, M_2, ... , M_n\}$ such that
(a) $\forall M_i \in FM$, $M_i \cap part = \emptyset$ and (b) $WP_0 - part \subseteq \cup FM$.

There are different ways of considering the blank in feature recognition. A casual treatment would be using a rectangular block (billet) that is effective the minimum enclosing box of the finished part for a prismatic part. Likewise, cylindrical stock (round bars) is used for rotational parts. A blank can be derived based on the geometry of the finished part. This is often done by considering the tolerance and surface finish requirements on the part. Sometimes, information about the machining operations is also needed. The latter approach may involve two steps. Starting with the component model, the machining operations which were thought to be suitable to generate machining, is first selected. These machining operations are then inversely executed for the component in a specific order, which in turn modifies the component, features, dimensions and surface roughness, until all the applicable inverse operations were executed (Figure 5.15). As a result, the component model was changed to the blank.

In the case of the raw workpiece being made available and made from a casting, forging or pre-machining process, feature recognition may face additional difficulties. This is due to the extra geometric information concerning the raw workpiece that has to be taken into account during reasoning processes.

CONCLUSION

Let it be no doubt that features are important information for CAD/CAPP/CAM. Feature recognition systems act as a mere interface between CAD and CAM. Depending on the representation scheme used, different methods are used. Among the popular algorithms are syntactic pattern recognition approach, geometric decomposition approach, expert system rule/logic approach and graph-based approach. Research in the field is still continuing, but with less momentum. This is partially due to the fact that there does not seem to exist a single method that can deal with a wealth of features with no major deficiency. A combination of methods may offer a final solution (Owodunni & Hinduja, 2002a, 2002b). There are also some common issues that need to be addressed, such as those regarding concave and convex properties of a geometric entity, optimal machining volumes, consideration of the geometry of the raw material and integrating feature recognition with process planning. Feature interactions lead to additional difficulties in feature recognition. This will be discussed in Chapter VI.

Figure 5.15. Modelling a blank

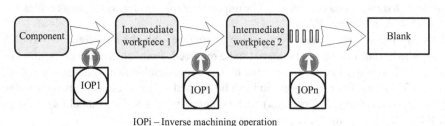

IOPi – Inverse machining operation

REFERENCES

Choi, B. K., Barash, M. M., & Anderson, D. C. (1984). Automatic recognition of machined surfaces from a 3-D solid model. *Computer-Aided Design, 16*(2), 81-86

Dong, X., & Wozny, M. (1991). A method for generating volumetric features from surface features. In *Proceedings of Symposium on Solid Modelling Foundations & CAD/CAM Applications, ACM.* (pp. 185-194).

Falcidieno, B., & Giannini, F. (1989). Automatic recognition and representation of shape-based features in a geometric modelling system. *Computer Vision, Graphics, & Image Processing, 48*(1), 93-123.

Gao, S., & Shah, J. J. (1998). Automatic recognition of interacting machining features based on minimal condition sub-graph. *Computer-Aided Design, 30*(9), 727-739.

Ibrahim, R. N., & McCormack, A. D. (2005). Robustness and generality issues of feature recognition for CNC machining. *International Journal of Advanced Manufacturing Technology, 25*(7-8), 705-713.

Kang, M., Han, J., & Moon, J. G. (2003). An approach for interlinking design and process planning, *Journal of Materials Processing Technology, 139*(1-3 SPEC), 589-595.

Kim, Y. S. (1992). Recognition of form features using convex decomposition. *Computer-Aided Design, 24*(9), 461-476.

Kim, Y. S., Pariente, F., & Wang, E. (1997). Geometric reasoning for mill-turn machining process planning. *Computers & Industrial Engneering, 33*(3/4), 501-504.

Kim, Y. S., Wang, E., & Rho, H. M. (2001). Geometry-based machining precedence reasoning for feature-based process planning. *International Journal of Production Research, 39*(10), 2077-2103.

Kyprianou, I. K. (1980). *Shape classification in computer-aided design.* PhD Dissertation. University of Cambridge. UK.

Owodunni, O., & Hinduja, S. (2002a). Evaluation of existing and new feature recognition algorithms. Part 1: Theory and implementation. *Proceedings of IMechE, Part B: Journal of Engineering Manufacture, 216*(6), 839-852.

Owodunni, O., & Hinduja, S. (2002b). Evaluation of existing and new feature recognition algorithms. Part 2: Experimental results. *Proceedings of IMechE, Part B: Journal of Engineering Manufacture, 216*(6), 853-866.

Pariente, F., & Kim, Y. S. (1996). Incremental and localised update of convex decomposition used for form feature recognition. *Computer-Aided Design, 28*(8), 589-602.

Sakurai, H., & Gossard, D. C. (1990). Recognising shape features in solid models. *Computer Graphics and Applications, IEEE, 10*(9), 22-32.

Shah, J. J. (1991). Assessment of features technology. *Computer-Aided Design, 23*(5), 331-34.

Shah, J. J., & Mäntylä, M. (1995). *Parametric and feature-based CAD/CAM – concepts, techniques and applications.* New York, USA: John Wiley & Sons, Inc.

Shah, J.J., Yan, Y., & Zhang, B.-C. (1998). Dimension and tolerance modeling and transformations in feature based design and manufacturing. *Journal of Intelligent Manufacturing, 9*(5), 475-488.

Singh, N. & Qi, D. (1992). A structural framework for part feature recognition: a link between computer-aided design and process planning. *Integrated Manufacturing Systems, 3*(1), 4-12.

Tseng, Y. J., & Joshi, S. B. (1994). Recognising multiple interpretations of interacting machining features. *Computer-Aided Design, 26*(9), 667-688.

Verma, A. K., & Rajotia, S. (2004). Feature vector: A graph-based feature recognition methodology. *International Journal of Production Research, 42*(16), 3219-3234.

Vosniakos, G. C. (1998). Feature-based product engineering: A critique. *International Journal of Advanced Manufacturing Technology,* 14(7), 474-480.

Woo, T. C. (1982). Feature extraction by volume decomposition. In *Proceedings of Conferefernce in CAD/CAM Technology in Mechanical Engineering.* (pp. 76-94).

Woo, Y., & Sakurai, H. (2002). Recognition of maximal features by volume decomposition. *Computer-Aided Design, 34*(3), 195-207.

Xu, X. (2001). Feature Recognition Methodologies and Beyond. *Australian Journal of Mechanical Engineering, ME25*(1), 1-20.

Xu, X., & Hinduja, S. (1997). Determination of finishing features in 2 1/2D components. *Proceedings of the IMechE, Part B: Journal of Engineering Manufacture, 211*(2), 125-142.

Chapter VI
Feature Interactions

ABSTRACT

Feature interaction tends to have a wide range of consequences and effects on a feature model and its applications. While these may often be intended, it is also true that feature validity can be violated, one way or another, by feature interactions (Shah & Mäntylä, 1995, Gao & Shah, 1998, Lee & Kim, 1998). They may affect the semantics of a feature, ranging from slight changes in actual parameter values, to some substantial alterations to both geometry and topology or even complete suppression of its contribution to the model shape.

To certain extent, successful applications of feature recognition and feature-based techniques have been hindered by interactions among the features. Feature interaction was first studied in relation to feature recognition systems. As an alternative to feature recognition, feature-based design methodology has also become prevalent in recent years. Although a number of successful and commercially available feature-based design systems have been reported, current CAD technology is still unable to provide an effective solution for fully handling the complexity of feature interactions. Very often in a feature-based design system, the interaction between two features gives rise to an unintended feature, nullifying the one-to-one mapping from design features to manufacturing features. The resulting manufacturing feature is usually of a form that the system cannot handle or represent. Thus feature interaction resolution is equally essential for a feature-based design system (Dereli & Baykasoğlu, 2004).

As discussed in Chapter IV, features can be represented either as a set of faces or as a volume. The interactions between surface features are different from those occurring between volumetric features. This chapter discusses different types of interactions that arise from these two feature representation schemes and uses the interacting entities to classify them. There are two types of surface feature interactions, basic feature interaction and complex feature interaction. Three types of basic feature interactions are discussed. They are nested, overlapping, and intersecting types. Interacting patches are used to classify volumetric feature interactions. These interacting patches can be of a containing, contained, or overlapping type. The significance of feature interactions lies in their effect on the machining sequence of the features involved. This is also discussed in this chapter. When features are close to each other but do not share any geometric entities, interactions may also happen for structural reasons. This type of feature interaction can be called interaction by vicinity. The main aim of this chapter is to take a holistic approach toward feature interaction solutions. The example parts used are from the "Catalogue of the NIST (National Institute of Standards and Technology) Design, Planning and Assembly Repository" (Regli & Gaines, 1996). A case study is provided in the end of the chapter.

SURFACE FEATURE INTERACTIONS

Surface features are readily available in a design model and they are the first type of features dealt with in the development of a feature recognition system. Surface feature interactions were also first studied by the researchers.

Surface Features

Surface features have been discussed in comparison to volumetric features in Chapter IV. This chapter discusses feature-feature interactions in a 2½D component. More specifically, a face in a 2½D feature is categorised as a top, base or side face. The top face is always open. A base face for a feature is opposite to the top face. The feature is blind if a base face exists; otherwise, the feature is through. The remaining faces are referred to as side faces. All side faces on a feature collectively form the boundary of the feature. If the boundary is closed, the feature is a closed feature; otherwise it is an open feature.

Classification of Surface Feature Interactions

In the following discussions, the interactions between surface features can be defined on the basis of interacting entity, I. An interacting entity is a collection of geometrical elements which are shared between the face(s) of the two surface features. Symbolically, the interacting entity between features F_1 and F_2 is expressed as, I_{1-2} (or I_{2-1}). An interacting entity can be a wire (i.e. one or more than one consecutive edges) or a face. Two classes of surface interactions are thus defined: *basic* feature interaction whereby the interacting entity is a wire, and *complex* feature interaction whereby the interacting entity is a face.

Basic Feature Interactions

An interacting wire can be open or closed; in the latter case it becomes an interacting loop. There are three types of basic surface feature interactions, *nested, overlapping*, and *intersecting*, partially dependent on the property of the interacting wire (Xu, 2005).

Nested Features

A feature is said to be nested within another feature, if:

(i)   the interacting wire is closed, i.e. the interacting entity becomes a closed loop;
(ii) all the edges comprising the loop are convex; and
(iii) the feature is not through.

Symbolically, "$\subset$" denotes "nested in". Hence, $F_0 \subset F_1$ reads "feature F_0 is nested in feature F_1". For example in Figure 6.1, pocket F_1 is nested in pocket F_2, which is in turn nested in pocket F_3. This can be expressed as,

$$(F_1 \subset F_2) \cap (F_2 \subset F_3) \text{ or } F_1 \subset F_2 \subset F_3$$

where I_{1-2} and I_{2-3} are the interacting loops respectively.

Overlapping Features

Overlapping features only apply to blind features. Two features are said to overlap, if:

(i) the interacting wire is open; and
(ii) two features do not share a common base.

Symbolically, "$\cap^o$" denotes "overlap". Hence, $F_0 \cap^o F_1$ reads "features F_0 and F_1 overlap". In Figure 6.2 (Xu, 2005), feature F_1 overlaps with features F_2 and F_3 at the same time, because the interacting wires (I_{1-2}, I_{1-3}) are open and the two features have different bases. This can be expressed as,

Figure 6.1. Nested features

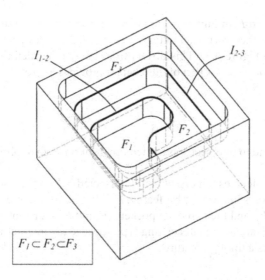

$$F_1 \subset F_2 \subset F_3$$

Figure 6.2. Overlapping features

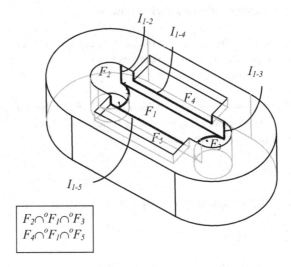

$$(F_2 \cap^o F_1) \wedge (F_1 \cap^o F_3) \text{ or } F_2 \cap^o F_1 \cap^o F_3$$

Similarly, we have,

$$F_4 \cap^o F_1 \cap^o F_5$$

In Figure 6.3, the interactions between F_1 and F_2, and F_1 and F_3 are also of the overlapping type (Xu, 2005), i.e.

$$F_2 \cap^o F_1 \cap^o F_3$$

Note that features F_4 and F_5 in Figure 6.2 are considered as two separate features simply because they each have their own interacting wires (I_{1-4}, I_{1-5}) with respect to F_1. The same applies to F_2 and F_3 in Figure 6.3. This differs from many other definitions that tend to treat these features as one. Latter part of this chapter provides a formal definition for such cases.

Intersecting Features

A through feature is said to intersect another feature, be it through or blind, if the interacting wire is open.

Symbolically, "$\cap^i$" denotes "intersect" or "intersected by". Therefore, $F_0 \cap^i F_1$ reads "feature F_0 intersects, or is intersected by, feature F_1". In Figure 6.4, three features interact with each other: step F_1, and the two open pockets (F_2 and F_3). The interactions between F_1 and F_2, and F_1 and F_3 are of the intersecting type because the interacting wires (I_{1-2}, I_{1-3}) are open and the step is a through feature.

Figure 6.3. Overlapped pockets

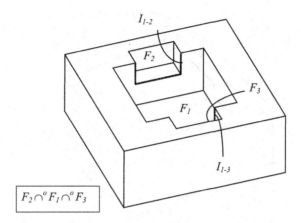

$$F_2 \cap^o F_1 \cap^o F_3$$

Figure 6.4. Feature intersections

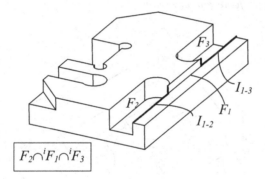

$$F_2 \cap^i F_1 \cap^i F_3$$

Complex Feature Interactions

Complex feature interactions occur when there exists at least one interacting face between the two interacting features. Symbolically, complex feature interaction is denoted as "$\cap^c$". Figure 6.5 shows a closed pocket (F_1) interacting with a step (F_2). This is of a complex feature interaction type as the interacting entities are two faces, also known as "bridging faces". In the part as shown in Figure 6.6, complex feature interactions are found between two pairs of features (Xu, 2005). They are the closed pocket (F_1) and step (F_4 or F_5), and the two closed pockets (F_1 and F_3). Note that the interactions between F_1 and F_2, F_2 and F_4 (or F_5) are of the intersecting type.

More Examples of Surface Feature Interactions

Two more parts (Figures 6.7 and 6.8) from the "Catalogue of the NIST Design, Planning and Assembly Repository" (Regli & Gaines, 1996) are used to further illustrate the concepts presented herein. The "PolyH_Castle" part has four slots (F_1, F_2, F_3 and F_4) and a pocket

Figure 6.5. Complex feature interactions

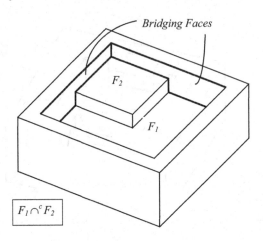

Figure 6.6. More complex feature interactions

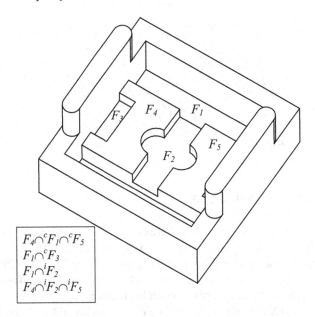

(F_5). It is evident that the pocket interacts with each of the four slots, but does it in two different ways. Slots F_1 and F_3 both intersect F_5: $F_1 \cap^i F_5 \cap^i F_3$. However, complex feature interaction occurs amongst F_2, F_4 and F_5. This is due to the fact that these three features all share the two bridging faces (f_1 and f_2). The part shown in Figure 6.8 contains all types of surface feature interactions that have been discussed so far. Interactions between pockets F_2 and F_3 are of dual nature – overlap ($F_2 \cap^o F_3$) and complex feature interaction ($F_2 \cap^c F_3$), as they are both blind features with different bases, and at the same time, share the bridging faces ($f_4 \sim f_7$). Pocket F_1 also interacts with F_2 in a complex manner. Faces f_1,

Figure 6.7. Feature interactions in the "PolyH_Castle" part

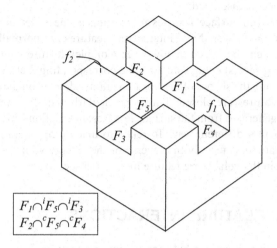

$$F_1 \cap^i F_5 \cap^i F_3$$
$$F_2 \cap^c F_5 \cap^c F_4$$

Figure 6.8. Feature interactions in the "DEMO05_wcr" part

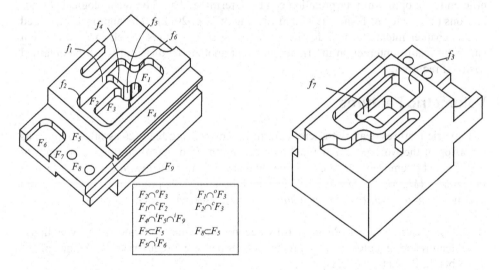

$$F_2 \cap^o F_3 \qquad F_1 \cap^o F_3$$
$$F_1 \cap^c F_2 \qquad F_2 \cap^c F_3$$
$$F_4 \cap^i F_5 \cap^i F_9$$
$$F_7 \subset F_5 \qquad F_8 \subset F_5$$
$$F_5 \cap^i F_6$$

f_2 and f_3 are the bridging faces between F_1 and F_2. Step feature F_5 intersects both step F_4 and slot F_9. There are also two nested holes F_7 and F_8 with respect to step F_5, i.e. $F_7 \subset F_5$, $F_8 \subset F_5$. Another feature interaction occurs between step F_5 and open pocket F_6, which is of the intersecting type.

Significance of Surface Feature Interactions

The true value of detecting surface feature interactions is its ability of providing necessary evidence and information for constructing its feature volume that in turn can be related to the machining operation and sequence. Hence, its impact on machining operation is indirect. In this section, only direct impact of a surface feature interaction, i.e. formation of the feature volume, is discussed.

Interactions between surface features often suggest the order in which the feature volumes are determined. Nested and intersecting features are normally closed first, but overlapping features can be closed in any order. Complex feature interactions inevitably result in the bridging face(s) being split once the corresponding feature volumes are constructed. Furthermore, the shapes of the feature volumes depend on the sequence in which these interacting features are closed. This is particularly true for overlapping features. Once volumes are generated from the surface features, interactions do not disappear; they present themselves in a different way. To relate to machining operations, the sequence of machining operations is usually the reverse of the feature volumes generation. More discussions follow in the volumetric feature interaction section.

VOLUMETRIC FEATURE INTERACTIONS

One way to deal with interactions between volumetric features is to generate several alternative feature sets, each of which is then evaluated by an operation-planning module (Chamberlain, Joneja & Chang, 1993, Shen & Shah, 1994, Tseng & Joshi, 1994). More efficiently, an optimum interpretation can be determined based on technological considerations (Yellowley & Fisher, 1994 and Li, Ong & Nee, 2002). The approach described in this chapter intents to provide one set of volumetric features which carry with them sufficient feature interaction information so that another set of features can be obtained easily, if required.

Volumetric Features

Volumetric features dealt with herein are in fact machining features as often defined as a portion of the workpiece generated by a certain mode of metal cutting, or volumes of material to be removed. A set of volumetric features is termed a *valid* volumetric feature model $M = \{M_1, M_2, ..., M_m\}$ if it satisfies the following three properties, where $-$, $\cup$ and $\cap$ denote *regularised set difference, union*, and *intersection* respectively:

(i)   Completeness: a part P can be fully decomposed when the union of all volumetric features M_i equates the stock removal S (S being the regularised difference of the blank, B and the part), i.e.

$$S = B - P = \bigcup_{i=1}^{m} M_i \, ;$$

(ii)   Part Nonintrusion: $M_i \cap P = \varnothing$, $(i=1, 2, ..., m)$;
(iii)   Feature Nonintrusion: $M_i \cap M_j = \varnothing$, $i \neq j$, $(i=1, 2, ..., m; j=1, 2, ..., m)$.

Based on the above prepositions, one can ascertain that only volumetric features generated from the depression type of surface features are considered. Protrusions are not accounted for because the second condition, i.e. *Part Nonintrusion*, would not have been met. Two such examples are an island (F_1) in a pocket and a protrusion (F_2) on the top of a face (Figure 6.9). In these cases, it is actually the surrounding material that constitutes valid volumetric features, e.g. F_3 and F_4, but not the protrusions themselves (Xu, 2005).

The last property is essential for a volumetric feature to be a machining feature that is equivalent to the actual material to be removed. Machining features illustrated in Figure 6.10(b) are not valid but those in Figures 6.10(c) and (d) are.

Interacting Patches

Since the volumetric features considered here do not have any common volume (Feature Nonintrusion requirement), interaction between any two features, e.g. F_1 and F_2, can occur only between faces, e.g. f_1 and f_2, one belonging to each feature. Therefore, unlike the surface feature interactions where interacting entities can be either a wire/loop or a face that is shared by the both interacting features, the interaction between a pair of volumetric features (F_1, F_2) is defined by a patch, p - the (surface) area common to both faces (f_1, f_2). Karinthi and Nau (1992) used patches to describe the faces of a feature and he classified these patches as "IN", "OUT", "WITH", and "ANTI". Examples of these patches are shown in Figure 6.11 and they are self-explanatory. As feature volumes considered in this research either have no contact or make contact only on external faces, only the ANTI type of patch is of interest. A patch, which is either totally or partially contained in a face, is called an ANTI patch with reference to the two bodies. In this work, an ANTI patch is further classified as being of the *contained* or *equal* type. Given two volumetric features, F_1 and F_2, and the different types of patches, three situations can arise,

(i)   If patch p is completely enclosed within a face (f_1) from feature F_1, and exactly coincident with a face (f_2) from feature F_2, then patch p is defined as being contained by face f_1 of F_1, and equal to face f_2 of F_2 (Figure 6.12), i.e.

$f_1 \supseteq p$: patch p is contained by face f_1 of F_1;
$f_2 \equiv p$: patch p is equal to face f_2 of F_2.

(ii) If p is equal to faces f_1 and f_2, then patch p is an equal patch for faces f_1 and f_2 (Figure 6.10(d)), i.e.

Figure 6.9. Valid and invalid volumetric features

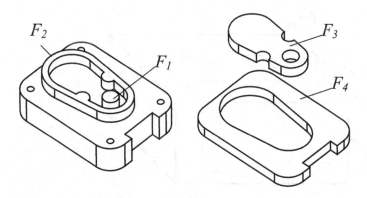

Figure 6.10. Valid and invalid volumetric features

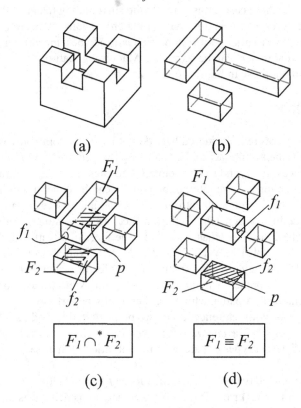

Figure 6.11. Different surface patches

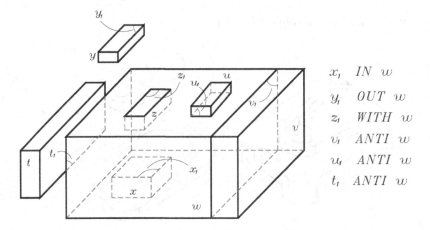

$f_1 \equiv p$: patch p is equal to face f_1 of F_1;
$f_2 \equiv p$: patch p is equal to face f_2 of F_2.

(iii) If p is completely enclosed within both faces, f_1 and f_2, then patch p is defined as being contained by f_1 and f_2 (Figure 6.10(c)) i.e.

$f_1 \supseteq p$: patch p is contained by face f_1 of F_1;
$f_2 \supseteq p$: patch p is contained by face f_2 of F_2.

Feature Interaction Types

The three situations described above give rise to four types of volumetric feature interactions: containing, contained, equal and overlap. Feature interaction type can be derived from the information associated with the interacting patch. Given two features, F_1 and F_2, and the interacting patch p between faces f_1 and f_2 ($f_1 \in F_1, f_2 \in F_2$),

(i) feature F_1 is of the containing type and F_2 is of the contained type, if $(f_1 \supseteq p) \cap (f_2 \equiv p)$. This is expressed as $F_1 \supset^* F_2$;

(ii) features F_1 and F_2 are of the equal type, if $(f_1 \equiv p) \cap (f_2 \equiv p)$. This is expressed as $F_1 \equiv^* F_2$;

(iii) features F_1 and F_2 are of the overlap type, if $(f_1 \supset p) \cap (f_2 \supset p)$. This is expressed as $F_1 \cap^* F_2$.

In Figure 6.12, feature F_1 is of the containing type and feature F_2, with respect to F_1, is of the contained type, $F_1 \supset^* F_2$. Similarly, $F_1 \supset^* F_3$. In Figure 6.10(d), both F_1 and F_2 are of the equal type, $F_1 \equiv^* F_2$. In Figure 6.13, F_1 and F_2 are of the overlap type, $F_1 \cap^* F_2$; the same is true for features F_2 and F_3, $F_2 \cap^* F_3$. Figure 6.10 (c) shows another example of feature overlapping, $F_1 \cap^* F_2$.

Significance of Feature Interactions

From the manufacturing point of view, feature interactions as considered here provide some insight into the machining priority. The interacting information associated with each feature is an additional factor that must be considered when determining the machining sequence. If this information is the only factor to be considered and invasive machining is not permitted, then a containing feature should always be machined prior to the contained feature. It should be possible to do this without penetrating the space of the contained feature. Therefore, the machining sequence for the part shown in Figure 6.12 is: $F_1 \Rightarrow F_2 \Rightarrow$

Figure 6.12. Volumetric feature interactions

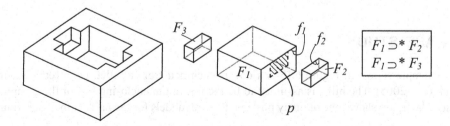

Figure 6.13. Overlapped volumetric features

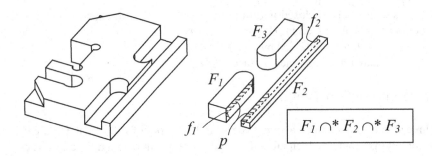

F_3 or $F_1 \Rightarrow F_3 \Rightarrow F_2$. Features of the equal interaction type are normally merged together to form a single machining feature. Figures 6.10(c) shows one of many combinations of the equal-type features in Figure 6.10(d). Overlapping features can be machined in any order, although invasion is often inevitable.

INDIRECT FEATURE INTERACTIONS

Both surface and volumetric feature interactions discussed above are resulted from them sharing a certain type of geometric entities, be it an edge, a wire or a surface patch. Therefore, they can be termed as "geometric feature interactions". There is another type of feature interaction that there is no common geometry shared between the concerning features, yet they need to be considered together when it comes to determining the machining sequences. The interacting medium in this case is effectively the distance between the two features. It is therefore called feature interaction by vicinity. Such interactions are largely due to structural requirements, in that when two features come close enough to form a thin wall between them, the feature machined second may encounter problems in maintaining the accuracy. Figure 6.14 shows a modified version of the part shown in Figure 6.8. In three occasions, the distance between two features has become too small (*t*), (Xu, 2005).

Different workpiece materials will have different minimal wall thicknesses to be observed. If the thickness is too small, the deflection around the thin region due to the cutting force and/or temperature rise will affect the quality the second feature. Dereli and Baykasoğlu, (2004) have studied the problem and calculated the minimum wall thickness for different materials based on factors such as the diameter of the cutter, the spindle speed and the strength of the material. If the minimum thickness value is exceeded, recommendations are issued to either (a) change the material, (b) shift or remove the feature(s), (c) change the machining parameters, (d) change the cutter, or (e) change the sequence of operations.

A CASE STUDY

The example shown in Figure 6.15 is a cover machined from a billet, i.e. a rectangular block (Xu, 2005). The billet is assumed to be the minimum enclosing box of the component. The figure shows one of many possible feature models for the part. It includes, four

Figure 6.14. Feature interactions by vicinity

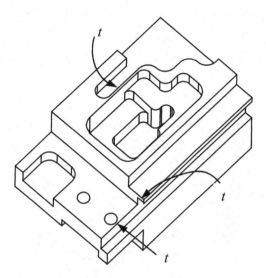

blind holes (1 - 4), five coaxial holes (5, 7, 9, 10 and 19); two cross-holes (6 and 8), four pairs of co-axial holes (11-12, 13-14, 15-16, 17-18), two steps 20 and 22, two slots 21 and 23 and a cross-slot 24. Two types of surface feature interactions are present. Holes 6 and 8 intersect hole 7, because they are through holes and also originate from a convex inner loop, which is effectively the interacting entity. Similarly, hole 9 intersects holes 7 and 10. However, hole 10 is nested in hole 19, since it originates from a convex inner loop and is not a through hole. The co-axial holes 12, 14, 16 and 18 are nested in holes 11, 13, 15 and 17 respectively.

The type of feature interaction dictates the sequence in which the features are closed to obtain volumes. For example, the nested features 12, 14, 16 and 18 are closed before features 11, 13, 15 and 17. Similarly, intersecting features 6 and 8, are closed before feature 7. Holes 1, 2, 3 and 4 are independent (i.e. non-interacting) features, and therefore they can be closed at any time. Slots 21 and 23 intersect steps 20 and 22. The surface interaction is of the intersect type because the interacting wire (labelled as w1, etc.) is open and lies on one planar face. The cross-shaped slot is an independent feature. Since the relationship of features 21 and 23 with 20 and 22 is of the intersecting type, the order in which the feature volumes are obtained is immaterial.

There also exist a number of volumetric feature interactions among the feature volumes as shown in Figure 6.15. Also shown in this figure are the interacting patches between the feature volumes. The classification for some of the interacting patches is shown in Table 6.1 (Xu, 2005).

These patch types are used in turn to classify the feature interactions, some of which are shown in Table 6.2. Features 1, 2, 3, 4 and 24 are not shown in the table, because they do not interact with any other features; 13 to 18 repeat the pattern of 11,12.

The type of interaction should be considered, along with other factors, to determine the machining sequence. If the feature interaction type was the only consideration, and for example, invasion by the cutter into another feature is not preferred, then containing features

Figure 6.15. Interacting wires and patches for the features in a part

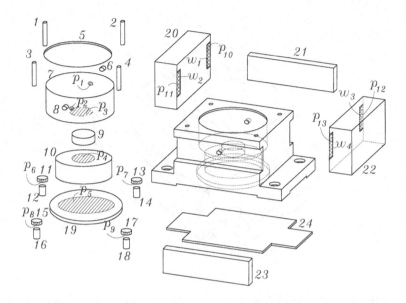

should be machined prior to the contained features. Therefore, considering features 6-10 and 19, one possible machining sequence would be 19, 10, 7, 6, 8 and 9. Features 20 and 22 should be machined before 21 and 23. Features 1-4 and 24 are independent and can be machined in any sequence. However, in practice, other factors are usually taken into account. For example, if calculation showed that the machining of the slots has a lower specific machining cost than that for the steps, then the slots would be machined first. This would require the feature volumes to be modified. The modified feature volumes for the slot and step are obtained firstly by extending the slot in both directions and subsequently by subtracting the extended slot from the step. The modified feature volumes are shown in Figure 6.16. Note that the relationships between the slots and the steps are reversed, i.e. modified feature 21 is now of the containing type with respect to features 20 and 22. The same is true for the modified features 23, 20 and 22.

Feature interaction by vicinity may also present a problem for this component. If hole 7 is large enough to reduce the wall thickness between features 21 and 23 and the hole,

Table 6.1. Interacting patches

Patch No	Reference Feature	
	Type of Patch	
	Contained	Equal
p1	7	6
p3	7	9
p6	11	12
p10	20	21

Table 6.2. Feature interaction types

Feature No.	Interacted Features		
	Type of Feature Interactions		
	Containing	Contained	Equal
5			7
6		7	
7	6, 8, 9		5
8		7	
9		7, 10	
10	9	19	
11	12		
12		11	
19	10		
20	21, 23		
21		20, 22	
22	21, 23		
23		20, 22	

Figure 6.16. Modified feature volumes

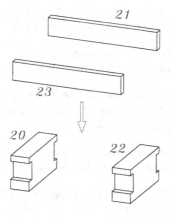

to a value below the minimal thickness for the type of material and the given machining conditions, either the designer or the machinist will need to make changes to the design model or the machining strategy.

CONCLUSION

Feature interactions have a wide range of consequences and effects on a feature model and its applications. They may affect the semantics of a feature, ranging from slight changes in actual parameter values, to some substantial alterations to both geometry and topology or even complete suppression of its contribution to the model shape. More importantly, feature interaction has a significant effect on, and is closely related to, both functionality and the assembly process, not to mention its profound impact on dictating the machining volumes and machining sequence of the features.

Surface feature interaction is different from volumetric feature interaction. The interacting entities between two surface features can be of either wire or face type, whereas those between two volumetric features are always of face type. The definition of surface feature interactions is generic as it is based on the interacting entities between the two interacting features. Knowledge of surface interaction type is a prerequisite for the order in which the feature volumes should be generated.

Features that do have interacting entities between them, may also interact indirectly, having an effect on the sequence in which they are machined. This type of feature interaction though not well researched, deserves particular attention. Other factors that may cause features to interact with each other include tolerances, fixture and cutting tools (Gao, Zheng, Gindy & Clark, 2005).

REFERENCES

Chamberlain, M. A., Joneja, A., & Chang, T-C. (1993). Protrusion-features handling in design and manufacturing planning. *Computer-Aided Design, 25*(1), 19-28.

Dereli, T., & Baykasoğlu, A. (2004). Concurrent engineering utilities for controlling interactions in process planning. *Journal of Intelligent Manufacturing, 15*(4), 471-479.

Gao, J., Zheng, D. T., Gindy, N., & Clark, D. (2005). Extraction/conversion of geometric dimensions and tolerances for machining features. *International Journal of Advanced Manufacturing Technology, 26*(4), 405-414.

Gao, S., & Shah, J. J. (1998). Automatic recognition of interacting machining features based on minimal condition subgraph. *Computer-Aided Design, 30*(9), 727-739.

Karinthi, R. R., & Nau, D. S. (1992). An algebraic approach to feature interactions, *Pattern Analysis and Machine Intelligence, IEEE. 14*(4), 469-484.

Lee, J. Y., & Kim, K. (1998). A feature-based approach to extracting machining features. *Computer-Aided Design, 30*(13), 1019-1035.

Li, W. D., Ong, S. K., & Nee, A. Y. C. (2002). Recognizing manufacturing features from a design-by-feature model. *Computer-Aided Design, 34*(11), 849-868.

Regli, W. C., & Gaines, D. M. (1996). *Catalogue of the NIST Design, Planning, and Assembly Repository.* Gaithersburg, USA: Engineering Design Technologies Group, NIST.

Shah, J. J., & Mäntylä, M. (1995). *Parametric and feature-based CAD/CAM – Concepts, techniques and applications.* New York, USA: John Wiley & Sons, Inc.

Shen, Y., & Shah, J. J. (1994). Feature recognition by volume decomposition using half-space partitioning, *Design Engineering Division (Publication), ASME. DE 69-1,* 575-583.

Tseng, Y.-J., & Joshi, S. B. (1994). Recognising multiple interpretations of interacting machining features. *Computer-Aided Design, 26*(9), 667-688.

Xu, X.W. (2005). Novel surface and volumetric feature interactions for process planning, *International Journal of Computer Applications in Technology, 24*(4), 185-194.

Yellowley, I., & Fisher, A. D. (1994). The planning of multi-volume rough machining operations, *International Journal of Machine Tools and Manufacture, 34*(3), 439-452.

Chapter VII
Integrated Feature Technology

ABSTRACT

Integrated feature technology promotes a closer connection between design and manufacturing through features. When machining features are determined, they may or may not be readily useable for a process planning system. In a feature-based design system, features in a design model are of design type of features. Further conversion is also needed to arrive at machining features. This chapter starts with a discussion on the issues of interfacing and integration. This is followed by some of the methodologies that can bring feature technologies one step closer to manufacturing processes.

Representing a machining feature in terms of its machining volume that can directly corresponds to a specific type of machining operation (e.g. finishing, semi-finishing, and roughing operations) is one of the methods introduced in this chapter. In order to achieve this, a number of machining operations is to be decided. For this, tolerances, surface, finish, and other design information are to be considered. The fuzzy nature of these data and the concerning knowledge means that an appropriate treatment of such information is also needed. A direct way of linking a feature-based design model with machining operations is to map the design features to machining features and perhaps further to the cutting tools that may be used to produce the features.

INTEGRATION VERSUS INTERFACING

There exist some confusions between integrated and interfaced feature technologies. Careful examination shows that many systems are mainly trying to interface various separated activities at the design, manufacturing, and planning phases. One difference between interfacing and integration is that interfacing can be achieved at the result-level, while integration must be addressed at the task-level. In other words, it would be too late to integrate a task when its sub-results have already been decided separately. To achieve truly integrated design and manufacturing, integration between them should be addressed at a much earlier stage than currently done.

Figure 7.1 shows a CAPP system adopting an interfaced approach (Xu, 2001). Features that have been recognised are first organised into a directed graph, generally known as feature access graph, which represents the precedence of the machining of features based on their accesses. This activity may be called routing sequence planning, or macro planning. At the routing sequence level only general machining processes, such as hole-making, pocket-milling and slotting, are decided. Detailed shop-floor operations, such as whether a hole should be centre-drilled, pre-drilled, drilled and reamed or just centre-drilled and drilled are yet to be determined. In order to generate a shop-floor operation plan, an operation planning module, also called a micro planning module, is needed later. The operation planning module decomposes the general machining processes into sequences of actual

Figure 7.1. CAPP between CAD to Shop-Floor

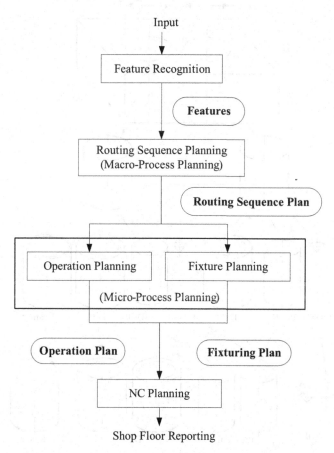

machining cuts, i.e. preliminary cuts (e.g. centre-drilling, pocket-opening and roughing), follow-up cuts (e.g. semi-finishing) and/or final cuts (e.g. finishing), with the same or different cutting tools or machining tools. The final operation plan for a part is then constructed by combining similar machining cuts into different operation clusters and performing them in a specific sequence, e.g. rough machining, semi-finish machining, and finish machining. At each machining stage, operations mainly of the same nature are grouped. In other words, a process plan is more operation-oriented than feature-oriented.

Figure 7.2 gives such an example (Xu, 2001). The two holes have differing tolerance requirements, hence different (number of) machining operations are required. The final machining sequence is dependent on the sub-operations that is to centre-drill (C'Drill) the two holes first and then pre-drill and drill the two holes. The final operation is to ream the second hole to meet the tighter tolerance requirement specified on the second hole. Clearly, the feature access graph is based on a set of intermediate results, i.e. features that have

Figure 7.2. Machining features grouped for different types of operations. ©2001, Engineers Australia used with permission.

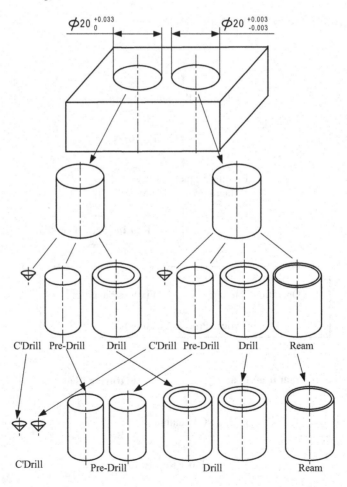

been provided by a feature recognition system. It is obvious that many existing systems merely act as an interface between CAD and CAM. It is too late to integrate CAD with CAM when so-called features have been decided separately.

In general there are three different types of integration. *Data Integration* is the ability to share part models (data files). This is the most important type of integration for CAD/CAM. *Interface Integration* refers to a common look and feel for different software modules. *Application Integration* provides different functions in the same computer program. This chapter discusses some of the requirements and methodologies of an integrated feature-based approach in the context of data integration. Both integrated feature recognition methods and feature mapping (for design-by-feature systems) will be discussed. Applications of integration will be discussed in details in Chapters X – XVII.

INTEGRATED FEATURE RECOGNITION

Clearly there is a need to recognise (machining) features that can be intimately associated with machining processes. From the constraint viewpoint, there are two basic types of machining operations, i.e. *geometry-constrained* and *technology-constrained* operations (Xu, 2001). Examples of the former are centre-drilling and slot drilling, as pilot operations for drilling a hole and opening a pocket respectively. Examples of the latter are roughing, semi-finishing and finishing operations. Product cost and quality are largely dependent on technology-constrained operations. Therefore, there is a need for a feature-based system to generate features with which specific technology-constrained operations can be associated. Such features, for example, in the case of hole-making, may comprise roughing (pre-drilling), semi-finishing (drilling) and finishing (reaming) features (Figure 7.2).

Machining Volumes for Different Operations

Determination of correct volume for different types of technology-constrained operations can be a non-trivial task. This is illustrated in Figure 7.3(a), which shows a component positioned in its billet. Assume that faces A, B and C require a finishing operation. The stock material as shown in Figure 7.3(b) can be decomposed in several ways, two of which are shown in Figure 7.3(c) and 7.3(e). For both these methods, the finishing volumes may be calculated as shown in Figures 7.3(d) and 7.3(f). In Figure 7.3(d), the majority of the finishing volume in V_1 would have been machined during the roughing operation. The same is true for the finishing volume in V_2 (Figure 7.3(f)). Obviously this is caused by the approach adopted in decomposing a stock. A more acceptable method is to subtract the finishing volume from the stock material and then decompose the remaining stock into roughing features (Figures 7.3(g) and 7.3(h)). Note that the finishing volume is also decomposed, in this case, into two finishing features.

Recognising features directly for roughing, semi-finishing and finishing operations is an essential step to achieve an integrated CAD/CAPP/CAM scenario. The remaining of this section attempts to illustrate some of the methods by which feature volumes are determined for different types of machining operations.

Figure 7.3. Subdivision of stock material into roughing and finishing features. ©1997, IMechE used with permission.

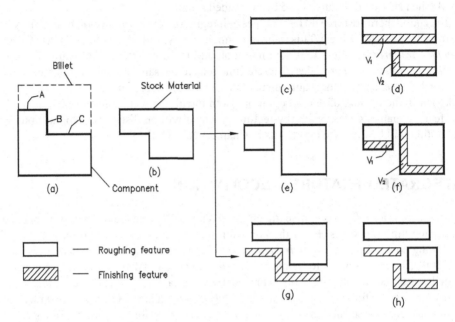

Features for Finishing Operations

It is easy to generate the (semi-)finishing features first. They are then used to arrive at an intermediate workpiece based on which features for roughing operations can be determined. Finishing features have a close relationship with the faces on a component. This is why the backward reasoning technique is best suited for generating finishing features. It should be pointed out that the term "finishing" is used liberally here to refer to any operation performed after a roughing operation, i.e. there can be two finishing operations for a surface, a semi-finishing and a (final) finishing operation. The first step towards recognising a finishing feature is to generate elementary finishing volumes. An elementary finishing volume is a unit volume removed by a finishing operation on a face. Hence, it is a face-based machining volume and also named as a face volume. An elementary finishing volume can be generated by "growing" the face back by an amount equal to the corresponding machining allowance.

It is likely that neighbouring elementary finishing volumes either overlap or have a void between them. An overlap occurs when two faces share a concave edge. A void occurs when two neighbouring faces share a convex edge. To bridge the gap, an *edge volume* is needed. Edge volumes can be generated after the face volumes, and linked to them so that they can be easily merged to form a finishing feature.

An elementary finishing volume may form a machining feature. In practice, several elementary finishing features are merged to form a single machining feature. This is discussed as follows, and definitions of concave and convex geometric entities discussed in Chapter V are utilised. If two neighbouring faces share a concave or smooth edge, their elementary finishing volumes are merged together because it is not possible to remove one of the face volumes without violating the other. In the case of smoothly-connected faces, machining the faces in separate passes will not guarantee tangency.

Intermediate Workpiece

Information regarding the state of the workpiece at each stage of manufacturing is important. The intermediate workpiece prior to the finishing operations is referred to as finishing workpiece; the workpiece prior to the semi-finishing operations is referred to as a semi-finishing workpiece. The semi-finishing workpiece is then necessary for recognising the roughing features. To generate an intermediate workpiece, the finishing or semi-finishing features are "glued" onto the current workpiece. The intermediate workpiece has no technological information attached to it but a link is usually needed so that each face on the intermediate workpiece can reference the original component from which data can be retrieved.

Machining Requirements

Many feature recognition systems recognise features based on the premise that all the faces on a component are to be machined. In reality, the near-net shape manufacturing techniques in the production of castings/forgings have always tried to keep the number of faces requiring machining to a minimum. This means that not every face on the design part needs a machining operation. Those that need may also require different machining regimes, e.g. roughing, semi-finishing and/or finishing operations. Machining requirement evaluation for each face therefore becomes a necessity. The ultimate goal is to identify (a) all the faces on the finished part that need to be machined in order to meet the surface requirements; (b) how many machining operations are required; and (c) the material (machining) allowance of each operation. Once this information is available, finishing and semi-finishing if any can be generated before the roughing features. Very few process planning systems consider the machining requirement for a face. Those that do, assign discrete values of machining allowance to faces which require machining. This process can be tedious and error-prone.

Surface-Targeted Operation Information

Every component has surface finish, fits, limits and tolerance requirements that must be satisfied. This type of information, often specified on the surfaces of a component, is crucial in determining the most efficient and economic method of machining the part. In order to achieve a good surface finish and tight tolerances, additional finishing operations as well as better control of processing parameters and the use of accurate machine(s) may be required. Table 7.1 shows the machining capabilities of some common hole-making operations using different types or the same type of cutting tools (Xu & Hinduja, 1997). Data was collected from various sources (Chang, Wysk & Wang 1991, Zeid 1991, Gu & Norrie, 1995, Wang & Li, 1992) and since the actual values differ, they are averaged and these average values are shown in the table. There are three types of information that is often present on a design drawings, dimensional and geometrical tolerances, and surface finish.

Table 7.1. Hole-making operations on a machining centre

OPERATION	CUTTING TOOLS	ATTAINABLE SURFACE FINISH	ATTAINABLE IT	ATTAINABLE STRAIGHTNESS	ATTAINABLE CYLINDRICITY	ATTAINABLE ROUNDNESS
DRILLING	Twist drill		IT11 (φ≤30)			
	Combined drills					
	Countersinks and Counterbores	> Ra3.2	IT12 (3<φ≤50)	0.003	0.02 (φ≤50) 0.03 (50<φ≤120) 0.05 (120<φ≤250)	0.005 (φ≤10) 0.015 (10<φ≤50) 0.030 (50<φ≤120)
	Centre drill		IT13 (10<φ≤80)			
	Spade drill					0.050 (120<φ≤250)
	Daecp-hole drill	>Ra12.5	IT9 (φ≤15)	0.012 in 15mm		
	Gun drills		IT10 (φ>15)			
ENLARGING	Core drill	Ra12.5 - Ra3.2	IT10 - IT11 (10<φ≤120)	0.003	0.01	0.008
REAMING	Long-flute machine reamers	SEMI-FINISHING: Ra3.2 - Ra1.6	SEMI-FINISHING: IT8 - IT9 (3<φ≤315)	0.003	0.003 (φ≤50) 0.005 (50<φ≤120) 0.008 (120<φ≤250)	0.003 (φ≤10) 0.005 (10<φ≤50)
	Machine chucking reamers					
	Shell reamers	FINISHING: Ra1.6 - Ra0.8	FINISHING: IT6 (3<φ≤18) IT7 (3<φ≤315)	0.001		
	Socket reamers					
	Machine taper pin reamers					
	Bridge reamers	ROUGHING: Ra25 - Ra12.5	ROUGHING: IT12 - IT13			
BORING	Boring tools	SEMI-FINISHING: Ra6.3 - Ra3.2	SEMI-FINISHING: IT10 - IT11	0.005	0.02 (φ≤50) 0.025 (50<φ≤120) 0.040 (120<φ≤250)	0.008 (50<φ≤120) 0.010 (120<φ≤250)
		FINISHING: Ra1.6 - Ra0.8	FINISHING: IT8 - IT9			
		HIGH-PRECISION: Ra0.4 - Ra0.1	HIGH-PRECISION: IT6 (10<φ≤120) IT7 (φ>10)			

Dimensional Tolerances

Dimensional tolerances are imposed on portion(s) of a design model to ensure functional and assembly requirements. Tolerances themselves, however, do not reflect a true accuracy level. They have to be considered together with the nominal dimensions. International tolerance grade (IT), specified in ISO as Standard Tolerance Grade (ISO 286-2, 1988), is referred to as a group of tolerances that vary depending on the basic size, but provide the same relative level of accuracy within a grade. The smaller an IT number, the tighter the tolerance, and the more liekly that a finishing cut is needed.

Surface Finish (Roughness)

Surface quality is another important factor affecting the choice of machining operations. A component with a high surface finish requirement together with a tight dimensional tolerance, may require several consecutive machining operations, such as roughing, semi-finishing and finishing operations. Otherwise, a roughing operation may be sufficient to achieve the required surface quality.

Geometrical Tolerances

A geometrical tolerance defines the size and shape of a zone within which a toleranced entity has to lie. It controls the form, attitude or location of a face. Geometrical dimensioning and tolerancing of a workpiece also impose important constraints on the selection and sequencing of operations although the ways geometric tolerances influence the selection and sequence of operations can be very complex. This chapter only discusses some of the common types of geometric tolerances and their influence over the decision on machining operations. Interested readers are referred to some of the publications listed at the end for more details (Gao, Zheng, Gindy & Clark, 2005, Geddam & Kaldor, 1998, Huang, Liu & Musa, 2004, Lin, Lin & Ho, 1999, Thimm, Britton & Lin, 2004, Wu, Gao & Chen, 2001).

There are 14 types of geometrical tolerances (Henzold, 1995) as listed in Table 7.2. Amongst them, form tolerances limit the deviations of an individual entity from its ideal geometrical shape, i.e. a line or a planar surface. Special cases of line forms are straightness and roundness (circularity). Special cases of surfaces are flatness (planarity) and cylindricity. These four types of geometrical tolerances influence the type of operations selected. Others, such as profile, orientation, location and runout tolerances, affect the operation sequence.

Decisions on Number of Cuts

Making decisions about the type and number of cuts, or machining operations is a complex, multi-attribute problem because the relationship between an operation and an attribute (conventional tolerances, surface finish etc.) is, in most cases, ill-defined. The data in Table 7.1 in fact, show the values (tolerances and surface finish) attainable with several different types of operations. The boundaries set by these values should not be interpreted as rigid because these data are imprecise. For example, a finishing operation should be considered if the required IT values are between 7 and 9. However, the certainty of selecting a finishing operation differs with different values falling in-between. A finishing operation is likely

Table 7.2. Geometric tolerances and their characteristic symbols

Type of feature	Type of tolerance	Characteristic	Symbol
Individual		Flatness	▱
(no datum	Form	Straightness	—
reference)		Circularity	○
		Cylindricity	⌀
Individual	Profile	Profile of a line	⌒
or related		Profile of a surface	◠
		Perpendicularity	⊥
	Orientation	Angularity	∠
Related		Parallelism	//
(datum		Position	⊕
reference	Location	Concentricity	◎
required)		Symmetry	⸗
	Runout	Circular runout	↗
		Total runout	⌀↗

to be deemed most suitable, i.e. a certainty of 1.0, when there is a requirement of IT8. Although acceptable, a finishing operation becomes unnecessary, and therefore uneconomical, when a requirement of IT9 has to be satisfied. At the other end, a finishing operation may encounter some difficulties in obtaining an IT grade of 7. The certainty values for the last two situations are bound to be smaller than 1. Furthermore, it would be grossly wrong to consider it impossible for a finishing operation to produce an IT grade of 6. The cause for the above impreciseness is mainly due to the fact that there is usually not a clear division among different types of operations. A certain value of surface finish or tolerance requires a particular operation type only to a degree of certainty. Absolute divisions and decisions do not exist. Expert systems which rely heavily on rules do not yield desirable solutions for the selection of machining operations, or sometimes even fail to yield a solution. Take the rule in Chapter III as an example,

"finishing_operation for a hole:
(IT (8, 9))
(Ra (0.8, 1.6))
(Roundness (0.003, 0.010))
(Cylindricity (0.003, 0.008))
(Straightness (0.0008, 0.0012))"

This rule may result in two problems. Firstly, given the following set of facts,

{IT (8), Ra (0.8), *Roundness (0.011)*, Cylindricity (0.003), Straightness (0.0008)},

the rule will not be fired, and consequently no decision is made. Secondly, given the two sets of facts shown below, the above rule will be fired yielding the same decision but giving no indication as to what extent a finishing operation is suitable.

{IT (8), Ra (0.8), Roundness (0.003), Cylindricity (0.003), Straightness (0.0008)} and
{IT (9), Ra (0.8), Roundness (0.010), Cylindricity (0.008), Straightness (0.0012)}

Therefore, a method that can handle imprecise and fuzzy information has become necessary to make decisions about the number/type(s) of cuts to be made on a particular face of a workpiece. A brief description of such a method dealing with fuzzy information is given below.

Dealing with Fuzzy Information

It is of a typical nature that in the design and manufacturing domain the information being dealt with is imprecise. Decisions are often made based on this type of fuzzy information.

Fuzzy Variables

In a multi-attribute decision-making system that deals with fuzzy data, five variables can be defined: A, T, W, $R(a_i)$ and $R(r_{ij})$. A is associated with the attribute fuzzy set, $A = \{(a_i, \mu_A(a_i) \mid a_i \in A\}$, where $A = \{a_1, a_2, \cdots, a_m\}$, a_i refers to the i-th attribute, and m the total number of the attributes. For example, in the case of a milling operation, the attributes that may be considered are the dimensional tolerance and roughness, hence $m = 2$. For a hole-making operation, the attributes that may be considered are the dimensional tolerance, roughness, straightness, roundness and cylindricity, hence $m = 5$.

T is defined based on the operation type fuzzy set, $T = \{(t_j, \mu_T(t_j)|t_j \in T\}$, where $T = \{t_1, t_2, t_3\}, t_1, t_2$ and t_3 refer to finishing, semi-finishing and roughing operations respectively. T, which is also called the fuzzy decision set, is the output of the system whereas A is the input.

Defined on A, W is a weighting vector, which assigns different contributions of the attributes $a_i (i = 1, 2, \cdots, m)$ toward the final decision $t_j (j = 1, 2, 3)$. $R(a_i)$ is the result of mapping $a_i \in A$ to T, and is referred to as the decision-making of an individual attribute, $R(a_i) = (r_{i1}, r_{i2}, \cdots, r_{im})$. This mapping is also called *defuzzisation*, which is carried out through membership functions. Set A, when mapped to the operation type fuzzy set T, results in a two-dimensional fuzzy relation matrix $R(r_{ij})$ *(i=1,2,...,m; j=1,2,...,n)*. All the fuzzy elements in the above fuzzy sets are normalised, which is a prerequisite for the fuzzy composition operations. The four common types of fuzzy composition operations are shown in Table 7.3.

Membership Functions

Membership functions are used to map (imprecise) attributes to fuzzy values that are often in the interval of [0,1]. Membership functions can have different shapes depending on the user's preference or experience. It is found in practice that triangular/trapezoidal and *S-functions* help capture the sense of fuzzy numbers. The former can simplify the computation; the latter behaves more naturally through out the interval [0,1]. An *S-function* is defined as follows,

Table 7.3. Fuzzy composition operators

Composition Operator	Fuzzy Operators $\begin{matrix}+\\ *\end{matrix}$	$\begin{matrix}\bullet\\ *\end{matrix}$	Formulae	Characteristics
I (max-min)	$\cap$	$\cup$	$v_j = \bigcup\limits_{i=1}^{m}(u_i \cap r_{ij})$	principal element dominating
II (max-product)	$\bullet$	$\cup$	$v_j = \bigcup\limits_{i=1}^{m}(u_i \bullet r_{ij})$	principal element
III (bounded sum-min)	$\cap$	$\oplus$	$v_j = \sum\limits_{i=1}^{m}\oplus(u_i \cap r_{ij})$	conspicuous
IV (bounded sum-product)	$\bullet$	$\oplus$	$v_j = \sum\limits_{i=1}^{m}\oplus(u_i \bullet r_{ij})$	weighed element

$$S(x;\alpha,\beta,\gamma) = \begin{cases} 0 & \text{for} \quad x \leq \alpha \\ 2\left(\dfrac{x-\alpha}{\gamma-\alpha}\right)^2 & \text{for} \quad \alpha \leq x \leq \beta \\ 1-2\left(\dfrac{x-\gamma}{\gamma-\alpha}\right)^2 & \text{for} \quad \beta \leq x \leq \gamma \\ 1 & \text{for} \quad x \geq \gamma \end{cases} \qquad (7.1)$$

In this definition, α, β and γ are parameters which may be adjusted to fit the desired membership data.

Another popular membership function is Π-*function*, which can be expressed in terms of *S-function*,

$$\Pi(x;\beta,\gamma) = \begin{cases} S(x;\gamma-\beta,\gamma-\beta/2,\gamma) & \text{for} \quad x \leq \gamma \\ S(x;\gamma,\gamma+\beta/2,\gamma+\beta) & \text{for} \quad x \geq \gamma \end{cases} \qquad (7.2)$$

Note that β is the *bandwidth* or *total width* at the crossover points which are at $x = \gamma \pm \beta/2$.

Table 7.4, which is based on Table 7.1 and other sources (Chang, Wysk & Wang 1991, Zeid 1991, Gu & Norrie, 1995), shows how the technological data influence the way decisions are made about machining operations. Again, the data in Table 7.4 can be modified for different practical machining environments. Depending upon the nature of the data, a Π- or *S-function* is used and this is discussed below.

Membership Functions for Dimensional Tolerances and Surface Finish

Π-*function* is suitable for dimensional tolerance (IT number) and surface finish (roughness) because there are bounding values available in these cases (Table 7.4). To define function $\mu_A(a_j)$, parameter β is set equal to the absolute value of a particular attribute range, while γ is the mean of this range. Consider attribute surface finish for finishing operations in peripheral milling (Table 7.4). β would be 0.8 (=1.6-0.8) and γ would be 1.2 (=(1.6+0.8)/2). Tables 7.5 and 7.6 show the values of β and γ in the case of tolerance grade and surface finish. The corresponding membership functions are plotted in Figures 7.4 and 7.5. Note that the membership functions also vary according to different types of cutting tools used.

Table 7.4. Influencing factors for machining operations

Operations	Finishing	Semi-finishing	Roughing	Note
Conventional tolerance(IT)	6~8	8~11	11~13	
Surface finish (Ra)	0.8~1.6	1.6~3.2	3.2~12.5	
Roundness	>0.0008	>0.0012	>0.008	Applicable to hole-
Cylindricity	>0.001	>0.002	>0.001	making operations
Straightness	>0.005	>0.015	>0.08	

Table 7.5. Machining operations and their Π-function parameters relating to IT numbers

Operations	Finishing	Semi-Finishing	Roughing
Value Range	6 ~ 8	8 ~ 11	11 ~ 13
Function Parameters	γ=7,	γ=9.5,	γ=12,
	β=2	β=3	β=2

Table 7.6. Machining operations and the Π-function parameters for surface finish (Ra)

Operations	Finishing	Semi-Finishing	Roughing
Value Range	0.8 ~ 1.6	1.6 ~ 3.2	3.2 ~ 12.5
Function Parameters	γ=1.2,	γ=2.4,	γ=7.8,
	β=0.8	β=0.8	β=9.3

Membership Functions for Geometrical Tolerances

More often than not, the geometrical tolerance attainable by a particular type of machining operation is a single value which denotes the minimum value this operation is capable of achieving. An *S-function* $f(x)$ can represent this single-value case by making the parameter γ equal to the minimum value. However, this function only reflects a degree of *machinability* pertaining to a particular type of machining operation. The concept of *economics* is missing. The machining economics is represented by the *complement* of the machinability membership function $f'(x)=1-f(x)$ shifted by a distance of γ-β, i.e. $f_i(x) = f'(x+γ-β)$ (Figure 7.6). For example, assume that the attainable roundness in a reaming (semi-finishing) operation is 0.0012, i.e. γ=0.0012 as shown in Table 7.4. A roundness value of 0.001 would be considered machinable only to a degree less than 1, whereas it is economical to a degree of 1. On the other hand, a value of 0.002 would be considered machinable to a degree of 1, but economical to a degree of less than 1.

Figure 7.4. Membership functions for IT. ©1997, IMechE used with permission.

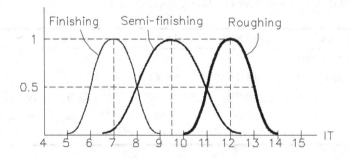

Figure 7.5. Membership functions for Roughness. ©1997, IMechE used with permission.

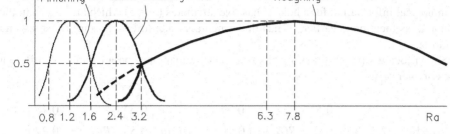

Figure 7.6. An S-function and its complements

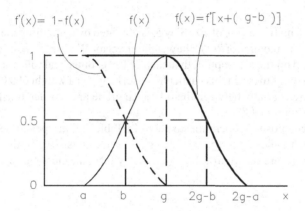

Let fuzzy sets M and E, represented by membership functions $f_m(x)$ and $f_e(x)$ respectively, be the machinability and economics fuzzy sets regarding a specific geometrical tolerance attainable by a certain machining operation. The overall suitability fuzzy set S is the *intersection* of the fuzzy sets M and E, i.e. $S = M \cap E$, where the membership function for S, $f_s(x)$, is related to those of M and E by,

$$f_s(x) = Min[f_m(x), f_e(x)], \ x \in X \tag{7.3}$$

Making Decisions Based on Fuzzy Data

Making decisions based on fuzzy data is effectively mapping A to T. The input data are first "fuzzified" into sets with membership functions, $\mu A(a_i)$. Secondly, fuzzy mapping from a_i to t_i is carried out for each data type, thus obtaining the fuzzy relation matrix, $R(r_{ij})$. Preliminary decisions are made based on this fuzzy relation matrix along with the weighting vector, W. After this the final decision is made by considering all the four preliminary decisions with a secondary weighting vector, W_T. The output is in the form of recommendations which are shown in Table 7.7; these recommendations are obtained by mapping the fuzzy qualifiers contained in T to fuzzy propositions as shown in the table.

An Example

The following example illustrates the decision-making procedure. Table 7.8 shows the technological information for a hole. *A* has five attributes (*m* = 5) which are shown in the table and, as mentioned earlier, *T* has three members, i.e. finishing, semi-finishing and roughing.

Shown below are the fuzzy results obtained by mapping the attributes to different types of operations.

$$R(a_1) = \begin{pmatrix} 1 \\ 0 \\ 0 \end{pmatrix}, \quad R(a_2) = \begin{pmatrix} 0.5 \\ 0.5 \\ 0 \end{pmatrix}, \quad R(a_3) = \begin{pmatrix} 0.21 \\ 0.79 \\ 0 \end{pmatrix}, \quad R(a_4) = \begin{pmatrix} 0.5 \\ 0.5 \\ 0 \end{pmatrix}, \quad R(a_5) = \begin{pmatrix} 0.78 \\ 0.22 \\ 0 \end{pmatrix}$$

$$(7.4)$$

The fuzzy relation matrix, $R(r_{ij})$, of size 3 by 5, is obtained by combining the above vectors, each vector becoming a column of $R(r_{ij})$. The weighting vector $W = (w_1 \quad w_2 \quad w_3 \quad w_4 \quad w_5)$ is calculated based on the assumption that each of the geometrical tolerances (roundness, cylindricity and straightness, in this particular case) be given a weight of 0.08. The remaining weight is shared equally between the tolerance grade and surface finish, i.e. $w_1 = w_2 = 0.38$ and $w_3 = w_4 = w_5 = 0.08$.

The four fuzzy composition operations, shown in Table 7.3, are performed on $R(r_{ij})$ and *W*. Each operation yields a preliminary decision vector consisting of three values. The four decision vectors are shown in Table 7.9 and they form the elements of the preliminary decision matrix, R_T.

Table 7.7. Mapping fuzzy values to fuzzy propositions

Fuzzy	values(qualifiers)	Fuzzy propositions
Above	Up to and include	
0.85	1.00	*ESSENTIAL*
0.60	0.85	*STRONGLY RECOMMENDED*
0.45	0.60	*RECOMMENDED*
0.30	0.45	*PREFERRED*
0	0.30	*NOT REQUIRED*

Table 7.8. Technological information for a hole

A	a_1	a_2	a_3	a_4	a_5
Attribute	IT number	Roughness	Roundness	Cylindricity	Straightness
Value	7	1.6	0.007	0.016	0.0012

Table 7.9. Preliminary decisions

Decisions	Operations		
	t_1	t_2	t_3
I	0.5	0.5	0
II	0.689	0.311	0
III	0.617	0.383	0
IV	0.689	0.311	0

Assuming that each of the four decisions be given an equal weighting, we have the secondary weighting vector $W_T = (0.25\ 0.25\ 0.25\ 0.25)$. The secondary decision-making is then performed on R_T and W_T using the second (max-product) fuzzy composition operation i.e.

$$T = W_T \circ R_T \tag{7.5}$$

where

$$R_T = \begin{pmatrix} 0.5 & 0.5 & 0 \\ 0.689 & 0.311 & 0 \\ 0.617 & 0.383 & 0 \\ 0.689 & 0.311 & 0 \end{pmatrix}$$

The result obtained gives the final decision vector, T.

$$T = (0.624\ 0.376\ 0) \tag{7.6}$$

This result is then mapped to the fuzzy propositions as shown in Table 7.7. The following recommendation can be made to the user,

"Roughing, Semi-finishing and Finishing Operations are strongly recommended."

The three corresponding operations could be drilling, reaming and fine reaming.

Had a set of given attributes led to a result of $T = (0.2\ 0.5\ 0.3)$, the recommendation would be:

"Roughing and Semi-finishing Operations are recommended."

Since semi-finishing is the last operation, it should be interpreted as the final operation to be performed on the face.

Machining Allowances for Different Cuts

A machining cut, be it roughing, semi-finishing or finishing, requires a specific amount of machining allowance. The workpiece prior to a machining operation should have an adequate amount of material. For example, in the case of castings, machining allowances depend on the type and size of the casting, and usually range from about 2 to 5 *mm* for small castings, to more than 25 *mm* for large castings. This machining allowance is actually the sum of all the machining allowances for the subsequent machining operations. The machining allowance for a particular cut plays a crucial role in generating the corresponding feature volume. Theoretically, machining allowances should be determined so that defects and errors left on the surface by the previous operation(s) are removed completely. Only by doing this can the precision and surface integrity be further improved.

The magnitude of the machining allowance can greatly influence the quality and the production efficiency of a machined part. Excessive machining allowance will increase the consumption of material, machining time, tool and power, and thus increase manufacturing cost. On the other hand, if there is an insufficient machining allowance, the surface roughness and defective surface layer caused by the preceding process may not be removed completely from the workpiece surface of the part. The factors contributing to the defects and errors, such as roughness, surface defects, positional deviation and dimensional deviation, are rather complex and difficult to quantify. This is also true in the case of the actual machining allowances for different operations. Table 7.10 gives some examples of machining allowances (Z) and their allowable variations (ΔZ).

A Case Study

This case study demonstrates a procedure for obtaining the finishing and semi-finishing features for the component shown in Figure 7.7. The component is located within the billet such that the bottom and side faces of the blank and component coincide, which means that all other faces have to be machined. The component has several features, i.e. a pocket, a protrusion, a *U*-shaped pocket, two steps and three holes, two of which are identical and threaded. Figure 7.8 shows a top view of the component.

Decisions on Number of Cuts

The machining evaluation procedure determines the amount of total amount of material that should be machined from each face. Since the bottom and side faces of the blank and component coincide, the machining allowance for each of these faces is zero. Next, the

Table 7.10. Default machining allowances and their allowable variations

Operation	$Z(mm)$	$\Delta Z(mm)$
Roughing	2.5	0.2
Semi-finishing	1.2	0.06
Finishing	0.25	0.002

Figure 7.7. A prismatic component. ©1997, IMechE used with permission.

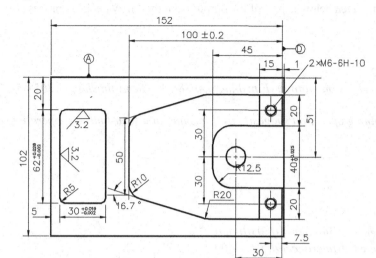

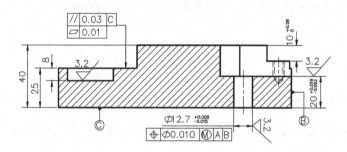

Figure 7.8. Component with some of its faces labelled

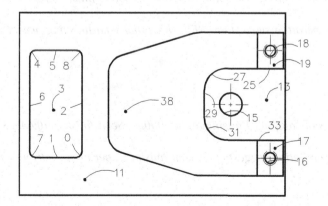

faces of the component with respect to the tolerances and surface finish requirements are examined. Given below is part of the output from the fuzzy decision process.

Face 0:
  IT: 7
  Ra: 3.2
  Fuzzy decision output: Finishing(0.403884), Semi-finishing(0.305585), Roughing(0.290531)
  Machining operation suggestion: "Finishing and semi-finishing operations are preferred."
....
....
Face 11:
  IT: 20
  Ra: 12.5
  Geometrical Tolerance[2]: 0.010000
  Geometrical Tolerance[9]: 0.030000
  Fuzzy decision output: Finishing(0.000000), Semi-finishing(0.000000), Roughing(1.000000)
  Machining operation suggestion: "No finishing operations are needed."
....
....
Face 13:
  IT: 7
  Ra: 3.2
  Fuzzy decision output: Finishing(0.403884), Semi-finishing(0.305585), Roughing(0.290531)
  Machining operation suggestion: "Finishing and semi-finishing operations are preferred."
....
....
Face 15:
  IT: 7
  Ra: 3.2
  Fuzzy decision output: Finishing(0.403884), Semi-finishing(0.305585), Roughing(0.290531)
  Machining operation suggestion: "Finishing and semi-finishing operations are preferred."

Face 16:
  IT: 10
  Ra: 3.2
  Fuzzy decision output: Finishing(0.000000), Semi-finishing(0.645833), Roughing(0.354167)
  Machining operation suggestion: "Semi-finishing operation is strongly recommended."

Face 17:
  IT: 10
  Ra: 12.5
  Fuzzy decision output: Finishing(0.000000), Semi-finishing(0.500000), Roughing(0.500000)
  Machining operation suggestion: "Semi-finishing operation is recommended."

Face 18:
  IT: 10
  Ra: 3.2
  Fuzzy decision output: Finishing(0.000000), Semi-finishing(0.645833), Roughing(0.354167)
  Machining operation suggestion: "Semi-finishing operation is strongly recommended."

Face 19:
  IT: 10
  Ra: 12.5
  Fuzzy decision output: Finishing(0.000000), Semi-finishing(0.500000), Roughing(0.500000)
  Machining operation suggestion: "Semi-finishing operation is recommended."
  ....
  ....
Face 38:
  IT: 10
  Ra: 12.5
  Fuzzy decision output: Finishing(0.000000), Semi-finishing(0.500000), Roughing(0.500000)
  Machining operation suggestion: "Semi-finishing operation is recommended."
  ....
  ....

Based on the recommendations given above, the following faces would require a finishing operation: the side and bottom faces of the pocket (faces 0~8), the side and bottom faces of the *U*-shaped pocket (faces 13, 25, 27, 29, 31 and 33), and the circular face of the central hole (face 15). In each pocket, the side faces are smoothly connected and hence integrated. The bottom face of each pocket is integrated with the side faces because it is concavely connected with them.

Elementary Machining Volumes

Having decided the machining allowances for the finishing and semi-finishing operations, the elementary finishing volumes are generated and then glued together to give the finishing features $f1$ and $f2$ (Figure 7.9(a)). The elementary volume for the central hole, $f3$, is also a finishing feature. $f4$ is the edge volume generated due to the circular convex edge shared by the *U*-shaped pocket and the central hole. $f4$ is glued to either $f2$ or $f3$ depending upon the order in which they are machined. The first intermediate workpiece is obtained by gluing these finishing features on to the component as shown in Figure 7.9(b).

The finishing operations associated with the above features (*f1* to *f4*) should be preceded by semi-finishing operations and the associated semi-finishing feature volumes are shown in the figure as *sf1* to *sf4* respectively. The top surface (face 38) of the protrusion, the bottom surface of the two steps (faces 17 and 19) and the circular surfaces (faces 16 and 18) of the two holes require two operations, i.e. a roughing and a semi-finishing operation. The corresponding semi-finishing features are *sf5, sf6, sf7, sf8* and *sf9* respectively. Although the latter is the only finishing operation, it is still referred to as a semi-finishing operation. Volumes *sf10* to *sf14* are edge volumes between the *U*-shaped pocket and the top surface of the pocket. Similarly, *sf15* and *sf16* are edge volumes between the side walls of the *U*-shaped pocket and the steps. *sf17* and *sf18* are the edge volumes for the two holes and steps. When the semi-finishing features are glued on to the first intermediate workpiece, the resulting workpiece as shown in Figure 7.9(c) becomes the starting point for determining roughing features.

Features for Roughing Operations

Based on the intermediate workpiece as shown in Figure 7.9(c), features for subsequent operations (i.e. roughing operations) can be generated. When these features are generated, the initial shape of the blank is considered. The importance of considering the blank is discussed in Chapter IV. It is particularly essential when a part were to be machined from a casting/forging which can take any arbitrary shape. The features for roughing operations (*rf1 – rf9*) can be generated in a backward fashion as shown in Figure 7.10 (Xu & Hinduja, 1998). Note that because of the blank that is being considered and the way it is positioned, a face-milling operation is needed which corresponds to feature *rf9*.

DETERMING MACHINING FEATURES FROM A FBD MODEL

An integrated approach for a feature-based design model is to transfer product information from a design-oriented feature model to a manufacturing-oriented model. Current CAD/CAM system adopting the feature-based design approach often requires a user to manually convert design features to manufacturing features, and the user himself has to be a domain-knowledgeable person, if not a domain expert. The automated feature transformation is clearly desirable.

Laakko and Mantyla (1993) made the first effort to determine machining features from a design feature model. They used an incremental feature recognition approach to dynamically compare the attributed graph of the evolved part with that of the previous part. Han and Requicha (1995) described a heuristic reasoning algorithm to recognize manufacturing features based on the combination of the nominal geometry, design features, tolerances and attributes of a design model. Lee and Kim (1998, 1999) proposed a geometric reasoning approach to recognize manufacturing features from a design feature model on the basis of STEP. Through re-orientation, reduction and splitting operations, alternative interpretations are generated. Recently, Li, Ong and Nee (2002), presented a methodology for recognizing manufacturing features from a design feature model that considered some common feature-feature interactions. In their system, a feature recognition processor first translates the design feature model of a part into an intermediate manufacturing feature tree by handling design features according to their properties and the interacting relationships between features. Through combination, decomposition and tool approach directions, alternative interpretations of manufacturing feature model for the part are then generated, and the manufacturing feature tree is updated and extended with AND/OR operators to

Figure 7.9. Finishing and semi-finishing features, and intermediate workpiece

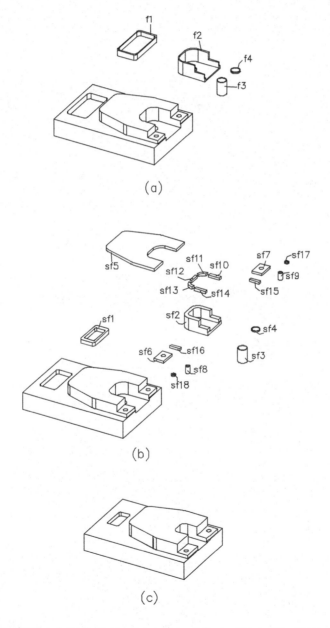

Figure 7.10. Roughing features generated

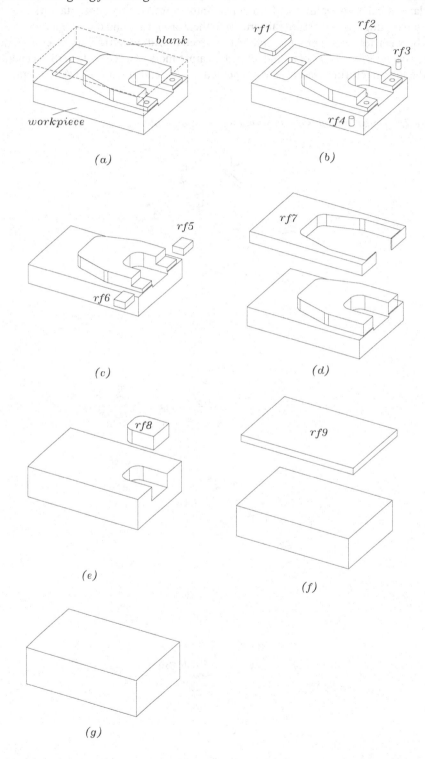

store these interpretations. Finally, a single interpretation with the lowest machining cost is selected in the manufacturing feature tree (Ong, Li & Nee, 2003).

This chapter discusses a method that transforms design feature models directly to manufacturing feature models for machining operations, and the methodology is showcased in a CAD/CAM system, i.e. Pro/E. This process is also termed *feature mapping*.

Mapping Design Features to Machining Features

In a typical feature-based design system, design features present in the model play little part in generating/constructing machining features. In other words, there exists no relationship between the design and machining features. This has not only resulted in the lost of the (design) information at the product design stage, but also unnecessarily increased the work load for the user at the process planning stage. It is one of the requirements for integrating design with manufacturing that re-interpretation of design information for manufacturing be carried out automatically. Mapping design features to machining features is one effective way of realising this re-interpretation.

A CAD/CAM system may offer different types of design features, such as Protrusion, Slot, Cut, Hole, Round, Chamfer, Tweak and Cosmetic features as in Pro/E. Within each type exist different kinds of constructing methods which, to certain extend, characterise different natures of a design feature within that type. Table 7.11 illustrates these feature types and some of their variations. These features are categorised into five groups: Positive, Negative, Modification, Implicit and Patterned features.

Table 7.11. Design features

Feature Categories	Design Features	Feature Variations
Positive	Protrusion	Extrude
		Revolve
		Blend
		Sweep
Negative	Slots and Cuts	
	Holes	Straight-Blind
		Straight-Through
		Sketched-Blind
		Sketched-Through
Modification	Rounds	
	Chamfers	
	Tweak Features	
Implicit	Cosmetic Features	Sketched
		Thread
		Groove
		ECAD Areas
Patterned	Set of any features	

Positive Features

A positive feature is an entity or a group of entities that are added to the existing model. Apparently, the starting feature for a design model has to be a positive feature. A typical positive feature is *protrusion*. *Protrusions* may come in four forms depending on how they are constructed: *extrude, revolve, sweep* and *blend*.

An extruded protrusion is defined by projecting a two-dimensional section at a specified distance normal to the sketching plane. A revolved protrusion is created by revolving a sketched section around a centre-line. Similarly, one can sweep a section along one or more selected trajectories to obtain a swept solid. Sweeping can be carried out using either a constant section or a variable section. A blended protrusion consists of a series of planar sections (usually at least two of them) that are joined together at their edges with transitional surfaces to form a continuous feature.

Negative Features

A negative feature is an entity or a group of entities that are removed or subtracted from the existing model. Therefore, they create depressions on a part. *Cuts, slots* and *holes* are some common types of negative features.

Slots and Cuts

The geometry of these two features is dependent on the 2D section from which they are created. This 2D section can be closed as for a *slot*, or open as for a *cut* (Figure 7.11).

Holes

Holes can be of different types, e.g. *counterbored, countersunk, blind* and *through*[1]. They can be classified as either a *straight* or *sketched* hole. A *straight hole* is created by an extruded slot with a circular section. It passes from the placement surface to the specified end surface. A *sketched hole* is created by a revolved feature defined by a sketched section. *Counterbored* and *countersunk holes*, for example, can be created as *sketched holes*. In addition, both types of holes can be either *blind* or *through*.

Figure 7.11. Close and open slot/cut

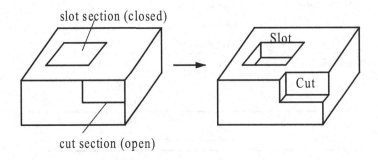

Modification Features

A modification feature alters an existing feature, or a portion of an existing feature. Examples of modification features are *Rounds, Chamfers* and *Tweak* features. *Round* and *Chamfer* features modify an edge or a vertex on a part whereas a *Tweak* feature modifies a face.

Rounds

The most common type of *Round* is a transitional face between two existing faces that share a common edge. This transitional face is normally of the cylindrical surface type. Dependent on the characteristics of this common edge, the *round* can be treated as material added to the original part if the edge is concave; or material removed from the original part if the edge is convex. Hence, a round can also be classified as *positive* as in the former case, or *negative* as in the latter case.

Chamfers

Chamfers are in many ways similar to *Rounds*. The main difference is that a *chamfer* creates a planar surface whereas a *round* creates a cylindrical surface. *Chamfers* can be created on an edge or a corner. Like rounds, a chamfer can also be material added to the original part or material removed from the original part.

Tweak Features

Tweak features deform or alter ("*tweak*") the surface of a part. For example, the *draft* feature adds a draft angle to a surface, or to a series of selected planar surfaces. The *Radius Dome* option allows a user to create a dome feature. Other *Tweak* features may include *section dome local push ear, offset* and *draft offset, replace, lip, patch, toridal* and *spinal bends,* and *free form.*

Implicit Features

Implicit features are sometimes called unevaluated or procedural features. They are unambiguously defined, for example by a generic description and a number of parameters for the specific occurrence, but are not evaluated into an explicit geometrical description. This type of features can be categorised as *Cosmetic* features.

There can be four types of *cosmetic* features: *sketched, thread, groove,* and *user-defined. Sketched cosmetic* features are "drawn" on the surface of a part. They include such things as company logos or serial numbers that are stamped on a part. A *cosmetic thread* represents the diameter of a thread. It can be *external* or *internal*, and *blind* or *through*. A *groove* is a projected cosmetic feature. The option *User Defined* allows a user to create a group of cosmetic features. Obviously, the *cosmetic thread* is most relevant to machining processes.

Patterned Features

Patterned features are those created from a pattern leader feature. They are identical instances of the leader and, along with the leader itself, behave as one feature. Depending on whether instances are located along a line or circumference, patterns can be rectangular or rotational.

Feature Mapping

The following section presents a unidirectional mapping from design features to machining features. The majority of these mappings are of the one-to-one type where a design feature can be directly and exclusively related to a machining feature.

Mapping Negative Features to Machining Features

The negative features considered are cuts, slots and holes. Cuts can be mapped to many Open Pocket/Slot machining features and some of the Through Hole and Free Features (Table 7.12). In many cases when a cut is mapped to a machining feature, the tool accessing direction(s) can be inferred.

A slot can be mapped to a Closed or Open Pocket, a Non-circular hole or Non-straight groove. When a slot is mapped to a Non-circular hole, it forms a through feature. When a slot is mapped to any one of the other machining features, it forms a blind feature. A Non-circular hole is accessible from both ends. An Open Pocket and a Non-straight groove are accessible from both top and side. A Closed Pocket, however, is only accessible from the top. Hence a "plunging" operation is normally required. Dependent upon the type of hole, a hole feature can be mapped to a Hole/Pocket feature or a Through Hole feature. Table 7.13 illustrates these mapping variations.

Table 7.12. Mapping Cuts to machining features

Machining Features	Instances	Tool Accessing Direction
Blind Partial Hole	One open edge, blind	perpendicular to cut
Blind Slot		
Notch	Two open edges, blind	
Simple Slot	One open edge, through	parallel to cut
Open Pocket	One open edge, blind	perpendicular to cut
Step	Two open edges, through	
Dovetail	One open edge, through	parallel to cut
V Slot		parallel to cut
T Slot		parallel to cut
Partial Circular Hole	One open edge, through	perpendicular to cut
Face Milling Feature	Three open edges, through	parallel to cut

Table 7.13. Mapping Holes to machining features

Design Features	Machining Features	Comments
Straight Holes	Hole/Pocket: Simple Hole	Blind
	Through Hole: Circular Hole	Through
Sketched Hole	Hole/Pocket: Stepped Hole	Blind
	Hole/Pocket: Counter-sunk Hole	Through
	Hole/Pocket: Counter-bored Hole	
	Through Hole: Circular Hole: Stepped Hole	
	Through Hole: Circular Hole: Counter-sunk Hole	
	Through Hole: Circular Hole: Counter-bored Hole	

Mapping Modification Features to Machining Features

A round or chamfer feature may or may not be directly mapped to a machining feature. This is dependent upon whether the round or chamfer is positive or negative. A negative round/chamfer requires a machining operation, and is therefore a machining feature; whereas a positive round/chamfer will always be part, or modification, of an existing machining feature, e.g. rounds(s) inside a pocket to be machined, as shown in Figure 7.12. Adjacent rounds or chamfers sometimes form a group feature because they can be machined by one cutter in one go. Tweak features such as *Local Push* and *Radius Dome* can be mapped to a Free Form feature. Machining of these features though often requires a 4 or 5 axes CNC mill.

Mapping Positive Features to Machining Features

Positive features, e.g. *protrusion* features, cannot be directly mapped to machining features as they are material added onto a part. However, depending on the shape of the 2D section from which a protrusion is generated, one or more than one machining features can be identified. One clue for detecting a machining feature would be the existence of a concave corner or edge. Discussions about concave corner and concave edge are given in Chapter V. A combination of more than one consecutive concave corners and/or edges often gives rise to a single machining feature. It is also worth mentioning that the shape of

Figure 7.12. Positive rounds in a pocket

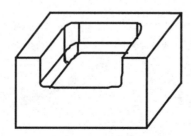

the machining feature(s) derived from a protrusion feature depends upon the stock shape, stock size, machining method, and sequence of machining operations.

Mapping Implicit Features to Machining Features

Among the four types of implicit (*cosmetic*) features, *cosmetic thread* is the most relevant to machining operations. An *internal thread* can be mapped to a tapped blind or through hole, whereas an *external thread* can be mapped to a sub-feature of the *Free Feature* class.

Mapping Patterned Features to Machining Features

Patterned features of the same geometry are often related to the same function from the design viewpoint. These features may also share the same machining information, i.e. they can be recursively machined by the same cutter, in the same setup. For instance, the rotational type of patterned holes (Figure 7.13(a)) and holes using a curve pattern (Figure 7.13(b)) can be machined using one cutter and possibly in one setup.

MACHINING FEATURES AND CUTTING TOOLS

One principal characteristic of a machining feature is its machine-dependence that is a machining feature can be defined as the material removed by a machine tool with a corresponding cutting tool (Figure 7.14). Therefore, given a machine tool, a machining feature becomes cutter-dependent to a certain extent. This is equally to say that there is an intrinsic relationship between a machining feature and the cutter(s) that can be used to produce the feature. Hence identifying the possible links between a machining feature and a cutting tool can be an effective approach to integrate design with manufacturing.

Cutting Tool Classification

Cutting tools that perform the same or similar kind of machining features can be grouped into one category, so that mapping can be carried out between the types of machining

Figure 7.13. Patterned holes

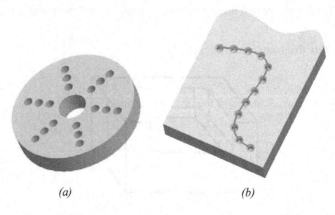

(a)   *(b)*

features and the types of the cutters that can machine the features. An ISO standardised cutter code (ISO 3002-1, 1992) consists of eleven symbols, the first four of them denoting *the cutter diameter, the type of cutter and the insert cutting edge angel (A-H, J-M, X and Y), the number of slots for inserts and the cutting direction (R, L and N)* respectively. Among them, *the type of cutter and the insert cutting edge angel* are considered to be a major identifier for a cutter, as it determines the structure and machinability of a cutter. Tables 7.14-7.17 illustrate the cutter classification, which is, in principle, in conformity to ISO 11529-2 (1998), except the Woodruff keyseat cutter(P), Dovetail cutter(Q), Inverse dovetail cutter(R), Tapered diesinking cutter(S), Ball-nosed tapered diesinking cutter(T), Drill, Counterbore cutter and Countersink cutter, which have also been included to cover a comprehensive range of cutters.

Mapping Design Features to Cutting Tools

This section discusses how to map a design feature in a CAD system (i.e. Pro/E) to a possible cutter that can produce the feature.

Figure 7.14. Machining features, processes and the corresponding cutting tools

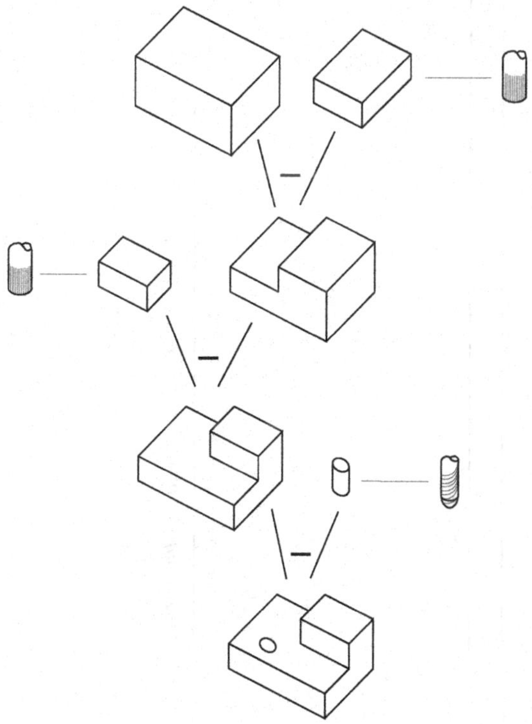

Table 7.14 Classification of milling cutters (1)

Type of Cutter	End mills				T-slot cutter		Side cutting end mill
	End mills						
Symbol	A*	B*	C*	D*	E*	F*	G*
Insert Cutting Edge Angel κ_r	90°	75°	60°	45°	-	-	90°
Figure							
No. of insert(s) per slot	1	1	1	1	1	1	>1

* -- In conformity to ISO 11529-2

Table 7.15. Classification of milling cutters (2)

Type of Cutter	Slotting drill	Side and face cutting end mill	Ball nose end mill	Ball nose side and face cutting mill	Spot facing cutter	Woodruff key seat cutter
Symbol	H*	J*	K*	L*	M*	P
Insert Cutting Edge Angel κ_r	90°	90°	-	90°	0°	-
Figure						
No. of insert(s) per slot	>1	1	-	-	-	-

* -- *In conformity to ISO 11529-2*

Mapping Cut Features to Cutting Tools

A *cut* can generate different types of machining features which, in turn, can be machined using different types of cutters. Basically, there are two factors that determine a machining feature: the construction options (e.g. Extrude, Revolved, Sweep, Through and Blind) and the sketched 2D section from which the cut is created. Figure 7.14 illustrates the relationship between a cut feature, a machining feature and one (or more than one) cutting tool(s). For instance, an extruded through (*ET/TH*) cut, once the 2D section is created accordingly, will give rise to a simple square slot, a (inverse) dovetail slot, a T slot or other general slot. The cutting tools that can be used to machine the feature are also given in the figure. To machine a simple square slot for example, a normal end mill (A), a side cutting end mill (G), a slotting cutter (H), or a side and face cutting end mill (J) can all be used, whereas only a dovetail cutter (Q) can be used to machine a dovetail.

Mapping Slot Features to Cutting Tools

As shown in Figure 7.15, a slot will give rise to a non-circular hole if it is created by extruding the 2D sketched section through the whole part; otherwise it gives rise to a closed pocket. Different types of grooves can be created by revolving or sweeping the 2D section. Depending on the size of the hole or pocket, there are two possible sets of cutting tools which could be used. A slotting drill (H) may suffice if the hole or pocket is relatively small. Otherwise, a slotting drill (H) can be used to perform a pilot operation to open up the feature, followed by either an end mill (A), a side cutting end mill (G) or a side and face cutting end mill (J) to finish off. Note that grooves herewith generated are not machinable on a conventional CNC mill, thus no cutter mapping attempted.

Mapping Holes to Cutting Tools

A simple straight-through hole is normally machined by a twist drill; however a slotting drill (H) can be another possible cutter if the hole is not too deep (Figure 7.16). A simple blind hole can be machined by a slotting drill (H) or a spot facing cutter (M). A twist drill could not be used in this case as it produces a conical bottom. A sketched hole (as in Pro/E) can give rise to different kinds of compound holes, of which counterbore and countersink holes are the most common ones. Both holes require a twist drill followed by a counterbore and countersink cutter to produce (Figure 7.17).

Mapping Rounds and Chamfers to Cutting Tools

A negative round/chamfer is considered as a machining feature itself; whereas a positive round/chamfer is always be part, or modification, of an existing machining feature. All the negative rounds are considered as part of the open pocket. Consequently when selecting the cutter for the pocket, one should also take the cutter's diameter into consideration. Depending on the angle at which the chamfer is created, an end mill A, B, C or D can be used. Adjacent rounds/chamfers sometimes form a feature group because they are often machined by one cutter in one go.

Table 7.16. Classification of milling cutters (3)

Type of Cutter	Dovetail cutter	Inverse dovetail cutter	Tapered diesinking cutter	Ball-nosed tapered diesinking cutter	Other cutter of special design	End mill of other cutting edge angels
Symbol	Q	R	S	T	X*	Y*
Insert Cutting Edge Angel κ_r	-	-	-	-	-	-
Figure						
No. of insert(s) per slot	-	-	-	-	-	

* -- *In conformity to ISO 11529-2*

Table 7.17. Classification of drilling cutters

Type of Cutter	Drill	Counterbored cutter	Countersink cutter
Figure			

Figure 7.15. Mapping cuts to machining features and cutting tools

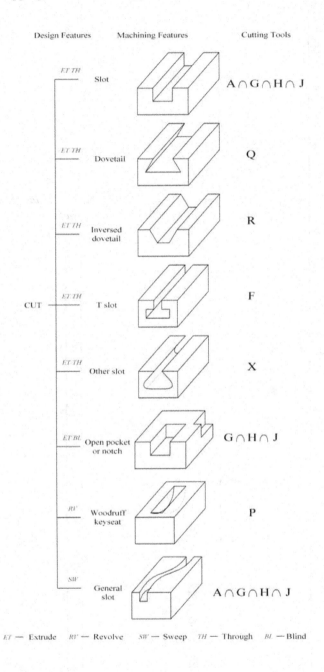

Figure 7.16. Mapping slots to machining features and cutting tools

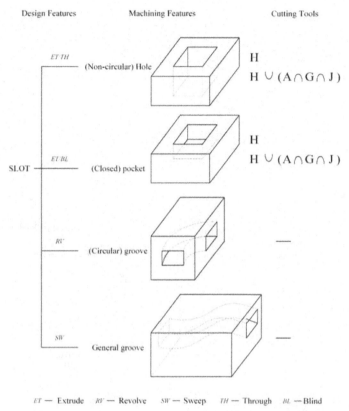

CONCLUSION

Features in design and manufacturing serve as an information carrier that no other individual geometric entities can replace. Equally important is its presentation that may also be dependent on the method to be used to remove the feature. When features are generated with no specific machining operations attached and/or considered, they may become invalid at a latter stage, i.e. machining stage. In this case, features are used as an "interface" between design and manufacturing. In order to achieve an integrated environment and to make sure the features formed can be directly related to machining processes, machining information has to be considered such as roughing and finishing operations, and cutting tools that may be used.

In a feature-based design system, feature mapping from design to manufacturing is considered necessary. In order to achieve an integrated scenario, a feature mapping

Figure 7.17. Mapping holes to machining features and cutting tools

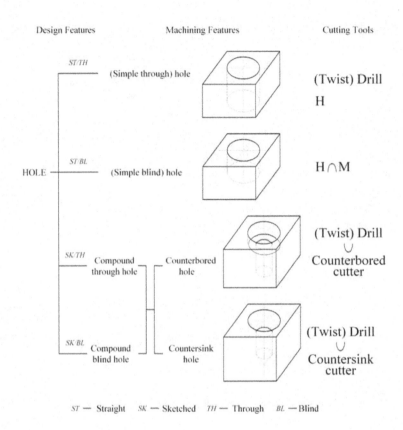

methodology should map design features to machining features, and for every machining feature, possible cutting tools that are capable of producing the feature are also designated to the machining feature concerned.

It is not difficult to appreciate that an integrated approach to CAD/CAPP/CAM takes into account both design and manufacturing information. The methods discussed herein that are applicable to 3-axis machining centres, may yield differing results when a 4 or 5-axis machining centre is assumed. For a more complete account on CNC machining centres, readers are encouraged to read the next chapter.

REFERENCES

Chang, T. C., Wysk, R. A., & Wang, H.-P. (1991). *Computer-aided manufacturing.* Englewood Cliffs, New Jersey, USA: Prentice Hall.

Gao, J., Zheng, D.T., Gindy, N., & Clark, D. (2005). Extraction/conversion of geometric dimensions and tolerances for machining features. *International Journal of Advanced Manufacturing Technology, 26*(4), 405-414.

Geddam, A., & Kaldor, S. (1998). Interlinking dimensional tolerances with geometric accuracy and surface finish in the process design and manufacture of precision machined components. *IIE Transactions (Institute of Industrial Engineers), 30*(10), 905-912.

Gu, P., & Norrie, D. H. (1995). *Intelligent manufacturing Planning*, 2-6 Boundary Row, London, SE1 8HN, UK: Chapman & Hall.

Han, J., & Requicha, A. A. G. (1995). Incremental recognition of machining features. In *Proceedings of ASME Computers in Engineering Conference*. (pp 569-78).

Henzold, G. (1995). *Handbook of Geometrical Tolerancing*, West Sussex, PO19 1UD, England: John Wiley & Sons Ltd.

Huang, S. H., Liu, Q., & Musa, R. (2004). Tolerance-based process plan evaluation using Monte Carlo simulation. *International Journal of Production Research, 42*(23), 4871-4891.

ISO 11529-2. (1998). *Milling cutters -- Designation -- Part 2: Shank type and bore type milling cutters with indexable inserts*. Geneva, Switzerland: International Organisation for Standardisation (ISO).

ISO 286-2. (1988). *ISO system of limits and fits. Tables of standard tolerance grades and limit deviations for holes and shafts*. Geneva, Switzerland: International Organisation for Standardisation (ISO).

ISO 3002-1. (1992). *Basic Quantities and Cutting and Grinding - Part 1: Geometry of the Active Part of Cutting Tools - General Terms, Reference Systems, Tools and Working Angles, Chip Breakers*. Geneva, Switzerland: International Organisation for Standardisation (ISO).

Laakko, T., & Mantyla, M. (1993). Feature modelling by incremental recognition. *Computer-Aided Design, 25*(8), 479-92.

Lee, J. Y., & Kim, K. (1998). A feature-based approach to extracting machining features. *Computer-Aided Design, 30*(13), 1019-35.

Lee, J. Y., & Kim, K. (1999). Generating alternative interpretations of machining features. *International Journal of Advanced Manufacturing Technology, 15*, 38-48.

Li, W. D., Ong, S. K., & Nee, A. Y. C. (2002). Recognizing manufacturing features from a design-by-feature model. *Computer-Aided Design*, 34(11), 849-868.

Lin, A. C., Lin, M.-Y., & Ho, H.-B. (1999). CAPP and its integration with tolerance charts for machining of aircraft components. *Computers in Industry, 38*(3), 263-283.

Ong, S. K., Li, W. D., & Nee, A. Y. C. (2003). STEP-based integration of feature recognition and design-by-feature for manufacturing applications in a concurrent engineering environment. International Journal of Computer Applications in Technology, *18*(1/2/3/4), 78-92.

Thimm, G., Britton, G., & Lin, J. (2004). Operation element-based efficiency for process plans and designs. *International Journal of Advanced Manufacturing Technology, 24*(5-6), 370-375.

Wang, H.-P. & Li, J.-K. (1992). *Computer-Aided Process Planning*, Sara Burgerhartstraet 25, P. O. Box., 1000 BZ Amsterdam, The Netherlands: Elsevier Science Publishers B. V.

Wu, Y., Gao, S., & Chen, Z. (2001). Automatic setup planning and operation sequencing for satisfying tolerance requirements. In *Proceedings of the ASME Design Engineering Technical Conference, 3*, 141-148.

Xu, X., & Hinduja, S. (1997). Determination of finishing features in 2½D components", *Journal of Engineering Manufacture, Proc. Instn Mech Engrs,* 211(B), 125-142.

Xu, X., & Hinduja, S. (1998). Recognition of rough machining features in 2½D Components, *Computer-Aided Design, 30*(7), 503-516.

Xu, X. (2001). Feature recognition methodologies and beyond, *Australian Journal of Mechanical Engineering, ME25*(1), 1-20.

Zeid, I. (1991). *CAD/CAM Theory and Practice*, USA: McGraw-Hill, Inc.

ENDNOTE

[1]   *Blind* and *through* are two basic types of depth options. A blind feature needs to specify a depth value. A through feature can be made to through to a selected surface or plane, named a terminating surface, or through all the surfaces in its way of projection.

Chapter VIII
CNC Machine Tools

ABSTRACT

The introduction of CNC machines has radically changed the manufacturing industry. Curves are as easy to cut as straight lines, complex 3-D structures are relatively easy to produce, and the number of machining steps that required human action has dramatically reduced. With the increased automation of manufacturing processes with CNC machining, considerable improvements in consistency and quality can be achieved. CNC automation reduced the frequency of errors and provided CNC operators with time to perform additional tasks. CNC automation also allows for more flexibility in the way parts are held in the manufacturing process and the time required to change the machine to produce different components. In a production environment, a series of CNC machines may be combined into one station, commonly called a "cell", to progressively machine a part requiring several operations.

CNC controller is the "brain" of a CNC machine, whereas the physical configuration of the machine tool is the "skeleton". A thorough understanding of the physical configuration of a machine tool is always a priority for a CNC programmer as well as the CNC machine tool manufacturers. This chapter starts with a historical perspective of CNC machine tools. Two typical types of CNC machine tools (i.e. vertical and horizontal machining centres) are first discussed. Tooling systems for a CNC machine tool are integral part of a CNC system and are therefore elaborated. Also discussed are the four principal elements of a CNC machine tool. They are machine base, machine spindle, spindle drive, and slide drive. What letter should be assigned to a linear or rotary axis and what if a machine tool has two sets of linear axes? These questions are answered later in the chapter. In order for readers to better comprehend the axis and motion designations, a number of machine tool schematics are given.

A HISTORICAL PERSPECTIVE

Computer numerical control refers specifically to a computer "controller" that reads some sort of machine control (e.g. G-code) instructions and drives the machine tool. The controller does numerically directed interpolation of a cutting tool in the work envelope of a machine. Numerical controllers (NC) were developed in the late 1940s and early 1950s by John T. Parsons in collaboration with the MIT Servomechanisms Laboratory.

The first NC machines, which are frequently referred to as being of the first generation, had been previously designed for manual or fixed cycle operations. These machines had numerical control systems added, but only for numerical control on positioning the work relative to the tool. Considerable time was saved, yet the operator had to select the tools, speeds and feeds.

Second-generation machines are those on which material removal occurs at the same time as control of the work/tool relationship. These NC machines were also termed tape-controlled machines, because the information was stored on either punched tape or magnetic tape. Figure 8.1 illustrates the characteristics of a punched type. It is very cumbersome to edit the information at the machine; the machines had only very limited memory capacity.

The development of computers has created the third-generation machines which are capable of an extended range of machining operations. These machines are commonly referred to as Computer Numerical Control and sometimes Direct Numerical Control (DNC) machines.

PRINCIPLES OF NUMERICAL CONTROL

A CNC system usually contains a machine-control unit (MCU) and the machine tool itself. The MCU is further divided into two elements: the data-processing unit (DPU) and the

Figure 8.1. NC punched tape. ©1969 (or 2003) Industrial Press. Used with permission.

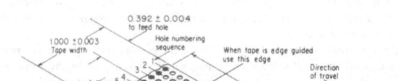

control-loops unit (CLU). The DPU processes the coded data and passes information on the position of each axis, its direction of motion, feed, and auxiliary function controls signals to the CLU. The CLU operates the drive mechanisms of the machine, receives feedback signals about the actual position and velocity of each of the axes, and announces when an operation has been completed. The DPU sequentially reads the data when each line has completed execution as noted by the CLU.

A DPU consists of some or all of the following parts,

- data-input device such as a paper-tape reader (as in the old says), RS-232-C port, and so on;
- data-reading circuits and parity-checking logic;
- decoding circuits for describing data among the controller axes; and
- an editor.

A CLU, on the other hand, consists of the following,

- an interpolator that supplies machine-motion commands between data points for tool motion;
- position-control-loops hardware for all the axes of motion, where each axis has a separate control loop;
- velocity-control loops, where feed control is required;
- deceleration and backlash take-up circuits; and
- auxiliary function control, such as coolant on/off, gear changes, and spindle on/off control.

TYPICAL CNC MACHINE TOOLS

CNC machine tool can be categorized as CNC mills, CNC lathes and CNC mill-turning centres. In fact, it has become customary to referring to the machines that are capable of multiple operations such as turning, milling, drilling, boring and tapping operations, and can work on more than one face of a component, as machining centres. They are among the most popular types of CNC machine tools these days. As the name itself implies, machining centres have a great deal of machining versatility.

Machines which are capable of a wide range of turning operations that are normally available on lathes may also be known as turning centres. CNC machines known as mill-turning centres are capable of what is termed complete machining. These machines have small power-driven rotary spindle heads mounted on the tool turret so that cross drilling and other milling operations can be performed while the component is still mounted on the turning centre.

It has to be pointed out that since machining centres are so designed to have the capability of doing both milling and turning jobs, there is a tendency that parts, no matter of what nature, (be it rotational and prismatic) can be machined on a single machine tool. By doing this, number of part set-ups and parts transportation will be reduced dramatically.

Machining Capabilities of a CNC Machine

Different CNC machine tools are specialised in different machining operations. A CAD/CAM system may also be supportive of different machining operations/machine tools. For example, it may support 2- and 4-axis CNC lathes, 3- to 5-axis machining centres and mill-turning centres (Table 8.1). Two dominant categories of machining centres are vertical and horizontal machining centres.

Vertical Machining Centres

A vertical machining centre has the spindle oriented in the vertical position. An automatic tool changer is mounted to the machine to allow tools to be loaded into the spindle without operator intervention. Basic vertical machining centres will allow three directions or axes of motion. The table can move left to right (the X axis), and in and out, or toward and away from the operator (the Y axis). The headstock or spindle can also move up and down (the Z axis). A detailed discussion on machine tool axis designation is provided toward the end of this chapter. Figure 8.2 shows the three basic axes of a vertical machining centre.

Some vertical machining centres have a rotary table or indexer mounted on the table to allow a part to be rotated during machining. These devices allow more than one surface of the workpiece to be machined during a machining cycle. If a true rotary table (axis) is attached, the rotation of the rotary table will provide additional dexterity. This rotary axis is commonly called the C axis, or possibly the B axis depending on how the rotary axis is mounted to the machine.

The biggest limitation of a vertical machining centre is that the spindle can only access one side of the workpiece at a time, unless a multiple part setup is made or if the machine has a rotary device attached. This means that if more than one side of the workpiece are to be machined, another setup must be made on the machine (requiring another program). This is also another reason why vertical CNC machining centres are considered easier to program.

Table 8.1. Machine tools and machining operations

Machine Tool	Description		Machining Operations
Lathe	2- or 4-Axis Turning and Hole-making	Turning	Area, Profile, Groove, Trajectory, Thread
		Hole-making	Drill, Face, Bore, Countersink, Tap, Ream
Mill	3- to 5-Axis Milling and Hole-making	Milling	Volume, Local Mill, Conventional Surface, Contour Surface, Face, Profile, Pocketing, Trajectory, Thread, Grooving
		Hole-making	Drill, Face, Bore, Countersink, Tap, Ream
Mill/Turn	Mill/Turn centre (2-Axis Turning to 5-Axis Milling and Hole-making)	Milling	Volume, Local Mill, Conventional Surface, Contour Surface, Face, Profile, Pocketing, Trajectory, Thread, Grooving
		Turning	Area, Profile, Groove, Trajectory, Thread
		Hole-making	Drill, Face, Bore, Countersink, Tap, Ream

Figure 8.2. Three basic axes of a vertical machining centre

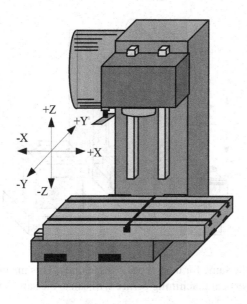

As depicted in Figure 8.2, the table moves to form the X and Y axis and the headstock moves to form the Z axis. Note that the headstock includes the spindle that holds the cutting tool. For this kind of machine, the polarity (plus versus minus) of the Z axis is easy to understand. As the tool (headstock) moves closer to the table top (down), the Z axis is moving in the minus direction. As it moves away from the table top (up), it is moving in the plus direction. However, with the X and Y axes, the cutting tool does not actually move. Instead, the table moves. This makes understanding the axis polarity a little more difficult. When considering axis polarity from the programmer's viewpoint, it is always best to think of axis polarity as if the tool is moving. In order for the tool to move in the plus direction (to the right), the table must move to the left. Whenever the tool is stationary during an axis movement, the axis polarity will be a little confusing. This is true of any kind of CNC machine tool, including vertical as well as horizontal machining centres.

Horizontal Machining Centres

A horizontal machining centre (Figure 8.3) has the spindle oriented in the horizontal position. Again, an automatic tool changer is equipped to allow tools to be automatically placed in the spindle. The table motion left to right as viewed from the spindle is still the X axis. But now the head motion up and down is considered the Y axis. The table motion toward and away from the spindle is the Z axis. Note that on some horizontal machining centres, the Z axis is the column motion, not the table motion. In either case, the Z axis is the motion direction from the spindle face to the workpiece. The table of most horizontal machining centres can rotate by either an indexer or a rotary axis.

At first glance, it may appear that the configuration for a horizontal machining centre is different from that of a vertical machining centre. However, notice that if you look at the machine from the perspective of a workpiece being machined, the basic layout for X,

Figure 8.3. The three basic axes of a horizontal machining centre

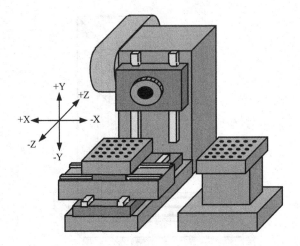

Y, and *Z* is essentially the same for both types of machines. This means motions (*X*, *Y*, and *Z*) programmed for a vertical machining centre will cause the same effect on a horizontal machining centre.

Many horizontal machining centres manufactured today will also have some form of automatic pallet changer to allow the whole table setup to be shuffled into and out of the work area. This allows the operator to be loading one workpiece while the machine is running another.

Generally speaking, horizontal machining centres require more work to program than vertical machining centres. Since the horizontal machining centre allows access to any side of the workpiece, more machining operations can be done per setup. This makes the typical horizontal machining centre program length much longer than one for a vertical machining centre.

TOOLING FOR CNC MACHINE TOOLS

Today's CNC machines are capable of working at a rapid metal-removal rate. The cutting tools are capable of withstanding higher loads and their indexing time can be as short as less than one second. The automatic tool changing may provide a "chip-to-chip" time of around five seconds. This is why tooling is being considered to be one of the most important aspects of machines.

Material for Cutting Tools

Many types of tool materials, ranging from high-carbon steel to ceramics and diamonds, are used to make cutting tools. It is important to be aware that differences do exist among tool materials, what these differences are, and the correct application for each type of material.

A cutting tool must have the following characteristics,

- **Hardness:** Hardness and strength of the cutting tool must be maintained at elevated temperatures. This is also called hot hardness.
- **Toughness:** Toughness of cutting tools is needed so that tools do not chip or fracture, especially during interrupted cutting operations.
- **Wear resistance:** Wear resistance means the attainment of acceptable tool life before tools need to be replaced.

High-speed steel is tougher than cemented carbide but not as hard and, therefore, cannot be used at a high rate of metal removal. On the other hand , the lack of toughness for cemented carbide presents problems, and this has meant that a tremendous amount of research has gone into developing carbide grades that, when adequately supported, are able to meet the requirements of modern machining techniques. The hardness of cemented carbide is almost equal to that of diamond. It derives this hardness from its main constituent, tungsten carbide.

Carbides when coated can give superior properties. Numerous types of coating materials are used, each for a specific application. The most common coating materials are titanium carbide, titanium nitride, ceramic coating, diamond coating and titanium carbon-nitride. In general the coating process is accomplished by chemical vapour deposition (CVD). The substrate is placed in an environmentally controlled chamber having an elevated temperature. The coating material is then introduced into the chamber as a chemical vapour. The coating material is drawn to and deposited on the substrate by a magnetic field around the substrate. Another process is Physical Vapour Deposition (PVD). This process is similar to chemical vapour deposition except that the raw materials/precursors, i.e. the material that is going to be deposited starts out in solid form. PVD often incorporates processes such as sputter coating and pulsed laser deposition (PLD). PVD processes are also carried out under vacuum conditions. There are four steps involved, evaporation, transportation, reaction and deposition.

In addition, diamond, Cubic boron nitride (CBN) and so-called whisker-reinforced[1] tools are also used in some extreme cutting conditions. Two types of diamonds may be used as cutting tools, industrial grade natural diamonds, and synthetic polycrystalline diamonds. Because diamonds are pure carbon, they have an affinity for the carbon of ferrous metals. Therefore, they can only be used on nonferrous metals.

CBN is similar to diamond in its polycrystalline structure and is also bonded to a carbide base. With the exception of titanium, or titanium-alloyed materials, CBN will work effectively as a cutting tool on most common work materials. However, the use of CBN should be reserved for very hard and difficult-to-machine materials. CBN will run at lower speeds, and will take heavier cuts with higher lead angles than diamond. Still, CBN should mainly be considered as a finishing tool material because of its extreme hardness and brittleness. Machine tool and set-up rigidity for CBN, as with diamond, is equally critical.

To further improve the performance and wear resistance of cutting tools to machine new work materials and composites, whisker-reinforced composite cutting tool materials have been developed. Whisker-reinforced materials include silicon-nitride base tools and aluminium-oxide base tools, reinforced with silicon-carbide (SiC) whiskers. Such tools are effective in machining composites and nonferrous materials, but are not suitable for machining irons and steels.

Tooling Systems

Production of a component invariably involves the use of a variety of cutting tools, and the machine has to cater for their use. The way in which a range of cutting tools can be located and securely held in position is referred to as a tooling system and is usually an important feature of the modern machine tools.

The use of tool holders with standard tapers can be very helpful in keeping tooling costs to a minimum. Figure 8.4 shows some of the flanges and collets in a tooling system for a machining centre. A tooling system for a machining centre will indicate the range of tooling which should be accommodated on the machine. Two such systems are illustrated in Figure 8.5.

A simple three-piece system typically involves a tool holder, an intermediate component such as a boring bar or insert type milling cutter body, and an indexable insert cutter (Figure 8.5). Automatic tool changer and tool holders are multipurpose devices that are designed to,

- Be easily manipulated by the tool changing mechanism;
- Ensure repeatability of a tool, i.e. place the tool in the spindle such that the tool's relation to the work is repeated within tolerance every time the tool is used; and
- Provide fast and easy off-line tool assembly.

Automatic Tool Changer System

Many different types of mechanisms have been designed for storing and changing tools. The three most important are turret head, carousel storage with spindle direct changing,

Figure 8.4. Tooling system for a machining centre

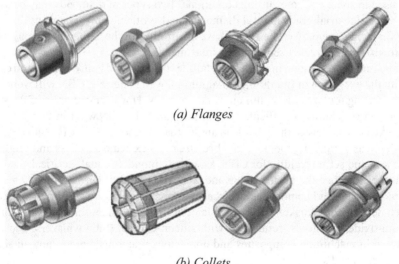

(a) Flanges

(b) Collets

Figure 8.5. Interface diagrams of tooling systems

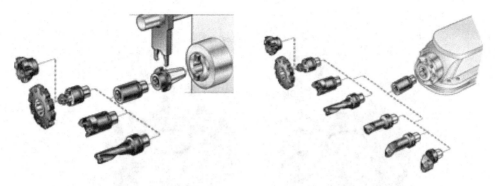

and matrix magazine storage with pivot insertion tool changer. Tool storage magazines may be horizontal or vertical.

Turret Head

The tools in this type of system are stored in the spindles of a device called a turret head (Figure 8.6). When a tool is called by the program, the turret rotates (or indexes) it into position. The tool can be used immediately without having to be inserted into a spindle. Thus, turret head designs provide for very fast tool changes. The main disadvantage of turret head changers is the limit on the number of tool spindles that can be mounted.

Carousel Storage with Spindle Direct Tool Changer

Systems of this type are usually found in vertical machining centres. Tools are stored in a coded drum called a carousel (Figure 8.7). The drum rotates to the space where the current tool is to be stored. It moves up and removes the current tool, then rotates the new tool into position and places it into the spindle. On larger systems the spindle moves to the carousel during a tool change.

Figure 8.6. Turret head tool changing systems

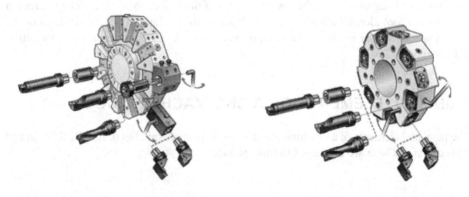

Figure 8.7. A carousel storage with spindle direct tool changer

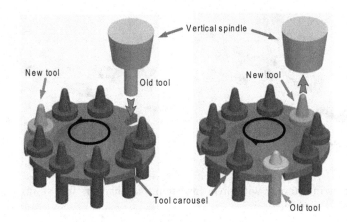

Horizontal Storage Matrix Magazine with Pivot Insertion Tool Changer

Chain-type storage matrix magazines have been popular in machining centres since the early 1970's. This type of system permits an operator to load many tools in a relatively small space. The chain may be located on the side or the top of the CNC machine. These positions enable tools to be stored away from the spindle and work. This will ensure a minimum of chip interference with the storage mechanism and a maximum of tool protection. Upon entering a programmed tool change, the system advances to the proper tool via the chain mechanism. The pivot arm rotates and picks up both the new tool in the magazine and the old tool in the spindle. The magazine then advances to the space where the old tool is to be stored. The arm executes a rotation again and inserts the new tool into the spindle and the old tool into the magazine. A final rotation returns the arm back to its parked position. These steps are illustrated in Figure 8.8.

Two methods of tool identification are currently in use. One is the bar code designation. The code is imprinted and fastened to the tool. When the program calls for a specific tool, the controller looks for a particular tool code, not a specific location. Another tool identification system uses a computer microchip, which is part of the tool or tool holder. The microchip contains the tool identification number and information related to the parameters of the tool. A special sensor reads the data and transfers it to the machine controller (Valentino & Goldenberg, 2003).

PRINCIPAL ELEMENTS OF A CNC MACHINE TOOL

The principal elements of a machine tool are machine base, spindle(s), spindle drive(s) and slide drive(s). These are discussed in this section.

Figure 8.8. A storage matrix magazine with pivot insertion tool changer

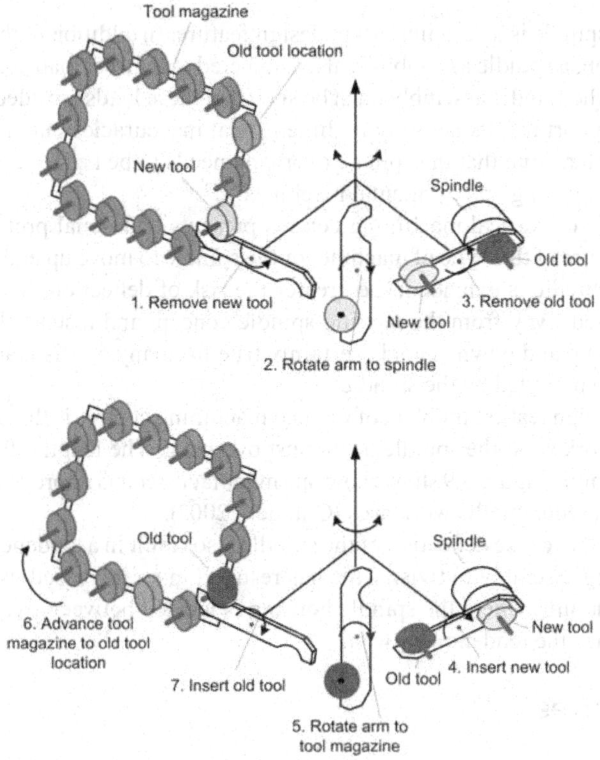

Machine Base

For many years cast iron was considered to be the only material suitable for the basic structure of a machine tool. It possessed adequate strength and rigidity and tended to absorb vibration. In addition, the complex shapes required were easier to produce by casting than by any other method. Cast iron is still extensively used, but its traditional position as the most suitable material is now challenged by steel and by concrete. Fabricated steel structures are increasingly being favoured for very large machines. Steel plates of the same thickness as a cast iron structure have approximately twice the strength. By reducing the plate thickness, the weight of the structure can be considerably reduced, yet still provide the necessary strength. In use, the rigidity of such structures has proved to be more than adequate. However, the general use of steel is limited by the problems of making complex shapes and by its resonant quality, which is not conducive to effective damping of vibration.

The use of concrete or ceramics as a machine base is a comparatively new development. The advantages of concrete are its low cost and good damping characteristics. Very large structures can be cast on site, thus reducing the overall cost even further, since no transport is involved. Smaller structures can be provided with steel tubing cast into the concrete to permit easier handling.

Machine Spindles

The machine spindle is a very important design feature. In addition to the radial loads that cause deflection, a spindle assembly is also subjected to a thrust load acting along its axis. The design of the spindle assembly must be such that these loads are adequately contained. Inadequate support results not only in dimensional inaccuracies but also in poor surface finish and chatter. Note that the spindle overhang needs to be kept to a minimum, a common feature of turning and horizontal machines.

The spindle of vertical machining centres presents additional problems, since it is a traditional feature of this type of machine for the spindle to move up and down. Obviously, the more the spindle is extended, the greater the risk of deflection. Some manufacturers have now moved away from the moving-spindle concept and instead the whole head assembly moves up and down. This is certainly true for many 5-axis machine tools whose rotary axes are provided by the spindle.

Another design feature problem of vertical machining centres is that in order to provide an adequate work area, the spindle head must overhang. The length of overhang must be kept to a minimum. Figure 8.9 shows how one manufacturer has improved on the traditional design without reducing the work area (Crandell, 2003).

The forces that cause deflection of the spindle also result in a tendency for the complete spindle housing assembly to twist. This has resulted in an increased use of bifurcated or two-pillar structures where the spindle housing is located between two substantial slideways that reduce the tendency to twist.

Spindle Drives

Two types of electric motors are used for spindle drives: direct current (DC) and alternating current (AC) . They may be coupled directly to the spindle or via belts or gears. Many machines have a final belt drive which is quieter and produces less vibration than a geared drive (Crandell, 2003).

Many modern machines use DC motors. By varying the voltage input, their speeds are infinitely variable as they rotate and so a constant cutting speed can be maintained. There are some machines fitted with specially designed AC motors that also provide for variable

Figure 8.9. Variations in the design of a vertical machining centre. ©2004, used with permission from the author, the copyright owner.

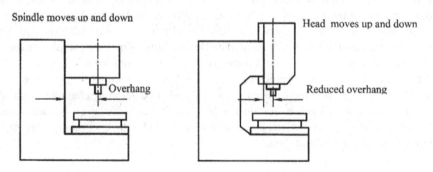

spindle speeds, but the use of AC motors usually involves a stepped drive, that is, a series of spindle speeds will be available and the selection of a particular speed may involve switching from one speed range to another.

New spindle drive and bearing designs are now allowing high-speed machining using rpms of tens of thousands. Manufacturers have developed fluid or air bearing high-speed spindle that provides higher stiffness, better running accuracies, full range of operation with high horsepower, lower runout, better dampening and lower vibration, along with unlimited bearing life. All of this is achieved through the use of hydrostatic/hydrodynamic/aerostatic spindle bearing technology. Simply put, they eliminate the rolling element spindle bearings and the spindle shaft runs on a film of oil or air (Crandell, 2003). The machine spindle becomes the motor shaft running on this film of oil/air. Also used, but not very widely, are hydrostatic bearings where the bearing surfaces are always separated by oil or air supplied under pressure.

Slide Drives

Both electric and hydraulic power is used to achieve slide motion. There are a number of very effective, responsive, and thoroughly proved hydraulic systems currently in use, but by far the most common power source is the electric motor, and so the text will be confined to dealing only with this method. Three types of DC motor are used,

- stepping motors (rotary);
- conventional, non-stepping motors (rotary);
- magnetic linear drive motors.

Stepping motors are a special type of motor designed so that they rotate in sequential finite steps when energized by electrical pulses. Stepping motor drive systems can be open-loop or close-loop. Open-loop stepping motor drive systems while simple to build have two major limitations, (a) limited horsepower and torque ratings to meet requirements; (b) need for the increment size-versus-slide velocity.

An example would be an 8000 pulse per second stepper motor with a system requiring 0.001 mm. The slide accuracy would have a velocity of 0.48 m/min. Therefore, the higher the machine slide accuracy required, the slower the feedrate obtainable. See open-loop servo control diagram in Figure 8.10. This type of motor was fitted to the earlier generation of machines but has now been largely superseded by the closed-loop servo drive system (Crandell, 2003).

The speeds of DC motors are infinitely variable. Constant torque is available throughout most of the speed range, which means that relatively small motors can be used, and when

Figure 8.10. Open-loop system block diagram

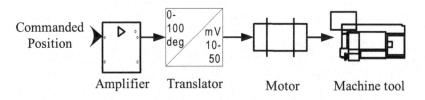

Amplifier Translator Motor Machine tool

they are directly coupled to the machine leadscrew a torsionally stiff drive is provided. The motors provide regenerative braking, resulting in a virtually nonexistent slide overrun.

The closed-loop system (Figure 8.11) is not drive-motor-dependent using stepper motors, AC motors, DC motors, hydraulic motors, or hydraulic cylinders. With this type of drive system, resolutions of 50 millionths and speeds higher than 10m/min are possible.

Considerable research is being carried out with AC servo motors. At present they are larger than DC motors providing equivalent power, and are also more costly. However, they need less maintenance and this is a factor very much in their favour. The newest slide drive system to appear on machinery is the magnetic linear drive system. Machine movement is obtained through the activation of magnetic forces alone, using high force linear motors. Using this direct axis drive system allows much higher machine acceleration and deceleration and velocity, as well as being stiffer and allowing improved control performance (Crandell, 2003).

Direct Numerical Control

DNC can be understood as a system containing a number of CNC machines rather than a single one. All the machines are linked to a mainframe computer which sends the information to the individual machines as required. There can be a number of different types of machines linked to the mainframe computer. To this point, DNC is also termed as Distributed Numerical Control. The computer is programmed to be able to select the order of manufacture of the components. DNC is capable of being integrated into the running of a flexible manufacturing system or even an automated factory.

Figure 8.11. Closed-loop system block diagram

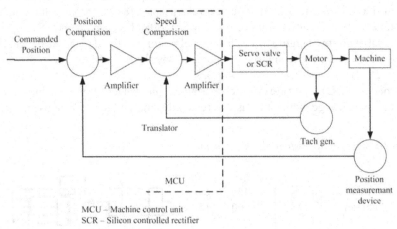

MCU – Machine control unit
SCR – Silicon controlled rectifier

DESIGNATION OF AXIS AND MOTION OF CNC MACHINES

Axis and motion designation have been briefly touched upon in the early sections of this chapter. For example, a 3-axis machining centre may have three linear axes: X, Y and Z. However, axis and motion nomenclature for a numerically controlled machine have been defined in various ways. The following discussion reflects the international standard (ISO 841, 2001), and has been widely accepted and applied.

Co-ordinate system and the machine movements are defined in such a way that a programmer can always assume that the tool moves relative to the co-ordinate system of the stationary workpiece. The standard co-ordinate system is a right-handed rectangular Cartesian one (Figure 8.12), related to a workpiece mounted in a machine and aligned with the principal linear slide-ways of that machine. When the machine is used for drilling or boring (using only its three principal linear movements), movement in the negative Z direction will drill or bore into the workpiece. When the machine cannot be so used for drilling or boring, special rules are provided to minimize inconsistencies on multi-purpose machines. On the schematic drawings of the machines, an unprimed letter is used when a tool movement is being dealt with. When a workpiece movement is being dealt with, a primed letter is used and the positive direction of this movement is opposite to the corresponding unprimed letter movement.

Z Axis of Motion

The Z axis of motion is identified by reference to a spindle which imparts main cutting power. It is usually the first axis to be identified. In the case of machines such as milling, boring and tapping machines, this spindle rotates the tool. In the case of machines such as lathes, grinding machines and others which generate a surface of revolution, this spindle rotates the work.

If there are several spindles, one should be selected as the principal spindle, preferably one perpendicular to the work-holding surface. If the principal spindle axis remains constantly parallel to one of the three axes of the standard three-axis system, this axis is the Z axis. If the principal spindle axis can be swivelled and if the extent of its motion allows it

Figure 8.12. Right-hand co-ordinate system

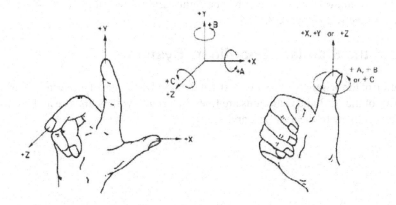

to lie in only one position parallel to one of the axes of the standard three-axis system, this standard axis is the Z axis. If the extent of the swivelling motion is such that the principal spindle may lie parallel to two or three axes of the standard three-axis system, the Z axis is the standard axis which is perpendicular to the work-holding surface of the work-table of the machine, ignoring such ancillaries as angles or packing pieces. If there is no spindle, the Z axis is perpendicular to the work-holding surface. Positive Z motion increases the clearance between the workpiece and the tool-holder.

X Axis of Motion

Where it is possible, the X axis of motion is horizontal and parallel to the work-holding surface. It is the principal axis of motion in the positioning plane of the tool or workpiece. It is usually the axis identified after Z axis. On machines with non-rotating workpieces and non-rotating tools (for example shapers), the X axis is parallel to, and positive in the principal direction of cutting. On machines with rotating workpieces (e.g. lathes, grinding machines, etc.), X motion is radial and parallel to the cross slide. Positive X motion occurs when a tool, mounted on the principal tool post position of the cross slide, recedes from the axis of rotation of the workpiece.

On machines with rotating tools, e.g. milling machines,

- If the Z axis is horizontal, positive X motion is to the right when looking from the principal tool spindle towards the workpiece.
- If the Z axis is vertical, positive X motion is to the right for single column machines when looking from the principal tool spindle to the column, and for gantry type machines when looking from the principal spindle to the left-hand gantry support.

Y Axis of Motion

Positive Y motion should be selected to complete with the X and Z motions a right-hand Cartesian co-ordinate system (Figure 8.12).

Rotary Motions *A, B* and *C*

A, B and C define rotary motions about axes respectively parallel to X, Y and Z. Positive A, B and C are in the directions to advance right-hand screws in the positive X, Y and Z directions respectively (Figure 8.12).

Origin of the Standard Coordinate System

The location of the origin ($X = 0$, $Y = 0$, $Z = 0$) of the standard co-ordinate system is arbitrary. The origins of the A, B and C motions are likewise arbitrary; they are selected, preferably, parallel respectively to the axes Y, Z and X.

Additional Axes

It has become a common feature for a modern CNC machine tool to be equipped with multiple spindles, slide-ways, pallets and other moving components.

Linear Motion

If, in addition to the primary slide motions X, Y and Z, there exist secondary slide motions parallel to these, they should be designated U, V and W, respectively. If tertiary motions exist, they should be designated P, Q and R, respectively. If linear motions exist which are not or may not be parallel to X, Y or Z, they may also be designated U, V, W, P, Q or R, as is most convenient. Figure 8.13 illustrates these axis designations.

In a boring mill the movement of the cutting-bit with respect to a facing slide is designated U or P, if these letters are available, the movement of the table already having been designated X; in fact, the cutting-bit movement, although close to the spindle, is an oblique movement. The origin and the direction are specified in the same way.

Preferably, the primary linear motions are those nearest the principal spindle, the secondary linear motions are those next nearest and the tertiary linear motions are the farthest from the spindle. In case of a radial drilling machine for example, motion of the spindle quill and that of the arm on the column are designated by Z and W respectively. With a turret lathe, motion of the tool slide and of the turret slide, which is farther from the spindle, are designated Z and W, respectively.

Rotary Motion

If, in addition to the primary rotary motions A, B and C, there exist secondary rotary motions, whether parallel or not to A, B and C, they should be designated D or E.

Figure 8.13. Primary, secondary and tertiary axes

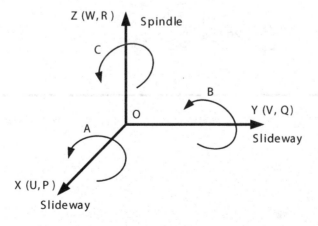

Table 8.2. Common CNC machining centres (ISO 841, 2001, reproduced with permission from ISO)

CNC Machine Tool	Schematic Drawing	Comments
Twin-turret lathe		This lathe has a secondary slide-way in the same direction of Z, hence W (Z2) is used. It also has a programmable tail-stock, hence R (Z3)
Vertical turning and boring lathe		This machine tool has three sets of tool carriages, primary (X, Z), secondary (U, W) and tertiary (P, R). The C' axis is vertical, hence the name of the lathe.
Boring and milling machine with horizontal spindle		Note the secondary Z – W'

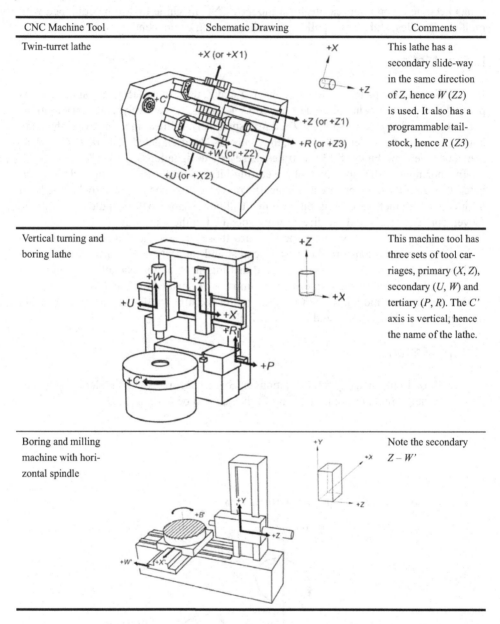

continued on following page

Table 8.2. continued

Gantry-type milling machine	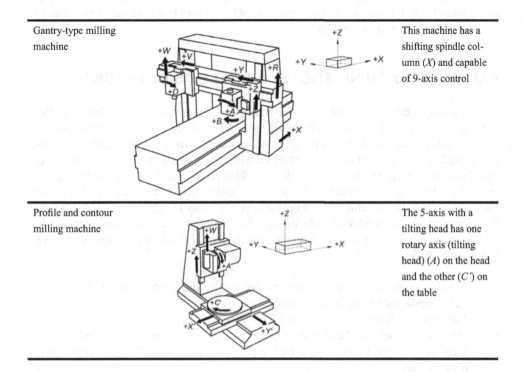	This machine has a shifting spindle column (*X*) and capable of 9-axis control
Profile and contour milling machine		The 5-axis with a tilting head has one rotary axis (tilting head) (*A*) on the head and the other (*C'*) on the table

Direction of Spindle Rotation

The convention is that clockwise spindle rotation is in the direction to advance a right-handed screw into the workpiece. If a machine element moves the workpiece instead of the tool, it must respond to the tape in the opposite direction to that defined above for moving the tool. In illustrating various machines, an arrow with a primed letter, such as + *X'*, is the direction of motion of a moving workpiece, for a command calling for positive motion, while an arrow with an unprimed letter, such as +*X*, is the direction of motion (for the same positive command) of the tool with respect to the workpiece.

SOME SCHEMATICS OF CNC MACHINE TOOLS

Table 8.2 shows five types of CNC machine tools with axis designations, selected from ISO 841 (2001). There are some 31 machine tools in total listed in the standards including grinding machines, flame cutting machines, punch press, drafting machine, EDM machines and even coordinate measuring machines. However, the list should not be treated as a comprehensive collection of the modern CNC machines that may take any variation of the structures shown in the table.

PARALLEL MACHINE TOOLS: A LITTLE "SIDETRACK"

Conventional machine tools are characterized by a serial arrangement of feed axes that are built one on top of the other. The lower axis carries those above it. Most of the machine structures are based on this principle. Since the feed axes are principally arranged orthogonally to one another as well as being serially arranged, the machine and workpiece coordinate systems generally match each other. This feature has helped to ease programming these types of CNC machine tools. The question is whether these machine tools meet the increased requirements with regard to productivity (e.g. high-speed cutting) and flexibility (e.g. reconfigurable manufacturing). Previous study seems to have suggested the following limitations associated with the conventional serial machine structure (Warnecke, Neugebauer & Wieland, 1998),

- Bending loads are the predominant type of load on the machine structure;
- Large masses are being moved around;
- The feed axes have poor dynamics performance;
- Errors are accumulated due to the individual axes that are arranged in serial;
- There is a stringent requirement for the precision of the individual structural components; and
- There are very few components that are inter-changeable.

Parallel structures represent one solution. This type of structure is made up of one or more closed kinematics chains whose end element (end effector) represents a platform. The platforms are coupled by guide chains which can be moved independent of each other. The guide chains (struts) are attached to a fixed platform or frame platform by means of joints. The other end of the struts is attached, again by means of joints, to a movable platform or end effector. The joints are capable of several rotational degrees of freedom. The struts can change in length, whereby through the variable length of the struts the end effector can be positioned in space in all six degrees of freedom.

Parallel structures can be classified in different ways, one of which is by the degree of freedom of the structure. Parallel structures with six degrees of freedom are called Hexapod structures. Another way of classifying them is by the type of feed drives, i.e. rotary drives or linear drives. No matter what type of drives are used, one would always have the final structure with either a variable-length strut or a fixed-length strut (Figure 8.14). In the case of structures with variable-length struts, the struts execute a telescopic movement used to position the end effector in space. Structures with fixed-length struts are equipped with struts of rigid design, and movement of the joint elements takes place.

Based on a triple-tripod concept called the Stewart platform, the hexapod design is easily the most radical departure from the conventional machine tool design (Rao, Saha & Rao, 2005, Zhang, Wang & Lang 2005, Pritschow & Wurst, 1997, Tlusty, Ziegert & Ridgeway, 1999). A Stewart platform has six degrees of freedom (*x, y, z*, pitch, roll and yaw) (Figure 8.15).

There are six independently actuated legs, where the lengths of the legs are changed to position and orient the platform. The forward kinematics problem, an equation which given the leg lengths, finds the position and orientation of the platform, has 16 solutions. However, the inverse kinematics problem (i.e. given the position and orientation of the platform, find the required leg lengths) has a unique and very simple solution. Because of this, hexapod machining centres have been developed by simply turning the platform into a tool holder and inverting the structure (Figure 8.16).

The biggest advantage of this design is volumetric accuracy because it is a parallel mechanism. Volumetric accuracy can be as much as two to three times better. That means

Figure 8.14. Design variants of a parallel structure

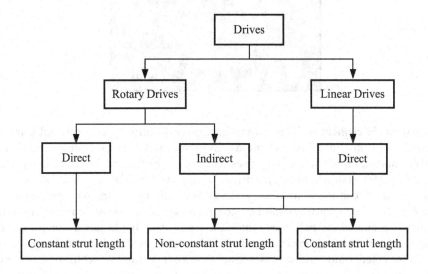

Figure 8.15. A Stewart platform

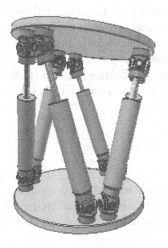

Figure 8.16. Hexel's Hexapod

the worst single element is the worst machine error. Contrarily, conventional Cartesian structures stack up errors. For example, a conventional mill may have one axis configured based on another. The error from both axes accumulates because of the serial arrangement. In the hexapod structure however, the drive elements work in parallel. Often no more than two elements are connected in series, so less error build-up occurs. Another major asset of the design is rigidity, because most of the stresses are in tension and compression rather than bending and all six ballscrews share the load. Thus, the hexapod can cut difficult aerospace materials more accurately because of its great rigidity. It is usually believed to be five times more rigid and four times faster than a conventional machine tool. Since it is modular in structure, manufacturers of hexapod machine tools are able to respond flexibly and quickly to customer needs.

The main design issues facing the builders seem to be the machine configuration (space frame or enclosed), optimum strut length, and thermal compensation. As in any machine, accuracy deviations due to thermal expansion represent a major area of concern because the rapid motion of the balls generates a lot of heat. The Hexapod also needs a lot of fast computing power, i.e. algorithms and processing speed are big problems. There are also questions of chip handling and part feeding. Further studies are also needed on the technological potential of parallel structures and suitable CAD/CAM processors for hexapod machine tools.

CONCLUSION

The transformation of conventional machine tools to numerically controlled machine tools and then to computer numerically controlled machining centres has made today's manufacturing world drastically different from that of half century ago. Some of the significant characteristics of a modern CNC system are the use of automatic tool handling facilities, real-time feedback capabilities and of course the multi-axis configurations that allow different machining operations to be performed on a single machine tool.

In order to work with today's sophisticated CNC machines, it is necessary to understand the axes and motions of these machine tools. These axes correspond to translational and rotational motions, and are often the indication of a CNC machine tool's machining capability. Close-loop control has become the norm for many modern CNC machines and it makes machining more accurate and reliable.

While the serial kinematics structure continues to dominate the structures of the mainstream machine tool, the problems associated with this type of machine tools are also evident and await solutions. Hexapod machine tools seem to offer such a solution. They are far more rigid structure-wise and can be built with high accuracy.

REFERENCES

Childs, J. J. (1969). *Principles of numerical control*. New York: Industrial Press.

Crandell, T. M. (2003). *CNC machining and programming: An introduction*. New York: Industrial Press.

ISO 841. (2001). *Industrial automation systems and integration - Numerical control of machines - Coordinate system and motion nomenclature*. Geneva, Switzerland: International Organisation for Standardisation (ISO).

Pritschow, G., & Wurst, K.-H. (1997). Systematic design of hexapods and other parallel link systems. *CIRP Annals, 46*(1), 291-295.

Rao, A. B. K., Saha, S. K., & Rao, P. V. M. (2005). Stiffness analysis of hexaslide machine tools. *Advanced Robotics, 19*(6), 671-693.

Tlusty, J., Ziegert, J., & Ridgeway, S. (1999). Fundamental comparison of the use of serial and parallel kinematics for machines tools, *CIRP Annals, 48*(1), 351-356.

Valentino, J. V., & Goldenberg, J. (2003). *Introduction to computer numerical control (CNC)*. Upper Saddle River, NJ: Prentice Hall.

Warnecke, H. J., Neugebauer, R., & Wieland, F. (1998). Development of hexapod based machine tool. *CIRP Annal, 47*(1), 337-340.

Zhang, D., Wang, L., & Lang, S. Y. T. (2005). Parallel kinematic machines: Design, analysis and simulation in an integrated virtual environment. *Journal of Mechanical Design, Transactions of the ASME, 127*(4), 580-588.

ENDNOTE

[1] Whisker material is micron or nanometer size filament made to be used as reinforcement materials. Examples of whiskers are micron size carbon whiskers and potassium titanate whiskers.

Chapter IX
Program CNCs

ABSTRACT

A CNC machine can be programmed in different ways to machine a workpiece. In addition to creating the cutting program, many other factors also need to be considered or programmed. These include workholding devices, cutting tools, machining conditions as well as the machining strategy. The first generation CNCs were programmed manually and punched tapes were used as a medium for transferring the machine control data (MCD), that is, G-codes into a controller. Tapes were later replaced by RS232 cables, floppy disks, and finally standard computer network cables.

Today's CNC machines are controlled directly from files created by CAD/CAM or CAM software packages, so that a part or assembly can go directly from design to manufacturing without the need of producing a drafted paper drawing of the component. This means that for the first time, bringing design and manufacturing under the same automation regime becomes a reachable target. Error detection features give CNC machines the ability to alert the operator in different ways including giving a ring to the operation's mobile phone if it detects that a tool has broken. While the machine is awaiting replacement on the tool, it would run other parts that are already loaded up to that tool and wait for the operator. The focus of this chapter is on a detailed account of the basics of CNC programming, and the emphasis is on G-code and Automatic Programming Tool (APT). G-code is still the dominant manual programming language for CNC machine tools. It is also the main form of control commands many CAD/CAM (or CAM) systems output. APT was developed soon after G-codes and CNC machine tools were developed to alleviate the drudgery work of straight G-code programming. Modern CAD/CAM systems these days are now becoming the main-stream tools for CNC programming.

PROGRAM BASICS

Today's full-blown machining centres allow the programmer to control just about any function required through programmed commands. This section lists the things that the programmer can usually control within a program. Also explained is how each function is controlled. The MCD format discussed here conforms to ISO 6983-1 (1982).

Program Format

The CNC machine program is structured in blocks of data. A fixed set of alphabetic, numeric and special characters is used. Any characters that are not to be processed are included within parenthesis. Characters ":" or "%" can be used for display purposes. To identify a machine program, an identifier may be placed immediately after the program start character and before the first "end of block" character.

A block of data consists of a sequence number word and one or more than one data words (also known as NC words). Tab characters, which are optional for the tabulation of a printed copy of the data, may be inserted between words but are usually ignored by the control system. A data word always starts with an address character. The characters are usually presented in the following sequence and are not repeated within one block,

- Preparatory words "G";
- "Dimension" words. These words are arranged in the following sequence: X, Y, Z, U, V, W, P, Q, R, A, B, C;
- "Interpolation or thread cutting lead words" I, J and K;
- "Feed function (F)" word;
- "Spindle speed function (S)" word;
- "Tool function (T)" word; and
- "Miscellaneous function (M)" words.

Some words may be omitted in a specific block of data, indicating that there is no change in the condition of the machine with respect to the function denoted by the omitted word. This word is named as a "modal" word. Table 9.1 summarises the address characters commonly used in a modal word.

NC Words

The address character is always the first in an NC word and it is followed by digital data, e.g. G01 X10. Most control systems accept implicit decimal sign programming. With explicit decimal sign format both leading zeros before the decimal sign and trailing zeros after the decimal sign may be omitted.

Preparatory Function

The preparatory function is expressed by the address character "G" followed by a coded number. Character G can form NC words for specifying spindle directions, types of feed-rate functions, dwell and many other functions. Therefore, this is one of the most important

Table 9.1. Commonly used address characters

Character	Meaning
A	Angular dimension about X axis
B	Angular dimension about Y axis
C	Angular dimension about Z axis
D	Second tool function
E	Second feed function
F	First feed function
G	Preparatory function
I	Interpolation parameter of thread lead parallel to X
J	Interpolation parameter of thread lead parallel to Y
K	Interpolation parameter of thread lead parallel to Z
M	Miscellaneous function
N	Sequence number
P	Tertiary dimension parallel to X or parameter
Q	Tertiary dimension parallel to Y or parameter
R	Tertiary dimension parallel to Z or parameter
S	Spindle speed function
T	First tool function
U	Secondary dimension parallel to X
V	Secondary dimension parallel to Y
W	Secondary dimension parallel to Z
X	Primary dimension X
Y	Primary dimension Y
Z	Primary dimension Z

groups of words in the programme. This is why the word "G-code" is often used to refer to the entire family of programming codes discussed herein. A detailed list of G-codes can be found in Table 9.2 later in the chapter.

Spindle Control

A programmer can control precisely how fast the spindle rotates in one rpm increments. An S word is used for this purpose. If 350 rpm is desired, the word S350 is used.

Spindle Activation and Direction

A programmer can control which direction the spindle rotates, forward or reverse. In case of a lathe, the forward direction is used for right hand tooling and the reverse direction is used for left hand tooling. Two M codes control this function. M03 turns the spindle on in the forward direction; M04 turns the spindle on in a reverse direction. M05 turns the spindle off. Both constant surface speed (G96) and constant RPM (G97) can be supported.

Spindle Range

Most larger machining centres have more than one spindle range. The low spindle range is used for slow speed and powerful machining, whereas the high spindle range is used for faster speed with less power available.

Feed-Rate

A programmer can control the motion rate for any machining operation. This is done with an F word. There are three types of feed functions supported, G93 Inverse time; G94 Feed per minute and G95 Feed per revolution. When the feed is independent of spindle speed, the digits represent directly the vectorial motion in mm/min or inch/min (G94). Otherwise, the digits represent directly the vectorial motion in mm/revolution or inch/revolution (G95). When the feed is applied to a rotary motion only, the digits represent directly the vectorial motion in degree/min (G93). The preparatory code G00 is used for rapid positioning.

Dwell

Dwell denotes a delay between moves and is programmed in a separate block starting with G04. The duration of the dwell time is specified by the F word. The delay is measured in seconds when G94 is operative and in revolutions of the spindle if G95 is operative. It is a common practice that the resolution of the F word should be 0.1 second or 0.1 revolutions, or as specified in the detailed format classification.

Coolant

A programmer can turn coolant on and off at any time from within a program. An M08 command turns coolant on and an M09 turns the coolant off.

Tool Changes

Most machining centres have automatic tool changers that allow tools to be loaded into the spindle automatically during the program's cycle. This, of course, allows a multitude of machining operations to be performed within one program cycle.

Though this function will change slightly from one machining centre to another, many machining centres use a T word to rotate the machine's tool magazine to the desired position. For example, T05 rotates the magazine to station number five. An M06 command is used to actually make the tool change and exchanges the tool in the ready position with the tool in the spindle.

NC Parameters

To increase programming flexibility, calculations of axis values or setting of parameters for a subroutine may be allowed. This type of feature is usually proprietary to a particular controller. The type of information required includes, (a) which address character is used, e.g. P, Q, R or #; (b) which operations are allowed, e.g. arithmetic, trigonometric, logical and (c) which memory addresses are used for the parameters. In these cases the parameter index is the memory location of the parameter. In all cases, address indexing will be mandatory. For example,

R11 = 22.2: the content of parameter R11 is set to 22.2
R29 = R9 + R15: parameter content addition; result stored in parameter R29
X2 = 105. + R9: X2 gets the result of addition of 105 and the content of R9

Other Controllable Functions

Other features that may be equipped on some machines include pallet changers, programmable chip conveyers, spindle probes, tool length measuring probes, and a variety of other application-based features.

COORDINATE SYSTEM AND PROGRAM ZERO

Understanding the coordinate system on a CNC machine is the basis of programming a CNC. It is also important to understand the two principal modes of control, absolute and incremental. Program zero is another important concept. It allows the programmer to input all coordinates within a program from a common and logical point. Failing to observe and specify a correct program zero could lead to wrong machining path or even damage of the machine tool.

Coordinate System

For CNC machining centres, the XY plane usually defines a horizontal plane for a machining centre. Figure 9.1 shows these two machining centre's axes, X and Y. The Z axis behaves in exactly the same manner as X and Y. When taken all together, the X, Y, and Z give you a three dimensional grid. It is within this grid that you will position (using coordinates) your tools for machining operations.

Plus and Minus

Machining may happen in any one of the eight quadrants of the co-ordinate system. Figure 9.2 show how a series of coordinates are determined to drill the 6 holes evenly spaced on a plate. The holes are specified relative to the centre of the co-ordinate system. Any hole to the left of the origin requires a minus X coordinate, and any hole below the origin requires a minus Y coordinate. Note that the CNC control will automatically assume that

Figure 9.1. Tool positioned in a 3D co-ordinate system

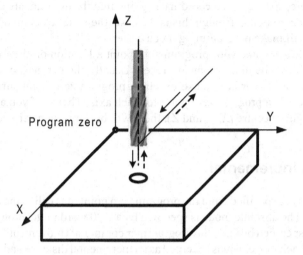

a coordinate is plus unless a minus sign (-) is programmed within the coordinate word. This means you never have to program a plus sign (+).

Program Zero

When programming a CNC, the origin point for each axis is commonly called the program zero point, also called work zero, part origin, and zero point. Program zero allows the programmer to input all coordinates within a program from a common and logical point.

Figure 9.2. Plus and minus coordinates

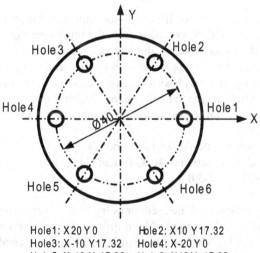

Hole1: X20 Y0   Hole2: X10 Y17.32
Hole3: X-10 Y17.32   Hole4: X-20 Y0
Hole5: X-10 Y-17.32   Hole6: X10 Y-17.32

The placement of program zero is determined by the programmer. Program zero could be placed anywhere, as long as the coordinates going into the program are taken correctly from the program zero point. Though this is the case, the wise selection of a logical program zero point will make programming much easier.

It is wise to always make your program zero point a location on the workpiece from which all (or most) of the dimensions are taken. Usually the surfaces of the workpiece that are used as location surfaces make excellent program zero point surfaces for each axis. Note that there is a program zero point for each axis. That is, if you are working on a three-axis machining centre (X, Y, and Z), there will be a program zero position in each of the three axes.

Absolute vs. Incremental

When coordinates are specified from the program zero point, it is called the absolute mode of programming. The absolute mode is specified by a G90 word in the program. In the incremental mode (specified by G91) the programmer commands movements from the tool's current position. Each movement is specified as an incremental distance and direction from the tool's current location. While at first this may seem easier than working from program zero, you will find that programs including incremental motions can be very difficult to follow. Also, if the programmer makes a mistake in a series of incremental motions, every incremental movement from that point on will be incorrect. If the programmer makes the same mistake in an absolute program, only one movement will be incorrect.

When programming, you will be specifying the coordinate to which you want to make the tool move. To do this, you must always specify the letter address, of the axes you wish to move (X, Y, and Z) along with the coordinate position to which the tool must move. The coordinate position value tells the control where along the axis to stop the tool (Figure 9.3).

COMPENSATIONS

In general, compensation is used to allow for some unpredictable (or nearly unpredictable) variation. With all forms of CNC compensation, the setup operators will do their best to perfectly determine the compensation values needed for perfect machining. But until machining actually occurs, the setup operators cannot be sure that compensation values are perfect. After machining, they may have to fine-tune them, due to some secondary variation (like tool pressure). After this second adjustment, machining will be more precise.

The three kinds of machining centre tooling compensation are

- Tool Length Compensation (G43, G44, and G49);
- Cutter Radius Compensation (G40, G41, and G42);
- Fixture Offsets (G54 - G59).

Tool length compensation will be used for every tool in every program you write. Cutter radius compensation is only applicable to milling cutters, and only when milling on the periphery of the tool (as when contour milling with end mills and shell mills). Cutter

Figure 9.3. Movement made in both absolute and incremental mode

Absolute				Incremental		
#	X	Y		#	X	Y
1	1.0	1.0		1	0.0	0.0
2	2.0	1.5		2	1.0	0.5
3	3.0	3.0		3	1.0	1.5
4	4.0	3.0		4	1.0	0.0
5	5.0	2.0		5	1.0	-1.0
6	6.0	2.0		6	1.0	0.0

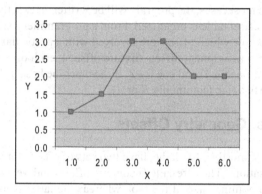

radius compensation allows you to work from the work surface as opposed to the cutter's centre line, meaning you can save yourself a great deal of work if you understand cutter radius compensation. Note that the first two kinds of compensation apply to the cutting tools. Fixture offsets relate to the work holding setup.

Offsets

All three compensation types use offsets. Offsets are storage locations for values. They are very much like the memories of an electronic calculator. The setup operator can *type* important values into offsets. When needed in the program, a special command will invoke the value of the offset.

Like the memories of most calculators, offsets are designated with offset numbers. Offset number one may have a value of 6.54. Offset number two may have a value of 6.29. Though it is not mandatory to do so, most offset numbers are made to correspond in some way to tool station numbers. For example, the tool length compensation value of tool station number one is commonly placed in offset number one.

CNC offsets are much more permanent. They will he retained even after the machine's power is turned off. This means that important values will be retained from day to day. Most CNC controls have at least 99 offsets. For most applications, only one offset is needed per cutting tool, e.g. tool length compensation. If using an end mill or shell mill, you may need a second offset for the tool for cutter radius compensation. Generally speaking, most CNC machining centres will have an ample supply of tool offsets.

Organization of Offsets

Machining centre controls vary with regard to how offsets are organized. Most have at least two distinct sets of offsets, one for cutting tools and another for program zero assignment (fixture offsets). When it comes to cutting tools, one offset will be needed for tool length compensation; another may be for cutter radius compensation. With most controls, there is but one value per offset. The program tells the control how to use the offset value, as a tool length or cutter radius compensation value. With other controls, one offset actually may contain two values, one for the tool length compensation value and the other for the cutter radius compensation value. Note that these offset discrepancies have little to do with programming. In most cases, the program will be written in exactly the same manner regardless of how the offset table is organized. From a programmer's standpoint, the most important thing is to know which offsets are involved with a particular cutting tool.

As for program zero assignment offsets (fixture offsets), each offset will have at least three values, one for X, one for Y, and one for Z. If the machine has a full rotary axis, each offset will have a fourth value (commonly B or A).

Wear Offsets vs. Geometry Offsets

Some CNC controllers, mostly CNC lathe, have two sets of offsets for the tool length and cutter radius compensations. They are called geometry offsets and wear offsets. The former is used to specify the nominal size of the tool, whereas the latter is used to specify any small discrepancy possibly caused by improper measurement, tool deflection, or tool wear. The wear offset value for the tool will be zero only if (a) the tool is measured perfectly, (b) the tool does not deflect during machining, and (c) no wear occurs.

Instate an Offset

With most CNCs, each offset includes only one value, and the offset value is invoked (instated) in the program by the corresponding offset number. The programming format which invokes an offset determines how the offset will be used. For example, if invoked in a tool length compensation command, the offset will be used as a tool length compensation value.

With almost all controllers, two digit H word is used to instate a tool length compensation offset, e.g. H01 for offset one and H02 for offset two. A two digit D word is used to instate a cutter radius compensation offset, e.g. D11 for offset eleven and D12 for offset twelve.

Offsets and Trial Machining

When machining critical surfaces with very tight tolerances, you can use offsets to trial machine. Prior to machining, it will always be possible to set an offset in such a way that when the tool does machine the surface, an extra amount of material is left behind. This will ensure that the surface will not be overcut. Once the surface is machined, it can he measured to determine just how much more material must be machined. The offset can then be adjusted accordingly and the tool can be rerun to machine the surface to the proper size.

Tool Length Compensation

Tool length compensation is an extremely important feature of a CNC program. You will use it for almost every tool in every program you write. For this reason, it is the most important of the compensation types.

The Need for Tool Length Compensation

Program zero is a location on the workpiece from which all coordinates in the program will be taken (note that program zero is a position relative to the workpiece). This allows you to reference all coordinates going into the program from a logical position, and this position is usually right on the workpiece itself. Take a vertical mill as an example. When programming a hole machining operation, one would specify coordinates based upon the spindle centre line. The program zero for both X and Y will stay consistent from tool to tool. Even after changing tools, the distance from the program zero point to the machine's zero return position in X and Y will remain the same since the tool's centre position in X and Y does not change from tool to tool. However, when it comes to the Z axis, this is not the case. Almost all tools will vary in length, as will the distance from the tip of each tool at the machine's Z axis zero return position to the program zero point in Z, commonly the top surface of the workpiece. Take a hole as an example that needs a drilling and tapping operation. The drill is 60.25mm long and the tap is 60.50mm long. The distance between the tool tip and the program zero point will be greater for the drill than the tap. If both tools begin from the zero return position in Z, the drill must travel further to reach the work surface. Therefore, tool length compensation is related only to the Z axis.

Figure 9.4 shows three cutters super-imposed in the spindle, each having its own offset value. The shorter ones must traverse a longer distance to get down to the workpiece. This is the reason why tool length compensation is so important. Since the lengths of your tools will vary, the distance each tool must travel in the Z axis to reach a given surface of the workpiece will also vary. In essence, tool length compensation eliminates the need for a programmer to be concerned with a tool's length as the program is written.

Use of Tool Length Compensation

When instating tool length compensation in the Z axis, the instating command will include a G45 word and an H word to invoke the related tool offset (Figure 9.4). The instating command must also contain a Z axis positioning movement. In the instating command, the control is being told to bring the nose of the spindle to the programmed Z position after adding in the tool length compensation value. The ending result is that the tip of the tool will stop at the programmed Z position. Note that once instated, tool length compensation will remain in effect until the next G43 command in the Z axis command of the next tool.

Figure 9.4. Cutter length compensation

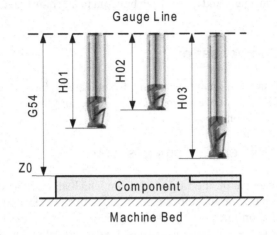

Cutter Radius Compensation

Similar to tool length compensation that lets you forget about each tool's actual length as you write the program, so does cutter radius compensation that lets you forget about the diameter of the tool as you write the program.

However, cutter radius compensation is used primarily only for milling cutters when the milling cutters machining on the periphery of the tool, e.g. milling a contour with an end mill or a shell mill. Clearly, you will not need cutter radius compensation for face milling operations. Cutter radius compensation, once mastered, you will find it to be one of the most valuable tools in CNC program. It may save countless programming hours and make life much easier for the people on the shop-floor who use.

Range of Cutter Sizes

Similar to tool length compensation, cutter radius compensation allows the diameter of the milling cutter to vary. If a programmer writes a program for a contour milling operation without using cutter radius compensation, they must specify the exact cutter size to be used. If that cutter size is not available and a replacement must be used, the program must be changed. For example, if a programmer plans on using a 12 mm diameter end mill, he will have to calculate the cutter's centre line path. When the program is finished, it will only work with a 12 mm end mill. If the setup person does not have such an end mill, the program will have to be changed to match the size of the end mill he does have. All coordinates related to the contour milling operation will have to he recalculated and changed to match the new cutter size. Otherwise, the workpiece will be either overcut or undercut (Figure 9.5).

Cutter radius compensation dramatically increases flexibility in this regard. Though there are still some limitations related to cutter size, i.e. the cutter must fall within a given range; a variety of milling cutters can be used without requiring changes to the program.

Figure 9.5. Cutting with no cutter radius compensations

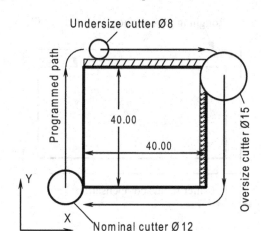

Adapt to Cutting Conditions

Consider a program that describes a perfect cutter centre line path. The shape may still not be perfectly cut. This is due to the end mill not perfectly concentric with its holder, so that it overcuts the workpiece. Or, if the milling cutter's holder is somewhat weak, it may deflect from the work surface slightly, and not machine enough material. If cutter radius compensation is not used, it will be very difficult to manipulate the program to handle these tiny tool path variations. As the cutter dulls, cutting conditions will change, requiring further program changes.

Cutter radius compensation allows the setup person or operator to handle this problem easily. Just as they can manipulate the tool length compensation offset to hold size for Z axis-related surfaces, so can they manipulate a cutter radius compensation offset to hold size for X/Y contour milling operations.

Cutter radius compensation also makes it possible to use the same work surface coordinates needed for finish milling a contour to be used to rough the contour. Though there are some limitations, this eliminates the need for the programmer to calculate two sets of coordinates. Only the finish contour coordinates need be calculated. Figure 9.6 shows this.

However, this reason for using cutter radius compensation applies only to manual programmers. A CAM system can calculate and generate the roughing contour just as easily as the finishing contour.

Two Types of Cutter Radius Compensations

A G-code is used to control the relationship of the milling cutter to the workpiece during the machining operation. Either the cutter will be on the left side (G41) or right side (G42) of the workpiece as it machines the contour (Figure 9.7). Once cutter radius compensation is properly instated, the control will keep the milling cutter to the left or right (depending upon your choice) of all motions programmed.

Figure 9.6. Finishing tool path used for rough cut

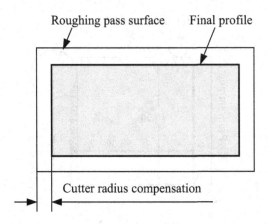

Roughing pass surface   Final profile

Cutter radius compensation

Figure 9.7. Two types of cutter radius compensations

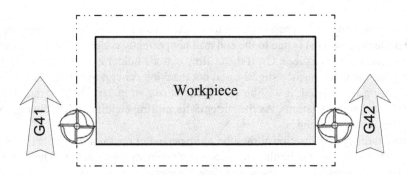

Two other things are worth noting. First is the instating movement. This movement requires the tool to be positioned to a location larger than the cutter radius away from the first surface to be machined. Second is the approach and retract of the tool. They do not actually cut the material but must be included in the program.

Fixture Offsets

There are two ways to assign program zero on machining centres: fixture offsets and the G92 command. The only good reason to use G92 is if your older CNC control does not support fixture off-sets.

Just as different companies have differing needs for cutter radius compensation, so do they have differing needs for assigning multiple program zero points. If a workpiece needs to be machined in multiple setups, multiple program zero point per setup is needed. Just as tool length and cutter radius compensation allow you to ignore cutting tool-related functions during programming, fixture offsets allow you to ignore work holding tooling (chucks, jigs, fixtures, vises, etc.) as you write a program.

PROGRAMMING METHODS FOR INTERPOLATION

Interpolation is the typical way that CNC machine tools deal with tool path generations and execution for a given curve. Interpolation is performed over a pre-determined portion of a given curve. The portion interpolated is called a "span" and may be covered by one or more blocks of information. Data necessary to define a span obeys one or more of the following principles:

- An appropriate G-code needs to be used to define the functional nature of the curve, i.e. linear (G01), circular (G02, G03) or parabolic (G06).
- The starting point of each span is identical to the end point of the previous span. Therefore, it is not necessary to repeat this point in a new block. Each subsequent point of the span for which coordinates are specified will require a separate block of information and will use a valid dimension address, e.g. X, Y or Z.
- Interpolation parameters are addressed by I, J or K and used for defining the geometric properties of the curve as defined for each interpolation method.
- In cases where an algebraic sign is required with the interpolation parameter word, it follows the address character and precedes the numeric characters.

Linear Interpolation

A straight line span is defined in one block which contains:

- The G function word (if not currently active), e.g. G01;
- The coordinates of the end point should be expressed as dimension words.

The example in Figure 9.8 shows the geometric properties of the span. Two examples are given below,

G90
G01 Xx1 Yy1 Zz1

G91
G01 Xx Yy Zz

where x = x1-x0; y=y1-y0; z=z1-z0.

Note that the first block of code corresponds to the absolute mode cutting whereas the second the incremental mode cutting; both yield the same result.

Circular Interpolation

Circular interpolation defines a circular span lying in a plane parallel to one of the three principal planes of reference. The example in Figure 9.9 shows the geometric properties of a typical circular span and gives an example of the coordinate and interpolation values to be programmed.

Figure 9.8. Linear interpolation

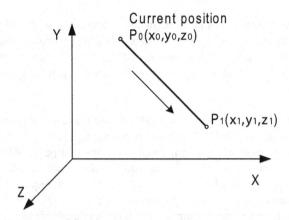

Figure 9.9. Example of circular interpolation in the XY plane (P0 to P1)

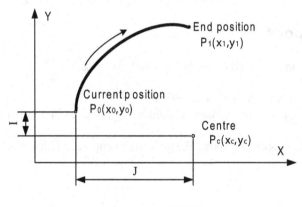

G02 X Y I J F

Absolute dimensions	Incremental dimensions
$X = x_1$	$X = x_1 - x_o$
$Y = y_1$	$Y = y_1 - y_o$
$I = x_c - x_o$	$I = x_c - x_o$
$J = y_c - y_o$	$J = y_c - y_o$

It is recommended that circular interpolation be programmed by defining the span (up to full circle) in one block. This block should contain,

- The G function word (if not currently active): G02 for circular interpolation arc clock wise (CW), and G03 for circular interpolation arc counter clock wise (CCW).
- The coordinates of the end point are to be expressed by any valid motion address such as X, Y or Z.

- The centre of the arc can be addressed by I, J and K

It is a common practice that the I, J and K words are the incremental (relative) dimensions from the starting point to the centre of the circle, irrespective of whether the dimension words are incremental or absolute, i.e.

- I for the dimension of the centre of the circle parallel to X,
- J for the dimension of the centre of the circle parallel to Y,
- K for the dimension of the centre of the circle parallel to Z.

When circular interpolation is to be combined with simultaneous linear interpolation, the plane of circular interpolation is selected by a preparatory function. Interpolation blocks shall be specified with the addition of a third dimension word, which should indicate the end point of the linear motion, and a third interpolation parameter addressed by the letter allocated to dimensions parallel to the linear motion (I, J and K). The value assigned should be the linear movement required per radian of arc.

Parabolic Interpolation

Parabolic interpolation defines a parabolic span lying in any plane. It is recommended that the method of programming of the span be by definition of three points. The intermediate point and the end point are programmed in successive blocks. The example in Figure 9.10 shows the geometric properties of the span.
    In this example, the first block contains,

- The G-function word (e.g. G06 for parabolic interpolation); and
- The coordinates of the intermediate point.
    i.e. G06 Xx1 Yy1 Zz1 (for absolute mode).

Figure 9.10. Example of parabolic interpolation in three axes

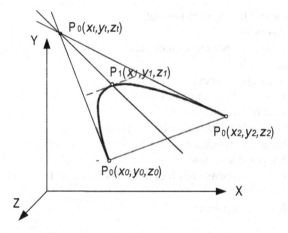

The second block contains the coordinates of the end point, i.e., Xx2 Yy2 Zz2 (for absolute mode).

Alternatively, the span may be defined in one block using interpolation parameters containing,

- The G-function word, e.g. G06;
- The coordinates of the end point, which are addressed by any valid motion address such as X,Y or Z, and
- The coordinates of the tangent intersection point addressed by I, J, K words.

SUMMARY OF SOME COMMON NC CODES

This section contains tables summarising most of the commonly used NC codes for the purpose of quick reference. Similar to the rest of this chapter, the definitions largely conform to the ISO 6983 standard. For an in-depth description of the NC codes discussed here, and their specific uses on a machining or turning centre, the interested readers are referred to the book *Computer Numerical Control: Machining and Turning Centres* (Quesada, 2005).

Lists of Some Common G Codes

Table 9.2 lists the common types of preparatory (G) function codes that are represented by the letter G followed by a two-digit integer (unsigned). Some modern controls may have extended the G code to a three or more digit integer.

G81 to G89 can be used to define a set of operations that may be repetitive such as boring, drilling, tapping or combinations thereof. These cycles of machining operations can then be called again and again. These fixed cycle words are listed in Table 9.3.

Reset States

There are certain operation modes that should be positioned at power turn-on. These modes correspond to some of the point to point and contouring motion controls.

- Point to point and line motion controls
    - G00 positioning
    - G40 cutter compensation/tool radius offset cancel
    - G71 metric data
    - G80 fixed cycle cancel
    - G90 absolute dimension data
    - G94 feed per minute
- Contouring controls other than those on lathes
    - G01 linear interpolation
    - G17 XY plane selection
    - G40 cutter compensation/tool radius offset cancel
    - G71 metric data
    - G80 fixed cycle cancel

Table 9.2. Assignment of preparatory function codes

Code	Function	Description
G00	Rapid positioning	A mode of control in which the movement to the programmed point occurs with the feedrate; a feedrate previously programmed is ignored but not cancelled.
G01	Linear interpolation	A mode of control, used for a uniform slope or straight line motion, that uses the information contained in a block to produce velocities proportional to the distances to be moved in two or more axes simultaneously.
G02	Circular interpolation arc (clockwise)	Circular interpolation in which the curvature of the path of the tool with respect to the workpiece is clockwise when the plane of motion is viewed in the negative direction of the axis perpendicular to it.
G03	Circular interpolation arc (counter-clockwise)	Same as G02 except the curvature of the path is counter-clockwise.
G04	Dwell	A timed delay of programmed or established duration, not cyclic or sequential.
G06	Parabolic interpolation	A mode of contouring control which uses the information contained in one or more blocks to produce a span of a parabola. The velocities of the axes used to generate this arc are varied by the control.
G08	Acceleration	An automatic velocity increase to the programmed rate starting at the beginning of the movement.
G09	Deceleration	An automatic velocity decrease to programmed rate starting on the approach of the programmed point.
G17	XY plane selection	Used to identify the plane for such functions as circular interpolation, cutter compensation and others as required.
G18	ZX plane selection	
G19	ZY plane selection	
G33	Thread cutting (constant lead)	Mode selection for machines equipped for thread cutting
G34	Thread cutting (increasing lead)	
G35	Thread cutting (decreasing lead)	
G40	Cutter compensation cancel	Command which cancels any cutter compensation (diameter or radius') or tool offset.
G41	Cutter compensation (left)	Direction of cutter compensation of the tool path looking from cutter in the direction of relative cutter motion.
G42	Cutter compensation (right)	
G43	Tool offset (positive)	The value of the tool offset to be added to
G44	Tool offset (negative)	the coordinate dimension of the relevant block, or blocks.
G53	Dimension shift cancel	Suppresses any program zero shift.
G54-G59	Zero shifts	Displaces the program zero relative to the machine datum.

continued on following page

Table 9.2. continued

G63	Tapping	The selection for the particular case shall be defined in the format specification.
G70	Dimension input (inch)	Mode selection for dimension input
G71	Dimension input (metric)	
G74	Home position	Move the axes specified to home position.
G80	Fixed cycle cancel	Fixed cycles discontinue.
G81-G89	Fixed cycle	A preset series of operations which direct machine axis movement and/or cause spindle operation to complete such action as boring, drilling, tapping or combinations thereof.
G90	Absolute dimension	Mode of control for interpretation of dimensions as relative to a speci-
G91	Incremental dimension	fied origin or relative to the previously programmed position.
G92	Preload registers	Used to modify or set registers by the programmed data words. No motion occurs.
G93	Inverse time federate	Feed input is reciprocal to the time to execute the block.
G94	Feed per minute	Feed-rate units are millimetres/inches per minute.
G95	Feed per revolution	Feed-rate units are millimetres/inches per revolution.
G96	Constant surface speed	The spindle speed codes specify the constant surface speed in meters/feet per minute. The spindle speed is automatically controlled to maintain the programmed value.
G97	Revolutions per minute	The spindle speed codes specify the spindle speed in revolutions per minute.

Table 9.3. Fixed cycles

Code	Movement in	At bottom		Movement out to feed start	Typical use
		dwell	spindle		
G81	Feed	-	-	Rapid	Drill spot drip
G82	Feed	Yes	-	Rapid	Drill counterbore
G83	Intermittent	-	-	Rapid	Deep hole
G84	Forward spindle feed	-	Reverse	Feed	Tap
G85	Feed	-	-	Feed	Bore
G86	Start spindle speed	-	Stop	Rapid	Bore
G87	Start spindle speed	-	Stop	Manual	Bore
G88	Start spindle speed	Yes	Stop	Manual	Bore
G89	Feed	Yes	-	Feed	Bore

- ○ G90 absolute dimension data
- ○ G94 feed per minute
- • Contouring controls on lathes
  - ○ G01 linear interpolation
  - ○ G40 cutter compensation/tool radius offset cancel
  - ○ G71 metric data
  - ○ G80 fixed cycle cancel
  - ○ G90 absolute dimension data
  - ○ G95 feed per revolution
  - ○ G97 revolutions per minute

Table 9.4. Miscellaneous (M) function coding

Code	Function	Description
M00	program stop	Cancel the spindle or other functions (for example coolant function) and terminate further processing after the completion of commands in the block.
M01	optional (planned) stop	Similar to M00 except that the control ignores the command unless the operator has previously pushed a button to validate the command.
M02	end of program	Cancel spindle or other function (e.g. coolant function) after completion of all commands in the block. Used to reset control and/or machine.
M06	tool change	Change of tool(s) manually or automatically, not to include tool selection. May or may not automatically shut-off coolant and spindle.
M10	clamp workpiece	Can pertain to machine slides, workpiece, fixture, spindle etc.
M11	unclamp workpiece	
M30	end of data	Cancel spindle or other function (for example coolant function) after completion of all commands in the block. Used to reset control and/or machine, which includes return to the program start character.
M48	cancel M49	
M49	bypass override	Deactivate a manual spindle or feed override and returns the parameter to the programmed value.
M60	workpiece change	Workpiece to be removed or reoriented; Cancel spindle and coolant functions after completion of all commands in the block.

Lists of Some Common M Codes

M codes are usually related to any actions controlled by a PLC unit. Table 9.4 lists the most common type of M codes.

EXAMPLES OF NC PROGRAMS

Examples of three common types of NC programs are included in this section, hole-making operations, programming linear profiles and circular profiles.

Programming Hole-Making Operations

The simplest operations to program are those related to producing holes. These include drilling, boring, tapping and counterboring. The simplicity of programming lies in the fact that the programmer only needs to specify the coordinates of a hole centre and the type of machine motions to be performed at the centre. A fixed cycle, if used properly, takes over and causes the machine to execute the required movements. The controller stores a number of fixed cycles that can be recalled for use in programs when needed. This reduces the programming time and the length of the code.

A fixed cycle is programmed by entering one block of information: the X and Y coordinates, the Z-axis reference plane (R), and the final Z-axis depth. A fixed cycle for hole operations will cause the following sequence of operations to occur,

- Rapid move to the X and Y coordinate of the hole centre.
- Rapid move to Z-axis reference plane (R).
- Feed to the Z-axis final depth.
- Rapid back to either the Z-axis initial position or the Z-axis reference plane (R).

Table 9.5. Part program and its explanation

Part Program	Explanation
N0010 G41 S1000 F5 M03	Begin compensation, set feed and speed, spindle on
N0020 G00 X6.000 Y6.000	Move to lower left corner
N0030 G01 Z-1.000	Plunge down the tool
N0040 Y46.000	Cut to upper left corner
N0050 X46.000	Cut to upper right corner
N0060 Y6.000	Cut to lower right corner
N0070 X6.000	Cut to lower left corner
N0080 Z1.000	Lift the tool
N0090 G40 M30	End compensation, stop the machine

Programming Linear Profiles

Shown in Table 9.5 is the program for machining the same part as shown in Figure 9.5 using a 10mm end-milling cutter (Figure 9.11). The lower left corner of the square (6,6) is set up as the start position. G40 is the code for cancelling tool-radius compensation. G41 stands for compensation-left – assuming cutter is on the left-hand side of the profile.

Programming Circular Profiles

When programming a circular profile, information such as start, end, centre points and radius is needed. However, there can be different ways of programming an arc. Different controllers may also have slightly different ways of coding.

Circular Interpolation Commands

The commands for circular interpolation direct the system to move the tool simultaneously in the X and Y directions such that a programmed circle or portion of a circle is cut. The programmer first defines the plane in which interpolation is to occur. The tool must then be moved to the start point of the circular arc to be cut. Upon receiving a command to execute circular interpolation, the controller will determine the radius between the start point and the centre of the circular arc. It will move the tool from the start point to the end point so that this radius is generated. Tool motion around the circular arc will occur in either the clockwise (G02) or the counter clockwise (G03) direction. If the circular arc is cut properly, the distance from the end point to the centre point will be equal to the radius.

The programmer can execute circular interpolation in either the absolute (G90) mode or the incremental (G91) mode. Below is one of the word address commands for circular interpolation on a vertical milling machine (Figure 9.12),

Figure 9.11. Machining a square shape based on the code in Table 9.5

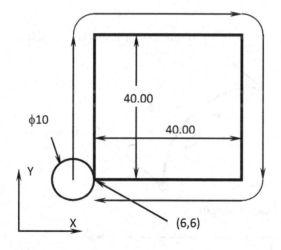

G90 G17 ---------------------------------- Set the XY plane
G01 X1.0 Y5.5 ------------------------ Go to start of arc
G02 X4.5 Y2.0 I0 J-3.5 ---------------- Clockwise circular move

Note that point (I0 J-3.5) specifies the incremental ± *X* and ± *Y* distance from the centre of the tool at the start of the arc (1.0 5.5).

Circular Interpolation via Direct Radius Specification

A programmer also has the option of coding the radius (R) of the circular arc instead of *I*, *J* and *K*. Below is an example (Figure 9.13),

G90 G17 ---------------------------------- Set the XY plane
G1 X1.0 Y5.5 ---------------------------Go to start of arc
G2 X4.5 Y2.0 R3.5 ----------------------Clockwise circular move

Note that R is used if the arc to be cut is smaller than 180°. Otherwise, -R is used.

CONTEMPORARY APPROACH TO PART PROGRAMMING

The previous sections in this chapter explain the basics of CNC programming in such a way that the programming would be done manually. In fact, CNC machine tools have been programmed in several ways. The most basic method and the original way of programming a CNC, is to simply do the necessary geometric calculations with a calculator and write the program directly using G-codes, M-codes, and so on. Figure 9.14 shows an example of such a programming sheet that is used to create the code in Table 9.5. The program is then keyed directly into the controller, i.e. Manual Data Input, or keyed into a computer and transferred

Figure 9.12. Program circular interpolation using an incremental centre

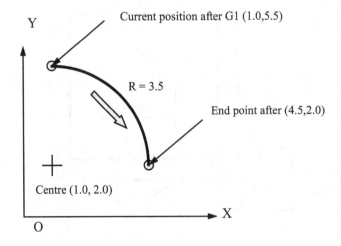

Figure 9.13. Program circular interpolation using a radius

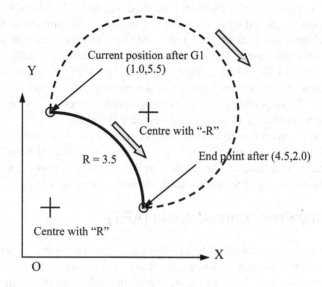

Figure 9.14. NC program work-sheet

						Part ID:	Bracket0281
		NC Program Worksheet				Program ID:	08372
N	*G*	*M*	*X (I)*	*Y (J)*	*Z (K)*	*F (S, T, H, L)*	*Remarks**
0010	G41					S1000, F5	Begin compensation, set feed and speed
0020		M03					Spindle on
0030	G00		X6.00	Y6.00			Move to lower left corner
0040	G01				Z-1.00		Plunge down the tool
0050				Y46.00			Cut to upper left corner
0060			X46.00				Cut to upper right corner
0070				Y6.00			Cut to lower right corner
0080			X6.00				Cut to lower left corner
0090					Z1.00		Lift the tool
0100	G40	M30					End compensation, stop the machine
%							

* -- In the real situation, there will not be remarks as detailed as these ones to the controller via an old-fashioned punched tape or some other medium. Some controllers can be programmed using a "conversational" method offered by the controller vendor. This may involve a more advanced language or hitting buttons with symbols on them.

Specialized languages such as APT and COMPACT II have been available since the sixties and continue to be used. These create a controller-neutral tool path, usually called a CL (Cutter Location) file, which is then converted to a CNC program acceptable to a given CNC control. A separate post-processor is generally used for each CNC control or control family. APT can perform some complex geometric calculations and has provided "modern" features like tool path associativity since its inception.

CAD/CAM systems for design and NC programming became generally available in the late seventies. Like APT, they also create a neutral file (i.e. CL file), although their CL file format is generally far different from traditional APT CL File formats. This section will briefly discuss these tools and formats. The discussions are by no means comprehensive.

Automatically Programmed Tools (APT)

APT programming language is a high-level computer programming language used to generate instructions for numerically controlled machine tools (Ross, 1977, ANSI, 1999).

The first prototype of the APT system was developed at MIT in 1956. The program was developed further by the cooperative efforts of 21 companies, sponsored by the Aerospace Industries Association (AIA) with assistance from MIT. As a result of these efforts, APT II was developed in 1958, and a more effective system, APT III, was made available in 1961. The Illinois Institute of Technology Research Institute (IITRI) was selected to direct the future expansion of the program, and the capabilities of APT are still being continually expanded (Lee, 1999).

APT can be considered as a CAM system based on a special-purpose language. It was created to simplify the task of calculating geometry points that a tool must traverse in space to cut the increasingly complex parts required in the aerospace industry. It was a direct result of the new CNC technology becoming available at that time, and the daunting task that a machinist or engineer faced calculating the movements of the CNC for the complex parts for which it was capable. APT had a large vocabulary of the general processor languages (IBM Corporation, 1986, Bedworth, Henderson & Wolfe, 1991). Unavailability of CAD systems at that time also means that APT had to be able to describe the design geometry in textual form. Therefore, there are three types of data defined in the APT language, part definition, machining specification and machining plan.

Part Definition

This branch of APT codes contains the elements for describing some of the simple geometry in a part to be machined. It is though not intended for an APT program to document the complete geometry of a part. The codes are only used to describe some of the key references and geometry necessary for the purpose of generating the CL data. For example, to describe a hole to be drilled, only a machining reference point and the centre point of the hole are needed.

The part geometry is defined in the Cartesian coordinate system, so coordinates are often used in defining geometry. The general format for geometric statement is,

<symbol> = geometric type / definitional modifiers

Table 9.6 shows some of the common types of APT geometry. It is to be noted that there can be more than one way of defining some of the geometry types.

Defining a Point

A point can be defined in many ways; only six of them are described below. Figure 9.15 shows all the examples of these definitions.

- *Define a point using a Cartesian point:*
  PTA = POINT / 40,10,0

Table 9.6. Typical APT geometry vocabulary words

Geometry type	APT vocabulary word
Point	POINT
Line	LINE
Plane	PLANE
Circle	CIRCLE
Patter (of parts)	PATERN
Cylinder	CYLNDR

Figure 9.15. Some APT point definitions

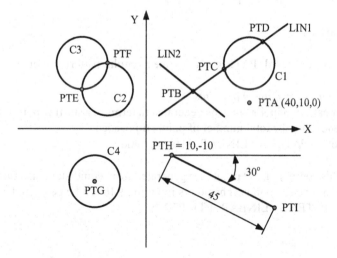

- *Define a point at intersection of two lines:*
  PTB = POINT / INTOF, LIN1, LIN2
  Note that INTOF is an APT modifier word for returning the intersection (point). The two lines, LIN1 and LIN2 would have been defined in advance in the x-y plane.

- *Define a point at intersection of a line and a circle:*
  In order to distinguish the two intersection points, one of the four modifiers can be used, YSMALL, YLARGE, XSMALL, XLARGE. The modifier gives the relative x or y-axis position of the point in relationship to the other possible point.
  PTC = POINT / YSMALL, INTOF, LIN1, C1
  PTC = POINT / XSMALL, INTOF, LIN1, C1
  PTD = POINT / YLARGE, INTOF, LIN1, C1
  PTD = POINT / XLARGE, INTOF, LIN1, C1

- *Define a point at intersection of two circles:*
  Similar to the previous case, we can have the following definitions,
  PTE = POINT / YSMALL, INTOF, C2, C3
  PTE = POINT / XSMALL, INTOF, C2, C3
  PTF = POINT / YLARGE, INTOF, C2, C3
  PTF = POINT / XLARGE, INTOF, C2, C3

- *Define a point to the centre of a circle:*
  Using the APT modifier word CENTER, we can have,
  PTG = POINT / CENTER, C4

- *Define a point using a reference point, radius and angle:*
  If the reference point is defined in the x-y plane as,
  PTH = POINT / 10, -10

  Then, we can define point PTI as,

  PTI = POINT / PTH, RADIUS, 45, ATANGLE, -30

Defining a Pattern

APT uses the pattern word (PATERN) to define a regular pattern of points.

- *Defining a linear pattern of points*
  A linear pattern of points may be generated in terms of a starting point (start), ending point (end), and the total number of points (n) needed,
  <symbol> = PATERN / LINEAR, <start>, <end>, <n>

  Using this command, n-2 points are generated in an equidistant fashion between the <start> and <end> points. The points in Figure 9.16 can be generated by,
  PATA = PATERN / LINEAR, PT1, PT2, 5

Note that the only points that have a symbolic name in the linear pattern are PT1 and PT2. If one of the other 3 points needs to be given a symbol, this can be handled by,

PT3 = POINT / PATA, 3

which gives the third point from the beginning <start>, point PT1, the name PT3 (Figure 9.16).

- *Defining a grid of points*
  A grid of points can be specified using the COPY modifier,
  <symbol> = PATERN / COPY, PATB, ON, PATA

Figure 9.17(a) shows how PAT1 may be attached to PAT2 if the following expression is given,

PAT3 = PATERN/COPY,PAT1,ON,PAT2

Since no further modifier is given, it is assumed that the first point generated in PAT1 be attached to each point, *in sequences,* on PAT2, i.e. (1,2,3), (4,5,6), (7,8,9), (10,11,12), (13,14,15).

If the grid of points represents the centres of 15 holes to be drilled, it should be apparent that drilling in this sequence will not minimize the travel distance. Fortunately, APT has a number of modifiers that one can use to arrange the point as preferred. Modifiers SAME and UNLIKE are the common ones. Modifier SAME placed *after* the pattern designator will force that pattern's sequence numbers to follow their original sequence. If SAME is used for the first pattern, it can be omitted (Figure 9.17(a)).

If we have SAME modifying the second pattern, i.e.

PAT4 = PATERN/COPY,PAT1,ON,PAT2,SAME

Figure 9.16. Forming patterns of points

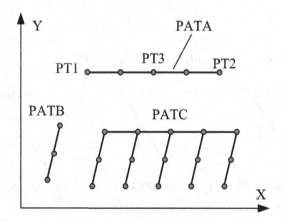

Figure 9.17. Forming patterns of points in different sequence

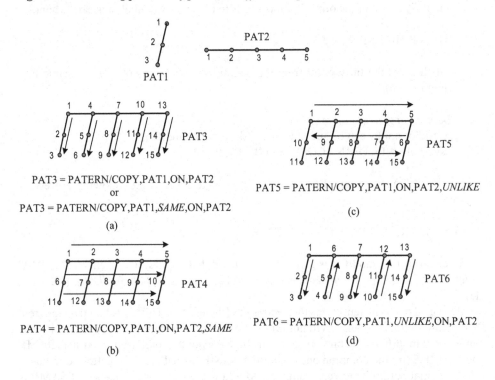

then the sequence of points for the three PAT2s is (1,2,3,4,5), (6,7,8,9,10), (11,12,13,14,15) as shown in Figure 9.17(b). This would probably still not be optimum as far as the tool path is concerned. The UNLIKE modifier can be of assistance in obtaining other sequences. UNLIKE says that the sequence of points will be reversed on the second cycle from that of the first and that the third will be the same as the first (or reversed from the second), and so on. Figure 9.17(c) shows this situation. Similarly, Figure 9.17(d) gives another preferred sequence.

Figure 9.18. Three common ways of defining a line in APT

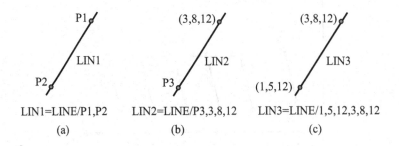

Figure 9.19. APT definitions of lines in terms of a circle and a point

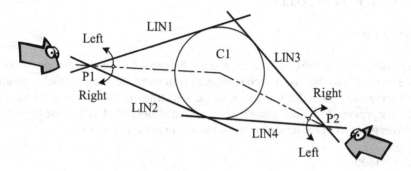

Defining a Line

There are also many ways in which a line can be defined. Figure 9.18 gives three somewhat obvious ways of definitions.

A line can be defined in many ways relative to a circle which has to be defined earlier.

Figure 9.19 shows how a line might be defined based on a single circle and a point. The lines are *tangent* to the circle, and the LEFT or RIGHT modifier indicates whether the line is at the left or right tangent point, depending on how one looks at the circle from the point.

LIN1 = LINE/P1,LEFT,TANTO,C1
LIN2 = LINE/P1,RIGHT,TANTO,C1
LIN3 = LINE/P2,RIGHT,TANTO,C1
LIN4 = LINE/P2,LEFT,TANTO,C1

A line can also be defined with reference to another line plus a given point. Figure 9.20 shows how a line can be defined in terms of a point through which it goes, as well as it is perpendicular or parallel to another line.

Figure 9.20. Some other APT line definitions

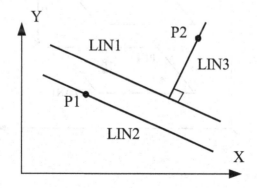

LIN2 = LINE/P1,PARLEL,LIN1
LIN3 = LINE/P2,PERPTO,LIN1

Defining a Plane

Three possible ways to define a plane are given in Figure 9.21. The most common is in terms of three non-collinear points. A second method is in terms of being parallel to an already defined plane and a point that the new plane passes through. The third is in terms of being parallel to a previously defined plane with an axis modifier (YSMALL in the figure) giving the relative position of the *new* plane with respect to the existing one.

P1 = POINT/-5,6.5,4
P2 = POINT/-4,9.5,4
P3 = POINT/-3,4.5,4
P4 = POINT/-6,7.5,8.5
PLAN1 = PLANE/P1,P2,P3
PLAN2 = PLANE/P4,PARLEL,PLAN1
PLAN2 = PLANE/PARLEL,PLAN1,ZLARGE,4.5

Defining a Circle

Figure 9.22 indicates how a circle can be defined in terms of points and/or a line. A circle can be represented by its centre point and radius. The centre point comes first in the definition and may be in terms of a symbolic or actual coordinates. A circle can also be defined in terms of its centre point and a tangent line or point on the circle.

C1 = CIRCLE/2,2,4,1.2
C1 = CIRCLE/CENTER,P1,RADIOUS,1.2
C2 = CIRCLE/CENTER,P2,TANTO,LN1
C3 = CIRCLE/CENTER,P3,P4

Figure 9.21. Some APT plane definitions

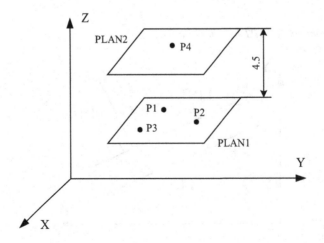

Figure 9.22. Some APT circle definitions

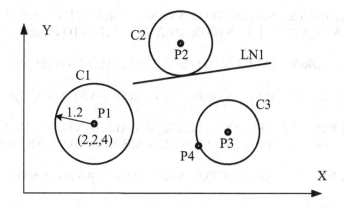

Figure 9.23. APT plane definitions

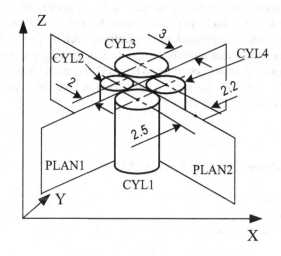

Defining a Cylinder

One of several ways to define a cylinder is as tangent to two planes. As can be seen in Figure 9.23, there are four possible ways this may happen. The definition structure becomes somewhat cumbersome as a few axis modifiers have to be used,

<symbolic> = CYLNDER/<axis modifier>, TANTO,<first plane>,<axis modifier>,TANTO,<second plane>,RADIOUS,<radius value>

The axis modifier depends on the relationship of the cylinder centre point to the tangent point of the plane the modifier proceeds. Examples for the cylinders in Figure 9.23 are,

CYL1 = CYLNDR/XLARGE,TANTO,PLAN1,YSMALL,TANTO,PLAN2,RADIUS,2.5,
or
CYL1 = CYLNDR/YSMALL,TANTO,PLAN2,XLARGE,TANTO,PLAN1,RADIUS,2.5
CYL2 = CYLNDR/XSMALL,TANTO,PLAN1,YSMALL,TANTO,PLAN2,RADIUS,2.0,
or
CYL2 = CYLNDR/YSMALL,TANTO,PLAN2,XSMALL,TANTO,PLAN1,RADIUS,2
.0
CYL3 = CYLNDR/XSMALL,TANTO,PLAN1,YLARGE,TANTO,PLAN2,RADIUS,3.0,
or
CYL3 = CYLNDR/YLARGE,TANTO,PLAN2,XSMALL,TANTO,PLAN1,RADIUS,3.0
CYL4 = CYLNDR/XLARGE,TANTO,PLAN1,YLARGE,TANTO,PLAN2,RADIUS,2.2,
or
CYL4 = CYLNDR/YLARGE,TANTO,PLAN2,XLARGE,TANTO,PLAN1,RADIUS,2.2

Machining Plan

There are three prime operating categories of numerical control, point-to-point, straight cut and contouring. *Point-to-point* refers to operations that require rapid movement to a point followed by, or after, a manufacturing operation at that point. Point-to-point is analogous to pick-and-place in robotic applications. Operations such as this include drilling and punching. *Straight cut* indicates motion along only a major axis; sawing is an application. *Contouring* refers to the complex, continuous removal of material in an application such as turbine-blade machining. APT has certain motion commands that relate to point-to-point and others used primarily for contouring.

Point-to-point

The three commands usually associated with ATP are:

FROM/<point location>
GOTO/<point location>
GODLTA/<coordinate increments>

<point location> may be given in terms of x, y, and z coordinates, or it may be a previously defined symbol. FROM/ denotes that the point location is a starting point for the tool, with the end of the tool being at that point. Motion from the starting point to the desired location is straight-line. GOTO/ refers to a rapid, straight-line move to the point location indicated, e.g. a point at which a drilling operation is to occur. GODLTA/ commands that the tool be moved an incremental distance from the current position. For example,

GODLTA/0,0,4

will cause the tool to be moved 4 mm in the z direction in a straight-line.

Figure 9.24 shows a workpiece on which three holes are to be drilled. The home point P0, has a 2 value for z to allow for clearance of the tool when it approaches the workpiece (the top surface has z = 0). Also, the three points as the centres of the holes will be given z-axis values of 2 for the same reason:

Figure 9.24. Hole-drilling operations

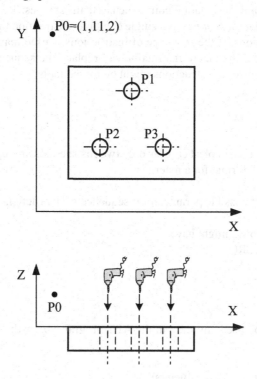

P1 = POINT/6.0,7.5,2.0
P2 = POINT/4.0,4.0,2.0
P3 = POINT/8.0,4.0,2.0

The motion statements to allow drilling the three holes through the 1.5mm-thick plate could be,

FROM/P0
GOTO/P1
GODLTA/0,0,-5.0
GODLTA/0,0,+5.0
GOTO/P2
GODLTA/0,0,-5.0
GODLTA/0,0,+5.0
GOTO/P3
GODLTA/0,0,-5.0
GODLTA/0,0,+5.0
GOTO/P0

The depth of motion is set to 5.0 to allow for the tool being 2.0 above the workpiece at the start of drilling as well as to ensure that the tool clears the bottom of the workpiece.

It is obvious that the use of looping of a subroutine would greatly facilitate point-to-point motion with many designation points such as drilling holes. This can be done by the use of *looping* and *macro*. A *macro* is a single computer instruction that stands for a given sequence of instructions. If the sequence of instructions is used many times in different sections of a program, the macro instruction can replace the sequence in each program section. Such a sequence of instructions might be for example,

```
GODLTA/0,0,-5.0
GODLTA/0,0,+5.0
```

This is obviously the simplest case, as only two instructions are replaced by *one* macro instruction. The APT format for a macro is:

```
<name> = MACRO/<possible parameters><sequence of instructions>
TERMAC
```
For our simple macro we might have,
```
DRILLHOLE = MACRO
GODLTA/0,0,-5.0
GODLTA/0,0,+5.0
TERMAC
```

The macro can be used any time in the APT program *(after* the MACRO is defined) by inserting,

```
CALL macro name (, list of parameters)
```
In our case this would be,
```
CALL DRILLHOLE
```

The original APT program for drilling the three holes in Figure 9.24 can therefore be written as,

```
P0 = POINT/1,11,2
DRILLHOLE = MACRO/DX,DY,DZ
GODLTA/DX,DY,0
GODLTA/0,0, -DZ
GODLTA/0,0, +DZ
TERMAC
FROM/P0
CALL DRILLHOLE/DX=2.0,DY=-3.5,DZ=5.0
CALL DRILLHOLE/DX=-2.0,DY=-3.5,DZ=5.0
CALL DRILLHOLE/DX=4.0,DY=0,DZ=5.0
GOTO/P0
```

The use of loops in APT can also allow one to position a tool to a large number of points with efficient programming. In a loop, commands such as IF and JUMPTO can also be used.

Contouring

More often than not, the workpiece to be cut requires the machining operation to follow some complex geometry, be it a 3D curve or surface. This can be a very complicated issue. This section explains the concept of contouring commands in APT, but not the programming method. Unlike the point-to-point commands GOTO/, FROM/, and GODLTA/ that all force straight-line motions from one position to the next, contouring is of course not restricted to such gross limitations on motion. As a result, APT requires that three surfaces be defined at all times to control tool movement. They are Part surface, Drive surface and Check surface.

Part surface is the surface on which the *end* of the tool is riding. Often, this is a hypothetical surface such as a plane lying some distance below the surface of the workpiece. Drive surface is the surface against which the edge of the tool rides; typically this is the actual part edge being cut by a milling tool. Check surface defines a surface at which the current tool motion is to stop. All three surfaces are shown schematically in Figure 9.25.

Machining Specifications

While APT has simplified the programming tasks in great deal, providing a standard tool for all CNC programs is another reason for APT to exist. However, the truth is that every CNC machine is different in many different ways. It may be that the controller is of a preparatory type; the cutters on the machine tool are handled differently and the spindles have differing power rating. As a result, a so-called post-processing step is needed so that an ATP program can be used on a particular CNC machine. Some of the typical post-processor commands are,

Figure 9.25. Three APT surfaces during contouring

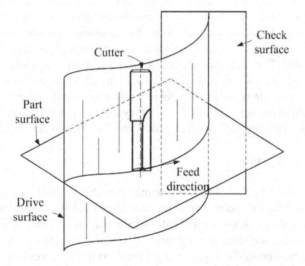

MACHIN/, COOLNT/, FEDRAT/, SPINDL/, TURRET/ and END.

- MACHIN/ is used to specify the machine tool and call the post-processor for that tool. For example, "MACHIN/ DRILL, 2" may specify the second NC drill in the shop.
- COOLNT/ allows the coolant fluid to be turned on or off. Typical modifiers to allow this to happen are,

  COOLNT/ MIST
  COOLNT/ FLOOD
  COOLNT/ OFF

- FEDRAT/ specifies the feed-rate of a cutting motion in mm per minute, e.g. FEDRAT/ 60.
- SPINDL/ gives the spindle rotation speed in revolutions per minute, e.g. SPINDL/ 2000.
- TURRET/ can be used to call a specific tool from an automatic tool changer, e.g. TURRET/ 8. There are modifications that allow for a tool identification to be specified as well as a tool holder location.

APT Programs: CL files

APT is sometimes called a compiler or an assembler. It is effectively a complex translator or processor. An APT program refers to an NC program written in the APT language, and often called Cutter Location (CL) data file, or APT CL file. An APT CL file is meant to be neutral because it was not formatted for any particular machine tool. There is though no single standard CL file format, and there is no single standard even for CL file contents.

The first generation APT translators handle APT programs in roughly four steps. Its translation module reads an APT program and builds tables containing the part geometry information. It verifies syntax and lists the program and geometry information if requested. The part geometry is now in canonical form. Its calculation module then takes this output and computes the tool path geometry. Tool offsets can be applied here. A preliminary CL file is then created. The third module allows users to modify and expand the preliminary CL file to arrive at a final version of the CL file. This CL listing may also be printed. The post-processing module is used to control any post-processing activities.

There are different versions of CL files; they all fall into three categories, traditional binary CL files, "full-fledged" ASCII CL files and CAD/CAM ASCII CL files.

Traditional APT CL files

A binary traditional APT CL file is not human readable without translating from an internal integer and floating point format into numbers and letters. The data itself is similar to other APT CL files, but some more information may be included, especially regarding circles. If a machine tool does not support circular interpolation (that is, has no G2 or G3 command), the post-processor must generate the short linear moves made to form the arcs. With a traditional APT CL file, this would not be necessary. For each arc, the APT CL file would contain a *type 3000* record containing the coordinates of the centre and the tool axis vector (angle), the radius, as well as the linear moves needed to make the arc if they are needed. For each actual move generated by a motion statement, a *type 5000* record would be present containing all points necessary to complete the motion.

For the statement reading GOTO/ -2.0, 1.2, 4.0 in a CL file (which would probably result in G0 X-2.0 Y1.2 Z4.0) the *type* 5000 record would contain the following,

3 5000 3 bb 0 -2.0 1.2 4.0

where,

3 -- Record number,
5000 -- Record type,
3 -- Code for the first record (also the only record in this case) in this move,
bb -- Geometry name used to create motion - blank in this case,
0 -- Subscript applied to name, if any,
-2.0 -- X
1.2 -- Y
4.0 -- Z

"Full-fledged" ASCII APT CL files

Since the APT language can define both geometry and tool motion data, a full-fledged CL file will also contain the geometry definition and motion data. Since it is of ASCII format it is human-readable.

The main benefit of having a full-fledged CL file is that tool path associativity can be had with the geometry concerned. Thus, changing a few values in geometry definitions (e.g. in a CIRCLE/ statement) can lead to changes made in tool path to reflect the geometry change. This tool path associativity has been a characteristic of APT since its inception and allows very simple but powerful macros to be written. These are especially useful for repetitive turning, drilling, and point to point operations. Such a useful feature later becomes not required as the contemporary CAD/CAM systems can do a much better job in relating tool path with to its driving geometry.

CAD/CAM ASCII APT CL files

CAD/CAM (or even CAM) systems now have taken over the job of manipulating almost any tricky geometry possible for machining purposes. There is therefore no good reason to have geometry described in an APT CL file. This type of CL file usually consists of only APT statements, i.e. mainly of post-processor commands such as linear moves (GOTO/ X,Y,Z) and arcs. This type of APT CL file is sometimes called "dumb APT". Since they are still of APT format, they can be processed by APT (creating yet another CL file) or in many cases, directly by a post-processor.

The CL files generated by a CAD/CAM system Processors such as APT eliminated much of the drudgery in preparing to machine complex parts in the days when CAM systems were non-existent or had limited functionalities. With today's CAD/CAM systems, design data can be easily used to generate machining information, and APT starts to fade away.

CAD/CAM Approach

In spite of APT's geometry description functionality, it would be impossible to produce a precise program to cut parts as complex as an engine blocs and cylinder head as shown in Figure 9.26.

Thanks to the rapid development of CAD/CAM software, this task of part programming is made much simpler. CAD/CAM systems enable translating a representation of the geometry of a component along with other related technological information first into a specification for the operations to be carried out by the machine tool, and then into a program of instructions for the controller.

Nowadays, comprehensive CAD/CAM packages such as Pro/Engineer®, SolidWorks® and Catia® can prepare the part program directly from a CAD part model. Figure 9.27 shows a typical procedure in a CAD/CAM system that brings the design and manufacturing under the same roof. The CAD/CAM approach has a number of advantages, of which the most important is the removal of the need to encode the part geometry and the tool motion manually. This eliminates the risk of error in interpreting or transcribing the geometry, and greatly reduces the time taken in tool-path data preparation. CAD/CAM also brings additional benefits to part programming through the use of interactive graphics for program editing and verification. It can provide facilities to,

- display the programmed motion of the cutter with respect to the workpiece (usually by means of a graphical representation of the cutter), which allows visual verification of the program; and
- interactively edit a tool path with the addition of tool moves, standard cycles and perhaps APT MACROS (or the equivalent from other languages).

The approach to part programming using CAD/CAM is thus broadly as follows:

- The aspects of the part geometry that are important for machining purposes, which are also known as machining features, are identified; geometry may be edited, or additional geometry added to define boundaries for the tool motion.

Figure 9.26. The "nightmare" for a CNC manual programmer

 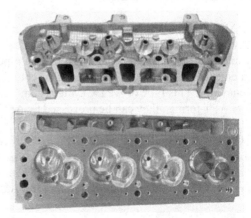

- Machine tools and cutting tools are defined in terms of their machinabilities and technological data.
- The desired sequence of machining operations is identified and the NC tool paths are defined (interactively) for the machining operations.
- The tool motion is displayed and may be edited, and MACRO commands or other details may be added for particular machining cycles or operations.
- A cutter location data (CL Data) file and/or an APT file are then produced.
- The CL Data file is post-processed to machine control data, also known as G-code, which is then used to drive the machine tool.

An APT processor is often used as one of the "back ends" for a CAD/CAM system which produces an APT source program (as shown in Figure 9.27). This CL file can be run through an APT translator. This is done for several reasons.

- **Allows use of existing post-processors** - Many companies used APT before. Now, they are migrating to using a CAD/CAM system. Yet, they still wish to retain their investment in post-processors.

Figure 9.27. From product design and manufacturing

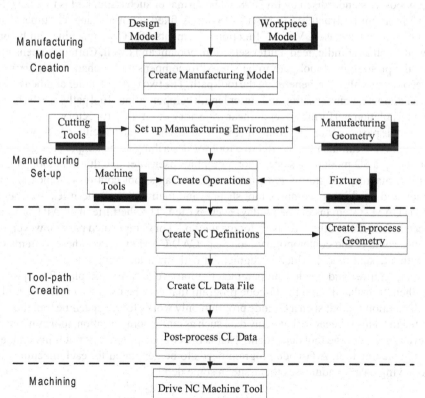

- **Allows use of APT features:** Some earlier CAD/CAM systems had limited or no ability to transform or to repeat portions of a tool path. For example, there was no way to drill a hole and then repeat that operation 10 times to create a bolt hole pattern. Instead, they would repeat the operation using APT INDEX/ and COPY/ statements which were inserted automatically into the output data.
- **Intelligent handling of arcs:** Some CAD/CAM systems did not know how the target machine tool handles circular interpolation. This often means that arcs are produced as a series of short linear moves, especially if not in the XY plane. APT does not know either but it can put *both* the arc definition and the short linear moves into the same CL file and lets the post-processor decide what to do. As CAD/CAM systems improve, this appears to be less of a problem.
- **Simpler post-processor library:** By using APT as a link to the post-processor, a company can use a single post-processor per machine tool, even if multiple CAD/CAM systems are in use.

CONCLUSION

When the designed product is produced using a CNC machine tool, the machine tool controller needs explicit instructions describing the type and order of individual steps required to perform machining task. CNC machine tools are programmed using G-code format which has been loosely standardised by ISO 6983. The format of such a standard is that the CNC machine program is structured in blocks of data. A fixed set of alphabetic, numeric and special characters are used. Various functional elements of a CNC machine can be programmed, such as spindle, feed, cutter selection, coolant and dwell. Cutter compensation enables the programmed tool-path to be altered to compensate for changes occurring to cutter geometry without re-generating the tool-path. The two types of cutter compensations are cutter diameter compensation and cutter length compensation. Tool paths are the results of the interpolation performed over a linear trajectory or circular trajectory.

For simple parts, manual programming is possible. One could use either APT or G-code to program. APT can also be an effective tool for describing some simple part geometry without using a 3D modelling system nor a graphics user interface. It offers tool path associativity, macros, transformations, pocketing, five axis tool control, complex surface definition and machining, complex tool shapes, and many other modern features before any CAD/CAM system (as defined today) even existed. The shelf life of an APT program far exceeds that of any other archival storage method. For complicated parts however, one has to use some of the contemporary tools, e.g. CAD/CAM systems. These systems can work with a design model, which is augmented with manufacturing information such as machining features and machining parameters to arrive at a process plan. This process plan is then "translated" into the G-code program that is to be used on a machine tool. It is worth mentioning that such a G-code program only works for the machine tool that was generated for. This is because that many data such as cutter compensation, tool number and fixed cycle, are machine tool dependent. That is the G-code program is not transferable to a second machine tool. A G-code program needs to be generated for each machine tool. The following chapter addresses this issue in some depth.

REFERENCES

ANSI INCITS 37. (1999). *Programming Language APT* (revision, re-designation and consolidation of ANSI X3.37-1995, ANSI X3.37-1995/AM 2-1998, ANSI X3.37-1995/AM 1-1998) (formerly ANSI NCITS 37-1999). Washington, DC. Headquarters: ANSI.

Bedworth, D. D., Henderson, M. R., & Wolfe, P. M. (1991). *Computer-Integrated Design and Manufacturing*, Columbus, OH 43272, USA: McGraw-Hill, Inc.

IBM Corporation. (1986). *System/370 Automatically Programming Tool – Advanced Contouring Numerical Control Processor: Program Reference Manual* (Program Number 6740-M53), 4th ed. White Plains, NY: IBM Corporation.

ISO 6983-1. (1982). *Numerical control of machines – Program format and definition of address words – Part 1: Data format for positioning, line motion and contouring control systems*. Geneva, Switzerland: International Organisation for Standardisation (ISO).

Lee, K. (1999). *Principles of CAD/CAM/CAE systems*. USA: Addison Wesley Longman, Inc.

Quesada, R. (2005). *Computer Numerical Control: Machining and Turning Centres*. Upper Saddle River, New Jersey, Columbus, Ohio, USA: Pearson Prentice Hall,

Ross, D. T. (1977). Origins of the APT Language for Automatically Programmed Tools. In 1981. R.L. Wexelblat (Ed.) *History of Programming Languages*, (pp. 279-367). New York: Academic Press.

Section II
Integration and Implementations

Chapter X
Integration of CAD / CAPP / CAM / CNC

ABSTRACT

Technologies concerning computer-aided design, process planning, manufacturing and numerical control, have matured to a point that commercialized software solutions and industrial systems can be acquired readily. These solutions or systems are, however, not necessarily connected in a seamless way, that is they are not fiintegrated. The term "islands of automation" has been used to describe these disconnected groups of systems with no obvious integration points other than the end user. As the engineering businesses are increasingly being run in a more globalized fashion, these islands of automation need to be connected to better suit and serve the collaborative and distributed environment. It is evident that the businesses are struggling with this integration strategy at a number of levels other than the underlying technology, including CAD, CAPP, CAM, and CNC for example. In some cases, where integration does not exist among these computer-aided solutions, promising product technologies may come to a sudden halt against these barriers.

The previous chapters have focused on these individual computer-aided solutions, e.g. CAD, CAPP, CAM, CNC, and feature technologies. Some localized integration such as integrated feature technology has been studied. The following chapters, will in particular, look at the integration issues, technologies, and solutions. This chapter starts with a general description of traditional CAD, CAPP, CAM, and CNC integration models. This is followed by an industry case study showcasing how a proprietary CAD/CAM can be used to achieve centralized integration. To illustrate CAM/CNC integration, three different efforts are mentioned. They are APT, BCL (Binary Cutter Location, (EIA/ANSI, 1992)), BNCL (Base Numerical Control Language, (Fortin, Chatelain & Rivest, 2004)) and use of Haskell language for CNC programming (Arroyo, Ochoa, Silva & Vidal, 2004).

MODELS OF INTEGRATING CAD/CAPP/CAM/CNC

In the effort to achieve CAD/CAPP/CAM/CNC integration, there have been two types of traditional models in use, centralized model (Model A) and collaborative model (Model B) (Xu & Mao, 2004). In a centralized model, manufacturing activities occur within a single manufacturer or a few manufacturers that have similar information infrastructure. In this model, proprietary data formats are commonly used. In a collaborative model, a middle tier is added using for example a neutral data exchange format. As such, collaborative activities in the manufacturing environment become easier. Figure 10.1 illustrates the data flows in these two models (Xu, 2006).

In Model A, both CAD and CAM systems use the same proprietary data format. Over the years, CAD/CAM system vendors have been successful in developing different proprietary data formats to support their systems throughout design and manufacturing processes. The benefits of this model are obvious. CAD and CAM systems are unified by the same data format so that data incompatibilities between them are eliminated. Furthermore, since there is no data-transferring barrier, system vendors have more freedom to model information. In addition to pure geometry, integrated CAD/CAM systems can cater for other activities ranging from design to NC programming. Some of such systems include Pro/E® (with Pro/NC®), Catia® and UGS.

A CASE STUDY OF INTEGRATING CAD/CAPP/CAM

This section presents a case study that highlights an integrated CAD/CAPP/CAM environment for a manufacturing company (Xu & Duhovic, 2004). It represents a classical example of how companies can use today's CAD/CAM systems to support a centralized integration model as shown in Figure 10.1.

Concurrent Product Modelling in a CAD/CAM System

The product in this case study is a small version of household refrigerator, usually mounted inside a cupboard. To allow for correct placement and adjustment, two foot levelling pads are fixed on the floor of the cupboard, into which the front levelling feet of the refrigerator sit (Figure 10.2). The case study starts from part design to all the down-stream activities related to manufacture of the part.

The foot levelling pad is designed using a 3D CAD/CAM system, i.e. Pro/Engineer®. Being a thermoplastic product, the pad is mass-produced using the injection moulding process. Tooling therefore becomes an important part of the entire manufacturing process. Design of the tooling is also carried out within the same CAD/CAM system, but using an additional module called Pro/MOLDESIGN®. The complete tooling model consists of the mould bases, insert core, insert cavity (within the top mould base), foot levelling pad and a number of small inserts (Figure 10.3). Most of the tooling components are machined on a CNC milling machine. Process planning and NC code generation are carried out within Pro/NC®, another integrated module of Pro/Engineer®.

A narrow deep circular slot, which corresponds to a small circular protrusion on the foot levelling pad (Figure 10.4) requires an EDM to produce. The tool used on the EDM

Figure 10.1. Two traditional models of integrating CAD/CAPP/CAM/CNC

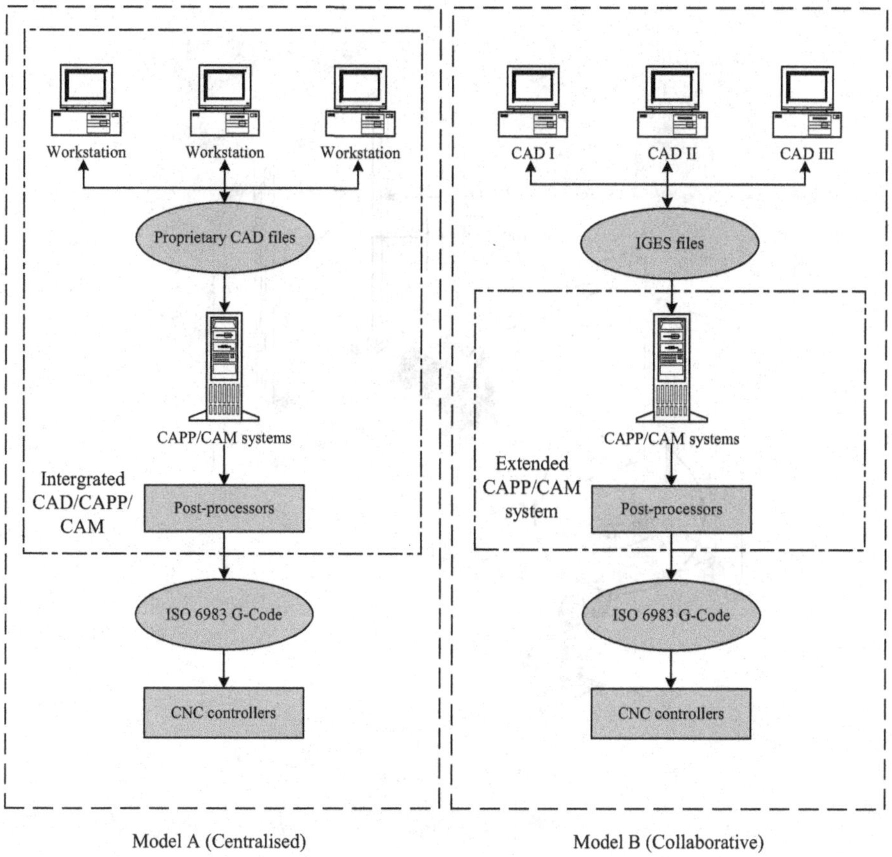

Model A (Centralised)   Model B (Collaborative)

machine is an electrode as shown in Figure 10.4, and is usually made from highly conductive materials such as graphite and copper.

Once again, design of the electrode is carried out in the same CAD/CAM system. Geometric modelling of the electrode part is done with reference to the corresponding faces on the insert core. This reference is deemed important as will be demonstrated later for the provision of a concurrent engineering environment. Electrode manufacturing is carried out on a high-speed CNC mill and its process planning and NC programming are also carried out in the Pro/NC® module.

A Bird's-Eye View of the Case Study

Figure 10.5 shows an overview of the entire manufacturing process concerning production of the foot levelling pad. The three highlighted routes are (1) Production; (2) Design information and (3) Manufacturing information. The Production route illustrates a sequence of different manufacturing activities on the shop-floor for the final production of the foot levelling pad. The Design information route describes the design activities for the foot levelling

Figure 10.2. The built-in type of refrigerator and its levelling assembly.   ©2004 IJEE for TEMPUS Publications, used with permission.

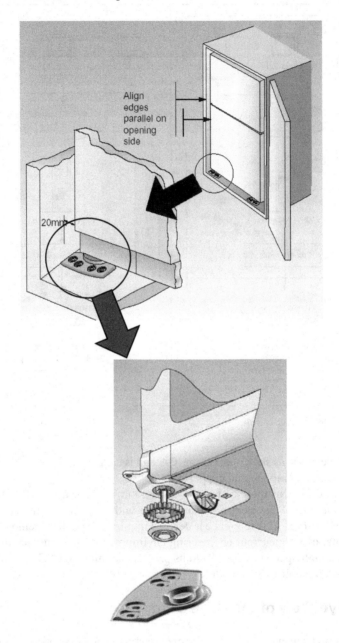

Figure 10.3. The tooling assembly ©2004 IJEE for TEMPUS Publications, used with permission.

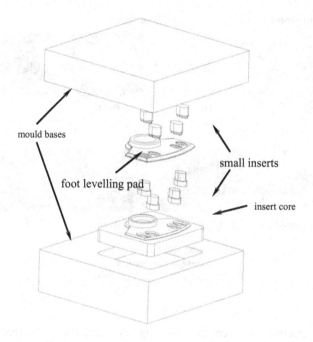

Figure 10.4. Mould insert core and the required electrode ©2004 IJEE for TEMPUS Publications, used with permission.

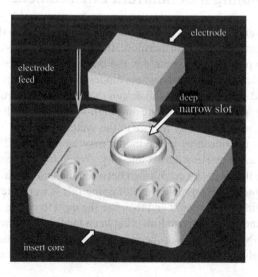

Figure 10.5. Design and manufacturing information flow ©2004 IJEE for TEMPUS Publications, used with permission.

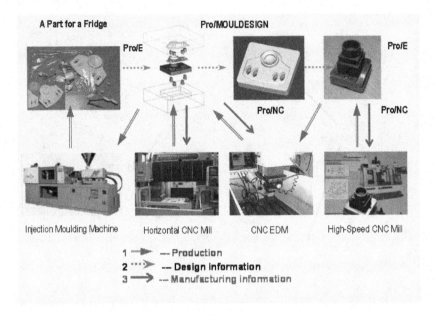

pad, tooling and electrode, whereby both Pro/Engineer® and Pro/MOLDESIGN® are used. The information flow from design to manufacturing follows the Manufacturing information route, primarily managed by the Pro/NC® module. It is worth noting that both design and manufacturing information is effectively managed by the same CAD/CAM system on a single database. Hence, the associativity among the different design and manufacturing models is guaranteed, which enables an integrated environment.

CAD/CAM Enabling a Concurrent Environment

Since design and manufacturing information resides in a common database, changes can be managed easily and quickly. Furthermore, these changes are bi-directional. A change made to the design part by a designer, e.g. the diameter of the seat on the foot levelling pad, can be propagated throughout the whole model chain all the way to the NC commands generated for mould manufacturing, the design model of the electrode part, the NC commands generated for electrode machining on a high-speed CNC mill and etc. This is made possible thanks to the associativity feature in the system.

Associativity or relationships in the model may be built in different ways. Making intended reference to an existing part is one way. When the electrode part is being modelled, it is desirable that links be established between the features in the tooling and those of the electrode. One of the possible ways of doing this is to create a surface quilt based on the faces belonging to the mould and then use the quilt to define the protrusion feature on the electrode. Another important link is between the foot levelling pad and the moulds. In Pro/MOLDESIGN®, the shape of the moulds is directly generated from a "reference" part that is effectively a duplicate of the foot levelling pad. Therefore, changes to the foot levelling pad, will be propagated through to the subsequent models and NC programs, i.e. the geometry on the moulds, electrode part and the NC programs for machining the moulds and the electrode part. Because of the associativity feature in the system, there is little revision work to carry out other than "re-generating" all the subsequent models based on the re-designed product model.

In brief, associativity makes it possible for different activities concerning manufacture of a part to happen simultaneously instead of sequentially. Tooling and electrode design, and process planning for tooling and electrodes can all commence at the early stage of the part design. Hence, the product development cycle time is shortened. Furthermore, product re-design at a later stage can be made less arduous and error-free.

For an injection-moulded part, Plastic Advisor in Pro/Engineer® allows users to check manufacturability of the foot levelling pad without the need for expertise in plastics processing. This is done by on-screen animations of mould filling. Pro/MOLDESIGN® provides some common tools for creating, modifying and analysing the mould components and assemblies, and also quickly updating them to the changes in the design model. Shrinkage can be applied corresponding to the design part material, geometry and moulding conditions. Once the basic mould assembly is completed, it can be populated with standard components such as the mould base, ejector pins, sprue bushings, screws, fittings and other components creating corresponding clearance holes. The system can advise users about how to best define feasible parting surface(s) and then split the workpiece using these surfaces. The module can also check interference of components during mould opening. To manufacture the moulds, insert core and electrode, Pro/NC® is used for process planning and NC machine data generation.

Reflections

The above case study provides a good example of contemporary CAD/CAM systems that can effectively integrate activities such as design and manufacturing. It is a typical case of Model A as shown in Figure 10.1. These systems are however not without problems. They assume that data exchanges during a product life cycle only occur within one manufacturer or among a few manufacturers that implement the same CAD/CAM system. When more manufacturers are involved in the product life cycle, it is hard, if not impossible, to unify those manufacturers with a specific proprietary data format. Therefore, the structure represented by Model A is deemed unfit for collaborative manufacturing due to data incompatibility.

Model B aims to solve this problem by using exchangeable neutral data formats such as IGES (1980). Neutral data formats provide a middle tier to connect CAD and CAM systems. With the help of neutral data formats, Model B creates a collaborative manufacturing environment and makes the design data exchange possible for large projects at the international level.

LIMITED EFFORTS TO INTEGRATE CAM AND CNC

The integration as shown in both Models A and B (Figure 10.1) terminates at the point when an NC code is generated. This NC code is usually produced by a built-in post-processor. This section discusses this problem as well as some "partial" solutions.

Post-Processor: A Source of Vexation

Post-processors are the software programs that "customize" a file of tool path data and related machine instructions for a particular machine tool. Once an NC program has been post-processed, it can be used to produce parts on the designated machine.

The same program may or may not be usable at other machine tools unless the machines are identical -- same configuration, same control unit, same home position, same clearance planes, same set of tools fitted and so on. This is rarely the case for most workshops since they are likely to have a variety of equipment from a variety of machine tool builders and CNC unit suppliers.

It is more than likely that a company will purchase machines and/or control units over a period of time. Yet, these machines are often intended to perform similar or same tasks. However, machines may be equipped with a variety of controls, each requiring its own post-processor. The greater the number of post-processors a shop must have, the greater the magnitude of associated problems.

Writing a post-processor is also a non-trivial task. Machine and control manuals must be digested. Great care must be taken to include a user's specific programming standards, such as start and end protocols, tool change sequences, and so on. Often, the post-processor writer must contact the machine tool builder and/or control manufacturer for specifics to a system as delivered to the end user. In fact, most CAD/CAM users probably underestimate the importance of acquiring post-processors when they order a new system. Whereas customer training on a new system may take several weeks, it may be several months before the necessary post-processors are received, tested and proved. Some machine tool builders are more responsive than others to such requests. The same is true of control manufacturers. The prompt delivery of a post-processor for a newly-introduced model of machine tool is often delayed because the CAD/CAM vendor is at the mercy of the machine tool builder or control manufacturer.

Furthermore, because it is virtually impossible for any CAD/CAM company to have all of these target machine and control combinations at its disposal, the end user is the one who must "check out" or exercise all of the functionality that is expected from the post-processor. This could mean several iterations before a post-processor is acceptable to the user. All of this valuable machine time is lost to the user. It is highly possible that a post-processor could be installed at a user site for several months before each and every feature has been tested.

Challenges

Most programming departments must have several post-processors to properly prepare an NC program for whichever machine tool will be producing the workpieces. The programming departments at larger shops may have fifty or sixty different post-processors to support a hundred NC machine tools. A small job shop may have a unique post-processor for every one of its machines.

The real challenges in the NC codes generated by the post-processor relate to the aspects of the code, semantics and syntax. The semantics-related problem is to do with the content of the code, or rather the lack of it. The NC codes (i.e. G-codes) carry little geometric information about the design model. Because of this, a truly integrated environment for CAD/CAPP/CAM/CNC is not possible. Every single change made to the design model requires re-production (or re-post-processing) of the NC codes. The syntax-related problem is to do with standardization of the syntax, or rather the lack of it. As a result of lack of standardization, proliferation of post-processors creates problems both on the shop-floor and in NC programming. The trend to computer-integrated manufacturing, which is driven by the pressures of global competition, only intensifies the difficulties created by this lack of standardization.

There have been some efforts to alleviate the problems. An early effort with APT language (ANSI INCITS 37, 1999) is to both standardize NC programming tools (to solve the syntax-related problem) and provide some level of associativity between the geometry part of a workpiece and its tool path (to solve the semantics-related problem). To solve the syntax-related problem, Binary Cutter Location (EIA/ANSI, 1992) and Base Numerical Control Language (Fortin, Chatelain & Rivest, 2004) have also been developed. Some other languages have been used to generate CNC programs, e.g. AutoLISP (Carr & Holt, 1998, Rawls & Hagen, 1998) and Haskell (Jones, 2003). The latter is discussed in this section, too.

The APT Effort

An early effort to standardize NC programming tools and languages is through APT (see Chapter IX for a detailed account for APT). APT was intended to be a general purpose language, not just oriented towards one type of machine tool or one manufacturer. It was therefore designed to create a machine tool independent, generic NC program called a Cutter Location file. The CL file is then read and processed by a post-processor supplied by someone with a good knowledge of the specific machine tool and its requirements and limitations.

The basic APT processor is public domain code and the language rigidly defined by an ANSI standard. Most APT processors were written in FORTRAN and were reasonably computer and operating system independent. The biggest issue, however, was post-processors. The APT designers did not want to have to support every machine tool available, yet they could not expect the tool companies and others to supply post-processors that supported every variety of APT CL file. Although the CL file format was similar from APT vendor to vendor, they were tailored to individual computer system characteristics. Therefore, they created a set of programming subroutines (may be called Application Programming Interfaces, APIs for short) that would insulate the post-processor from the actual CL file format. APT post-processors traditionally do not read the CL file directly, but use the APIs to access the CL data. This method lets a single post-processor function with multiple APT systems, operating systems, and computers and has allowed many post-processors written for mainframes run on PCs with only minor changes.

The associativity in a full-fledged ASCII APT CL file has realized some level of integration between the geometry to be made and its tool path. This is made possible by having both the geometry definition and tool path definition included in a APT file as shown in the previous section. Changing a few values in some types of geometry definitions (e.g. in a CIRCLE/ statement) will lead to changes in its tool path so as to reflect the geometry change. This tool path associativity allows simple but powerful macros to be written. This is the first attempt to have geometry drive the machining process.

The BCL Effort

BCL is the numerical control data format standard initiated by North American Rockwell in the mid-1970's, and later became EIA Standard RS-494 in 1983. It has a number of names associated to it, "Binary Centre Line", "Binary Cutter Location" and "Basic Control Language" to name a few. At revision "B" level the standard was also adopted by the American National Standards Institute (ANSI) and was renamed EIA/ANSI-494. This revision still supported both binary and ASCII data transfer. Revision "C" has dropped binary and now only supports ASCII data exchange which is more in line with today's data exchange technology.

The purpose of BCL was to provide part program compatibility across a variety of NC machines and to fulfil industry's need for a "neutral" NC part program language. The work was prompted by the complexity of systems and lack of standardization experienced at North American Rockwell, Los Angeles Division, where seven different types of NCs and 23 post processors had to be used to create part programs for 31 NC machines. The concept of BCL is to move the post-processor function out of the computer room into the NC unit and provide a standard set of rules for handling and transmitting part program data. This permits generic APT CL data from section III of an APT processor to be formatted into a 32 bit binary exchange format for transferring to an NC machine having the BCL input feature. With the post-processor function embedded in the NC unit, the part program can be generic and thus compatible for machines within a given class such as milling or turning.

The underpinning principle is that data used as input to the machine tool remains oriented to the part coordinate system, not to the coordinate system of the machine tool. Use of the BCL format requires that the control unit itself be equipped to perform all machine-geometry dependent functions, which may have been previously performed by a post-processor.

The BCL converter in a BCL-enabled NC machine tool is a part-oriented post-processing program, which converts the contents of a CL file to the BCL format file. The BCL format represents NC machining input data as a series of records that are groups of 32-bit binary integer words. It performs no machine-dependent functions such as orienting data to the origin of the machine's coordinate system or computing tool length values. The calculations for machine coordinate data and tool length compensation are performed "on the fly" in the BCL control unit during program execution. Therefore, as long as a workpiece can be machined with a particular machine/control combination, the NC data files are interchangeable between different BCL machines. An idle five-axis machine with BCL capability can be utilized to offset a priority job that is overloading a three-axis BCL machine. This flexibility would be impossible without the exchangeability of NC programs in BCL.

The BCL format was originally developed for use with the APT NC processor. It is designed to utilize the integer codes defined for major and minor words from the CL data files. All of the post-processor commands are represented as integer codes.

An NC program is literally the link between design and manufacturing, realising some low-level integration for design and manufacturing. The NC program is ultimately how designers and engineers convey their intent to the shop-floor. The NC program represents a description of the production process whereby an abstract set of dimensional data and feature characteristics takes material form as a workpiece. Hence, the best way to look at an NC program is from two points of view at once--from where it originates and from where it is executed. To a CAD/CAM system user, the NC program is output. To the shop-floor, it is input to the machine tool.

Most discussions of BCL have concentrated on its significance to the shop-floor. BCL is a viable approach to creating neutral machine tool input. At the same time, it is also a viable approach to creating neutral CAD/CAM output. Because it works both ways at the same time, BCL brings CAD/CAM and the shop-floor closer together by offering benefits mutually attractive to both. The basic-level integration enables designers, engineers, NC programmers, production supervisors and machine operators, to work together as a single, coherent, flexible, profit-making team.

The BNCL Effort

Base Numerical Control Language (BNCL) is based on a low-level simple instruction set-like approach (Fortin, Chatelain & Rivest, 2004). The entire architecture is designed around two concepts -- the BNCL Virtual Machine (BVM) and the BNCL Virtual Hardware (BVH). The former acts as a virtual microprocessor and the latter is an abstraction of the machine tool.

The BNCL architecture is proposed to improve information flow between CAM and CNC through a low-level approach to machine control. According to Fortin, Chatelain & Rivest (2004), there are two categories of computer languages, high-level and low-level languages (Figure 10.6). High-level languages offer a great deal of abstraction, and are further away from any direct interaction with a machine. High-level languages designed for machining operations can therefore solve the problem of portability, and offer an abstraction of the entire machining process. Among these machining languages are BCL and STEP-NC[1](ISO 14649-1, 2004). Low-level languages on the other hand, attempt to emulate the functions of the instruction set of a microprocessor. They form the basis of what is called a low-level architecture. This approach has the advantage of abstracting only the particularities of each machine, not the entire machining process. Any higher-level construct can be built on top of it, and any machining process can also be used or easily modified. The STEP-NC standard is a good example of a high-level structure that can be built on top of this kind of architecture. BNCL has been developed as a low-level language. It is a new architecture designed with machine control in mind. This language mimics the binary syntax of the instruction set of a microprocessor. This binary syntax is standardized across

Figure 10.6. Low-level and high-level components of architecture

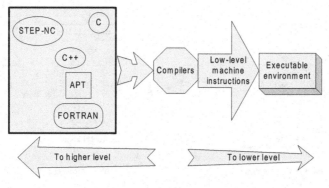

all machines, and therefore allows the use of any programming environment that the user considers adequate for his work.

The BVM is the virtual microprocessor to be targeted by a compiler of any language or programming tool. The BVH is the part of the architecture that makes abstractions of the machine it sits on. To make an analogy with a computer (Figure 10.7), the BVM would be the CPU for which programs are compiled, and the BVH would be the chipset around the microprocessor, which allows it to communicate with hardware connected to, or residing in the computer (Fortin, Chatelain & Rivest, 2004).

The BVH is the component that virtualizes a specific machine. It was designed with hardware in mind. The concepts used are mapped directly from hardware features found in computing systems. For instance, the BVM communicates through hardware ports with the BVH, which in turn abstracts the different functionalities of the real machine. The concept of hardware ports is already used in several systems, the port map being an address space used to send values from device to device. This concept of I/O ports is used extensively in the PC architecture (Intel Corporation, 1999). Each port address has a specific meaning. For example, on a graphic card, a port can be used to change the video mode currently in use. Different graphics cards equipped with the same set of ports can thus be controlled in the same way. The CPU only has to send a certain value to that port in order to change the mode. The BVH works in the same way: ports have specific values, and the BVM, which is the equivalent of the CPU in a real hardware system, sends values to these ports. In the graphic card example, one port in the BVH port map can represent the kind of coolant that is to be used on the machine. Such hardware concepts are used in the BNCL architecture in order to stay as close as possible to the real machine being abstracted (Fortin, Chatelain & Rivest, 2004).

A user does not have to code in such a low-level language. It is the compiler that transforms any high-level language into these basic BNCL instructions. Being close to a real CPU also allows for a rapid physical implementation of a BVM into a real microprocessor. In the BNCL architecture therefore, programs are compiled to be executed on the BVM. The tools needed to access a machine are thus a CAM software application to create BNCL source code and a BNCL Assembler to create the executable code that will be executed on a BVM.

Figure 10.7. Similarities between computer hardware and the BNCL architecture (Fortin, Chatelain & Rivest, 2004, Reproduced with permission from Elsevier)

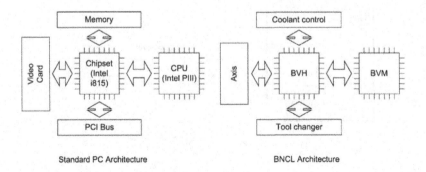

Intermediate Languages for CNC Programming

Being a low-level language, G-codes have no control statements, procedures, and many other advantages of modern high-level languages. In order to provide portability to CNC programs and to raise the abstraction level of the language, there have been several proposals of intermediate languages, such as APL (Otto, 2000) and OMAC (Michaloski, Birla, Yen, Igou & Weinert, 2000), from which G-codes can be automatically generated with compilers and post-processors. Unfortunately, the lack of a clean semantics in these languages prevents the development of formal tools for the analysis and manipulation of programs. AutoLISP (Carr & Holt, 1998, Rawls & Hagen, 1998) allows us to completely specify CNC programs but does not enable program property analysis such as termination, or use of heuristics when defining the behavior of a CNC machine. Functional language Haskell (Jones, 2003) has been used to design CNC programs. Use of a high-level language such as Haskell provides a framework to produce, formally analyze and verify an NC program. It enables control sequence, recursion, rich data structures and polymorphism (Arroyo, Ochoa, Silva & Vidal, 2004). Haskell also provides several advanced features like higher-order combinators, lazy evaluation, type classes, etc.

CONCLUSION

Both centralized and collaborative models have been used to achieve CAD/CAPP/CAM/CNC integration. The centralized model suits companies that have similar information infrastructure. The collaborative model can better support collaborative activities in the manufacturing environment. The case study showcases a centralized model. In this case study, the CAD/CAM software helps streamline the engineering process in a manufacturing company from conceptual design to tooling and manufacturing by allowing different people in the factory to enjoy bi-directional data associativity throughout the entire product development process. The case study also demonstrates the role that concurrent engineering plays in a modern manufacturing company which is product-centric and multi-dimensional.

In the effort to bridge CAM with CNC via a neutral interface language for NC machine tools, APT and BCL have made some inroads. In the case of APT, the APT CL file was meant to be machine-neutral. An APT CL file can also provide some level of associativity and integration between the geometry to be made and its tool path. In the case of BCL, the idea is to move the post-processors out of a CAD/CAM system and put them into the CNC's control unit. Thus, the part program can be generic and compatible for machines within a given class. An NC program in the BCL format is neutral with respect to both the machine tool and the programming system that generated that program.

Cost has been the major hindrance to up-taking of both APT and BCL, but more so with BCL. Machine tool and controller manufacturers have been treating BCL as an optional feature to support and are of the view that implementing them would involve extra cost hard to justify. Large companies have huge investments in post-processors. The knowledge accumulated throughout the years in managing these post-processors is commonly regarded as company's important assets and represents critical competitive advantage.

BNCL is a newer effort in achieving CAM/CNC integration. The philosophy of BNCL is abstraction of different machine tools in a common manner. The language offers some attractive features an open architecture, e.g. flexibility and extensibility. The BNCL architecture allows software development portability and is able to support multiple programming languages. This leads to creating flexible and efficient software architecture for machine tool control.

Use of high-level computer programming languages is another branch of research in the effort of making CNC programs more portable and more manageable. These languages include AutoLISP, APL, OMAC and Haskell. There is still a long way these high-level languages find their way into the main stream programming tools.

Leaving this chapter to move onto the next, the author wishes to point out that there has been no effort to integrate the entire chain of CAD/CAPP/CAM/CNC. None of the discussed approaches and methodologies has an international standard behind them. The next a few chapters intend to address the integration issues with the help of an international standard.

REFERENCES

ANSI/INCITS 37. (1999). *Programming Language APT* (revision, re-designation and consolidation of ANSI X3.37-1995, ANSI X3.37-1995/AM 2-1998, ANSI X3.37-1995/AM 1-1998) (formerly ANSI NCITS 37-1999). Washington, DC. Headquarters: ANSI.

Arroyo, G., Ochoa, C., Silva, J., & Vidal, G. (2004). Towards CNC programming using Haskell, In C. Lemaître, C. A. Reyes, & J. A. Gonzalez (Eds.), *Lecture Notes in Artificial Intelligence (Sub-series of Lecture Notes in Computer Science)*, 3315, pp. 386-396. Springer-Verlag, Berlin Heidelberg.

Carr, H., & Holt, R. (1998). The AutoLISP platform for computer aided design. In *Proceedings of 40th Anniversary of Lisp Conference: Lisp in the Mainstream*, Berkeley, California.

EIA/ANSI. (1992). *32 Bits Binary CL (BCL) and 7 bit (ACL). Exchange input format for numerically controlled machines.* Electronics Industries Association (EIA) and American National Standards Institute (ANSI) RS-494 Standard. Washington, DC. Headquarters: ANSI.

Fortin, É., Chatelain, J-F., & Rivest, L. (2004). An innovative software architecture to improve information flow from CAM to CNC. *Computers & Industrial Engineering, 46*(4), 655-667.

IGES. (1980). *ASME Y14.26M. Initial Graphics Exchange Specification (IGES)*. Gaithersburg, USA: National Bureau of Standards.

Intel Corporation. (1999). *Intel's architecture software developer manual: Basic architecture*, (Vol. 1). USA: Intel Corporation.

ISO 14649-1. (2003). *Data model for Computerized Numerical Controllers: Part 1 Overview and fundamental principles*. Geneva, Switzerland: International Organisation for Standardisation (ISO).

Jones, S. P. (2003). *Haskell 98 Language and Libraries: The Revised Report*. Cambridge University Press

Michaloski, J., Birla, S., Yen, C. J., Igou, R. & Weinert, G. (2000). An Open System Framework for Component-Based CNC Machines. *ACM Computing Surveys, 32*(23).

Otto, T. P. (2000). An APL Compiler. In *Proceedings of International Conference on APL*, Berlin, 186–193. ACM Press -New York, NY, USA.

Rawls, R., & Hagen, M. (1998). *AutoLISP Programming: Principles and Techniques*. Goodheart-Willcox Co.

Xu, X. (2006). STEP-NC to complete product development chain, In *Database Modeling for Industrial Data Management: Emerging Technologies and Applications*, edited by Z. Ma, pp. 148-184. IGI Global. ISBN 1-5914-0684-6.

Xu, X., & Mao, J. (2004). Development of the client tier for a STEP compliant CAPP system, In *Proceedings of the 6th International Conference on Frontiers of Design and Manufacturing (ICFDM'2004)*, 21-23 June, Xi'an, China.

Xu, X., & Duhovic, M. (2004). Computer-Aided Concurrent Environment for Manufacturing Education, *International Journal of Engineering Education, 20*(4), 543-551.

ENDNOTE

[1] STEP-NC will be discussed in details in the following chapters.

Chapter XI
Integration Based on STEP Standards

ABSTRACT

The integration model (Model B) as discussed in the previous chapter makes use of exchangeable neutral data formats such as IGES (1980). Neutral data formats provide a middle tier to connect CAD and CAM systems. Thus, Model B can create a collaborative manufacturing environment and make the design data exchange possible for large projects at the international level. Yet, some problems still remain. IGES was designed to exchange geometrical information only, so additional design or manufacturing information (such as feature information) within a proprietary model is ignored. During data exchange, some information may become astray during data transfer; geometry stitching or model repair is often needed. Plus, IGES is not an international standard.

As previously discussed, there are also problems common to both Models A and B (Figure 10.1). Different data formats (e.g. IGES and ISO 6983-1, 1982) are used in the design-to-manufacturing chain. Data loss occurs in the transaction from design to manufacturing because only low-level, step-by-step sequential machining commands are passed onto the CNC controllers, leaving the complete product model behind.

Of particular significance has been the endeavour made by the International Organization for Standardization to introduce the STEP Standard (i.e. ISO 10303-1 [1994]). Major aerospace and automotive companies have proven the value of STEP through production implementations resulting in savings of US $150 million per year (Gallaher, O'Connor & Phelps, 2002, PDES, Inc. 2006). Moreover, STEP has recently been extended to cater to manufacturing data modelling and execution with an aim to fill the information gap between CAD/CAPP/CAM and CNC. The standard is informally known as STEP-compliant Numerical Control, or otherwise STEP-NC for short. It was given an ISO name of "ISO

14649: Data model for Computerized Numerical Controllers (ISO 14649-1, 2003)", which defines the STEP-NC Application Reference Model. With STEP being extended to model manufacturing information, a new paradigm of integrated CAD/CAPP/CAM/CNC is emerging. This is illustrated in Figure 11.1. The key to this paradigm is that no data conversion is required and the data throughout the design and manufacturing chain are preserved.

This chapter focuses on the use of STEP standards to support data exchange between CAD systems as well as facilitate data flow between CAD, CAPP, CAM, and CNC systems. Also discussed are the specific integration issues between CAD and CAPP, CAPP and CAM, and CAM and CNC using STEP standards. STEP-NC data model is a relatively new member in the STEP family, but it completes the entire suite of STEP standards from design to NC machining. Both Physical File Implementation Method (ISO 10303-21, 1994) and XML Implementation Method (ISO/TS 10303-18, 2004) are presented as the two popular ways of implementing STEP and STEP-NC.

DATA EXCHANGE USING STEP AND STEP-NC

STEP has been briefly introduced in Chapter II. This section discusses the standard from the perspective of being a useful tool to support data exchange and integration. The keys

Figure 11.1. Integrating CAD/CAPP/CAM/CNC

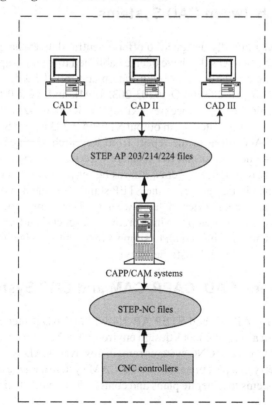

to the STEP standard are, (a) its generic nature, (b) computer-interpretable format, and (c) consistent data implementations across multiple applications and systems. They permit different implementation methods to be used for storing, accessing, transferring and archiving product data. The specification of a representation of product information is provided by a set of integrated resources. Each integrated resource comprises a set of product data descriptions, written in EXPRESS (ISO 10303-11, 1994) known as resource constructs. One set may be dependent on other sets for its definition. Similar information for different applications is represented by a single resource construct. The integrated resources are divided into two groups: generic resources and application resources. The generic resources are independent of applications and can reference each other. The application resources can reference the generic resources and can add other resource constructs for use by a group of similar applications. Application resources do not reference other application resources.

The integrated resources define a generic information model for product information. They are not sufficient to support the information requirements of an application without the addition of application specific constraints, relationships and attributes. STEP defines Application Protocols in which the integrated resources are interpreted to meet the product information requirements of specific applications, in other words Application Reference Model. The interpretation is achieved by selecting appropriate resource constructs, refining their meaning, and specifying any appropriate constraints, relationships and attributes. This interpretation results in an Application Interpreted Model. It is these AIMs that STEP brings data of differing applications under the same roof.

Data Exchange between CAD Systems

The STEP standard was initially designed to offer a neutral data exchange method in replacement of IGES. The two APs that have been established to mainly support design data exchanging and sharing are the AP for configuration controlled 3D designs of mechanical parts and assemblies (AP 203) (ISO 10303-203, 1994), and the AP for the core data for automotive mechanical design processes (AP 214) (ISO 10303-214, 1994). Currently, most of the commercial CAD systems can output STEP AP-203 and/or STEP AP-214 files via STEP translators. According to the report from Research Triangle Institute (1999), when STEP is used as a neutral format to exchange wireframe and surface data between commonly used commercial CAD systems, it fares better than IGES. This indicates that STEP is ready to replace IGES. However, the STEP standard is much more than a neutral data format that translates geometrical data between CAD systems. The ultimate goal of STEP is to provide a complete computer-interpretable product data format, so that users can integrate business and technical data to support the whole product life cycle: design, analysis, manufacturing, sales and customer services.

Data Flow between CAD, CAPP, CAM and CNC Systems

By implementing STEP AP-203 and STEP AP-214 within CAD systems, data exchange barriers are removed in a heterogeneous design environment. Yet, data exchange problems between CAD, CAPP, CAM and CNC systems remain unsolved. CAD systems are designed to describe the geometry of a part precisely. CAPP/CAM systems, on the other hand, focus on using computer systems to generate plans and control the manufacturing operations according to the geometrical information present in a CAD model and the existing resources on the shop-floor. The final result from a CAM system is a set of CNC programs that can be executed on a CNC machine. The neutral data formats such as STEP AP-203 and STEP AP214 only unify the input data for a CAM system. On the output side of a CAM system, a fifty-year-old international standard ISO 6983 still dominates the control systems of most CNC machines. Outdated yet still widely used as discussed in the previous chapter, ISO 6983 has become an impediment for the contemporary collaborative manufacturing environment. Some of the technical limits and problems found with ISO 6983 are summarized as follows (Xu & He, 2004),

(a)   The language focuses on programming the path of the cutter centre location with respect to the machine axes, rather than the machining tasks with respect to the part.

(b)   The standard defines the syntax of a program statement, but in most cases leaves the semantics ambiguous.

(c)   Vendors usually supplement the language with extensions that are not covered in the limited scope of ISO 6983; hence the CNC programs are not exchangeable.

(d)   It only supports one-way information flow from design to manufacturing. The changes made at the shop-floor cannot be directly fed back to the designer. Hence, invaluable experiences on the shop-floor can not be preserved and reused.

(e)   There is limited control over program execution and it is difficult to change the program in the workshop.

(f)   CAD data are not utilized at a machine tool. Instead, they have to be processed by a machine-specific post-processor, only to obtain a set of low-level, incomplete data that makes verifications and simulation difficult, if not impossible.

(g)   ISO 6983 does not support the spline data, which makes it incapable of controlling five or more axis milling.

These problems collectively make CNC machining a bottleneck in the concurrent manufacturing environment. G-codes are now considered as standing in the way of increased productivity expected by customers from state-of-the-art machine tools (Fortin, Chatelain & Rivest, 2004). Figure 11.2 shows the effect of an inadequate programming interface (i.e. G-codes) on the manufacturing information chain. Modern CAD/CAM systems can handle complex programs. On the other side of the chain are the CNC controllers which are also able to perform complex work. Between them, the programming interface used, the G-Codes can only perform tasks that are limited in complexity and transfer little information regarding design and manufacturing data. Since the G-Codes programming interface is currently used in the industry, the net result is that the controllers are not used to their full potential. It also means that a desired CAD/CAPP/CAM/CNC train is broken at the link between CAM and CNC.

Features as a Common Thread

The significance of features has been extensively discussed in Chapters IV-VII. This section discusses the features within the context of the STEP standard. Features have been used as a common thread in STEP, and a consistent approach has been used to develop the structure of a feature. In STEP, features are primarily defined as the combination of a profile shape and a path shape. Feature profile shapes are two dimensional implicit or explicit shape

Figure 11.2. Impact of using the G-Code programming interface (Fortin, Chatelain & Rivest, 2004, Reproduced with permission from Elsevier).

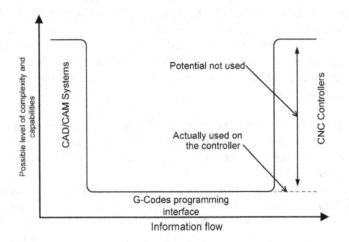

definitions with attributes such as length, width, height, corner radius, radius and diameter, combined to define a two dimensional shape. Feature paths are much like profiles; they are implicit shape definitions or three dimensional explicit shape definitions that define a path in which the entire feature profile is defined. In cases where features are created and the shape path cannot be defined in clear-cut distinct shapes, general shape paths are explicitly defined with three-dimensional geometry, such as curves or splines.

Besides path and profiles, features contain additional structural elements to further define their semantics. Each feature has an orientation attribute to define location and direction for placement of the feature on the part. Features may also have a taper element to define a tapered feature such as a tapered hole, draft, pocket or boss. In addition, certain features have implicit or explicit shape definitions to define feature end conditions. A slot feature has slot end type definitions, pocket feature has bottom type definitions, boss feature has a top definition, and a hole has a bottom definition. By combining paths, profiles, tapers and end conditions a large variety of machining features are defined.

Besides representing the semantics of the shape, machining features also carry some essential information. When a part is designed, there is valuable design information that is directly related to the specific features on the part. Much of this design information is provided to control the form, fit and function of the part during the manufacturing process. Geometric dimensioning and tolerancing is the means used by the APs to relate the information about the precision of the manufactured part. In addition, certain property specifications and conditions may be apart of the design information supplied to the manufacturing domain. For example a cylindricity tolerance applied to a hole feature, or a hardness property applied to a planar face feature. Exchanging this information to manufacturing processes gives a more complete and precise definition of the feature with its associated tolerances and properties.

Integration through STEP AP Harmonization

A number of Application Protocols have been developed to define industry data for design and manufacturing. Some of them are,

- AP203 - Configuration controlled 3D designs of mechanical parts and assemblies (ISO 10303-203, 1994).
- AP214 - Core data for automotive mechanical design processes (ISO 10303-214, 1994).
- AP219 - Dimensional Inspection Information Exchange (ISO 10303-219, 2007).
- AP223 - Exchange of Design and Manufacturing Product Information for Cast Parts (ISO/CD 10303-223, 2006).
- AP224 - Mechanical product definition for process planning using machining features (ISO 13030-224, 2001).
- AP238 - Application interpreted model for computerized numerical controllers (ISO 10303-238, 2007).
- AP240 - Process plans for machined parts (ISO 10303-240, 2006).

An integral part of the development of APs for design and manufacturing is to harmonize elements of requirements that are common across the entire product development domain. All of the abovementioned APs define different data representations for different stages of a product life cycle. However these APs all have data within their scope and context that is common with the other APs, e.g. dimensional and geometric tolerances, boundary representation geometry, properties, raw material data, and machining features. The intention of the standards organization is that vendors will supply software products which will exchange and interpret product data according to the specification prescribed in an application protocol. A primary criterion will be a product's adherence to one or more STEP APs. Therefore harmonization of "like" concepts such as machining features ensures data integrity of product data throughout the CAD/CAPP/CAM/CNC domain. Figure 11.3 shows such a scenario. Note that this scenario may be called "STEP in, STEP out, STEP throughout".

Figure 11.3. An integrated CAD/CAPP/CAM/CNC environment based on STEP

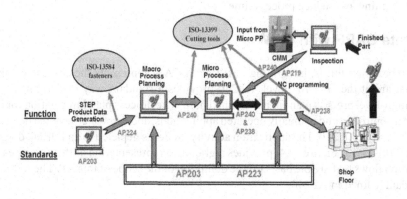

Integrate CAD with CAPP

AP224 was developed to bridge the gap between CAD and CAPP by providing machine part information that ensures the design information is at the same time 100-percent complete, accurate, computer-interpretable and reusable. Thus, automated process planning from product data in a digital format is made possible. The AP224 standard provides the mechanism to define the digital data that contains the information necessary to manufacture a required part. This includes information such as,

- CAD geometry and topology;
- Machining feature information (e.g. hole, boss, slot, groove, pocket, chamfer and fillet);
- Dimensional and geometric tolerances;
- Material properties and process properties; and
- Administrative information (e.g. approval, part name and ID, delivery date and quantity).

More specifically, AP224 defines the implicit information about machining features and other APs (such as AP203) define the explicit geometry using boundary representation (B-rep). Therefore, the dimensional and geometric tolerances defined in AP224 can reference either the B-rep geometry, or the implicit feature definitions. AP224 also defines part, process, material and surface properties that can reference B-rep geometry or the implicit feature definitions. Also defined in this AP is the implicit or explicit base shape of the part, in other words, the starting raw stock definition from which to manufacture the part. The explicit shape may be considered as a cast or forged shape, the implicit shape is defined as a piece of bar stock. These raw stock definitions also reference the machining features that define the material removal.

A manufactured assembly was added in the second edition of this AP, and machining features play an important role when several parts in an assembly have features in common. For example, there may be two parts that require several holes to be machined through both parts. These hole features and associated data such as tolerances and properties can be defined across both parts. A process plan would contain product data for both parts to be placed together on a machine, so that the hole could be machined through both parts at the same time. Creating a hole feature that has a relationship with both parts will aid process planning and reduce process time.

Integrate CAPP with CAM

In somewhat loose terms, integrating CAPP with CAM represents the process planning tasks that are at the "macro" level. AP240 provides a standard way of defining such a macro, high-level process plan for a machined part. The process plan information for both numerical controlled and manually operated applications, and associated product definition data is defined in AP 240. The application activity model as depicted in an IDEF0[1] diagram (IEEE 1320.1-1998) (Figure 11.4) provides a graphical representation of the processes and information flows that are the basis for the definition of the scope of this AP. The following are the data defined in AP240,

- information out of the planning activity that is contained in the process plans for machined parts, e.g. numerical controlled and manual machines;
- manufacture of a single piece or assemblies of single piece parts;
- interface for capturing technical data out of the upstream application protocols, e.g. product definition data and initial material definition data;
- technical data for and/or out of the process planning for machined pats, e.g. machining features, geometric and dimensional tolerances of the parts, materials, and properties of the parts being manufactured;
- work instructions for the tasks required to manufacture a part, including references to the resources required to perform the work, the sequences of the work instructions and relationships of the work to the part geometry;
- information required to support NC programming of processes specified in the process plan, e.g. product definition, administrative data, machine, tooling, and material requirements;
- information required to support in-process inspection specified in the process plan, e.g. tasks such as using gauge blocks or performing a probing operation to verify the dimensional constraints placed upon the part;
- shop-floor information specified in the process plan;
- information for production planning specified in the process plan.

A part may have features on several sides of the part, requiring several setups on one or more machines. The AP240 process plan defines the sequence of machine processes; each of them identifies the machine tool, machine setup, clamping positions, a list of machine

Figure 11.4. Application activity model for macro CAPP

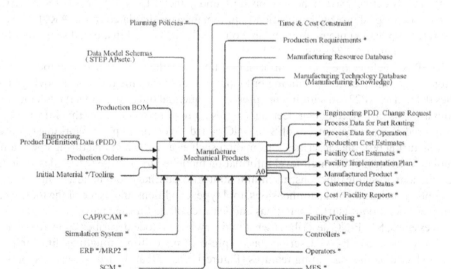

*Terms marked with * are outside the scope of this application protocol.*
ERP – Enterprise Resource Planning   MRP2 – Manufacturing Resource Planning
SCM – Supply Chain Management   MES – Manufacturing Execution System

operations, and a list of machining features that are eligible to be machined per process. This list of machining features is not the list of all features on the part, but a subset of the part features that are eligible to be machined for a particular machine setup and machining process on a specified machine. Each machining setup identifies one or more machining operations. A machine operation may be rough mill, finish mill, drill, tap or countersink. A list of machining features is specified for each operation. For example a countersink operation would identify a countersunk hole, or a rough mill operation would identify a pocket.

Also defined are the type of clamp to use, location on either the machine tool or fixture, and what portion of the part shape is being affected by the clamp position. If there are no machining features at this clamping location, the geometric shape is identified and machining continues. Otherwise, the feature on which the clamp location is positioned, may not be machined during that setup. When machining a part certain features require machining prior to the machining of others. For example, if there is a counterbore hole feature in the bottom of a pocket feature, the pocket would need to be machined first, and the counterbore hole afterwards. The process plan information includes essentially a feature dependency tree. This tree is an ordered list of machining features indicating a sequential order for processing features.

Integrate CAM with CNC

After macro process planning comes the micro process planning, which is closely related to a CNC machine. This is done by AP238 (ISO 10303-238, 2007) or ISO 14649 (ISO 14649-1, 2004), both are collectively known as STEP-NC. The former is the AIM of STEP-NC whereas the latter the ARM of STEP-NC. Being the ARM model, ISO 14649 provides a detailed analysis of the requirements of CNC applications. The specific objects are accurately defined; so are the relationships among them. The AIM model of STEP-NC, i.e. AP-238, maps these NC application requirement data stipulated in the ARM into an integrated application protocol. From now on, STEP-NC is used in a broad sense to refer to both or either of AP 238 and ISO 14649.

STEP-NC defines the process information for a specific class of machine tools, such as turning, milling, drilling, reaming or tapping. It describes the tasks of removing volumes defined as AP224 machining features in a sequential order, with specific tolerances, and with tools that meet all engineering and design requirements. All of this information is captured in a unique concept of STEP-NC called "Workingstep". A Workingstep is a manufacturing task that describes information such as a single manufacturing operation, a tool or a strategy. Other high-level information modelled by STEP-NC includes various NC functions, machine functions, machining strategies, auxiliary commands, technological description such as tool data (dimensions, tool type, conditions and usage of the tool), and workpiece definitions (surfaces, regions and features of the finished part).

In essence, STEP-NC describes "what to do", while G-code describes "how to do" for CNC machines. STEP-NC describes tasks (pre-drilling, drilling, roughing, finishing…) that are based on the machining features (Figure 11.5), so that the part program supplies the shop-floor with higher-level information, i.e. the information about machining tasks and technological data on top of pure geometrical and topological information. As a result, modifications at the shop-floor can be saved and transferred back to the planning department that enables a better exchange and preservation of experience and knowledge.

Some of the benefits with using STEP-NC are as follows (Xu & He, 2004).

- STEP-NC provides a complete and structured data model, linked with geometrical and technological information, so that no information is lost between the different stages of the product development process.
- Its data elements are adequate enough to describe task-oriented NC data.
- The data model is extendable to further technologies and scalable (with Conformance Classes) to match the abilities of a specific CAM, SFP (Shop-floor Programming) or NC systems.
- Machining time for small to medium sized job lots can be reduced because intelligent optimization can be built into the STEP-NC controllers.
- Post-processor mechanism will be eliminated, as the interface does not require machine-specific information.
- Machine tools are safer and more adaptable because STEP-NC is independent from machine tool vendors.
- Modification at the shop-floor can be saved and fed back to the design department hence bi-directional information flow from CAD/CAM to CNC machines can be achieved.
- XML files can be used as an information carrier hence enable Web-base distributed manufacturing.

STEP-NC Data Model

Like other parts of the STEP standard, the STEP-NC EXPRESS information model is organized into schemas. These schemas contain model definitions and serve as a scooping mechanism for subdivision of STEP-NC models. EXPRESS also gives STEP-NC an object-oriented flavour. Its inheritance can be illustrated by the definition of manufacturing features defined in STEP-NC (ISO 14649-10, 2004) (Figure 11.6). For every 2½D manufacturing feature, there is always a feature placement value. Therefore, it is defined at the top-level (in the Two5D_manufacturing_feature entity). This attribute is inherited by all the "child" entities, i.e. machining, replicate and compound features. Similarly, each sub-type of machining features will have an elementary surface to define its depth, and it is defined once for all at the machining_feature level.

In STEP-NC, all geometrical data for workpiece, set-ups and manufacturing features are described based on other STEP APs, e.g. AP 203. These data are also expected to be used directly by the CNC machines to avoid conversions between different data formats that may result in reduced accuracy and provide an integrated environment. Tooling information including tool type, tool geometry, expected tool life and etc. is also included in a STEP-NC file. Figure 11.7 illustrates part of the internal structure of the STEP-NC data, showing how design and manufacturing information comes together in one hierarchy.

Data Access Implementation Methods

As briefly touched upon, EXPRESS language does not define any implementation methods. Therefore, additional implementation methods are defined to describe all STEP instances for building product exchange models, e.g. STEP AP 224, AP 238 and ISO 14649 mod-

Figure 11.5. Comparison of G-code with STEP-NC (Xu, 2006)

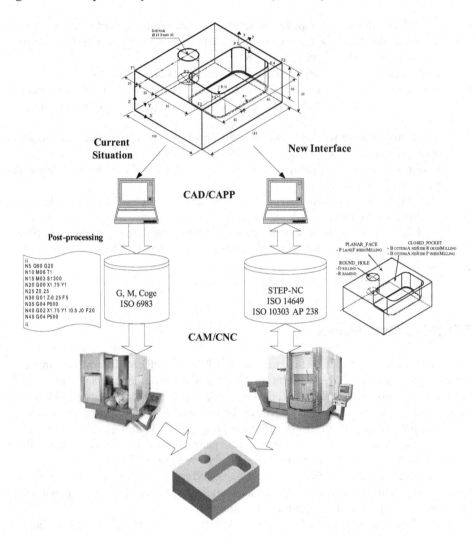

els. These implementation methods are called STEP Data Access Interface (SDAI) (ISO 10303-22, 1998). SDAI reduces the costs of managing integrated product data by making complex engineering applications portable across data implementations. Currently, four international standards have been established for SDAI,

- Standard data access interface (Part 21) (ISO 10303-21, 1994);
- C++ language binding to the standard data access interface (ISO 10303-23, 2000);
- C language binding of standard data access interface (ISO 10303-24, 2001); and
- Java Programming language binding to the standard data access interface with Internet/Intranet extensions (ISO 10303-27, 2000).

Figure 11.6. EXPRESS-G illustration of STEP-NC manufacturing features (ISO 14649-10, 2004. Reproduced with permission from ISO)

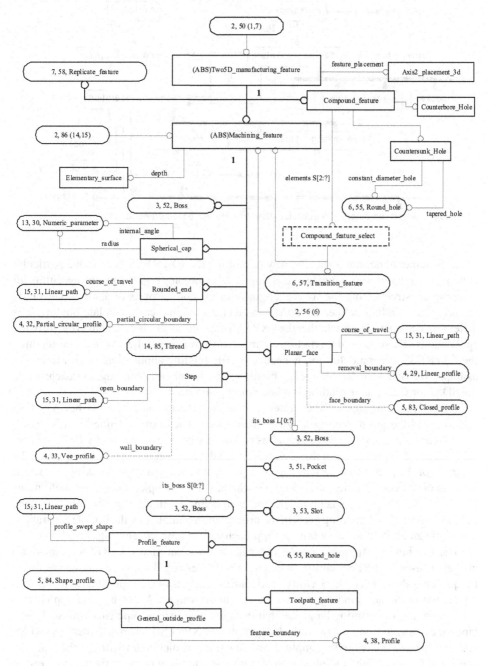

Figure 11.7. Geometry, technology and process information in STEP-NC

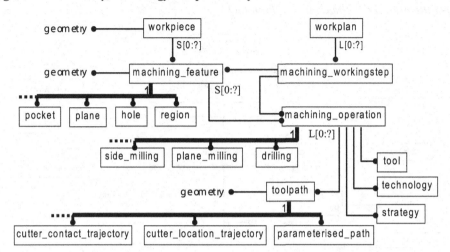

Each standard defines a specific way of binding the EXPRESS data with a particular computer programming language. Binding is a terminology given to an algorithm for mapping constructs from the source language to the counterparts of another. Generally speaking, the binding defined in SDAI can be classified into early and late binding. The difference between them is whether the EXRESS data dictionary is available to the software applications. There is no data dictionary in an early binding, whereas in a late binding, the EXPRESS schema definition is needed by late binding applications at run-time. For example, the SDAI for C++ language binding is a typical early binding approach; while the SDAI for C language binding is a late binding approach.

The early binding approach generates specific data structure according to the EXPRESS schemas and the programming language definitions. The entities defined in EXPRESS schemas are converted to C++ or Java classes. The inheritance properties in the EXPRESS schemas are also preserved in those classes. The advantage of an early binding is that the compiler of the programming language can perform additional type checking. However, because of the complexities of EXPRESS schemas (for example, the average definitions in a STEP-NC AIM model is up to 200 and each definition in the early binding approach needs to have a corresponding class in the programming language), the initial preparation, compiling and link of an early binding approach can be time-consuming.

The late binding approach on the other hand, does not map EXPRESS entities into classes. It uses EXPRESS entity dictionaries for accessing data. Data values are found by querying those EXPRESS entity dictionaries. Only a few simple functions need to be defined in the late binding approach to get or set values. A late binding approach is suitable for a programming language that does not have strong type checking such as C language or an environment that may have multiple EXPRESS schemas (when EXPRESS schema changes, a late binding application can use a new dictionary without changing the application itself). Late binding is simpler than early binding because there is no need to generate the corresponding classes. However, the lack of type checking destines that the late binding approach is not suitable for large systems.

A mixed binding approach may provide the advantages of an early binding (compile-time type checking and semantics as functions in a class) and late binding (simplicity). For example, a mixed binding takes advantage of the observation that applications rarely use all of the structures defined by an AP AIM. The subset of structures that are used, called the working set, can be early-bound, while the rest of the AP is late-bound. All data is still available, but the application development process is simplified. The number of classes and files that are needed are reduced dramatically, resulting in quicker compilations, simpler source control and more rapid development.

Part 21 Physical File Implementation Method

STEP Part 21 is the first implementation method (ISO 10303-21, 1994). It defines the basic rules of storing EXPRESS/STEP data in a character-based physical file. Its aim is to provide a method so that it is possible to write EXPRESS/STEP entities and transmit those entities using normal networking and communication protocols, e.g. FTP (File Transfer Protocol), e-mail and HTTP (Hyper Text Transfer Protocol). Clearly, STEP Part 21 files can be made to support Internet-based, distributed manufacturing environment. This has been further discussed in the latter chapters of this book.

A Part 21 file does not have any EXPRESS schemas included. It only defines the relationships between entities that are defined by external EXPRESS schemas. The Part 21 file format uses the minimalist style that was popular before the advent of XML. In this style the same information is not written twice so that there is no room for any contradictions in the data. The style assumes that normally the data will only be processed by software that people will only look at the data to create test examples or find bugs, and that making the data more easily readable by these people is less important than eliminating redundancies.

The Part 21 format is therefore simple and elegant. Each entity instance in a Part 21 file begins with a unique Entity ID and terminates with a semicolon ";". Entity ID is a hash symbol "#" followed by an integer and has to be unique within the data exchange file. Entity ID is followed by an equal symbol ("=") and the name of the entity that defines the instance. The names are always capitalized though EXPRESS is case insensitive. The name of the instance is then followed by the values of the attributes listed between parentheses and separated by commas. The following is the exert of a STEP-NC ARM file.

```
ISO-10303-21;
HEADER;
FILE _ DESCRIPTION(('A STEP-NC demo file'),'1');
FILE _ NAME('sample _ part.stp',$,(IIMS),('\'),'CNC Mill','',''');
FILE _ SCHEMA(('STEP-NC milling schema'));
ENDSEC;
DATA;
// Project and Workplan
#1=PROJECT('Contour',#2,(#3));
#2=WORKPLAN('Work plan',(#4),$,#5);
#3=WORKPIECE('Workpiece',#6,0.01,$,$,#8,());
// Workingsteps
#4=MACHINING _ WORKINGSTEP('Rough Contour',#13,#16,#17);
#5=SETUP('main _ setup',#44,#48,(#51));
```

```
#6=MATERIAL('ST-50','Steel',(#7));
#7=PROPERTY _ PARAMETER('E=200000 N/mm^2');
#8=BLOCK('Block',#9,260.000,210.000,110.000);
// Geometric data
#9=AXIS2 _ PLACEMENT _ 3D('BLOCK',#10,#11,#12);
...........
// Manufacturing features
#16=GENERAL _ OUTSIDE _ PROFILE('Profile',#3,(#17),#18,#22,$,$,$,$,#23,$,$);
// Operation data
#17=SIDE _ ROUGH _ MILLING($,$,'Contour profile',#38,10.000,  #39,#40,#43,$,
$,$,20.000,5.000,0.000);
#18=AXIS2 _ PLACEMENT _ 3D('Position of contour',#19,#20,#21);
#19=CARTESIAN _ POINT('Position of contour',  (40.000,90.000,100.000));
#20=DIRECTION('',(0.0,0.0,1.0));
#21=DIRECTION('',(1.0,0.0,0.0));
#22=TOLERANCED _ LENGTH _ MEASURE(20.000,$,$,$);
#23=COMPOSITE _ CURVE('Contour Profile',(#24,#25,#56),.F.);
...........
// Tool data
#40=CUTTING _ TOOL('Endmill 10mm',#41,(),(50.000),50.000);
#41=TAPERED _ ENDMILL(#42,3,.RIGHT.,.F.,$,$);
#42=TOOL _ DIMENSION(10.000,$,$,$,$,$,$);
// Machining technology
#43=MILLING _ TECHNOLOGY($,.TCP.,$,3.3333,$,0.10,.T.,.F.,.F.);
#44=AXIS2 _ PLACEMENT _ 3D('Reference  point  to  Machine  zero',
#45,#46,#47);
#45=CARTESIAN _ POINT('',(20.000,30.000,10.000));
...........
#56=COMPOSITE _ CURVE _ SEGMENT(.CONTINUOUS.,.T.,#57);
#57=POLYLINE('Second cut of the contour',(#29,#30,#31,#32,#33,#27));
ENDSEC;
END-ISO-10303-21;
```

In this Part 21 file, a number of entities defined in STEP-NC can be found such as those related to Project, Workplan, Workingstep, Manufacturing features, Operation data, Tool data and Machining technology.

XML Implementation Method (Part 28 Edition 1)

XML consists of different rules for defining semantic tags that break a document into parts and identify different parts of the document. Furthermore, it is a meta-markup language that defines a syntax in which other field-specific markup languages can be written (Harold, 2002). Essentially, XML defines a character-based document format. The following is a simple XML document defining a milling cutter,

```
<?xml version="1.0"?>
   <MILLING _ TOOL>
      MILL 18MM
   </MILLING _ TOOL>
```

The first line is the XML declaration. It is usually made up of an attribute named "version" and its value "1.0". Lines two to four define a "MILLING_TOOL" element with "<MILL-ING_TOOL>" as the start tag and "</MILLING_TOOL>" the end tag. "MILL 18MM" is the content, or in another word, the value of the element. XML is flexible because there is no restriction to those tag names. Hence, it is possible to assign more human-understandable tag names in an XML document, while computers just interpret an XML document according to a pre-defined formula. It is obvious that the use of meaningful tags can make an XML document human-understandable as well as computer-interpretable.

When representing EXPRESS schemas, Part 28 (Edition 1) (ISO/TS 10303-28 (Edition 1), 2003) specifies an XML markup declaration set based on the syntax of the EXPRESS language. EXPRESS text representation of schemas is also supported. The markup declaration sets are intended as formal specifications for the appearance of markup in a conforming XML document. These declarations may appear as part of Document Type Definitions (DTDs) for such a document.

Like the method used in SDAI, STEP Part 28 (Edition 1) defined two broad approaches for representing the data corresponding to an EXPRESS schema. One approach is to specify a single markup declaration set that is independent of the EXPRESS schema and can represent data of any schema. This approach is called XML late binding. The second approach is to specify the results of the generation of a markup declaration set that is dependent on the EXPRESS schema. This approach is called XML early binding. STEP Part 28 (Edition 1) defines one late binding approach and two early binding approaches.

XML Implementation Method (Part 28 Edition 2)

It has soon become evident that the use of DTD syntax to specify mappings of EXPRESS to XML as prescribed in Part 28 (Edition 1), may result in a sub-optimal solution. Recognizing the limitations of the first edition, ISO has developed a second edition Part 28 (ISO 10303-28 (Edition 2), 2007) employing W3C XML Schema. The main theme of the new implementation method is its two-level method. At the lower-level CAD authoring systems can continue to read and write STEP data sets. The only difference at this level is that these data sets can now have an XML format to make them more compatible with the higher level. At the upper level the data sets are modularized by inserting information from the mapping tables into the XML data to explain the meaning of each entity sequence. The new method can open up the definition of an Application Protocol into a series of interconnected XML schemas. As shown in Figure 11.8, each XML Schema defines the representation required for one of the STEP-NC ARM objects.

This method is implemented using two languages, a configuration language for describing how to map EXPRESS information into an XML defined form, and the existing STEP mapping table language converted into an XML form.

CONCLUSION

First published in 1994, the initial scope of STEP covered geometry, product structure and technical drawings. Since then, the standard has been extensively implemented on major commercial projects in the aerospace, automotive and other industries. Typical implemen-

Figure 11.8. Definitions generated by the new method

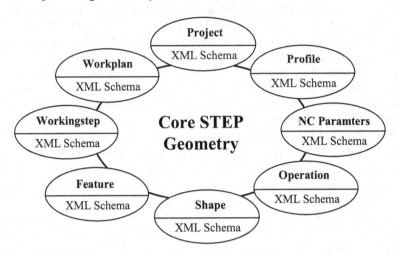

tations are the use of STEP to combine the information on shape and other characteristics of individual parts with assembly structures to form a single integrated representation of a complex assembly or product. This information is gathered from a range of application systems and consolidated into a STEP file which can be transferred to other companies and unloaded into their corresponding systems. The advantage from combining this data is that it guarantees consistency for information deliveries, and avoids the administrative cost of ensuring that data is consistent between multiple systems (Srinivasan, 2008). SCRA's STEP Application Handbook gives some more insight of STEP applications (SCRA, 2006).

Now STEP is on the verge of a new success with the release of a specification for defining the data input to CNC controllers – STEP-NC. STEP-NC along with other APs such as AP203 and AP224 provides an integrated environment for CAD, CAPP, CAM and NC, avoids data exchange and entails a truly exchangeable format. Machine operators can now be supported at the machine tool-level by complete information containing understandable geometry (machining features), task oriented operations (Workingsteps and Workplans), strategies and tool definitions. A bi-directional information flow throughout the design and manufacturing chain can now be realized, i.e. design information in its entirety is available in the manufacturing model. The STEP Data Access Interfaces help reduce the costs of managing integrated product data by making complex engineering applications (in C++, C, Java and XML, for example) portable across data implementations.

REFERENCES

Fortin, É., Chatelain, J-F., & Rivest, L. (2004). An innovative software architecture to improve information flow from CAM to CNC. *Computers & Industrial Engineering, 46*(4), 655-667.

Gallaher, M. P., O'Connor, A. C., & Phelps, T. (2002). Economic impact assessment of international Standard for the Exchange of Product Model Data (STEP) in Transportation

Equipment Industries, *NIST Planning Report 02-5*, Retrieved July 28, 2009, from http://www.mel.nist.gov/msid/sima/step_economic_impact.pdf.

Harold, E. R. (2002). *XML Bible Gold Edition*, Hoboken, NJ, USA: Hungry Minds. Inc.

IEEE 1320.1, (1998). *IEEE Standard for Functional Modeling Language—Syntax and Semantics for IDEF0*. New York: IEEE.

IGES. (1980). *ASME Y14.26M. Initial Graphics Exchange Specification (IGES)*. Gaithersburg, USA: National Bureau of Standards.

ISO 10303-1. (1994). *Industrial automation systems — Product data representation and exchange —Part 1: Overview and fundamental principles*. Geneva, Switzerland: International Organisation for Standardisation (ISO).

ISO 10303-11. (1994). *Industrial automation systems and integration – Product data representation and exchange – Part 11: Description methods: The EXPRESS language reference manual*. Geneva, Switzerland: International Organisation for Standardisation (ISO).

ISO 10303-203. (1994). *Industrial automation systems and integration – Product data representation and exchange – Part 203: Application protocol: Configuration controlled 3D designs of mechanical parts and assemblies*. Geneva, Switzerland: International Organisation for Standardisation (ISO).

ISO 10303-21. (1994). *Industrial automation systems and integration – Product data representation and exchange – Part 21: Implementation methods: Clear text encoding of the exchange structure*. Geneva, Switzerland: International Organisation for Standardisation (ISO).

ISO 10303-214. (1994). *Industrial automation systems and integration – Product data representation and exchange – Part 214: Application protocol: Core data for automotive mechanical design processes*. Geneva, Switzerland: International Organisation for Standardisation (ISO).

ISO 10303-219. (2007). *Industrial automation systems and integration – Product data representation and exchange – Part 219: Application protocol: Dimensional inspection information exchange*. Geneva, Switzerland: International Organisation for Standardisation (ISO).

ISO 10303-22. (1998). *Industrial automation systems and integration – Product data representation and exchange – Part 22: Implementation methods: Standard data access interface*. Geneva, Switzerland: International Organisation for Standardisation (ISO).

ISO 13030-224. (2001). *Industrial automation systems and integration – Product data representation and exchange – Part 224: Application protocol: Mechanical product definition for process plans using machining features*. Geneva, Switzerland: International Organisation for Standardisation (ISO).

ISO 10303-23. (2000). *Industrial automation systems and integration – Product data representation and exchange – Part 23: C++ language binding to the standard data access interface*. Geneva, Switzerland: International Organisation for Standardisation (ISO).

ISO/CD 10303-223. (2006). *Industrial automation systems and integration – Product data representation and exchange – Part 223: Application Protocols: Application interpreted model for casting.* Geneva, Switzerland: International Organisation for Standardisation (ISO).

ISO 10303-238. (2007). *Industrial automation systems and integration – Product data representation and exchange – Part 238: Application Protocols: Application interpreted model for computerized numerical controllers.* Geneva, Switzerland: International Organisation for Standardisation (ISO).

ISO 10303-24. (2001). *Industrial automation systems and integration – Product data representation and exchange – Part 24: C language binding of standard data access interface.* Geneva, Switzerland: International Organisation for Standardisation (ISO).

ISO 10303-240. (2006). *Industrial automation systems and integration – Product data representation and exchange – Part 240: Application protocol: Process plans for machined products.* Geneva, Switzerland: International Organisation for Standardisation (ISO).

ISO 10303-27. (2000). *Industrial automation systems and integration – Product data representation and exchange – Part 27: Java programming language binding to the standard data access interface with Internet/Intranet extensions.* Geneva, Switzerland: International Organisation for Standardisation (ISO).

ISO 14649-1. (2004). Data model for Computerized Numerical Controllers: Part 1 Overview and fundamental principles. Geneva, Switzerland: International Organisation for Standardisation (ISO).

ISO 14649-10. (2004). Data model for Computerized Numerical Controllers: Part 10 – General process data. Geneva, Switzerland: International Organisation for Standardisation (ISO).

ISO 6983-1. (1982). *Numerical control of machines – Program format and definition of address words – Part 1: Data format for positioning, line motion and contouring control systems.* Geneva, Switzerland: International Organisation for Standardisation (ISO).

ISO/TS 10303-28 (Edition 1). (2003). *Product data representation and exchange: Implementation methods: EXPRESS to XML binding, Draft Technical Specification.* Geneva, Switzerland: International Organisation for Standardisation (ISO).

ISO 10303-28 (Edition 2). (2007). *Product data representation and exchange: Implementation methods: XML representations of EXPRESS schemas and data, using XML schemas,* Geneva, Switzerland: International Organisation for Standardisation (ISO).

PDES, Inc. (2006), *STEP Success Stories*, Retrieved July 28, 2007, from http://pdesinc.aticorp.org/success_stories.html.

Research Triangle Institute. (1999). *Interoperability Cost Analysis of the U.S Automotive Supply Chain.* NY, USA: Final Report.

SCRA (2006). STEP Application Handbook ISO 10303 Version 3, Retrieved April 14, 2008, from http://pdesinc.aticorp.org/

Srinivasan, V. (2008). Standardizing the specification, verification, and exchange of product geometry: Research, status and trends, Computer-aided Design. In press

Xu, X. (2006). STEP-NC to complete product development chain, In *Database Modeling for Industrial Data Management: Emerging Technologies and Applications*, edited by Z. Ma, pp. 148-184, IGI Global.

Xu, X., & He, Q. (2004). Striving for a total integration of CAD, CAPP, CAM and CNC. *Robotics and Computer Integrated Manufacturing, 20*, 101-109.

Chapter XII
Function Block–Enabled Integration

ABSTRACT

Function blocks are an IEC (International Electro-technical Commission) standard for distributed industrial processes and control systems (IEC 61499, 2005). It is based on an explicit event driven model and provides for data flow and finite state automata-based control. Based on previous research, function blocks can be used as the enabler to encapsulate process plans, integrate with a third-party dynamic scheduling system, monitor process plan during execution, and control machining jobs under normal and abnormal conditions. They are also considered to be suitable for machine-level monitoring, shop-floor execution control, and CNC control. Combination of STEP-NC and Function Blocks can be seen as a "natural marriage". This is because the former provides an informationally complete data model but with no functionality, whereas the latter can embed intelligence and provide functionality in the data model for a more capable CNC regime. This chapter introduces the function block architecture which has been implemented in two types of integrations. The first brings together CAD, CAPP, and CAM. The key is to embed machining information in a function block system that is based on the concept of machining features. The second integration connects CAM with CNC. This is in fact an open CNC architecture that is function block driven, instead of G-code driven.

FUNCTION BLOCK STRUCTURE

Being an atomic distributable and executable control function unit, a function block instance can encapsulate a part of machining process data (e.g. slot roughing, pocket finishing, and hole drilling, etc.) for a given machining feature. It comprises of an individual, named copy of the data structure specified by its function block type, which persists from one invocation of the function block to the next. Figure 12.1 illustrates both the basic (left) and composite (right) function blocks.

A function block, especially the basic function block, can have multiple outputs with internal state information hidden. This means a function block can generate different outputs even if the same inputs are applied. This characteristic is of vital importance for automatic cutting condition generation/modification, after an NC program has been downloaded to a CNC controller, by changing the internal state of a function block (a machining process). For example, an NC program for the same *pocket roughing* can be used by two different milling machines with different cutting conditions, simply by adjusting the internal state variable of the function block instances. Similar to object-oriented definitions, a function block type can be considered as a class, and a particular function block is the instance of that class. For example, a pocket milling function block can be used for either roughing or finishing depending on the message received. However, different from the object-oriented approach, the behaviour of a function block is controlled internally by a state machine whose operation can be represented by an execution control chart (ECC). Each basic function block is an atomic unit for execution. Composite function blocks may require a multi-threaded concurrent execution model due to the complex event flow. The event flow determines the scheduling and execution of machining operations specified by the algorithms (methods) in basic function blocks. It can also provide signals to maintain or change the internal state variables. In terms of machining process encapsulation, basic function blocks encapsulate both the data and functions of machining process, whereas composite function blocks only encapsulate basic function blocks.

Figure 12.1. Function block structure ©2006, IEEE used with permission

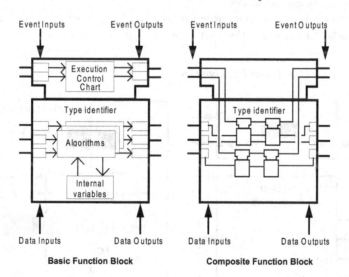

Not only can function blocks encapsulate machining processes, they can also provide support for their communications. The ECC for the state machine of a function block can be used to control their internal algorithms. Figure 12.2 shows a typical example of an ECC for pocket roughing (Xu, Wang & Rong, 2006). Being a (representation of a) finite state machine, an ECC is made up of EC (Execution control) states, EC transitions, and EC actions. The initial EC state, START in this example, cannot have any EC actions associated with it. The occurrence of an event input, such as PI_Init and PI_Cut, causes the ECC to be invoked and the input variables (tool#, key_para, etc.) to be mapped. The EC transitions use a Boolean combination of conditions that may be comprised of event inputs, input variables, output variables, and internal variables. A triggered EC transition causes a change of EC state and this leads to the execution of an associated EC action, Init or Cut in this case. The EC action then sends out an event, PO_Init or PO_Cut, upon completion.

It is anticipated that in the future CNC controllers may have function blocks as part of their device firmware or provide function block libraries from which function blocks can be selected and downloaded. However, to better utilize the legacy machine tools, vendor or user extensions to the standard G-codes could be encapsulated by function blocks and distributed to end-users to be directly utilized by their machining applications.

In addition, function block-based process plan encapsulations enable and facilitate transparent distribution and dynamic scheduling of machining processes over a group of machine tools. As shown in Figure 12.3, a combined process plan represented by three function blocks may be assigned to a single machine controller or may be distributed over several machine tools, depending on the process plan and the availability of each machine, with no interruption to the entire machining operation. The communication (event or data flow) between the function blocks can be realized by a well-established message passing mechanism, such as XML, to keep machining tasks on schedule. This capability is crucial for improving system performance and for rapid fault recovery in a machining shop-floor, where run-time process planning and dynamic rescheduling can be done in parallel whenever a run-time exception occurs.

In addition to basic and composite function block types, service interface (SI) function block is to provide an interface between function blocks and resources (machines) for

Figure 12.2. Execution control mechanism

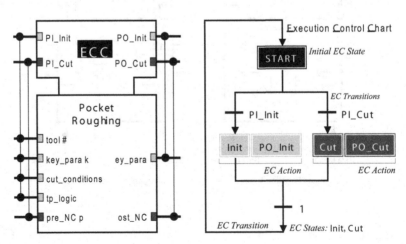

Figure 12.3. Function block distribution ©2006, IEEE used with permission

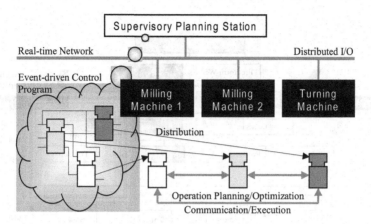

data/event communication. In fact, wherever any form of interaction is required between function blocks within the resource and the external world, there is a requirement for an SI function block. Such interactions include reading values of current cutting parameters, setting a spindle speed, publishing machining status for monitoring, and facilitating dynamic scheduling.

FUNCTION BLOCK-ENABLED CAD/CAPP/CAM INTEGRATION

Similar to STEP-NC, function blocks can also be coupled with machining features. Each function block type corresponds to one machining feature class. By selecting an appropriate function block, a process planner implicitly tells a CNC controller "what-to-do" and leaves the "how-to-do" to the algorithms embedded in the function block. In other words, a function block knows how to fabricate a defined machining feature with which it is coupled. As shown in Figure 12.4, the concept of function blocks can be easily integrated with STEP-NC through Workingsteps. From this perspective, function blocks can be used as a new class of NC control language to replace the G-codes.

Figure 12.5 depicts the function block design and embedded machining information of a typical machining feature – a 4-side pocket (Wang, Liu, Shen & Lang, 2004). The algorithms ALG_INI, ALG_ROU, ALG_FIN, and ALG_MON are responsible for initialization, roughing, finishing, and machining process monitoring respectively.

Along the CAD/CAPP/CAM/CNC chain, function blocks play an important role between CAPP and CNC. They can be used as information and function carriers with process plans embedded and bridge the gap between CNC machines and shop-floor execution control. Today, more and more CNC machines are linked to network, making distributed and interoperable manufacturing possible. In a distributed environment, function blocks are transmitted through network to remote machines whereas run-time machining status can be monitored by triggering the function block embedded monitoring algorithms. Figure 12.6 illustrates one scenario of data sharing enabled by function blocks and machining features. In this case, the tasks of process planning can be divided into two groups and accomplished

Figure 12.4 From machining features to function blocks. ©2006, IEEE used with permission.

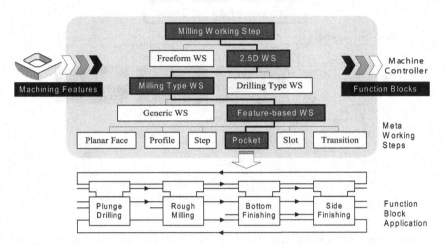

at two different levels: shop-level supervisory planning and controller-level operation planning. The former focuses on product data analysis, machining feature decomposition, setup planning, machining process sequencing, fixture and machine selection. The latter considers the detailed Workingsteps for each machining operations, including cutting tool selection, cutting condition assignment, tool path planning, and control code generation. From design to NC machining, machining features are used for information retrieval, data exchange, and decision-making support at different levels. At the supervisory planning level, the system outputs are a set of function blocks with machining data embedded. They are downloaded to appropriate controllers for low-level operation planning and execution. At the operation planning level, the function blocks are finalized by assigning actual tool data and cutting conditions. As a result, the resultant function blocks are able to describe the detailed operations for the corresponding machining features fabrication.

INTEGRATING CAM WITH CNC

In order to support CAM/CNC integration, an open CNC architecture is presented here. It is based on the STEP-NC data model and function blocks. The architecture (i) intends to support bidirectional information flow in the design-manufacturing chain; (ii) adopts the concept of feature-based machining for CNCs so that higher-level information is made available at CNC machines; (iii) enables an autonomous and intelligent CNC; and (iv) supports a distributed process planning scenario. The ultimate goal is to make the CNC system modular, reusable, open, scalable, extensible and portable.

Model-View-Control Design Pattern

The function block's object-oriented Model-View-Control (MVC) design pattern was adapted by Christensen (2000) for industrial control. Its applicability has been proven for the IEC 61499 architecture. More details on implementing MVC with function blocks can

Figure 12.5. Embedded machining information of a function block. ©*2006, IEEE used with permission*

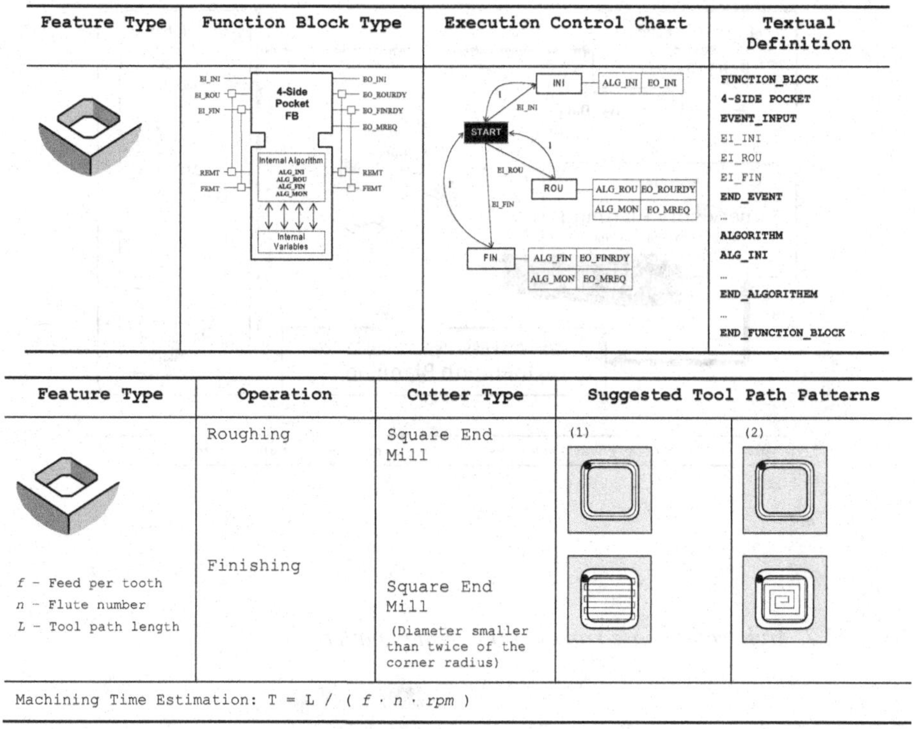

Feature Type	Function Block Type	Execution Control Chart	Textual Definition
			FUNCTION_BLOCK 4-SIDE POCKET EVENT_INPUT EI_INI EI_ROU EI_FIN END_EVENT ALGORITHM ALG_INI ... END_ALGORITHM ... END_FUNCTION_BLOCK

Feature Type	Operation	Cutter Type	Suggested Tool Path Patterns	
	Roughing	Square End Mill	(1)	(2)
	Finishing	Square End Mill (Diameter smaller than twice of the corner radius)		

f – Feed per tooth
n – Flute number
L – Tool path length

Machining Time Estimation: $T = L / (f \cdot n \cdot rpm)$

be found in Vyatkin (2007). The pattern is represented graphically in Figure 12.7. The core part of the pattern is the closed-loop object – controller interconnection. In software, the object is represented by an *interface* to its data sources (say sensors) and signal consumers (actuators). The object can be substituted by its model – a software entity having the same interface and simulating object's behaviour. Several models can be used depending on the required accuracy and the purpose of modelling.

The proposed CNC architecture is developed using the concept of MVC, which enables full simulation and rendering of the CNC system, driven by the actual control code.

Software Implementation: FBDK and FBRT

Function Block Development Kit (FBDK) (Holobloc, 2007) is a software tool that has been widely used in the IEC 61499-related research projects. The tool allows for the graphical

Figure 12.6. Data sharing through function blocks and machining features ©2006, IEEE used with permission.

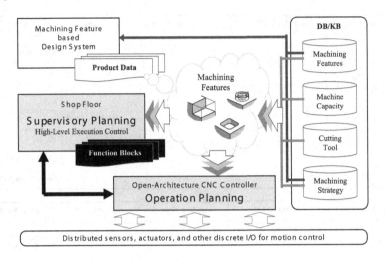

Figure 12.7. Architecture based on the MVC design pattern

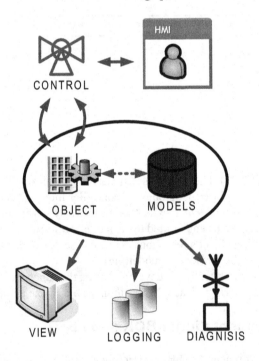

development of both function blocks and function block-based systems. FBDK compiles the developed function block types into Java programming language. The object-oriented nature of this language enables consistent implementation of function blocks. In addition, the platform independence of Java leads to portability of the implemented controller.

The use of FBDK can be combined with other Java development tools, for example, Eclipse Integrated Development Environment, especially when sophisticated Java code (e.g. 3D visualization) or interfacing peripheral devices (e.g. parallel port) need to be encapsulated into function blocks. The function block applications, designed using FBDK, are executed with Java Virtual Machine and the Function Block Runtime (FBRT) library of standard FB types.

Layered Architecture of the CNC System

The use of the layered software architecture as the framework for CNC design enables flexibility in adopting the controller to new machines and computer hardware/software platforms. The layers are selected to separate the functional units into a hierarchical structure so that the controller becomes more readily maintainable, as modifications can be done to a particular layer without compromising the functionality of other layers. Each layer is designed to utilize the services of the lower one.

There are three groups of functions that serve as the backbone of the layers. They are (i) input and data distribution of machining features, (ii) data storage/buffering and (iii) output of physical signals and process execution. The entire architecture consists of 5 layers as shown in Figure 12.8. In addition to the layers that correspond to the three groups of functions mentioned above, two more layers are added -- process planning (Layer 5) and 3D co-ordinates (Layer 3). Functionalities of all layers are encapsulated in function blocks. Communications between all of the layers are implemented by the communication function blocks *Publish* and *Subscribe*.

The layers are further divided into two categories as shown to the right-hand side of the diagram: "Input Model and FB Generic Data Program" and "Machine Specific/Native Program". The former contains primarily generic data whereas the latter contains machine specific data. All layers (5 to 1) are described as follows.

The process planning layer (Layer 5) is to provide definitions on settings and definitions such as security plane, cutting tool, Workplan, workpiece, clamping position and so forth. Layer 4 (Machining features) is implemented by a library of function blocks that parameterize machining features and machining data. It generates the tool paths required for the respective features. Function blocks are used for directing and managing features and shape coordinates to accept or collect data entered either manually by a user, or automatically from other data sources.

The input types required for initialization purposes include,

- Travel limits (maximum traverse of each axis).
- Workpiece dimensions
- Workpiece origin
- Tool start and home positions

An additional set of input options is used to enable the operator to customise a tool path. It consists of,

Figure 12.8. Layered CNC architecture of the novel CNC architecture ©2009 Elsevier Limited, used with permission.

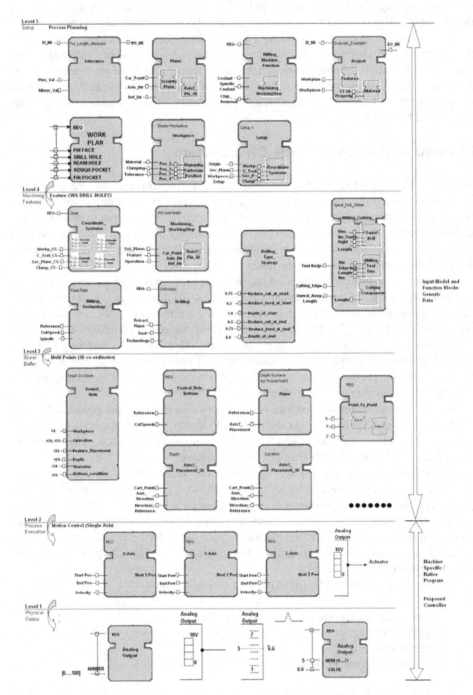

- **Parameterised shape blocks:** Each block represents a basic shape such as a rectangle or a circle. Each of those blocks generates the sequence of coordinates, required to construct the shape using intended dimensions.
- **Text file:** The library of this layer also contains a file reader block designed to read the geometric data of a design part from a text file.
- **Point-to-Point:** Manual point-to-point mapping can be performed to build a tool path.

The 3D co-ordinate layer (Layer 3) is an optional layer; it is there to cater for additional axes of a CNC machine tool (e.g. 4 and 5 axis machine tools). Layer 2 (Store/Buffer) stores all the points, feed-rates and other data required to carry out a machining job on a machine tool.

Layer 1 (Physical Outputs and Process Execution) is designed to calculate the feed-rate for each individual axis, using the feed-rate vector. It is responsible for point coordination and for sending updated physical signals to the output device. Implementation is realized as two separate function block resources. The first resource acts as a coordinator, with function blocks sending requests to, and receiving requests from, the co-ordinate memory storage. The velocity data are then sent to the second resource, whose responsibility is to activate the motion control. In the case of a milling machine, the required frequency and number of pulses are calculated from the given distance and feed-rate.

The Prototype CNC System

A prototype of the proposed CNC architecture has been implemented on a testbed, a PC controlled, 3-axis CNC vertical mill. The machine is supplied with a PC-based EMC (Enhanced Machine Control) controller and a motor control unit that drives the three stepper motors. The hardware of the PC and the motor control unit are used for the prototype system. A PC is used to run a Java-based function block execution platform. It is envisaged that embedded devices, capable of running function blocks, will be capable of deploying the same solution.

Software Implementation

The functional layers of the proposed CNC are encapsulated in function blocks as discussed in the previous section. Based on the design data of a part, the corresponding function block application is generated. STEP-NC data are translated into the function block application in Layer 5. The features, implemented by function blocks in Layer 4, are then translated into trajectories, i.e. sequences of points (Layer 3). Movement between the points is implemented by the motion controller function blocks in Layer 2. This is done through calculating an output for the axis motors from the sampled positions, generated by the calculated trajectory points. The output, generated from the motion controller is passed onto the discrete Input/Output (I/O) interface function blocks in Layer 1, which send the control signals to the motor's drivers.

The proposed CNC structure is presented in Figure 12.9. The CNC is implemented as a system configured by four devices (in IEC 61499 terminology): DISPLAY3D, Model, Controller and PhysicalOut, corresponding to View, Model, Control and Interface as in the extended MVC architecture. The process starts with interpreting the STEP-NC data for a part that are then captured by the function blocks in Layer 5. It is then translated to the function block application Control, which is composed of the function blocks from Layer 4 and uses services in Layer 3. For better structuring, the control application is distributed across 8 execution containers (resources in IEC 61499 terminology): MACHINE, WORKPIECE, WORKPIECE_START, TOOL_START, POINTS_AUTO, POINTS_FILE, POINTS, and INTERFACE. The Control device also includes 3 resources, corresponding to Layers 1 and 2.

The "Model" device contains function block applications, modelling uncontrolled behaviour of a machine tool. Given input control signals the model changes its state as a real machine tool does. It feeds the parameters of the current state to the device DISPLAY3D which can render function block applications.

The PhysicalOut device sends the control signals generated by the function blocks in Layer 1, to the parallel port of the PC. The devices communicate one with another by means of communication function blocks.

This system configuration, with minimal changes, can be executed on any computing platform supporting the IEC 61499 function blocks. As shown in Figure 12.9, it can be a personal computer with direct peripheral connection to a machine tool (right-hand side), or an embedded device with a distributed architecture (left-hand side). In the latter case, the motor drives, corresponding to three axes and the display are connected to the main

Figure 12.9. System structure based on the MVC pattern ©2009 Elsevier Limited, used with permission

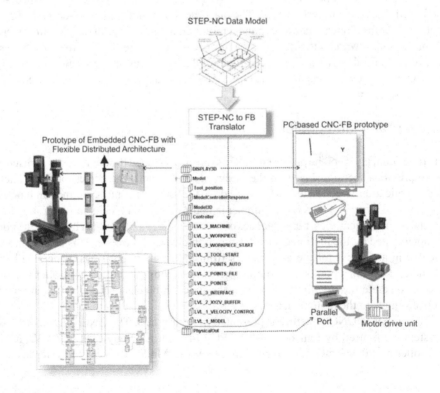

processing unit via a fieldbus. With this motor control, only a directional signal and a single pulse are required to move a motor a single step in a given direction. The desired behaviour of the physical interface is to utilize the raw data calculated in the controller (feed-rate) to control the real machine (i.e. to produce the signals required to drive the motors).

In this system, the physical interface of the PC with the motor drives is implemented using its parallel port. The dependency on this particular hardware solution was captured by creating an abstract device model, called *ParallelPortDev*. The device model is identified by a specific library of function blocks providing user interfaces to the motor drives via the parallel port of the PC. The *ParallelMotor* function block maps the motor control signals to the parallel port of the computer. The implementation of this function block is based on the *ParallelPortMapper Java* class which enables control of the parallel port data pins. A *ParallelPortMapper* object was designed to use classes in the RXTX Java library (2008) to build functions required to send data through the data pins of a parallel port. Function block libraries were implemented to encapsulate direct communication to any or all output pins of the parallel port. It is designed to access the *SendData* function in *ParallelPortMapper* to force the 8 data lines of a parallel port to a certain value. It can be noticed from the *ParallelMotor* block, that the inputs required are pulse period, number of steps required to be achieved and rotation direction of each individual motor.

A composite function block, using the services of the ParallelMotor function block, is designed to handle velocities and number of steps of all three motors. It can be easily extended to accommodate a fourth motor. This function block generates an output sequence which is written to the parallel port, and in turn drives the motors on the machine.

Implementation of the MVC Design Pattern

Model is the core part of the Model-View-Control architecture. A CNC machine is modelled by taking into account machine's structure, its physical dimensions, number of axes available and type of inputs, outputs and other specifications. The geometry of the part in terms of features is used as input for the corresponding function blocks. The workpiece model provides the data for tool path generation, similar to the Tool Path Generator in a traditional CNC. The controller generates signals such as co-ordinate and velocity signals (one set for each individual axis).

The *Movement_Estimator* function block (Figure 12.11 (a)) calculates the data for the planned path, which is then fed into the axis model block that estimates the next point for the axis. In order to have a modular design for the system, the *Axis_Model* (Figure 12.10 (b)) function block is used to represent a linear axis control unit to define an axis in the system. In this case, three *Axis_Model* function blocks are needed to denote the (X, Y, Z) coordinates of a point. This function block deals with data such as speed and directional input for an axis and updates the coordinate position. It can then be used for each of the X, Y and Z axis control.

Further limits were added to the model to reflect the capability of the machine tool. These include the rapid traversing speed and the maximum travel distances along each of the three axes.

Figure 12.10. Movement_Estimator function blocks (a) and Axis_Model function blocks (b)

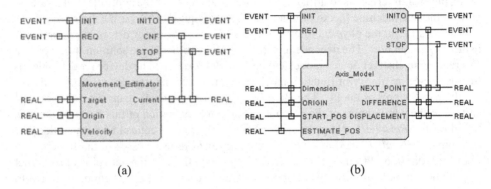

(a)   (b)

Visualisation

The Visualisation component of the MVC architecture is implemented in a 3D virtual environment through a Java extension, i.e. Java3D. The objects are rendered in a hierarchical manner. At the topmost level is the 3D universe. Rooted from it are branches. At the end of the branches are the leaf nodes, which represent 3D shapes. Branches themselves can contain other branches as well as leaf nodes. A simplified view of this hierarchy is shown in Figure 12.11. This structure is embodied in the function block visualization implementation.

The developed visualisation engine is primitive and wireframe-based. The purpose is to demonstrate the feasibility of using Java3D for graphic display. The engine renders workpieces and cutting tools. Travel constraints and axes relationships are also modelled. The engine consists of device models such as *SampleFrame3D* and *ImageDev3D*, and

Figure 12.11. Simplified overview of Java3D

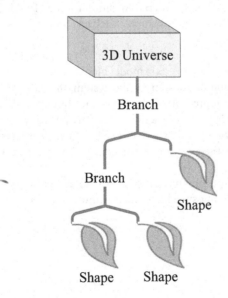

function block types such as *RenderAxis3D, RenderWireBox3D, RenderCylinder3D* and *RenderLine3D*. The *RenderAxis3D* function block draws 3 axes to represent the positive direction of the movement of each axis in the system. *RenderWireBox3D* function block draws a simple workpiece and travel constrains. The *RenderCylinder3D* function block draws the cutting tool. The *RenderLine3D* function blocks are used to render the tool path by joining two points, current and next, with a line.

3D rendering is achieved in a three-step process. First a JFrame object is extended to support 3D rendering. This is done by creating a 3D Universe within it. JFrame itself is a native object in the 2D library Java.Swing, and handles the creation of a window object in which to render. Next, an interface to the function block environment is created. This interface is called the ImageDev3D. This is encapsulated by a function block device (as it represents a separate subsystem). An extended JFrame object is added as a child of the ImageDev3D. In the final step, separate function blocks are created that define a particular shape. These function blocks construct Shape3D objects which can be rendered in the 3D Universe. The geometric data are transferred to the JFrame that exists in the ImageDev3D. The entire process is depicted in Figure 12.12 (Mohamad, Xu & Vyatkin, 2009). In this way it is possible to render multiple instances of any shape, as long as there is a function block for each instance. Furthermore it allows other more complex geometries to be created with ease.

Figure 12.13 shows interfaces of the function blocks encapsulating the visualization functions. Each shape added to the 3D Universe is coupled with a transform object that allows a user to manipulate the translation, rotation and scale of the shape. By modifying the transformation object it is possible to model dynamic motion of a system. The 3D visualization supports some typical navigation abilities as seen in many other 3D packages – namely rotate, zoom and pan. This enhances the user-friendliness of the interface.

A Test Part

The starting point of the process is the STEP-NC data, containing information such as Workplan, Workingstep, machining strategy, machining features and cutting tools. The system is tested by manufacturing several parts, one of which is the first example in the annex of ISO 14649-11 (2004) as shown in Figure 12.14. The data shown in the figure are included in a STEP physical file.

Figure 12.12. Overview of function block 3D rendering

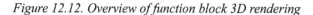
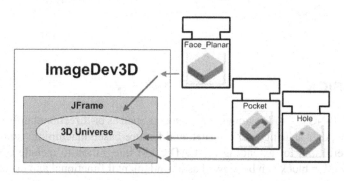

Figure 12.13. Samples of the library of 3D shape function blocks

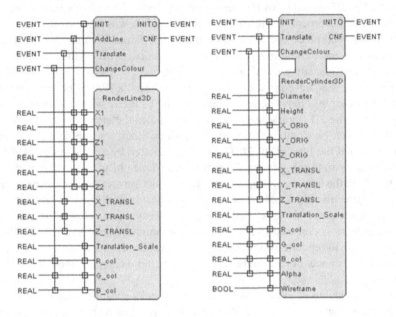

Figure 12.14. Sample part from ISO 14649-11

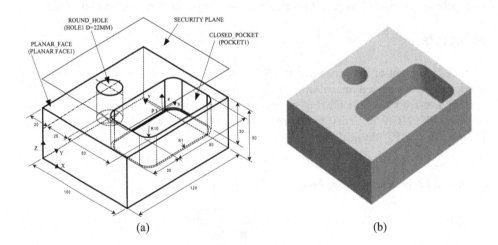

(a)   (b)

CONCLUSION

Whereas STEP-NC is good at supporting concepts such as bi-directional information flow in CAD/CAM, data sharing over Internet, and feature-based machining, function blocks provide a useful tool for extending the CAD/CAM integration to include CNC. This is because a function block can be viewed as a fundamental functional and executable unit.

Function blocks can be designed to match individual machining features and have needed algorithms and data embedded to decide the best cutting conditions and tool path once a machine and cutting tool are selected. This makes function blocks best suited for CNC controls. They have an edge over STEP-NC in supporting an intelligent and autonomous CNC. In short, STEP-NC can be viewed as a "job-setter" (providing all the necessary information), whereas function blocks can be viewed as a "job-doer" (executing the machining commands) for interoperable manufacturing. To this end, STEP-NC and function blocks can work hand in hand in supporting interoperable manufacturing.

The proposed CNC controller uses the IEC 61499 architecture as its development platform and STEP-NC as the input data model. Compliance with the STEP-NC standard helps transfer the data across different companies without the need of data conversion and manufacture the corresponding part on different machine tools. The prototype system has a layered structure. This type of organisation simplifies the transition between simulation and real machining, and substitution of one milling machine by another.

It is proved that use of function block technology allows development of an open and distributable CNC system. This also enables separate functional units of the controller to be implemented on other devices. In addition to the distributable nature of the prototype system, the proposed controller can also support remote management and configuration, a feature that could be useful in an environment featuring multiple machine tools (e.g. flexible manufacturing systems). Thanks to the successfully implemented Model-View-Control design methodology, the architecture and its prototype system can also support real-time machining simulation. Hence the system can also be used as a virtual machine tool, or software CNC.

REFERENCES

Christensen, J. H. (2000). Design patterns for systems engineering with IEC 61499. In *Proceedings of Conference in Distributed Automation* (Verteile Automatisierung), Magdeburg, Germany.

Holobloc. (2007). *Function Block Development Kit*. Retrieved July 28, 2007, from www.holobloc.com

IEC 61499. (2005). *Function blocks for industrial-process measurement and control systems - Part 1: Architecture*, Geneva, Switzerland: International Electro-technical Commission.

ISO 14649-11. (2003). *Data model for Computerized Numerical Controllers: Part 11 – Process data for milling. International Standards Organization*. Geneva, Switzerland: International Organisation for Standardisation (ISO).

Vyatkin, V. (2007). *IEC 61499 Function Blocks for Embedded Control Systems Design*. USA: Instrumentation Society of America.

Wang, L., Liu, Z., Shen, W., & Lang, S. (2004). Function-block enabled job shop planning and control with uncertainty, in *Proceedings of ASME International Mechanical Engineering Congress & Exposition, IMECE2004-59279*, Anaheim, California, Nov. 13-19, 2004.

Xu, X. W., Wang, L., & Rong, Y. (2006). STEP-NC and function blocks for interoperable manufacturing. *IEEE Transactions on Automation Science and Engineering, 3*(3), 297-307.

Minhat, M., Vyatkin, V., Xu, X., Wong, S., & Al-Bayaa, Z. (2009). A novel open CNC architecture based on STEP-NC data model and IEC 61499 function blocks. *Robotics and Computer-Integrated Manufacturing* (in press).

Mohamad M., Xu X, & Vyatkin, V. (2009). STEPNCMillUoA – A CNC System Based on STEP-NC and Function Block Architecture. *International Journal of Mechatronics and Manufacturing Systems.* (in press).

Chapter XIII
Development of an Integrated, Adaptable CNC System

ABSTRACT

In order to prepare manufacturing companies to face increasingly frequent and unpredictable market changes with confidence, there is a recognized need for CNC machine tools to be further advanced so that they become more integrated with design models and adaptable to uncertain machining conditions. For a CNC system to be able to access any design information, this design information has to be at the task-level, that is what-to-do. For a CNC system to produce the final part, it has to turn the task-level information into method-level information which effectively is the machine control data. These topics are discussed at the beginning of this chapter.

The rest of the chapter discusses a CNC native database used for converting the task-level data to method-level data, the methodology of converting the task-level data to method-level data, and implementation of the methodology to a conventional CNC machine that employs G-codes. Again both STEP-NC (ISO 14649-1, 2003) and function blocks (IEC 61499, 2005) are used.

TASK-LEVEL DATA VS. METHOD-LEVEL DATA

An important feature of the STEP-NC concept is that of "machine tool independency"; this makes STEP-NC codes interoperable across various CNC systems. This is because a STEP-NC data model mainly captures the task-level or the what-to-do information. Although it is possible to define data at the method-level or the how-to-do level, such as machine tool trajectory, the main aim of STEP-NC is to allow these decisions to be made by a STEP-NC-enabled controller. This way, STEP-NC part programs may be written once but can be used on different machine tools providing that the machine tool has the required process capabilities. Figure 13.1 shows these two categories of data defined in the STEP-NC data model. The first two columns depict the manufacturing task information. The process-level data describe abstract manufacturing tasks at the macro-level. The geometry-level data are represented in terms of *manufacturing_features*. The how-to-do data are also divided into two types. Machine tool core data spell out the manufacturing requirements. Machine tool auxiliary data are method-level data and they are in fact defined in the STEP-NC data model as optional data. Both categories of how-to-do data take different forms when different machine tools are used.

The central issue is therefore the 'transition' from the task-level data to the method-level, or from the what-to-do data to the how-to-do data. Since STEP-NC is utilized as a CNC machining data model, implementation of STEP-NC is effectively a process of adapting its data model for different CNC systems. This is illustrated in Figure 13.2.

Such a system may have three stages. First of all, a native version of STEP-NC program is generated based on the information in a generic STEP-NC program. Then, low-level, local NC commands can be generated based on the native STEP-NC information. This provides a direct interface with the targeted CNC machine, hence a "CAM-CNC transition". This transition is intended to be hidden away from the user and ideally synchronised with the subsequent execution process. Finally, a STEP-NC enabled controller executes the STEP-NC program through the above native CNC commands.

GENERATE A NATIVE STEP-NC PROGRAM

The key in this phase is to "map" a generic STEP-NC program to a native one. In other words, the main task is to convert what-to-do information in a generic STEP-NC program,

Figure 13.1. What-to-do and how-to-do data in STEP-NC ©2008, Taylor and Francis Journals, http://www.informaworld.com, used with permission from the authors.

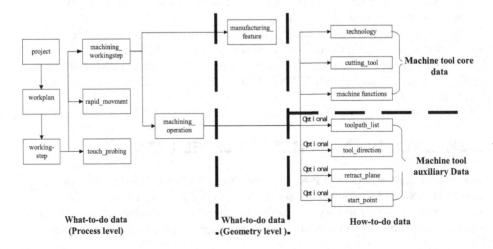

Figure 13.2. Implementation of STEP-NC manufacturing ©2008, Taylor and Francis Journals, http://www.informaworld.com, used with permission from the authors.

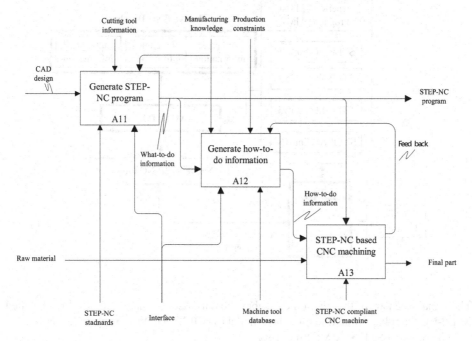

into the how-to-do information for a specific CNC machine. Different CNC machines have differing machining capabilities and native parameters. Until a STEP-NC program takes into account all the information specific to a CNC system, it will not be possible to execute the Workplan(s) specified in the STEP-NC program. The mapping process is also a "checking" process to evaluate the manufacturability of the job on a particular machine tool. In the distributed manufacturing environment, this "plug-and-play" feature gives a process plan the mobility and portability that are desired.

Figure 13.3 shows the logical structure of the system (Wang, Xu & Tedford, 2006). The three main functional units are the Native CNC database, Adaptor and Human-Machine (HM) interface.

MODELLING NATIVE MACHINING FACILITIES

CNC machining centres are vendor-specific and vary in their hardware configuration and control software. Numerous data are preloaded onto a machine tool during production to cater for different machine functions. In order for the Adaptor to work with different machine tools, it is essential to have a database structure that is capable of modelling the native information of different machine tools. Based on this database, the Adaptor can be developed with ease. When a new machine tool arrives, the only task would be to store the information of the new machine tool into the native database. The Adaptor, which has been developed to work with the database of a fixed structure, does not need to be altered.

Figure 13.3. Logical structure of the system

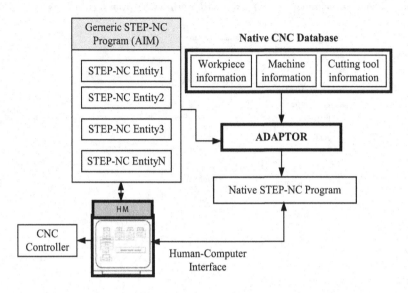

The remaining part of this section describes the database that has been developed, called STEP-NC compliant Machine tool Data model (STEP-NCMtDm) (Yang & Xu, 2008).

The scope of STEP-NCMtDm covers,

* machine tool data required by process planning, production planning and CNC machining. These data are not intended for machine tool vendors but for supporting process planning tasks. Thus, all related information about a machine tool required by process planning and production planning is included.
* machine tool data required to define the method-level information based on the task-level data. Four different STEP-NC based manufacturing scenarios (Figure 13.1) are supported. They correspond to the STEP-NC models at four different detail levels – those with
  (a) only the detailed level what-to-do information (i.e. manufacturing feature information from the design stage).
  (b) both types of the what-to-do information.
  (c) both types of the what-to-do information and the machine tool independent how-to-do information. The STEP-NCMtDm is required to evaluate whether a machine tool is suitable for this task.
  (d) all what-to-do and how-to-do data.
* the proposed STEP-NCMtDm is harmonized with the other machine tool data models defined in other standards (e.g. ISO and ASME).

Machine tool resources may be classified into two types: static and dynamic. If the data stay unchanged during the lifecycle of a machine tool, they are classified as 'static machine tool data', e.g. machine loading capacity and machine tool dimensions. These data are mainly machine tool's specifications, giving a gross indication of the machining capability of a machine tool. On the other hand, if the data change during different stages of machine tool usage, or take on different values for different applications, they are classified as 'dynamic machine tool data'. Dynamic machine tool data are the key information for realizing flexible process planning and manufacturing. There may be two causes to the change of machine tool's dynamic data. The first is to do with the machine tool wear, which may lead to an accuracy drift. The second is to do with the changes or re-configuration of a machine tool setup. For example, adding a new cutting tool or tool holder will affect its machining capability. With both types of dynamic data captured, STEP-NCMtDm becomes adaptable to the ever-changing shop-floor environment.

Separation of static and dynamic data in STEP-NCMtDm makes it more convenient to manage and utilize the machine tool data. The static machine tool data, once modelled, can stay unchanged. For the two types of dynamic machine tool data, different data processing and updating procedures are followed. The first type of dynamic data needs to be updated on a more regular basis due to the factors such as machine tool wear, whereas the second type is updated at irregular intervals.

STEP-NCMtDm

Six sets of data are modelled in STEP-NCMtDm: 1) Machine tool general data; 2) Machine tool component data; 3) Machining capability data; 4) Machine tool performance data; 5) Machining cost data; and 6) Machine tool kinematics data.

Machine Tool General Data Set

This data set represents the general information about a machine tool. The root is ENTITY *machine_tool*. The general information modelled about a machine tool includes its id, location, machine tool origin, axes, spindle, the cutting tool handling devices, etc. Since attribute *machine_tool*.its_spindle is defined by a set of ENTITY *spindle*, STEP-NCMtDm can support modelling multi-spindle CNC machine tools. In the current version of STEP-NCMtDm, ENTITY *machine_tool* can be utilized to model milling machine tools (including drilling machine tools), turning centres and mill-turn centres, and according to machine tool performance data, the model only represents machine tool's accuracy information.

Machine Tool Component Data Set

This data set represents the information about each individual component of a machine tool. It is further divided into machine tool axis data, spindle data, workpiece handling device data, cutting tool handling device data and auxiliary device data.

1. *Axis data set*: The main Entity for this data set is the abstract ENTITY *axis*, which represents the general concept of a machine tool axis. The name and its origin are represented as two attributes: axis_name and its_origin. The definitions of axis' orientations conform to Australian Standard AS 115-1985 (AS1115, 1985) and it is identified by a defined type axis_name. Entity *axis* has two subtypes: *traveling_axis* and *rotary_axis*. They inherit their supertype Entity *axis*'s attributes. Entity *traveling_axis* defines a linear movement axis, alongside its characteristics such as trav-

elling range, allowable movement directions (positive/negative axis movements), feeding information and rapid movement speed. *rotary_axis* represents a rotated axis with its movement type (*continous_rot_movement*, *index_rot_movement*, or *limited_swing_rot_movement*), the rotation directions, and the maximal rotation speed data.

2. *Spindle data set*: This data set represents the spindle data for assisting process planning activities. Similar to the axis data set, the main ENTITY *spindle* is also an abstract supertype. Two types of spindles are represented as subtypes, *milling_type spindle* and *turning_type_spindle*. The maximum workpiece or cutting tool allowed for these spindles are defined in them respectively. The main parameters of a spindle include: its_id, its rotation speed range, its orientations, its spindle nose information, the spindle nose to column/table distance, its coolant information, its max power and torque, and whether being capable of synchronizing spindle rotation with feeding.

3. *Workpiece handling device data se*: This data set is for various workpiece holding devices and their specifications as needed for process planning. The origin of the workpiece_handling_device (attribute its_origin) is defined in accordance with the STEP-NC definition of the workpiece origin. Attribute its_moving_orientation shows which axes (travelling axes and rotary axes) a *workpiece_handling_device* can move along. The OPTIONAL attribute its_driving_spindle indicates the driving information for the device. ENTITY *workpiece_handling_device_restricted_area* is used to determine information of a workpiece_hanlding_device's restricted area, which can be used for collision detection. Six types of devices are considered, *chuck*, *collet*, *chuck_tailstock_combination*, *bar_feeder*, *table*, and *pallet*. The capacity data for these devices are further defined, for example, max_part_diameter, min_part_diameter, max_allowed_part_length, workpiece_offset, and number_of_jaw for a *chuck*.

4. *Cutting tool handling device data set*: This data set contains information such as id, tool capacity, available tool list, its current machining tool, its moving orientations (along travelling axis or rotary axis), maximum tool length and weight, and allowed diameter range of cutting tools. In process planning, this data set can be used for cutting tool selection and handling of tool offsets. The related restricted area for avoiding collision is defined by ENTITY *cutting_tool_handling_device_restricted_area*. Two specific types of cutting tool handling devices are modelled: *turret* and *tool_magazine*. Note that the *turret*.index_time (existing when value of *turret*.auto_change is true) and *tool_magazine*.tool_change_time are two critical pieces of information for estimating production time.

5. *Auxiliary device data*: This data set includes the information about coolant and chip removal. Coolant information is required by ENTITIES *milling_functions* and *turning_functions* in a STEP-NC data model. It includes data such as coolant type, maximum pressure, and coolant through spindle or not.

Machine Tool Capability Data Set

This data set contains the information which can be used to determine machining capability of a machine tool. In process planning, these data are the key to determining whether a machine tool is suitable for a particular machining job. The machining capability, represented by ENTITY *machining_capability*, includes machine tool's possible operation types, restricted area for avoiding collision (including restricted areas for workpiece, workpiece handling device, cutting tool handling device, etc.), table loading capability, machinable workpiece size, feeding capability and maximum cutting depth data.

Machine Tool Performance Data Set

Machine tool performance data set is used along with some other data, in selecting a proper machine tool for machining. Only machine tool accuracy data is shown in the diagram. They are machine tool resolution (ENTITY *resolution*) and axis repeatability (ENTITY *repeatablility_accuracy*).

Machining Cost Information Data Set

This set of data is modelled by ENTITY *machine_tool_cost_information* for estimating machining cost in process planning. It keeps the data such as the average cost per setup (attribute setup_cost) and machining hourly rate (attribute machining_cost_per_hour). The process planning system can use these data to calculate the corresponding manufacturing cost.

Kinematics Model of a Machine Tool

Kinematics model is a core part in support of implementing STEP-NCMtDm in process planning and simulation. The kinematics model can be developed as a chain structure (Suk, Seo, Lee, Choi, Jeong & Kim, 2003), in which the information of each node and the relationships between them are modelled. ENTITY *k_component* is a fundamental element to determining each node of a machine tool's kinematics chain. The name, geometry information and the movement information of a *k_component* are modelled in attributes its_name, its_geometry, and its_degree_of_freedom. Two *k_components* form a *k_jointed_pair* with a start-end sequence. A sequenced list of *k_jointed_pairs* forms the entire kinematics chain of a machine tool (ENTITY *k_chain*), which can be either a tool oriented chain or workpiece oriented chain (indicated in attribute its_type).

Static and Dynamic Data

As discussed previously, machine tool data can be divided into two categories: static and dynamic. Different data acquisition and updating methods are required and implemented for different categories. The dynamic machine tool data can be further divided into two groups according to their updating frequency, regular or irregular. Classification of static and dynamic data is essential for later model implementation.

In general, such classification is based on the following guidelines:

- The machine tool's general information and the data related to machine tool or its components' capability are considered as static data.
- The machine tool data related to the machine tool's performance, such as accuracy data, belong to the first type of machine tool dynamic data. Frequency of updating this type of data depends on the usage of the machine tool.

- The machine tool data related to cutting tool and workpiece handling devices are of the second type of dynamic data that need to be updated on a regular basis. This is due to the fact that different cutting-tool handling devices or workpiece handling devices may be utilized for machining a different part. The data are often situational subject to the changes at the shop-floor.

AN ADAPTOR

There are three functional units in the Adaptor: a Pre-processor, Encoder and Function blocks Mapping unit (Figure 13.4). The Adaptor is therefore effectively a "Plug-and-Play" mapping unit.

STEP-NC Pre-Processor

As a supporting module, the STEP-NC Pre-processor reads the STEP-NC data and organizes them into three groups: Machining features, Machining technology data and Production resource data. Machining features are directly used by the Encoder. Machining technology and production resource data are stored in their respective databases. The feature information conforms to the STEP-NC standard. It therefore consists of features such as planar face, pocket, slot, step, round hole, tool path feature, profile feature, boss, spherical cap, rounded end and thread. This makes the system "feature-based". In the Machining technology database (MTDB), information such as feed-rate, feed-rate reference, cut speed, spindle speed, feed-rate override, spindle override, and feed-rate per tooth is stored; all is necessary for defining a machining operation. The Production resource database (PRDB) stores the specific CNC machine resources and setup information, e.g. the cutting tools, workpiece and setup data. These production resources help the mapping system to choose the suitable cutting tools and generate appropriate tool paths according to the setup information. There is also a Maintenance database that is responsible for collecting feedback information from a CNC machine. It acts as a buffer between the MTDB, PRDB and CNC machine. The information collected updates the MTDB and PRDB. This is done in real-time so that when an error is encountered while executing an early part of the STEP-NC code, the system can make corrections to a latter part of the code.

STEP-NC Encoder

STEP-NC Encoder reads the STEP-NC data from the Pre-processor and encodes the STEP-NC data into function blocks (FB) (IEC 61499, 2005). Meanwhile, the STEP-NC Encoder also organizes the data into three groups: Shared information, Workingstep and Workplan.

Shared information contains data about Workpiece information, Setup, Manufacturing function, Cutting tools and Security-Plane, all from a STEP-NC file. This information is shared by all Workingsteps. Being the basic machining unit, Workingstep is almost "self-sufficient" in fully defining a machining operation. The information contained in a Workplan indicates the machining sequence of the Workingsteps. This sequence, however, can be subject to changes when necessary.

Because STEP-NC and G-codes (ISO 6983-1, 1982) represent geometry at different levels, it is necessary to map the feature and tool path information represented in STEP-NC into that of the G-code format. As a high-level CNC control language, STEP-NC has the ability to describe complex geometric information using definitions such as ploy line and composite curves. G-code on the other hand is a low-level machine language which has only three geometry description modes --- G01 (Linear interpolation), G02 (Arc interpolation clock-wise) and G03 (Arc interpolation counter clock-wise). An important task for the Encoder is to generate the tool path based on the complex geometry in STEP-NC in terms of G-codes.

There are two types of tool paths being dealt with individually,

- Approach and retract tool paths
  The approach tool path defines the trajectory of a cutter prior to cutting. Similarly, the retract tool path defines the trajectory of a cutter after machining the part. In STEP-NC, approach and retract strategies are defined relative to the start or end point

Figure 13.4. Structure of the Adaptor Structure of the Adaptor. ©2007 Taylor & Francis Journals, http://www.informaworld.com, used with permission from the authors)

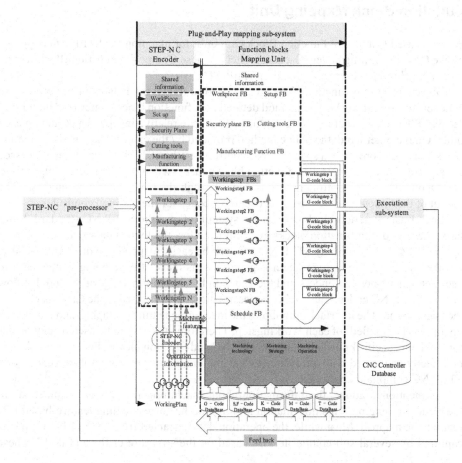

of the cutting operation. The feed-rate for the approach or retract path is the feed-rate specified for the related start or end point of the cutting operation respectively.

- Machining tool paths

   A machining tool path defines the tool's machining trajectory. It is defined according to the information about the machining feature and machining strategy. Machining feature defines the machining area, whereas machining strategy defines the cutting "style", be it overlap, allow_multiple_passes, unidirectional, bidirectional, contour parallel, bi-directional contour, contour spiral or centre milling.

Corresponding to these two types of tool paths, two modules are developed to generate the necessary information for outputting G-codes. They are Auxiliary Tool Path engine and Geometry engine. The former gets the tool path information from the setup data stored in the Production resource database and the approaching & retracting strategy data in the Machining technology database. Through analysis and calculations, the cutter's approaching and retracting tool paths are interpreted in G-codes. The Geometry engine receives the geometric data from the machining features and the machining strategy. Through the internal algorithms, the geometric data of a feature is converted into fragments of lines or arcs which are ready to be used for generating the G-codes.

Function Block Mapping Unit

Feature-based Composite Function Blocks are built for mapping the STEP-NC code into native CNC machining codes (G-codes). Each of these Composite Function Blocks represents a machining feature as defined in STEP-NC.

Objects used in a function block can be used to model the behaviour of entities and concepts in the real world. The method defined by a function block's internal data follows the STEP-NC data structure. Note that these FBs have relative independence among each other. On the other hand, the public method provided by the external data makes function block behave according to a specific CNC controller. When STEP-NC codes are processed for a particular CNC controller, function blocks just "switch to" the internal algorithms corresponding to the controller. This is done through the CNC controller database. The output of the system will be the correct set of G-codes for the targeted controller.

Each Basic function block built in the system follows the STEP-NC standard. Similarly, the Composite function blocks are built to follow the logical data structure defined by STEP-NC. Therefore, any STEP-NC code can be easily mapped into different G-codes. In other words, the mapping system is generic. This makes the mapping system easy to use. There is no need to understand the function blocks' internal algorithm and dataflow or even STEP-NC codes. The final G-codes are directly connected to the CNC machine in the background. The interface only shows the machining features (graphic) and machining operations (simplified) of each Workingstep. Therefore, it is easy to be used by any operators without specific knowledge about STEP-NC and function blocks. Function blocks can be directly connected with hardware such as motors, pumps etc. in a future version of a STEP-NC compliant controller.

As mentioned above, the information about machining features is "channelled" to the Geometry engine. This information is stored in the corresponding feature-based FBs ready to be mapped. Meanwhile, the operation data extracted from the STEP-NC code is captured by several sub-composite FBs based on the structure of the STEP-NC. These function blocks are Machining Technology FBs, Machining Strategy FBs and Machining Operation FBs, each containing lower-level FBs or basic FBs. For example, the Machining Technology FB contains nine basic function blocks according to the structure defined in STEP-NC, each representing one aspect of machining technology.

Each basic entity in STEP-NC has its corresponding Basic function block. Each basic function block has an internal algorithm responsible for mapping STEP-NC codes into G-codes. The structure and working principle of these basic function blocks are discussed in the next section.

When different machining information such as machining technology, machining function, and machining strategy is given to the feature-based function blocks, they are automatically mapped into the Workingstep-based FBs. Through these FBs, the STEP-NC codes are mapped into different G-code blocks representing Workingsteps and used directly by the targeted CNC machine.

As discussed in Chapter XII, a basic function block is built based on an explicit event driven model and provides for data flow and finite state automata based control. It can have multiple outputs and can maintain internal hidden state information. This means that a function block can generate different outputs even if the same inputs are applied while the algorithm built internal of function block is changed. For example, a function block for milling operations can be used by different machine tools with different controllers. This is done by adjusting the internal state variables of the function block according to different controllers. The adjustment is carried out by tuning the algorithms in the function block based on the external resources, i.e. the CNC controller databases. Figure 13.5 shows a Milling basic FB with inputs to the left and outputs to the right. The upper section shows the event input and output, whereas the lower section indicates the data connections.

The behaviour of a function block is controlled by an internal finite state machine, whose operation is represented by an execution control chart. The occurrence of an event input, such as Event_INIT or Event_REQ, causes the function block to be invoked and the input variables to be mapped. A function block actions based on a combination of Boolean conditions which may be comprised of event inputs, data inputs, and internal state variables. In this system, different combination of these Boolean conditions will result in different internal algorithm calls to the relevant data from a specific CNC controller database. This way, the input data which represents STEP-NC data is mapped into the output data, i.e. the G-codes for the specific CNC controller. Meanwhile, The EC action sends out an event Event_INITO or Event_CNF for another basic function block, or "flagging" that the execution cycle of the function block is completed.

HUMAN-MACHINE INTERFACE

The Human-Machine interface acts as a console that the operator of a CNC system can use to (a) load a STEP-NC part program, (b) set up the native database and (c) generate a native STEP-NC program. It enables communications with other modules and acts as a "bridge" between a CAPP system and a CNC machine. It can also provide the functions to edit both generic and native STEP-NC programs. When the tool-path simulation reveals an error, the operator can easily locate and fix it.

The proposed framework can be implemented on the Windows® platform using a set of development tools and technologies, such as Microsoft Visual C++®, Microsoft Foundation

Figure 13.5. Basic FB for Milling Function ©2007 Taylor & Francis Journals, http://www. informaworld.com, used with permission from the authors.

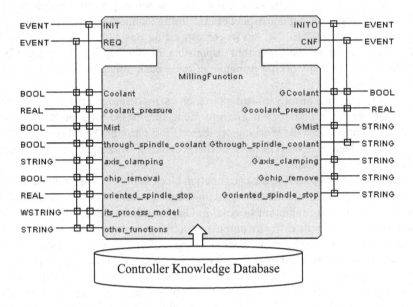

Figure 13.6. The HM interface window

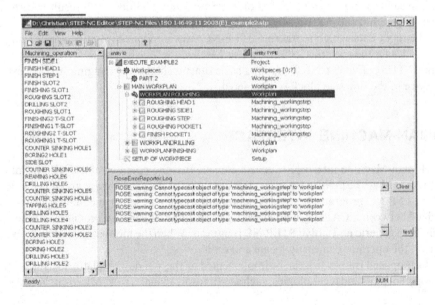

Classes and Microsoft Access™. Figures 13.6 shows a screen shot of the Human-Machine interface developed.

As part of an integrated system, the framework has a close link to the CAPP system. A typical working session includes the following four steps,

- Load and display a generic STEP-NC program.
- Load the native manufacturing database. The native manufacturing information can either be retrieved from STEP-NCMtDm or entered on-the-fly at the interface.
- The Adaptor converts the generic STEP-NC program to a native STEP-NC program. On completion, the new Workingsteps are displayed on the HM interface, along with the STEP Part 21 file.
- The native STEP-NC program is manually edited when necessary, before being sent to the CNC machine for execution.

CONCLUSION

The system described in this chapter can take STEP-NC as input and interface with a legacy CNC system. There is no need to modify the configuration of the current CNC machines. This is being viewed as a viable but intermediate step toward a fully STEP-NC enabled CNC controller.

Integration and interoperability are realised in the system. The input to the system is STEP-NC data regardless of what machine tools are to be used. The Adaptor incorporates a CNC native database called STEP-NCMtDm, which captures the specific information about different CNC machines. This effectively enables a "mapping" process, i.e. mapping the STEP-NC data (common input data) to specific G-code data (machine dependent data). Users only work with STEP-NC data as G-code data is hidden behind the scene. This has the merit of providing the operators with more information and "freedom" than G-code. Any changes can also be recorded and fed back to the design stage. From the controller end, though G-code is still used, its generation is automated and optimised as complete, feature-based product models can be utilised in the decision-making. The use of function blocks has the advantage of modulising and "mobilising" the system in that it becomes easy to reconfigure the system and allow real-time machining to take place. Again, the combination of STEP-NC and function blocks is proven to be an effective marriage in achieving integrated, interoperable and adaptive CNC machining.

REFERENCES

AS1115. (1985). *Numerical Control of Machines – Axis and Motion Nomenclature*, 2nd edition. Sydney, Australia: Standards Australian.

IEC 61499. (2005). *Function blocks for industrial-process measurement and control systems - Part 1: Architecture*, Geneva, Switzerland: International Electro-technical Commission.

ISO 6983-1. (1982). *Numerical control of machines – Program format and definition of address words – Part 1: Data format for positioning, line motion and contouring control systems*. Geneva, Switzerland: International Organisation for Standardisation (ISO).

ISO 14649-1. (2003). *Data model for computerized numerical controllers: part 1—overview and fundamental principles.* Geneva, Switzerland: International Organisation for Standardisation (ISO).

Suk, H. S., Seo, Y., Lee, S. M., Choi, T. H., Jeong, G. S., & Kim, D. Y. (2003). Modelling and implementation of Internet-Based Virtual Machine Tools, *International Journal of Advanced Manufacturing Technology, 21*, 516-522.

Yang, W., & Xu, X. (2008). Modelling Machine Tool Data in Support of STEP-NC Based Manufacturing. *International Journal of Computer Integrated Manufacturing.* (in press)

Wang, H., Xu, X., & Tedford, J.D. (2006). Making A Process Plan Adaptable to CNCs. *International Journal of Computer Applications in Technology, 26*(1/2), 49-58.

Wang, H., Xu, X., & Tedford, J.D. (2007). An Adaptable CNC System based on STEP-NC and Function Blocks. *International Journal of Production Research, 45*(17), 3809-3829.

Chapter XIV
Integrating CAD/CAPP/ CAM/CNC with Inspections

ABSTRACT

A logical step after CNC machining is inspection. With inspections, Closed-Loop Machining (CLM) can be realized to maximize the efficiency of a machining process by maintaining a tight control in a manufacturing system. CLM is normally regarded as the highest level of CNC automation. CLM however, requires a tight integration between CAD, CAPP, CAM, and CNC, in particular CAM and CNC and inspections. The questions that are to be answered are (a) what type of inspections is fit for CLM and (b) is there a good data model that one can use to bring machining and inspections together? This chapter tries to provide some possible solutions to these questions. Prior to this, a brief review of the past research work is given. Toward the end of the chapter, a conceptual framework for integrating machining with inspections is presented.

CLOSED-LOOP MACHINING AND ON-MACHINE INSPECTION

Inspection is an essential element in any closed-loop machining system. It can gather data to achieve precise measurement and monitor machine tool's performance during machining operations. In most CLM systems, Coordinate Measuring Machine is widely employed as a way of collecting the measurement data from a machined part. However, there are problems in this type of CLM systems. These problems relate to time, data compatibility and data modelling.

- Inspection using CMM is an off-line operation. It leads to increasement in machining cycle time due to relocating workpiece between machines and CMMs.
- Inspection using CMM is typically a three stage activity: programming, execution of the program and evaluation of the results. These activities are often carried out on separate systems which cause complex interface problems.
- The inspection results cannot be easily incorporated into the current NC programme, which is G-code-based. This is because G-code is a low-level programming language. Geometrical information about the part being machined and inspected is not preserved.

On-machine inspection (OMI) offers an attractive alternative solution. On-machine inspection enables measurement taking, data collection as well as data feedback and process adjustment fully automated and integrated. With on-machine inspections, a part can be measured at the machine and corrected there to avoid relocation between CNCs and CMMs. Small samples can be made and then checked immediately. Problems such as overcompensation and under-compensation can be identified at an early stage.

The benefits of CLM incorporating on-machine inspection are multiple (Jesse, 2001),

- It can reduce the reject rate by proofing fixture and part setups, automating offset adjustments, and monitoring the machine's "health" through machine self-checks;
- It can reduce part cost by promoting tooling standardization and reducing operator intervention;
- Inspection costs can be reduced through eliminating hard gauging, increasing the flexibility of measuring methods, avoiding cost of acquiring a CMM, and overcoming the CMM bottlenecking problems; and
- Data about parts, processes and equipment collected can be used for real-time, adaptive control.

The common data model for OMI is G-code-based. Using G-code, inspection and machining operations are characterized by a complex sequence of manual and automated activities. The measurement results from inspections cannot be fed back to the CAM system directly. The STEP-NC (ISO 14649-1, 2004) data model in contrast, provides higher level information for manufacturing processes including the part geometry and tolerances, hence enables a bi-directional information flow. STEP-NC (ISO 14649-10, 2004) provides the control structures for the sequence of programme execution, mainly the sequence of Workingsteps and associated machine functions. The "machining_schema" entity contains the definition of data types which are generally relevant for different technologies (e.g. milling, turning and grinding) (ISO 14649-10, 2004). Probing Workingstep is also defined in this part for inspection operations. However, the probing operations are specified in ISO 14649-16 (2004). The dimensional inspection data model is specified in ISO 10303 AP219 (2007).

PAST RESEARCH

In the past forty to fifty years, research work has been carried out in all aspects of CLM and OMI such as different ways of carrying out inspection operations, condition monitoring and machine reliability. The intention has been to prevent the equipment from breaking down during production, and facilitate robust process. However, most of the research is based on data models using G-code for data exchange with CNCs. Therefore, they fell short of achieving integration of inspection operation and machining process in a seamless, integrated process chain. With design, manufacturing and inspection consolidated on one platform, i.e. STEP (and STEP-NC), the above mentioned problems can be solved. STEP and STEP-NC can now be used to realize a true CLM with bi-directional information flow, including feedback of inspection results to process planning.

Brecher, Vitr and Wolf (2006) in the Laboratory for Machine Tools and Production Engineering (WZL) at Aachen University, Germany developed a system for a closed-loop process chain which integrated inspections into the STEP-NC information flow. The research presents a system that supports milling a workpiece, inspection of several workpiece features and feeding back the measured results to the product model. Their research focused on the closure of a broad process chain by integrating inspection activities into the STEP-NC-based process chain, and feeding the results of the manufacturing operation in terms of the obtained measurement data, back to process planning. The STEP-NC inspection data were converted into suitable format using for example, DMIS (Dimensional Measuring Interface Standard) (ANSI/CAM-I 104.0 Part 1, 2001) and DML (Dimensional Markup Language) (DML, 2004).

In the United States, a group of software vendors, industry partners and a government agency worked on a STEP-enabled CLM using ISO 10303 AP 238 to support probing capabilities of CLM (Hardwick, 2005). Note that ISO 10303 AP 238 is the AIM of STEP-NC ARM. A demonstration in May 2005 highlighted the use of probing results collected on a CNC machine to generate modified AP238 data. At the demonstration, offsets were coupled due to the possible misalignment, and resident single-axis offsets could not be used to accomplish the full transformation. Thus, one AP238 program was used for the probing, a second AP-238 program specified the machining in nominal coordinates, and the STEP-NC converter generated NC code using the nominal AP238 program and the acquired transformation just prior to machining. Conformance Classes 1 (CC1) and 2 (CC2) of AP238 were experimented.

Ali, Newman and Petzing (2005) from the Loughborough University, UK developed an inspection framework for closing the inspection loop through integration of information across the CAx process chain. The major feature of the proposed STEP-compliant inspection framework is the inclusion of information such as inspection Workplan and Workingstep. STEP-NC (ISO 14649-16, 2004), DMIS and AP219 are used as the basis for representing product and manufacturing models. This research has a focus on the utilization of CMMs.

A DATA MODEL FOR OMI

As aforementioned, the ISO 14649 standard has its Part 10 (ISO 14649-10, 2004) describing the general machining data and Part 16 (ISO 14649-16, 2004) describing the data for touch probing-based inspections. This means that the Part 16 data model of ISO14649 needs to be used to support a closed process chain by enabling the machining processes to be integrated with inspections so that automated, seamless data feedback of the measurement results to the product model can be achieved. This is considered important for process optimization and documentation.

Part 16 focuses on touch probing operations, which can either be executed with a touch probes on a CNC machine tool or a CMM. It provides an interface between a CNC controller and a programming system for inspections. In this chapter, only on-machine touch probes are discussed. Figure 14.1 is a simplified EXPRESS-G diagram describing the functionality of STEP-NC enabled on-machine inspection, integrated with machining operations (Zhao, Xu & Xie, 2008).

In Figure 14.1, four types of probing operations are defined: workpiece_probing, workpiece_complete_probing, tool_probing and probing_workingstep. They are specified in Parts 10 and 16 respectively. Their EXPRESS schema definitions are as follows.

```
ENTITY touch _ probing
    ABSTRACT SUPERTYPE OF (ONE OF (workpiece _ probing,
    workpiece _ complete _ probing, tool _ probing))
    SUBTYPE OF (Workingstep, OPERATION);
    measured _ offset:          nc _ variable;
END _ ENTITY;
```

Entity touch_probing is the supertype of workpiece_probing, workpiece_complete_probing, tool_probing, and probing_workingstep. It defines a single inspection task and is inserted into a sequence of executables including machining operations.

```
ENTITY workpiece _ probing
SUBTYPE OF (touch _ probing);
    start _ position: axis2 _ placement _ 3d;
    its _ workpiece:        workpiece;
    its _ direction:        direction;
    expected _ value:       toleranced _ length _ measure;
    its _ probe:            touch _ probe;
END _ ENTITY;
```

Entity workpiece_probing defines the probing of a dimension on a workpiece, with one axis movement from a starting location (start_position) to a nominal (expected) distance (expected_value). The starting location is known to be free of the workpiece along a direction (its_direction). The difference between the distance the actual probe travels and the nominal distance is recorded in the inspection result. This result can be used to determine possible corrective actions, such as re-machining, or to compute setup offsets.

```
ENTITY workpiece _ complete _ probing
    SUBTYPE OF (touch _ probing);
    its _ workpiece:        workpiece;
    probing _ distance:     toleranced _ length _ measure;
    its _ probe:            touch _ probe;
    computed _ offset:      offset _ vector;
END _ ENTITY;
```

Entity workpiece_complete_probing defines a complete measurement cycle at six locations of the workpiece. The six probing locations are determined by NC controller

Figure 14.1. EXPRESS-G diagram of on-machine inspection. ©*2008 Elsevier Limited, used with permission.*

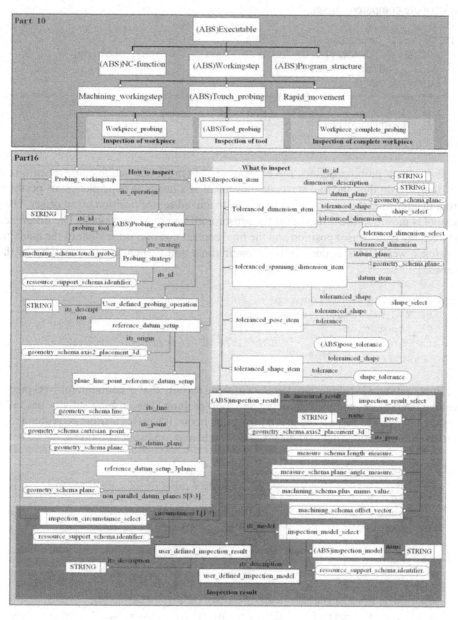

automatically based on the geometry of the workpiece. The translation and rotational offset of the workpiece is inspected and computed in comparison with the design data and kept in Attribute computed_offset.

```
ENTITY tool _ probing
    ABSTRACT SUPERTYPE OF (ONE OF (tool _ length _ probing,
    tool _ radius _ probing))
    SUBTYPE OF (touch _ probing);
    offset:         cartesian _ point;
    max _ wear:     length _ measure;
    its _ tool:machining _ tool;
END _ ENTITY;
```

Entity tool_probing defines the probing of the length and width/diameter of a tool (its_tool). To do this, the tool starts its movement at a machine dependent start position. From that position the tool position is shifted to a fixed sensor position by an offset. Then the tool is moved in the direction of the sensor until coming to a contact. The difference between the fixed sensor position and the final contact position is the wear of the machine tool (max_wear). This is done in both longitudinal and perpendicular directions of the tool-axis.

```
ENTITY probing _ workingstep
    SUBTYPE OF (touch _ probing);
    its _ operation:       probing _ operation;
    its _ items:           SET [1:?] OF inspection _ item;
END _ ENTITY;
```

Entity probing_workingstep defines a probing activity that is common for workpiece_probing, workpiece_complete_probing and tool_probing. The probing activity has to be executed in order to inspect the given inspection items. It has two attributes: probing_operation and inspection_item. Their EXPRESS schemas are listed as follows.

```
ENTITY probing _ operation
    ABSTRACT SUPERTYPE OF (user _ defined _ probing _ operation);
    its _ id:              STRING;
    reference _ datum:     reference _ datum _ setup;
    its _ strategy:        OPTIONAL probing _ strategy;
    probing _ tool:        touch _ probe;
END _ ENTITY;

ENTITY inspection _ item
    ABSTRACT SUPERTYPE OF (ONEOF(toleranced _ dimension _ item,
    toleranced _ spanning _ dimension _ item, toleranced _ pose _ item,
    toleranced _ shape _ item));
    its _ id:                  STRING;
    toleranced _ result:       OPTIONAL inspection _ result;
END _ ENTITY;

ENTITY inspection _ result
```

```
ABSTRACT SUPERTYPE;
its _ measured _ result:        inspection _ result _ select;
its _ model:                    inspection _ model _ select;
circumstances:                  LIST [1:?] OF inspection _ circumstance _ se-
lect;
END _ ENTITY;
```

Entity probing_operation contains operational instructions and circumstances of the probing inspection operation (reference_datum and its_strategy). They describe the way of carrying out an inspection operation. Inspection_item can be considered as containing two parts: toleranced items and inspection result. Toleranced items denote the nominal values and tolerances of a workpiece. They make reference to one or several machining features on which the inspection operation is performed. Entity inspection_item describes the items to be inspected in the inspection operation, and provides a "container" to attach tolerances to geometrical elements. These toleranced elements can be attributes of features (e.g. diameter of a round hole), relations within one feature (e.g. distance between two sides of a pocket) or relations between two different items (e.g. distance of the centre-lines of two holes and perpendicularity of a hole with reference to a plane). Inspection results are stored in a container—inspection_result so that it can be fed back to instruct subsequent machining operations.

In Figure 14.1, all the attributes in these entities are defined by various schemas in ISO 10303, e.g. machining schema, geometry schema, measure schema and resource support schema. The information modelled by these schemas can be shared through a database without having to modify the underlying structure of the database. In ISO 14649, these schemas are treated as "referred schema"; thus re-defining in ISO 14649 is not necessary.

Dimensional inspection can occur at any stage of the life cycle of a product where checking for conformance with a design specification is required. In order to enable the exchange of inspection data between various systems, STEP AP219 information model – Dimensional Inspection Process Planning for CMMs—for dimensional inspection may be used. This application protocol specifies information requirements to manage dimensional inspection of solid parts or assemblies, i.e. administering, planning, and executing dimensional inspection as well as analyzing and archiving the results.

Discussions in this chapter is however based on a combined STEP schema, including ISO 14649-10, 11, 12 and 16. This schema defines both STEP-NC inspection data and machining data (milling and turning). As the inspection_result entity and inspection_model entity are Abstract Supertype, and they have no subtypes, new entities are created,

```
ENTITY user _ defined _ inspection _ result
    SUBTYPE OF (inspection _ result);
    its _ description:              STRING;
END _ ENTITY;

ENTITY user _ defined _ inspection _ model
    SUBTYPE OF (inspection _ model);
    its _ description:              STRING;
END _ ENTITY;
```

Entity user_defined_inspection_result is defined as a subtype of the abstract supertype inspection_result. It is designed to be the entity for storing inspection results. The inspection result from the inspection operation is specified in this entity. The information of the inspection result includes the description of the measured feature and the circumstances in which the result is obtained. Entity user_defined_inspection_model is defined as a subtype of the abstract supertype inspection_model. This entity stores the specification(s) of the evaluation of the measured values.

AN INTEGRATED MACHINING AND INSPECTION SYSTEM

Use of ISO 14649-16 alongside other parts in ISO 14649 makes it possible to consolidate machining and inspection operations in one single program by including inspection Workingsteps amongst a sequence of machining Workingsteps. When and how the inspection should be carried out is a different decision to make. This is regarded as "how-to-do" information and should be decided when the hardware specifications, e.g. machine tools and probes, become known.

There are four types of inspections that can be considered:

- *INSPECTION TYPE* I: Inspections that are carried out prior to the machining operations. This type of inspection is needed to provide the positional information of the workpiece to the CNC controller; hence the controller knows the actual location of the workpiece so that cutter paths can be planned/altered accordingly.
- *INSPECTION TYPE* II: Inspections that are carried out at the completion of machining the part. This inspection is to make sure the planned operations have been successfully and accurately executed.
- *INSPECTION TYPE* III: Inspections that are carried out during the machining process. This type of inspection is necessary to detect any abnormity on the workpiece or the tools, so that the controller can make changes in time. At what stage the inspection should be carried out during the machining process depends on the requirement of the part. Parts that have very tight tolerances may need additional inspections during the machining processes, whereas parts that have looser tolerances may not need any inspection at all.
- *INSPECTION TYPE* IV: Inspections that are carried out for multiple setups. In this situation, inspections are necessary for each setup to provide accurate workpiece location information and new reference information after the previous machining operation.

The feature-based approach is adopted when representing inspection data. Whereas different types of features have been defined for design and manufacturing, they may not be utilized for inspection purposes. For example, a simple rectangular pocket in design may have been defined by removing a cuboid volume from a block and in NC machining the outer contour, the direction and the depth of the pocket are of interest. However, for pocket inspection, two pairs of apposing faces may be used as "inspection features". This means that the data model needs to be able to deal with both machining and inspection features.

In the data model, attribute inspection_item provides a "container" to attach tolerances to geometrical elements by referencing features of the workpiece. That means each inspection_item links an explicit, toleranced geometrical element (e.g. toleranced length measure) to a specific parameterised or semantic attribute of a feature. For example, these tolerated geometrical elements can be attributes of features (e.g. diameter of a round hole), relations within one feature (e.g. distance between two sides of a pocket) or relations between two different items (e.g. distance of the centrelines of two holes). User and application-specific views can then filter the data according to the specific demands on the data and its representation. The inspection result as well as the circumstances in which the result was generated are stored in the inspection_result entity. This information is fed back to the STEP-NC data model to be compared with the required data so that necessary changes can be made to the subsequent machining operations. Figure 14.2 shows the framework of this CAD/CAPP/CAM/CNC/Inspection process chain.

In such a system, design work can be carried out in a CAD system (e.g. Pro/E® and SolidWorks®), and saved in the format of STEP AP203. Based on the features conforming to STEP AP224, the STEP-NC compliant CAPP software generates information for machining and inspection processes. This information is represented in a STEP-NC file. This file therefore contains the information about machining features, materials, Workingsteps, Workplan, tool path, machining operations, and inspections. This information is fed into a CNC controller for execution. During the machining process, depending on the design requirements, different inspections may need to be carried out. In each inspection operation, (1) the feature and dimension items that need to be measured are inspected; (2) the inspection results are then analysed; (3) the analysed results are compared with the

Figure 14.2. Integration of machining with inspections

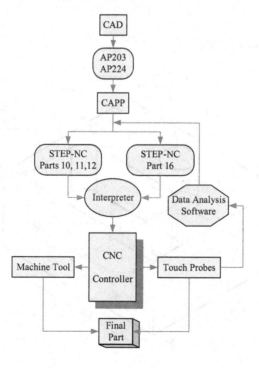

required design specifications; (4) required changes are fed to the STEP-NC data model; and (5) new machining operations are generated by updating the STEP-NC data model.

IMPLEMENTATION

The implementation is based on the example in ISO 14649-11 (Figure 14.3), "enriched" with some inspection data. There are five machining Workingsteps in this example part. They are for milling the top surface of the workpiece; drilling and reaming the hole; and rough and finish milling the pocket.

The following set of codes shows the first machining Workingstep.

```
#10= MACHINING_WORKINGSTEP('WS FINISH PLANAR FACE1',#62,#16,#19,$);
#19= PLANE_FINISH_MILLING($,$,'FINISH PLANAR FACE1',10.000,$,#39,#40,#41
,$,#60,#61,#42,2.500,$);
#39= MILLING_CUTTING_TOOL('MILL 18MM',#29,(#125),80.000,$,$);
 #29= TAPERED_ENDMILL(#30,4,.RIGHT.,.F.,$,$);
  #30= MILLING_TOOL_DIMENSION(18.000, $,$, 29.0, 0.0, $,$);
 #125= CUTTING_COMPONENT(80.000,$,$,$,$);
#40= MILLING_TECHNOLOGY(0.040,.TCP.,$,-12.000,$,.F.,.F.,.F.,$);
#42= BIDIRECTIONAL(0.05, .T., #43, .LEFT., $);
   #43= DIRECTION('STRATEGY PLANAR FACE1: 1.DIREC-
TION',(0.000,1.000,0.000));
#60= PLUNGE_TOOLAXIS($);
#61= PLUNGE_TOOLAXIS($);
```

Figure 14.3. Example workpiece

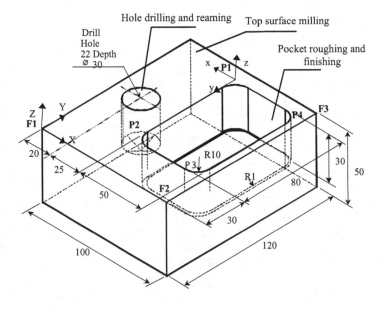

```
/************************************************************/
#16= PLANAR_FACE('PLANAR FACE1',#4,(#19),#77,#63,#24,#25,$,());
 #24= LINEAR_PATH($,#54,#55);
  #54= TOLERANCED_LENGTH_MEASURE(120.000,#56);
  #55= DIRECTION('COURSE OF TRAVEL DIRECTION',(0.000,1.000,0.000));
 #25= LINEAR_PROFILE($,#57);
  #57= NUMERIC_PARAMETER('PROFILE LENGTH',100.000,'MM');
 #63= PLANE('PLANAR FACE1-DEPTH PLANE',#80);
 #80= AXIS2_PLACEMENT_3D('PLANAR FACE1',#107,#108,#109);
  #107= CARTESIAN_POINT('PLANAR FACE1:DEPTH ',(0.000,0.000,-5.000));
  #108= DIRECTION(' AXIS ',(0.000,0.000,1.000));
  #109= DIRECTION(' REF_DIRECTION',(1.000,0.000,0.000));
 #77= AXIS2_PLACEMENT_3D('PLANAR FACE1',#104,#105,#106);
  #104= CARTESIAN_POINT('PLANAR FACE1:LOCATION ',(0.000,0.000,55.000));
  #105= DIRECTION(' AXIS ',(0.000,0.000,1.000));
  #106= DIRECTION(' REF_DIRECTION',(1.000,0.000,0.000));
/************************************************************/
```

In the above code, the Workingstep (#10) defines a face (finish) milling operation (#19). The milling cutting tool is defined in lines #39, #29, #30 and #125. The strategy and technology for this milling operation are defined in lines #40, #42 and #43. The approach strategy and the retract strategy are defined in lines #60 and #61. The section from lines #16 to #106 defines the plane feature information of this milling operation.

Four inspection Workingsteps are added to the file (Figure 14.4), each for a different purpose.

- Inspection Workingstep for setup. This Workingstep is to provide necessary information for set-up, e.g. the size and shape of the workpiece.
- Inspection Workingstep carried out after the first machining Workingstep (top surface milling). This Workingstep is to check the dimensional tolerance of the top surface.
- Inspection Workingstep checking the true position of the bottom of the pocket. This is done after the pocket rough milling Workingstep. The purpose is to determine the accurate finishing allowances for the finishing operation.
- Inspection Workingstep to check the dimensions of the finished pocket. The inspected items include depth, width and the length of the pocket.

As an example, the following code shows the first inspection Workingstep inserted after the first milling Workingstep.

```
#200=PROBING_WORKINGSTEP('SETUP    INSPEC-
TION',$,$,#62,$,#201,(#202,#203,#204));
 #201=USER_DEFINED_PROBING_OPERATION('SETUP PROBING',#205,$,#20
6,'SETUP PROBING');
  #205=REFERENCE_DATUM_SETUP(#71);
  #206=TOUCH_PROBE('NUM 01');
 #202=TOLERANCED_DIMENSION_ITEM('WORKPIECE DEPTH',#207,'workpiece
```

Figure 14.4. Machining and inspection Workingsteps and the data flow. ©2008 Elsevier Limited, used with permission.

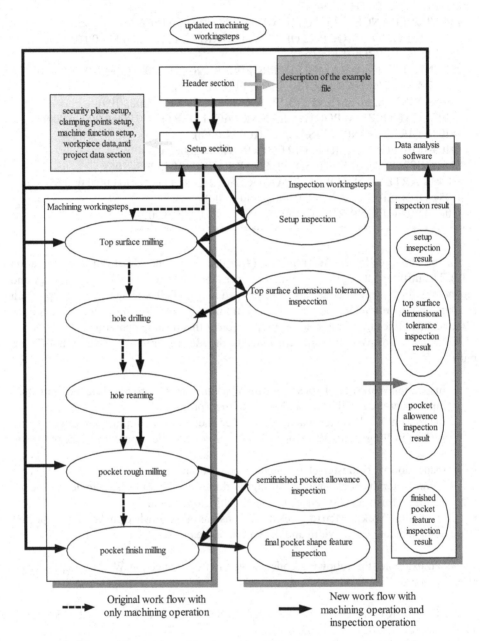

depth',#210,$,$);   #210=TOLERANCED_LENGTH_MEASURE(50.000,#56);

#203=TOLERANCED_DIMENSION_ITEM('WORKPIECE WIDTH',#208,'workpiece length',#211,$,$);   #211=TOLERANCED_LENGTH_MEASURE(120.000,#56);

#204=TOLERANCED_DIMENSION_ITEM('WORKPIECE LEGNTH',#209,'workpiece width',#212,$,$);   #212=TOLERANCED_LENGTH_MEA-SURE(100.000,#56);

#207=USER_DEFINED_INSPECTION_RESULT(0.000,'INSPECTION RESULT OF SETUP PROBING',(#200),'workpiece depth');

#208=USER_DEFINED_INSPECTION_RESULT(0.000,'INSPECTION RESULT OF SETUP PROBING',(#200),'workpiece length');

#209=USER_DEFINED_INSPECTION_RESULT(0.000,'INSPECTION RESULT OF SETUP PROBING',(#200),'workpiece width');

Line #200 defines the probing_workingstep for setup. Lines #205 and #206 define the reference datum and the probing tool of this probing operation. Lines #202, #203 and #204 define the features to be inspected. They are the depth, width and length of the workpiece, respectively. Lines #207, #208 and #209 describe and record the inspection results.

Due to the insertion of the inspection Workingsteps, the top-level Workingstep list is updated. Entity inspection_item contains the toleranced item and provides a container (entity inspection_result) for storing the inspection results and the circumstances of the inspection activity. The measured results are kept in the container and updated when further inspections are carried out. The circumstances entity is an inspection operation. It refers to the probing_workingstep entity. In this way, inspection result is recorded after each of the inspection Workingsteps and analysed by data analysis software. These analyzed results are fed back to certain machining Workingsteps for them to be updated. Figure 14.4 shows such as data flow alongside the machining and inspection Workingsteps.

CONCLUSION

A STEP-NC enabled, closed-loop machining system may require no data conversions. Hence data loss is minimized; both production time and cost are reduced. With STEP-NC data, geometry (e.g. machining features) can be used to define inspection tasks. The results of the process-integrated inspection tasks can be used for adjustment of workpiece positioning as well as for data acquisition to decide optimal machining operations or for other quality assurance purposes. The results can be finally used for planning subsequent manufacturing operations, for example to compensate for system errors. Furthermore, based on the integrated STEP data, changes made to the shape of the workpiece for example can automatically be taken into account for the provision of a new measuring strategy and/or procedure.

It is necessary to define a way of relating measurement results with machining features and operations. This is possible through use of a STEP-NC data model with which design data can be embedded and measurement can be carried out in a more informed and controlled manner. This is one of the fundamental differences between the traditional so-called in-cycle gauging and the system described in this chapter. Once analyzed and post-processed, inspection results can be fed back to the machining processes in real time to update the machining parameters. This could support a real-time, closed-loop machining process to be integrated with on-line inspections. The combined schema developed in this research can be used for applications other than the example in the case study. For example, it also caters for turning operations. The extended Part 21 file with inspection operations inserted can also be used for applications such as a genuine STEP-NC compliant inspection system.

REFERENCES

Ali, L., Newman, S. T., & Petzing, J. (2005). Development of a STEP-compliant inspection framework for discrete components. *Proceedings of the IMechE Part B Journal of Engineering Manufacture, B7*, 557-564

ANSI/CAM-I 104.0 Part 1. (2001). *DMIS 4.0 Standard, Part 1.* Gaithersburg, USA:, NIST.

Brecher, C., Vitr, M., & Wolf, J. (2006). Closed-loop CAPP/CAM/CNC process chain based on STEP and STEP-NC inspection tasks, *International Journal of Computer Integrated Manufacturing, 19*(6), 570-580.

DML. (2004). *DML - Dimensional Markup Language,* Version 2.0. USA: DML specification committee.

Hardwick, M. (2005). STEP-NC Probing Demonstration, *EASTEC 2005 Exposition & Conference*, 24-26 May 2005, West Springfield, MA USA, Retrieved June 28, 2007, from http://www.isd.mel.nist.gov/projects/stepnc/

ISO 14649-1. (2003). *Data model for Computerized Numerical Controllers: Part 1 Overview and fundamental principles.* Geneva, Switzerland: International Organisation for Standardisation (ISO).

ISO 14649-16. (2004). *Data model for Computerized Numerical Controllers: Part 16: Data for touch probing based inspection.* Geneva, Switzerland: International Organisation for Standardisation (ISO).

ISO 14649-10. (2003). *Data model for Computerized Numerical Controllers: Part 10 – General process data.* Geneva, Switzerland: International Organisation for Standardisation (ISO).

ISO 10303-219. (2007). *Industrial automation systems and integration – Product data representation and exchange – Part 219: Application protocol: Dimensional inspection information exchange.* Geneva, Switzerland: International Organisation for Standardisation (ISO).

Jesse, C. (2001). Process Controlled Manufacturing at Pratt & Whitney, *Aerospace Manufacturing Technology Conference & Exposition*, September 2001, Seattle, WA, USA.

Zhao, F. Xu, X., & Xie, S. Q. (2008). STEP-NC Enabled On-line Inspection in Support of Closed-loop Machining. *Robotics and Computer-Integrated Manufacturing, 24*(2), 200-216.

Chapter XV
Internet–Based Integration

ABSTRACT

Today, companies often have operations distributed around the world, and production facilities and designers are often in different locations. Increased use of outsourcing and geographically dispersed supply chains further complicates the manufacturing world. The globalization of manufacturing business means that companies should be able to design, build, and maintain, anywhere at any time.

Manufacturing engineers are seeking effective tools during planning to help improve production processes, plant designs, and tooling, and to allow earlier impact on product designs. Collaboration may exist in a number of activities such as (a) reviewing designs with the design team; (b) interfacing with tooling designers; (c) verifying tooling assembly and operation; (d) reviewing manufacturing process plans and factory layouts; and (e) discussing manufacturing problems with suppliers.

In larger companies, collaboration is becoming increasingly important in design and manufacturing. Everyone knows something, but no one knows everything. There is an evolution from individuals working independently to functioning in workgroups, as well as enterprise collaboration and collaboration throughout a supply chain. Within a supply chain, sharing knowledge has become paramount.

This chapter describes the methods of developing an Internet-enabled, integrated CAD, CAPP, CAM, and CNC system to support collaborative product development. The main goal is to provide a team environment enabling a group of designers and engineers to collaboratively develop a product in real time. STEP can be used to represent product data for heterogeneous application systems and data formats, and the Web-based Product

Structure Manager developed can be an effective function module to co-ordinate collaborative activities.

A COLLABORATIVE FRAMEWORK

The aim is to achieve a STEP-compliant system for collaborative manufacturing (Xu & Mao, 2004). Figure 15.1 shows the basic system architecture (Xu, 2006). The system used STEP (ISO 10303-21, 1994, ISO/TS 10303-28, 2003) and STEP-NC (ISO 10303-238, 2007) standards to construct a universal data model.

In the design phase, STEP (ISO 10303-203, 1994, or ISO 10303-214, 1994) is used as the neutral data format to exchange design data between different CAD systems or between CAD and CAPP systems. Two different manufacturing information databases (generic and native) are needed to support data exchange for collaborative manufacturing. The generic manufacturing databases are abstract information about machine tools and cutting tools of any kind to be used during manufacturing activities. Hence, process plans generated using generic manufacturing resources cannot be executed directly at the shop-floor. This is because a STEP-NC based process plan at this stage has only information about "what-to-do", i.e. the tasks. Examples of what-to-do information include machining features and the description of requirements of machine tool(s) and cutting tool(s). At this stage, no information about selection and determination of specific machine tool(s) and cutting tool(s) is present in the program. The native manufacturing databases reflect the actual conditions of a shop-floor including existing machine tools and cutting tools that can be used for populating and optimizing a generic process plan or generating native process plans for final execution. To this end, a native manufacturing database can be considered as a "DNA" bank for all the available manufacturing facilities.

As aforementioned, the basic element of a STEP-NC file is Workingstep instead of cutter locations. Workingsteps are built based on machining features. The system can use inputs from CAD systems, feature recognizer, CAPP algorithms and manufacturing resources to generate a STEP-NC file. As the CAPP system is designed based on a three-tiered architecture, it has the ability to switch between different manufacturing databases to generate generic or native STEP-NC files to provide a maximal flexibility to support collaborative manufacturing. As shown in dashed lines in Figure 15.1, when the CAPP system is connected to a generic database, the output STEP-NC files will be universal and machine tool independent. Under this condition, the CAM system can later populate and optimize a generic STEP-NC file according to the native manufacturing database on the shop-floor to obtain a suitable STEP-NC file for a specific CNC machine. When the CAPP system is directly connected to a native manufacturing database, it will be able to optimize the machining sequence, select machine tools and cutting tools at the process planning stage and generate a STEP-NC file which can be directly used by a targeted CNC machine. Figure 15.2 shows the detailed information flow in the proposed system (Mao, 2003).

In this scenario, CAM systems are more likely to be integrated with STEP-NC enabled CNC machines or rather their controllers. The main functions of a CAM system are therefore to optimize the generic STEP-NC information and offer data connections to a CAPP system instead of calculating tool trajectories and generating CNC programs, which will be handled by the built-in functions of the STEP-NC controller.

Figure 15.1. STEP-compliant collaborative manufacturing model

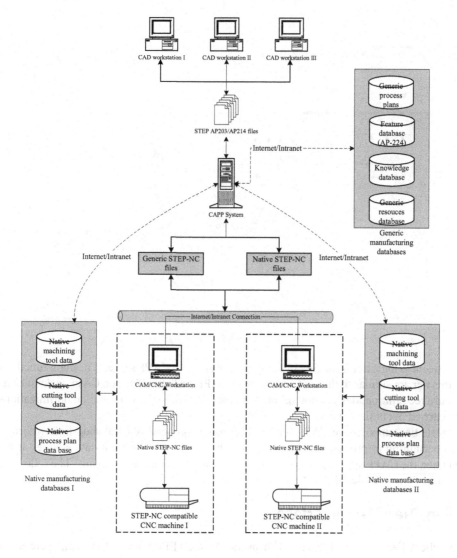

SYSTEM MODEL

The abstract model of the proposed system is illustrated in Figure 15.3 (Xu, 2006). As can be seen, the system is of a three-tiered network hierarchy. This helps to set up an integrated collaborative manufacturing environment.

The client tier is effectively a GUI, consisting of a set of applications and a Web browser to enable interactions between users and the system. The main functions of the client tier are to analyze the necessary interactions between users and the entire system as well as to provide an effective way to realize the interactions using existing technologies.

Figure 15.2. IDEF0 diagram of the STEP-compliant collaborative manufacturing model

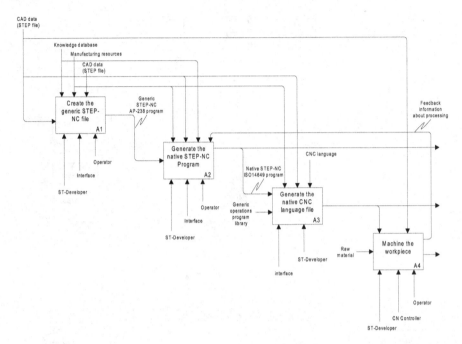

Business logic tier is the core of the system. It acts as a CAPP server. The main functions in this tier are similar to those of a traditional CAPP system. Common CAPP tasks such as feature recognition, designation of machine tool/cutting tool and operation optimizations are carried out at these tiers.

Data tier supports the CAPP server. It represents generic or local shop-floor information pertaining to process planning. By switching between different data sources at the data tier, the CAPP system can better support collaborative manufacturing. The following sections discuss in detail how to develop these tier.

Client Tier: User Interface

The client tier directly interacts with users. As a STEP-compliant system, there are a number of different modules that are needed to provide the required functions in the client tier. They are,

- A user interface that can view process plans through a specific query statement;
- A STEP physical file interpreter that interprets the STEP and STEP-NC structures;
- A GUI that displays 3-D models based on the geometric information in a STEP file;
- A module that presents manufacturing plans in STEP-NC terms, e.g. Workplans and Workingsteps;
- A module that presents, and allows the user to modify manufacturing information such as features, machine tools, cutting tools and tolerances within a Workingstep;

Figure 15.3. Abstract system model of the STEP compliant CAPP system

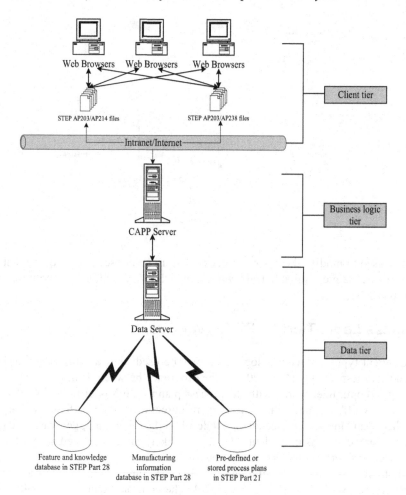

- A module that allows the user to alter the sequence of Workingsteps and/or Workplans; and
- An XML interpreter that can interpret both the generic manufacturing information from the CAPP server and native manufacturing information from a database in the XML format.

Figure 15.4 illustrates the information flow among different modules (Mao, 2003). The client tier starts with listing the existing process plans in a process plan database through a query statement. When a specific process plan is selescted, the Workplans and the solid models in the plan can be presented to the user via GUI. At this stage, the XML interpreter provides the interpreted XML manufacturing information to the clients. XML DTD, XSLT (Extensible Style-sheet Language Family Transformation) and XML Schema are the controls for keeping the XML data retrieved from the manufacturing databases in a desired manner. In doing so, the manufacturing information within the XML data can

Figure 15.4. Information flow in the client tier

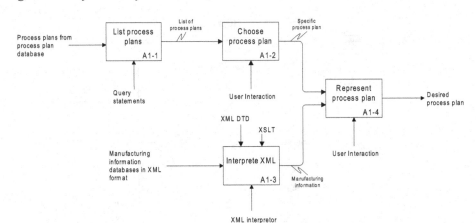

be easily used to modify the current process plan. In response to the requirements from the client tier, the most suitable framework in which those modules can be implemented is a Web browser.

Business Logic Tier: CAPP Server

Two different types of business logic tiers may be used; they are illustrated in Figures 15.5 and 15.6 respectively (Mao, 2003). The difference between them is the way that the Workingstep optimizer works with the process planner. In Model I, the CAPP server is able to access different native manufacturing resources to generate different native process plans, hence an "integrated" scenario. Model II on the other hand, generates the generic and native process plans in tandem. The latter is likely to be generated at the shop-floor. Therefore, it supports an "interfacing" scenario.

In both models, feature recognition is the first task. Inputs to this module are data files conforming to ISO 10303 AP-203 or AP-214. The controls include ISO 10303 AP-203, AP-214, AP-224 (ISO 13030-224, 2001). AP-203 and AP-214 are used to describe pure geometric information of a part, whereas AP-224 is used to describe machining features in a process plan. The goal of using AP-224 as a control here is to provide a universal and STEP-compliant machining feature library in place of different proprietary feature libraries from different system vendors.

The main function of the process planning module in Model I is to assign manufacturing resources to the features generated by the feature recognizer. The controls of the process-planning module include ISO 10303 AP-238, Workingstep optimizing algorithms and native manufacturing resources databases. The native manufacturing resources databases conform to ISO 14649 Part 111 (tools for milling) (2003) and Part 121 (tools for turning) (2003). As manufacturing information is stored in the STEP Part 28 (Edition 1) XML format, the connection between the CAPP server and the native resources databases is via the Internet. If the native shop-floor manufacturing resources are connected, the process planning module can directly assign specific manufacturing resources such as machine tools and cutting tools to each feature for creation of Workingsteps. Workingsteps

Figure 15.5. CAPP server Model I (Integrated model)

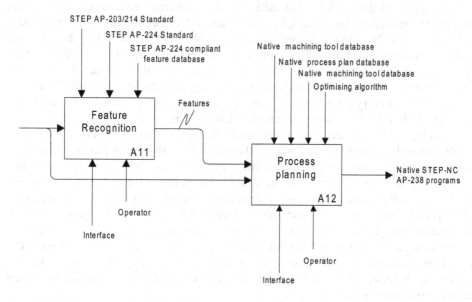

Figure 15.6. CAPP server Model II (Interfacing model)

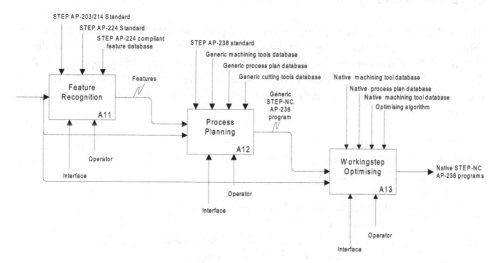

are optimized and properly sequenced to generate a process plan which can be executed immediately at the shop-floor.

In Model II, the Workingstep optimization mechanism is separated from process planning and forms a new module. This may be due to the fact that the native manufacturing resources are still pending. In this case, the outputs of the process-planning module are generic process plans. They will be "populated" in the Workingstep optimization module with the information from an identified native manufacturing resource to give a native process plan. Essentially, generic process planning is a process of "enriching" machining features, represented as the AP-224 format in this case, with the necessary syntax information to form entities defined by AP-238, e.g. Workplans and Workingsteps. Some preliminary decisions such as Workingstep ordering and set-up planning will be mainly based on the feature information and the information from a generic manufacturing database. Note that whatever decision is reached at this stage, changes can be easily made once the native manufacturing information becomes available. Many data entries in an AP-238 file can remain empty or carry default values at this stage. This is intended by the standard, that is STEP-NC has the ability to just model task-level information.

Both Models I and II seem to perform similar functions. There is however a fundamental difference between them. In Model I, the output from the CAPP server is a specific, how-to-do process plan, which can be directly used by a specific manufacturing facility. This how-to-do information may not be used by other manufacturing facilities. In Model II, there is an intermediate result from the process-planning module, i.e. a generic process plan. This generic process plan contains what-to-do instead of how-to-do information. It is therefore machine tool independent. The what-to-do information maintains its generic nature until the last moment when the CAM system of the chosen machine tool populates it with the native manufacturing information so as to generate a specific (how-to-do) process plan. Therefore, Model II possesses the required flexibility and mobility to support collaborative manufacturing.

Data Tier: Data Model

The databases in the data tier are constructed by applying the Part 28 rules to the EXPRESS schemas. For example, the feature database is constructed by applying the Part 28 rules to ISO 10303 AP-224 schemas. The cutting tool database is constructed by applying the Part 28 rules to ISO 14649 Part 111 and Part 121 schemas. The following XML codes from the cutting tool database define a centre drill. Figure 15.7 shows such information in a Web browser (Mao, 2003).

```
<STEP-XML xmlns:ceb="urn:iso10303-28:ceb">
<cutting_tool ceb:id="66" ceb:copies="4">
    <id>CENTER_DRILL_5MM</id>
    <its_tool_body>
        <center_drill ceb:id="65" ceb:copies="4">
            <dimension>
                <tool_dimension ceb:id="59" ceb:copies="4">
                    <diameter>5.000000</diameter>
                    <tool_top_angle>0.000000</tool_top_angle>
                    <tipcutting_edge_length>0.000000</tipcutting_edge_length>
                        <edge_radius>0.000000</edge_radius>
                        <edge_center_vertical>0.000000</edge_center_vertical>
                        <edge_center_horizontal>0.000000</edge_center_horizontal>
                </tool_dimension>
            </dimension>
            <number_of_teeth>2</number_of_teeth>
```

```
            <hand_of_cut>
                    <hand>right</hand>
            </hand_of_cut>
        </center_drill>
    </its_tool_body>
    <overall_assembly_length>50.000000</overall_assembly_length>
    <angle_for_spindle_orientation>0.000000</angle_for_spindle_orientation>
    <tool_holder_diameter_for_spindle_orientation>0.000000</tool_holder_diameter_
for_spindle_orientation>
</cutting_tool>
</STEP-XML>
```

Databases such as RDBMS (Relational DataBase Management System) can be used in the data tier. In order to keep the original structure within an XML document, the entire XML documents can be stored as a whole in the database or as an external file outside the database. Once such a database is constructed, the information required by the CAPP server can be carried by the XML documents and transferred via the Internet. The XML documents are readily viewable in Web browsers and/or interpreted by a STEP-XML interpreter in the CAPP server to obtain specific manufacturing information.

FRAMEWORK DEVELOPMENT

In the interest of space, only two types of development work are discussed in this section. The objectives are to (a) enable a process planner to view and manually edit the existing process plans/STEP-NC programs in the STEP AP-238 file format using manufacturing resources provided in the STEP Part 28 XML format, and (b) enable access to, and modification of, manufacturing databases across the Internet.

Client Tier Implementation

The prototype of the client tier can be developed and implemented under the Microsoft Windows® environment. This way, all client applications can be unified within Microsoft Internet Explorer®. A set of development tools and technologies may be used,

- Microsoft Visual C++® and Microsoft Foundation Classes (MFC);
- ST-Developer® (STEP Tools, 2004) and STIX (STEP Tools, 2005);
- OpenGL® (Open Graphics Library);
- ActiveX® technology.

ST-Developer® is a software development package for developing and working with STEP applications. It offers libraries for reading, writing, processing and checking STEP data of Part 21 formats. It also provides EXPRESS early binding with C++ classes. These features help to develop additional STEP compatible applications. Other software tools may also be used to process STEP data. Applications written in C++ can offer functions to read and write STEP Part 21 files, as well as create, delete, traverse and change any EXPRESS

Figure 15.7. Cutting tool information in the XML format

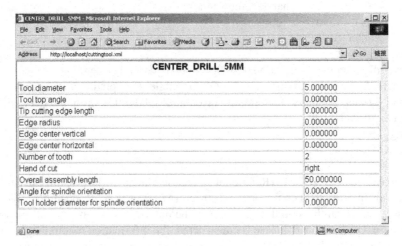

defined data sets compiled as objects in the C++ style. STIX is a STEP IndeX library for STEP AP-238 from the same company. It contains a C++ library which provides useful functions to process manufacturing data in the STEP AP-238 format. Therefore, STIX simplifies implementation and processing of the STEP AP-238 information in programs written in C++.

Business Logic Tier Implementation

In the business logical tier, a Web server is needed. Internet Information Server (IIS), Visual Basic® IIS application and Active Sever Pages (ASP) may be used to generate dynamic Web pages for different client users. The Web server separates users into two groups: the process planners and database administrators.

A process planner can access a list of existing process plans generated by the Web server. The process planner can then choose the desired process plan to modify. Each hyperlink leads to one existing process plan represented in a STEP AP-238 file and stored in the data tier. Once a process plan is chosen, the process plan file is downloaded into the ActiveX® control and represented in a Web browser for viewing and modifications. New process plans can be uploaded back to the data server after modifications.

For database administrators, the tier functions differently. The STEP Part 28 XML documents that contain manufacturing information are parsed by the Web server before transmission. Hence, database administrators can focus on the manufacturing information in the XML file. The generated dynamic Web page for database administration is illustrated in Figure 15.8 (Mao, 2003).

The left frame in the interface is a tree menu structure presenting the structure of an XML document. The upper-right frame represents the extracted manufacturing information. The lower-right frame is the editing area, in which the "Name" section represents tags in an XML document and the "Value" section refers to the detailed manufacturing information in XML tags. Once the modifications are submitted, the Web server generates a new

Figure 15.8. Interface for database administration

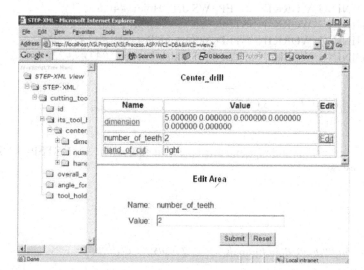

XML document based on the new values. The corresponding values in the manufacturing databases are also synchronized to reflect the changes.

Data Tier Implementation

The data tier may be implemented using different database management tools. Should Microsoft Access™ be used, the manufacturing information can be stored as XML files in the operating system on which the data tier is implemented. The complete file paths of those XML files are stored. Some important attributes such as tool diameter, tool length and tool name by which the manufacturing information can be identified are also extracted and stored in the tables to enable quick and more specific query statements. The main benefit of such an implementation method is that the database is easy to construct, and both the original XML structure and the flexibility provided by SQL can still be preserved. For example, a simple query statement, "*Select filepath from drilltools where tooldiameter=5.0 and overallasslength=50.0*", will return the file path for the existing drilling tools with a diameter equal to 5.0 and overall assembly length 50.0. The CAPP server can then extract the detailed manufacturing information from the XML documents according to these file paths. Figure 15.9 illustrates an implemented table which describes tools for drilling (Mao, 2003).

STEP-NC data is represented in XML by adding a definition of entities and attributes found in STEP-NC EXPRESS schema. A tag name is defined for each entity to indicate the attribute name of its super-type entity. The following is a fragment of a Part 21 file defining a Workplan, whose explanation is given in Table 12.1.

...

#1= PROJECT('EXAMPLE1',#10,(#4),$,$,$);

...

#10=WORKPLAN('Main Workplan',(#11,#12,#13,#14,#15),$,#36,$);

#11=MACHINING_WORKINGSTEP('WS finish Planar Face1',#46,#4,#16);
#12=MACHINING_WORKINGSTEP('WS drill Hole1',#46,#5,#19);
#13=MACHINING_WORKINGSTEP('WS ream Hole1',#46,#5,#20);
#14=MACHINING_WORKINGSTEP('WS rough Pocket1',#47,#7,#21);
#15=MACHINING_WORKINGSTEP('WS finish Pocket1',#47,#7,#22);
...
...
#36=SETUP('Setup1',#38,#45,(#37));
...

Using the corresponding tags and attributes, an equivalent XML STEP-NC file can be obtained as follows.

Figure 15.9. An implemented table describing tools for drilling

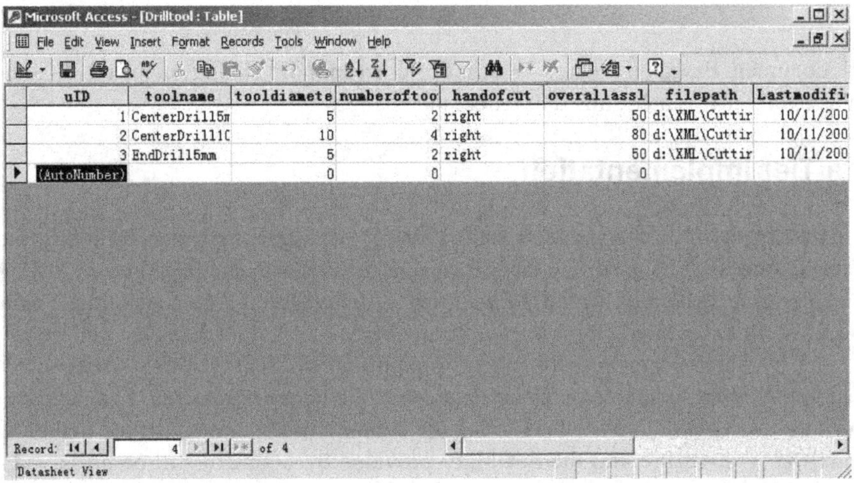

Table 12.1. Explanation of the "Workplan" entity

Attribute name	Attribute value	Data structure	Attribute type
ITS_ID	'Main Workplan'		identifier
ITS_ELEMENT	#11,#12,#13,#14,#15	LIST [1:?]OF	executable
ITS_CHANNEL	$	OPTIONAL	channel
ITS_SETUP	#36	OPTIONAL	setup
ITS_EFFECT	$	OPTIONAL	in_process_geometry

```
<?xml version="1.0" ?>
- <STEP-XML>
  - <PROJECT name="PROJECT" id="#1">
    <its_id name="identifier">'EXAMPLE1'</its_id>
    - <main_workplan name="WORKPLAN" id="#10">
      <its_id name="identifier">'MAIN WORKPLAN'</its_id>
      + <its_elements name="MACHINING_WORKINGSTEP" id="#11">
      </its_elements>
      + <its_elements name="MACHINING_WORKINGSTEP" id="#12">
      </its_elements>
      + <its_elements name="MACHINING_WORKINGSTEP" id="#13">
      </its_elements>
      + <its_elements name="MACHINING_WORKINGSTEP" id="#14">
      </its_elements>
      + <its_elements name="MACHINING_WORKINGSTEP" id="#15">
      </its_elements>
      <its_channel name="channel" />
      + <its_setup name="SETUP" id="#36">
      </its_setup>
      <its_effect name="in_process_geometry" />
    </main_workplan>
    + <its_workpieces name="WORKPIECE" id="#4">
    </its_workpieces>
    <its_owner name="person_and_address" />
    <its_release name="date_and_time" />
    <its_status name="approval" />
  </PROJECT>
</STEP-XML>
```

CONCLUSION

An integrated and collaborative CAD/CAPP/CAM/CNC scenario can be realised by an XML-based, STEP-compliant CAPP system. The system described in this chapter can support a bi-directional information flow throughout the design and manufacturing chain. Design information in its entirety is available in the manufacturing model. Manufacturing information is feature-based and task-oriented. In a collaborative manufacturing environment, designers and manufacturers are often geographically dispersed. Therefore, the system that adopts a three-tiered, Web-based network architecture can provide an open and integrated structure. This architecture provides convenient ways in exchanging design and manufacturing data in STEP Part 21 and/or Part 28 file format through the Internet. The client user interface implemented within a Web browser reduces the implementation and maintenance costs. Manufacturing information databases implemented in STEP Part 28 XML format enabled the CAPP server to switch between geographically dispersed shop-floor resources through Internet connections to realize collaborative manufacturing. Other benefits this system promises include effective and timely business transaction, enabling collaborative environment, virtual prototype and simulate, and best use of manufacturing tools, knowledge bases, product information, and regardless of location.

REFERENCES

ISO 10303-203. (1994). *Industrial automation systems and integration – Product data representation and exchange – Part 203: Application protocol: Configuration controlled 3D designs of mechanical parts and assemblies.* Geneva, Switzerland: International Organisation for Standardisation (ISO).

ISO 10303-21. (1994). *Industrial automation systems and integration – Product data representation and exchange – Part 21: Implementation methods: Clear text encoding of the exchange structure.* Geneva, Switzerland: International Organisation for Standardisation (ISO).

ISO 10303-214. (1994). *Industrial automation systems and integration – Product data representation and exchange – Part 214: Application protocol: Core data for automotive mechanical design processes.* Geneva, Switzerland: International Organisation for Standardisation (ISO).

ISO 13030-224. (2001). *Industrial automation systems and integration – Product data representation and exchange – Part 224: Application protocol: Mechanical product definition for process plans using machining features.* Geneva, Switzerland: International Organisation for Standardisation (ISO).

ISO 10303-238. (2007). *Industrial automation systems and integration – Product data representation and exchange – Part 238: Application Protocols: Application interpreted model for computerized numerical controllers.* Geneva, Switzerland: International Organisation for Standardisation (ISO).

ISO/TS 10303-28 (Edition 1). (2003). *Product data representation and exchange: Implementation methods: EXPRESS to XML binding,* Draft Technical Specification, ISO TC184/SC4/ WG11 N169, Geneva, Switzerland: International Organisation for Standardisation (ISO).

ISO 14649-111. (2003). *Data model for Computerized Numerical Controllers: Part 111 – Tools for milling.* Geneva, Switzerland: International Organisation for Standardisation (ISO).

ISO 14649-121. (2003). *Data model for Computerized Numerical Controllers: Part 121 – Tools for turning.* Geneva, Switzerland: International Organisation for Standardisation (ISO).

Mao, J. (2003). *A STEP-compliant collaborative product development system.* Master of Engineering Thesis, Department of Mechanical Engineering, School of Engineering, The University of Auckland, New Zealand.

STEP Tools. (2004). Retrieved on November 26, 2004 from http://www.steptools.com/products/stdev/

STEP Tools. (2005). Retrieved on October 21, 2005 from http://www.steptools.com/stix/

Xu, X. (2006). STEP-NC to complete product development chain, In *Database Modeling for Industrial Data Management: Emerging Technologies and Applications.* edited by Z. Ma, pp. 148-184. IGI Global. ISBN 1-5914-0684-6

Xu, X., & Mao, J. (2004). A STEP-compliant collaborative product development system, In *Proceedings of 33rd International Conference on Computers and Industrial Engineering.* Ramada Plaza, Oriental Hotel, Jeju, Korea. 25-27 March, 2004, CIE598.

Chapter XVI
From CAD/CAPP/CAM/ CNC to PDM, PLM and Beyond

ABSTRACT

Companies that have been practicing CAD, CAPP, CAM, and CNC integration have now realized that there is a need to operate in a much broader scope with wider boundaries and more functionality. To foster innovation in a product development lifecycle, change in the early stage is good, and, in fact, should be encouraged. The more iteration a product design can experience at this stage when change is inexpensive, the lower cost our final product will become. At a later stage when hardware set-up is committed against a design, change becomes expensive and should be discouraged. Therefore, there is a need for an effective way of managing product-related information as well as the product development action flow, which captures actions that need to be done, have been done, and what other parts are affected. Engineers that subscribe to a portion of a design also need to be working with other collaborators and then automatically be notified when changes occur. This leads to increased implementation of Product Data Management (PDM) and Product Lifecycle Management (PLM).

PDM systems are used to control information, files, documents, and work processes required to design, build, support, distribute, and maintain products. Using PDM, people can contribute at the early stages of product design and development. In addition, PDM can be seen as an integration tool connecting many different areas, which ensures that the right information is available to the right person at the right time and in the right form throughout the enterprise. In this way, PDM improves communication and cooperation between diverse groups in an organization, and between organizations and clients (Peltonen, Pitkanen & Sulonen, 1996, Liu & Xu, 2001). PDM is strongly rooted in the world of CAD, CAPP, CAM, and CNC in a more specific sense as well as in the world of engineering and design in a more general sense.

In recent years, more focus has also been on the improvement of the entire product lifecycles. The major concern here is time-to-market, as it reflects the competitiveness of a company. In response to the new area of focus, new generation PDM systems are developed to support the entire product lifecycle; from the initial concept to the finishing product. This has subsequently led to the birth to PLM systems. From the information context, PLM should cater for the management of the information throughout the lifecycle of a product, including multiple domain views, different business processes scattered across enterprises and different representations of a multitude of native product-, resource- and process-models (Stark, 2004, Rosén, 2006).

This chapter starts with introduction to and discussions about product data management systems. Topics covered include PDM's capabilities, its benefits, Web-based PDM and PDM standardization. The concept of integrated and extended PDM is also introduced. This is followed by discussions on product lifecycle management, for example definitions of PLM, its solution model, benefits, and implementation are among the topics covered. Like PDM, issues regarding PLM standardisation are also addressed. Share-A-space™ is a practical case of PLM. The core features and its architecture are discussed. Toward the end, the concept and some of the techniques of "grand" integration are introduced.

PDM'S CAPABILITIES

In terms of capabilities, five basic user functions should be supported by a PDM system,

- Data vault and document management, which provides for storage and retrieval of product information;
- Workflow and process management, which controls procedures for handling product data and provides a mechanism to drive a business with information;
- Product structure management, which handles bills of material, product configurations, associated versions and design variations;
- Parts management, which provides information on standard components and facilitates re-use of designs; and
- Program management, which provides work breakdown structures and allows coordination between processes, resource scheduling and project tracking.

There are some other utility functions that can enhance a PDM system. Communication capabilities such as links to e-mail provide for information transfer and event notification. Data transport functions track data locations and move data from one location or application to another. Data translation capability exchanges files in a proper format. Image services handle storage, access and viewing of product information. Administration functions control and monitor system operation and security.

The PDM user can search company's data or information through his or her desktop computer. The actual searching and finding process are handled by the server, using the meta-database search engine. The files are stored in the managed files or data vault. The server finds the specific information and then transfers it back to the user's screen with a proper format. The functional view of a PDM system is shown in Figure 16.1.

Evolution of PDM Methodology

CAD systems originally provided electronic drawings, but then evolved to creating designs in 3D. In the 70's and 80's, CAD users can build a 3D virtual prototype and with digital mock-up interactively simulate product performance and check for system interferences. Since the late 80's, other product development functionalities such as manufacturing have been introduced to CAD systems to provide manufacturing industry with tools doing design, process planning and manufacturing all under the same roof, hence the birth of CAD/CAM systems. It is however worth noting that the focus has been mainly on managing part geometry and other geometry-related information. For example, when assembly modelling is done, there is little to manage elements like versions and configurations, maturity and affectivities', or the relationships and links to other information that is being generated during the innovation phase of the design process.

Many large corporations, often the leaders in manufacturing industry, soon found their efficiency severely downgraded by the abovementioned insufficiency. CAD systems did not

Figure 16.1. Functional view of a typical PDM system. ©2001 Elsevier Limited, used with permission.

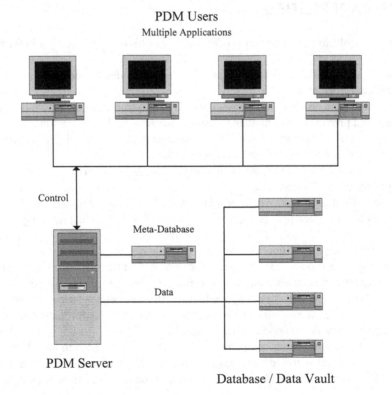

provide secure locations for others to universally access product data. There was not support for structured workflows with which to evolve a product design through its lifecycle, and share it with downstream manufacturing and other legacy applications. With no commercially available systems at that time, they started to develop their own data management solutions. Some were successful, others not. Meanwhile, a number of software companies started to realise the problems associated with so-called "automation islands" (e.g. CAD and CAM tools) and the potential market of efficient data management methodologies. They began to introduce the first generation commercial PDM systems. The majority of those vendors were already involved in the CAD/CAM/CAE software market. They focused on developing the data management solutions, and added PDM to their product lines.

BENEFITS OF PDM SYSTEMS

In general, organisations that successfully implement PDM can achieve multiple advantages in terms of productivity and competitiveness. The benefits can be summarised as follows (Hameri & Nihtila, 1998).

Interdisciplinary Collaboration

At the earliest stage of product definition a PDM system can aid marketers, designers and project planners in defining the manner in which they will collaborate and identify the relationships between the new product and other products currently in production. A PDM system can lead to collaborative development of new products as well as improvements on existing products.

Reduced Product Development Cycle Time

Due to the increased collaboration with all areas of an organisation and its supply chain and the easy access to product information, the product development time can be greatly reduced. This enables organisations to respond to the market with greater effectiveness and consistently provide their customers with new and initiative products.

Reduced Complexity of Accessing the Information of a Company

When properly implemented, PDM can simplify many day-to-day user operations by managing and automating routine tasks such as searching for drawings, tracking approvals and completing status reports. This improvement dramatically decreases the user's non-value-added time.

Improved Project Management

Project management is made easier using a PDM system as all those involved in the project have access to the same information and can work with a common product model. A PDM system also allows project managers to track the progress of a project more effectively and therefore ensure that the work being carried out is correct, on schedule and on target.

Improved Lifecycle Design

The easy access to information on new product development can assist organisations to exercise DFX philosophy. It allows manufacturing staff and production engineers to access design information at a much early stage of the product development, hence making it easier for problems to be identified earlier rather than later.

Supply Chain Collaboration

PDM systems are considered to have a strong impact on supply chain relationships by linking subcontractors, vendors, consultants, partners and customers and giving them access to the same information. PDM systems can also act as a data store for internally developed parts and external parts available from suppliers. By utilising a PDM system's database of existing parts, a designer can eliminate duplicating work and therefore considerably reduce development time and cost.

Despite numerous benefits, there are some shortfalls of traditional PDM systems. Firstly, the implementation of a PDM system, in order to get noticeable benefits, is no easy task. In fact, PDM is now more complicated, broader in scope, and more rapidly changing than ever before. Users often undergo a long learning curve when a new PDM system is implemented. Secondly, there has been a lack of global communication within a PDM system. In today's business world, multinational organisation is becoming more common with project teams spread all over the globe. Therefore, an efficient communication infrastructure becomes a must. Traditional PDM systems make the local or inter-organisational communication easy, yet they lack global cooperation support.

Last but not the least is the lack of user-friendly interface. A large number of PDM products on the market today have their proprietary user-interfaces. Users often have to spend a significant period of time to become familiar with new software. Consequently, instead of concentrating on their daily tasks, they have to focus on how to use the new PDM product. Unfamiliar user-interface is one of the main causes for end-users' hesitation to implement PDM systems.

WEB-BASED PDM

Based on Web-technology, the Internet presents a set of information technologies that provide a mechanism for the globalised electronic information sharing. PDM on the Internet can be considered as a natural extension of this distributed arrangement. The Web browser essentially becomes a new kind of client, one that is uniform across all applications. Internet and Web-technology are reshaping the PDM software business. Just a few years ago, Internet capabilities had barely made a dent in the way engineering companies managed information. Today, HTML/Java-based Web user interfaces and Web-based server access are increasingly becoming the norm for PDM systems.

Web-technology has been discussed in Chapter XV in a collaborative CAD/CAPP/CAM/CNC system. The following sections take a closer look at the similarities in architecture between Web-technology and PDM methodology.

Tiered-Architecture

Tiered-architecture has been touched upon in Chapter XV when an integrated and collaborative CAD/CAPP/CAM/CNC system is discussed. This section takes a look at the tired-architecture from the context of PDM. Like other database management systems, PDM also follows the tiered-architecture. One-tier architecture was widely used prior to the 1980s. The typical feature of the one-tier architecture is its self-contained monolithic program that consists of a GUI, processing logic and data store as a whole. Two-tier approach took over in the mid-1990s. This architecture divides an application into two separate tiers, namely, client and server tier. Users interface and logic processing both reside in the client tier, whereas its associate data vault resides on the server side. The major benefit of a two-tiered system over a one-tiered system is that it makes the client side "thinner". Therefore, two-tiered architecture allows faster processing than a single-tiered system. The drawback is however that the client can still become "too fat" as the application gets more complex. This will result in slow response and processing from the server.

In the early 1996, a revolutionary change in computer networking took place – the emergence of the three or multi-tier architecture. This is an open, distributed approach that separates the "fat" client into two parts -- user interface and logic processing. The result is a three-tiered structure which allows faster response and processing of users' requests. A systematic diagram of this multi-tier system is shown in Figure 16.2. A classic example of the three tier architecture is the World Wide Web, whereby Web Browsers form the client tier, the Database Server forms the third tier, and the TCP/IP serves as the second tier (Chu & Fan, 1999).

Similarities between Web-Technology and PDM Methodology

As PDM systems move toward a three-tiered distributed architecture, it is with no surprise to see a number of similarities between Web-technology and PDM methodology, in terms of both architecture and conceptual module (Figure 16.3 and Table 16.1).

Figure 16.2. Three-tier architecture in networking. ©2001 Elsevier Limited, used with permission

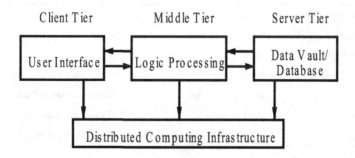

Figure 16.3. Logical architectures of Web and PDM

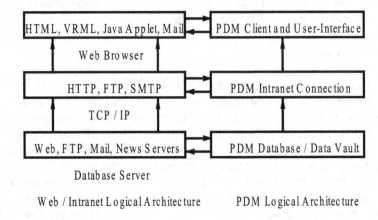

Web / Intranet Logical Architecture   PDM Logical Architecture

From Figure 16.3 and Table 16.1, it is evident that Web-technology resembles PDM methodology in many respects. The Web was firstly developed to provide a new lifestyle and better communication between people, making the transaction better implemented. Its ultimate goal is the same as PDM's basic starting point -- better management within the enterprise enhancing departmental collaboration through breaking down the boundary (formed by space and time) between them. Therefore, the Web technology is an enabling tool for overcoming the obstacles mentioned previously, as well as improving PDM's capabilities and efficiency.

Capability Improvements

There are many advantages of utilising Web-based technologies in PDM systems, some of them are summarised as follows.

Table 16.1. Comparison between Web and PDM's conceptual module

	Web-Technology	PDM-Technology
Software Architecture	Client/Server	Client/Server
Technologies Applied	Many	Many
Scope of Application	Huge	Big
Objective Handled	Any information	Engineering information
Security	Sharing and secure	Sharing and controllable
Openness	More extendable	Much more extendable
End User	Any hierarchy of the society	Any hierarchy of the enterprise

User-Friendliness

The development of Web-based front-end software has made them more user-friendly and easier to interact with. As such, a Web-based PDM system requires minimal training in comparison to other systems; hence the overall cost of system implementation is reduced. Simple, inexpensive Web browsers continue to expand the use of PDM to many people in the enterprise who can barely find any other equally convenient on-line access to such a broad base of information. By enabling users to become active quickly, browsers provide a "jump start" in achieving early success with PDM in organisations that might otherwise lose enthusiasm. Browsers used with PDM are the same ones used with the WWW (such as Microsoft Explorer, Netscape Navigator, and so on) for accessing data on the Internet as well as on the Intranet.

Greater Accessibility and Applicability

A rapidly growing number of companies have recognised that utilising Web browsers as the PDM interface is incredibly cost-effective, simple to comprehend, and capable of supporting almost all users. These browsers run on all types of computers, from UNIX machines to PCs and Macintoshes, providing the same look and feel across all platforms. Furthermore, the use of these Web browsers can eliminate the need to install and maintain specialised "client" software on each machine.

Effective Linking to the Supply Chain

Web-based PDM systems also have a great advantage over non Web-based systems in that they link the supply chain together more effectively, and subsequently lead to the improved supply chain collaboration. This allows the organisation to more easily share vital information with their suppliers and partners. The information available within a Web-based PDM system will assist the company - supplier relationship by effectively communicating any new product data and product change data to suppliers so that they can react accordingly.

Effective Linking to Geographically Diverse Organisations

A Web-based PDM system allows geographically diverse teams to work simultaneously on the same project. Project teams are able to view and with some systems to actually change information entered by others in different divisions or even different countries. This kind of co-ordination will enable an organisation to pool the expertise of their staff; no matter where in the world they are, at minimal costs and disruption to those involved. The ability to spread project teams around the world also allows an organisation to utilise the whole 24-hour day by taking advantage of time zone differences.

Making Virtual Organisation Possible

A virtual organisation is defined as a temporary union of companies that possess expertise in a specific field and gather for a particular project. After the project ends, the group disbands and the companies return to their daily business until a new project arises.

Virtual organisation has many advantages over the conventional type of companies. It mainly provides greater flexibility, and sharing expertise between project teams. The most important requirement for a successful virtual organisation is efficient communication between diverse project groups. By using Web-based PDM systems, the efficiency of global communication can be dramatically improved. Hence, the Web-technology enables companies to form a virtual organisation where partners or workers located over a wide area are linked seamlessly.

Further Challenges

In spite of many advantages of implementing PDM, in particular, a Web-based PDM system, there also exist some drawbacks or challenges. Firstly, a Web-based PDM system is constrained by the Web-technology currently available, and the speed at which it can transfer information. Although Web-technology is faster at transferring information to geographically diverse sites than the traditional postal service or courier, it still cannot compare to the speed of a local area network (LAN) or a wide area network (WAN).

Secondly, the potential to make mistakes during transferring data or information is not totally eliminated. If the system is not utilised correctly, mistakes relating to acquiring the correct information can still occur. As mentioned earlier, a PDM system can result in a reduction in product lead times. As the pace of product development and product change increases, the potential for human error may also increase.

Thirdly, there is a growing concern of security issues as the information flow between companies increases. Identifying the level of information transfer necessary for a project without jeopardising the company's security and exposing trade secrets is a crucial step for successfully implementing Web-technology in a PDM system. This would be dependent on the closeness of the supply relationship and level of information required for effective communication (Kovacs & Goff, 1998).

PDM STANDARDIZATION

With STEP being an international standard for exchanging product model data, it makes sense that STEP is used for PDM standardization. The STEP PDM Schema (PDM Implementer Forum, 2002) is such an example. It is a reference information model for the exchange of a central, common subset of the data being managed within a PDM system that uses STEP for product modelling.

The STEP PDM Schema represents the intersection of requirements and data structures from a range of STEP Application Protocols, all generally within the domains of design and development of discrete electro/mechanical parts and assemblies. In other words, the STEP PDM Schema is *not* a specification for the functionality required for the complete scope of all PDM system functionality – i.e., it is *not* the union, but the intersection, of functionality present in the set of STEP Application Protocols, e.g. AP203, AP212, AP214 and AP232 (Figure 16.4). There exists functionality important for complete PDM functionality that is not represented in the PDM Schema, but is in other units of functionality present in STEP APs. Clearly, the PDM Schema can promote interoperability between STEP APs in the area of product data management.

Figure 16.4. Relationships between the PMD Schema and other STEP APs

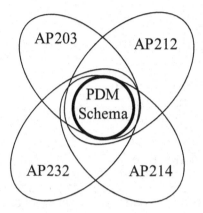

The product data management requirements addressed by the STEP PDM Schema are organized into groupings of related concepts. These groups provide logical clustering of AIM entities for the purpose of a clear structure within the PDM Schema. The groups also suggest a modular structure for the PDM Schema in line with the current direction towards modularization of the technical contents of STEP integrated resources and Application Protocols. The modular semantic units of functionality include,

- Part Identification, Classification, Properties, Structure and Relationships,
- Document Identification and Classification,
- External Files,
- Relationships Between Documents and Constituent Files
- Document and File Properties,
- Document and File Association to Product Data,
- Document and File Relationships,
- Alias Identification,
- Authorization,
- Configuration and Effectivity Information,
- Work Management Data.

The following shows the STEP Part 21 (ISO 10303-21, 1994) file of an instance model about a part called "BRAKE021". The information recorded include the part name (Line #10), identification (Lines #20 - #40), revisions (Lines #50 - #70), relationships with the other two parts (Lines #130 and #150), revisions about the other two parts (Lines #160 and #170), and so on.

```
ISO-10303-21;
HEADER;
FILE _ DESCRIPTION(('BRAKE part', 'file'), '2;1');
FILE _ NAME('brake021a.stp', '2008-06-03T10:03:10+00:00', ('X.X.'), (''),
'', '', '');
FILE _ SCHEMA(('PDM _ SCHEMA {1.2}));
```

```
ENDSEC;
DATA;

/* part #1 */
#10 = PRODUCT('BRAKE021', 'RAV6-1', $, (#20));

/* part context */
#20 = PRODUCT _ CONTEXT('', #30, '');
#30 = APPLICATION _ CONTEXT('');
#40 = APPLICATION _ PROTOCOL _ DEFINITION('version 1.2', 'pdm _ schema',
2000, #30);

/* part versions for part #1 */
#50 = PRODUCT _ DEFINITION _ FORMATION('02', 'valve modified', #10);
#60 = PRODUCT _ DEFINITION _ FORMATION('03', 'housing modified', #10);
#70 = PRODUCT _ DEFINITION _ FORMATION _ RELATIONSHIP('', 'sequence', $,
#50, #60);

/* definition of view on version 03 of part #1 */
/* primary life _ cycle _ stage = design, primary application _ domain
= mechanical design */
#80 = PRODUCT _ DEFINITION('/NULL', $, #60, #90);
#90 = PRODUCT _ DEFINITION _ CONTEXT('part definition', #100, 'design');
#100 = APPLICATION _ CONTEXT('mechanical design');

/* association of the id owner for part #1 */
#130 = APPLIED _ ORGANIZATION _ ASSIGNMENT(#140, #150, (#10, #160,
#170));
#150 = ORGANIZATION _ ROLE('id owner');

/* information on person and organization */
#140 = ORGANIZATION('CONCEPTCAR', 'FSAE', 'location');
#540 = PERSON('ravesix@fsae.com', 'Clark', 'Kay', $, $, $);
#550 = PERSON _ AND _ ORGANIZATION(#540, #140);

/* part #2 and part #3 */
#160 = PRODUCT('H24-1123.1', 'Fixture RX25B', '', (#20));
#170 = PRODUCT('NZ 222', 'Screw M3x15', '', (#20));

/* part versions for part #2 and part #3 */
#180 = PRODUCT _ DEFINITION _ FORMATION('B', 'larger screw holes',
#160);
#190 = PRODUCT _ DEFINITION _ FORMATION('15', '', #170);

/* view definition for version of part #2 */
#200 = PRODUCT _ DEFINITION('/NULL', $, #180, #210);
#210 = PRODUCT _ DEFINITION _ CONTEXT('part definition', #215, 'de-
sign');
#215 = APPLICATION _ CONTEXT('mechanical design');

/* view definition for version of part #3 */
#220 = PRODUCT _ DEFINITION('/NULL', $, #190, #230);
```

```
#230 = PRODUCT _ DEFINITION _ CONTEXT('part definition', #240, 'de-
sign');
#240 = APPLICATION _ CONTEXT('mechanical design');

/* part discriminator for parts #1 - #3 */
#250 = PRODUCT _ RELATED _ PRODUCT _ CATEGORY('part', $, (#10, #160,
#170));
#260 = PRODUCT _ CATEGORY _ RELATIONSHIP('', $, #250, #270);
#270 = PRODUCT _ RELATED _ PRODUCT _ CATEGORY('detail', $, (#160));
#280 = PRODUCT _ CATEGORY _ RELATIONSHIP('', $, #250, #290);
#290 = PRODUCT _ RELATED _ PRODUCT _ CATEGORY('assembly', $, (#10));
#300 = PRODUCT _ CATEGORY _ RELATIONSHIP('', $, #250, #310);
#310 = PRODUCT _ RELATED _ PRODUCT _ CATEGORY('standard', $, (#170));

ENDSEC;
END-ISO-10303-21;
```

INTEGRATED AND EXTENDED PDM

Between traditional CAD/CAM and PDM, a gap exists. CAD/CAM systems provide some level of data management, but not nearly that provided by PDM systems, whereas PDM systems can interface with CAD/CAM systems to control design files, but are too structured to function well in situations such as a conceptual design environment. This relates to two crucial goals that companies are striving to achieve -- fostering an environment of innovation and fostering an environment of collaboration. To achieve these two goals, a traditional PDM needs to be integrated with some other engineering tools and systems. These may include a Virtual Product Development Management (VPDM) system and an ERP system. The former encourages innovations in design, whereas the latter ensures a broader integration in a company.

Until recently, many intelligent design changes could only be made after performing simulations on physical prototypes. VPDM provides product knowledge much earlier in the design cycle, when the cost of change and design experimentation is minimal. VPDM enables engineering activities to occur in parallel, because it supports modelling dependencies among various engineering disciplines, carefully tracking design changes. With VPDM, engineers can become more efficient by finding required product data more quickly. VPDM also uses advanced tools for digital mock-up, behaviour simulation, and visualization, allowing engineers to spot defects or manufacturing difficulties early.

For companies that design the products they build, extending PDM to interface ERP can offer multiple benefits. While ERP systems may be able to model some product manufacturing, they are not designed to facilitate dynamic change. They assume a fixed product definition, and do not understand exploring options during conceptual design. By feeding more accurate and more detailed information into the ERP system, PDM facilitates additional efficiencies in manufacturing, procurement and other production elements.

PRODUCT LIFECYCLE MANAGEMENT

To consistently provide innovative products, the manufacturing company needs an effective product development process. This product development process should engage a variety of cross-functional participants from marketing, engineering, procurement, manufacturing, sales, and service departments. Furthermore, due to the increasing levels of outsourcing of the company, suppliers and business partners should also join this process; at the same time a strong customer focus has necessitated the customers' direct involvement as well. In this case, the product development process forms a distributed, extended enterprise value chain (Xu, Chen & Xie, 2003).

During the product development process, this cross-functional value chain works collaboratively to generate the intellectual property that represents a new product or product variant. When this intellectual property is transacted digitally through software applications, it begins to form a digital representation of the product. Normally, it is called "digital product". This "digital product" is now recognized as a manufacturing company's most important intellectual asset to its business because it does not only include the definition of the complete product, from mechanical and electronic components, to software and documentation, but also contains the entire set of information that defines how the product is designed, manufactured, operated, or used, serviced, and then retired and dismantled when it becomes obsolete (Clarke, 2002).

However, developing digital products in a collaborative environment—under intense time and cost pressure—is certainly not an easy task. The PDM delusion discussed early in this chapter has a limited scope. While it is sufficient for pure product data, it does not add to a suitable enterprise infrastructure that supports efficient collaborative product development process. This problem can be best solved through the proper application of product lifecycle management approach. This is because that PLM is a strategic business approach that applies a consistent set of business solutions to support the collaborative creation, management, dissemination, and use of digital product definition information and to improve the effectiveness of the product development process in an extended enterprise value chain environment (Grieves, 2005, Saaksvuori & Immonen, 2005). Once implemented, PLM will help manufacturer increase its flexibility and agility to respond swiftly to changing market pressures and competitors to:

- Reduce product costs, improve quality, and shorten time to market, while achieving the targeted Return On Investment (ROI);
- Deliver more innovative products and services tailored to customer needs;
- Establish more comprehensive, collaborative, and improved relationships with their customers, suppliers, and business partners.

Definition of PLM

PLM can be defined as a strategic business approach that applies a consistent set of business solutions to (CIMdata, 2002):

- Support the collaborative product development process in a virtual value chain with no time, distance, or organizational boundaries; and

- Collaboratively create, manage, disseminate and use digital product definition information across the extended enterprise through the complete product lifecycle from the concept to the end of life of a product when it becomes obsolete.

From the definition, it can be concluded that the essence of PLM is to solve the problem of managing the complete set of digital product definition information—creating that information, managing it through its life, and disseminating and using it throughout the lifecycle of the product.

In order to better understand the role of PLM to a company, it is necessary to know what product-related lifecycles the manufacturing companies need to manage with today's PLM solution. Within any industry, the overall enterprise lifecycles can be divided into three primary and tightly intertwined lifecycles shown in Figure 16.5:

In the PLM context, it focuses on the product definition lifecycle—the creation and management of all product-related information. As within the overall enterprise lifecycle, this lifecycle begins at the earliest point of customer requirement and product concept, and extends until the product is obsolete and field support is ceased. The contents of information contain the definition of the complete product, from mechanical and electronic components, to software and documentation, and the entire set of information that defines how the product is designed, manufactured, operated, serviced, retired and dismantled when it becomes obsolete. Furthermore, this product definition is continually updated throughout the entire lifecycle. The second lifecycle, product production, is concerned with all activities associated with production and distribution of the product. Enterprise Resource Planning system, which addresses product production, how to produce, manufacture, handle inventory, and ship, is mainly responsible for this lifecycle. The third one is support lifecycle. It focuses on managing the enterprise's core resources like its people, finances, and other resources required to support the enterprise.

For a company that needs to achieve business success, there must be close coordination and communication among all three lifecycles so that a seamless product lifecycle is created to bring innovative products to market effectively (Susman, 1998).

Figure 16.5. Three primary enterprise lifecycle

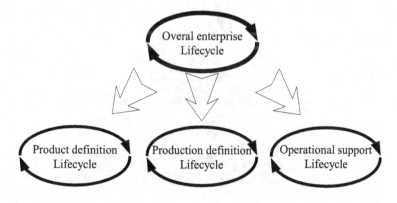

PLM Solution Model

As shown in Figure 16.6, a complete PLM model is made up of appropriate components of technology foundation, management and process. Across the bottom of the PLM model is technology foundation, it is an integral part of any PLM solution. In this technology foundation, there are many important elements such as standards, security, communication, visualization, and collaboration, which are applied to construct PLM's core functions such as design automation (e.g., the authoring and analysis tools and processes used to create, simulate and analyze a product), product structures and Bills of Materials, work flow and process management, information and content management and vaulting. Sequentially, these core functions are employed to build functional applications such as workflow and configuration management. Finally, an enterprise PLM solution is built by using these functional applications, together with best practices, methods, and processes pertinent to an enterprise's market and specific industrial sector that can be fine-tuned to meet company requirement (CIMdata, 2002, PTC, 2002, Susman, 1998).

Currently, a lot of PLM software with different focuses and specialties are available on the market. In most cases, these PLM products/systems can be divided into three classes depending on their functions to business. Each class of these PLM systems also encompasses elements that are used to deliver the related business function.

- Systems that focus on product and process definition (e.g. systems such as requirements management, CAD, DFM (Design for Manufacturability), CAPP, CAM, CAE (Computer-aided Engineering), NC programming, BOM systems, routing definition, plastic behaviour analysis, rapid prototyping, factory simulation, parts library systems.
- Interface systems that make product and process definition information available for use later in the product lifecycle (for example in sales catalogues, sales configurations, NC controllers, ERP systems and technical publishing systems).

Figure 16.6. Standard PLM model

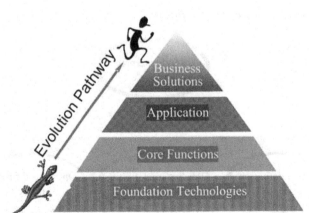

- Support systems used in many activities, i.e. systems such as viewers, QFD (Quality Function Deployment), process mapping, project management, Configuration Management, Engineering Data Management, PDM, visualization, collaborative workspace systems, and data exchange and translation systems.

Benefits of PLM

PLM is a strategic business approach and promises to deliver substantial benefits to manufacturing companies taking advantage of it. PLM applies its powerful business solutions that include a set of enabling technologies to help the manufacturing company improve its business performance. The followings summarize some improvements and cost savings resulting from implementing PLM (CIMdata, 2002, PTC, 2002, Susman, 1998). Some may agree with those of PDM systems, but many extend to a much broader scope.

- PLM provides an opportunity for the manufacturing company to improve its internal business process and organizational relationships with its business partners, suppliers and customers. By taking full advantage of PLM, the manufacturing company would become more innovative and competitive in today's distributed global and collaborative business environments.
- PLM can improve a company's business performance by helping manage all classes of digital product definition information and associated business processes. As an enterprise infrastructure, it can become a practical enabler and a means of support for key management initiatives that can make or break a company. Without PLM, some of these initiatives will be difficult to achieve.
- PLM fosters innovation by creating an infrastructure for collaboration that spans all level of a company, as well as its business partners, suppliers and customers. It provides a rich communication infrastructure for sharing ideas and information between them in the design and supply chain, enabling them to maintain, understand and use this data to advantage while its competitors waste time chasing the information.
- PLM helps increase a company's ability to innovate on product families and related services through the entire product lifecycle. Increasing the ability to innovate means competitive differentiation that grows revenue and expands markets, and can eventually result in a company becoming a whole product generation ahead of its competitors. In addition, PLM helps offer better customer service, thus increasing service revenues.
- PLM helps reduce product costs all the way along the product lifecycle. For instance, it reduces the number of error during product development, thus reducing unwanted engineering changes. It allows for more simulation and virtual prototyping of new products, thus reducing the need for production of costly physical prototypes. It enables examination of the detailed descriptions of all parts and products, resulting in identification and elimination of duplicate parts.

PLM Implementation

It must be pointed out that successfully implementing product lifecycle management is no easy task. A lot of factors affect the performance of PLM. Therefore, a company that wants to benefit from PLM should pay attention to the following six factors.

Top Management Commitment and Support

Product lifecycle management cannot be implemented successfully unless top management creates conditions that support its implementation and demonstrates a consistent commitment to the concept. Therefore, it is important that top management articulates and reinforces values that support a product lifecycle management culture. This can be done, for example, either by publicly praising employees whose actions are consistent with product lifecycle management and designating them as role models to be emulated by others, or by building an appraisal and compensation systems by top management to reward employees who carry out actions that are consistent with product lifecycle management (Susman, 1998).

Developing Appropriate Skills and Business Processes

Another key determinant for the successful implementation of product lifecycle management is the skills and business process that a company applies. The company must develop enough ability to (1) make effective use of a widely-distributed worldwide organization, creating a virtual value chain with no time, distance, or organizational boundaries; (2) ensure that corporate acquisitions and merges work together; (3) leverage the intellectual assets in these dispersed teams and organizations; and (4) enable 24 hours × 7 days development and product support using global teams (CIMdata, 2002).

Cross-Functional Collaborative Product Development Teams

Cross-Functional collaborative product development teams should be formed that include specialists who collectively possess a diverse and well-rounded set of experiences, information and skills. These teams are mainly responsible for an entire product development cycle from customer needs to final full-volume production. The biggest advantage of such teams is that they avoid the "throw it over the wall" mentality that is pervasive among product designers in organizations with function-based structures, where products are designed without much concern for problems such as manufacturability, environment and disposal.

Performance Measurement and Reward Systems

Top management will need to modify the conventional reward system to encourage behaviour that is consistent with the demands of product lifecycle management. For example, in a collaborative product development team, people who are responsible for developing new products can be rewarded on the basis of profits generated from new product, and those who focus on product enhancements and derivatives could be rewarded on the basis of the profit retention rather than on increases (Susman, 1998).

Continuous Employee Education

Continuous education of all employees can reinforce and increase the effectiveness of all the product lifecycle concepts and practices, and creates employees with multiple skills and broad product perspectives. In the long term, the probability of a company's success is increased by having employees who are better able to contribute to the fast development of high quality, innovative products. This requires employees with skills that enable them to be innovative. However, it must address here that although education is one of the prerequisites to implementing product lifecycle management successfully, it will not assure that managers are flexible enough to change their priorities and actions with transitions in lifecycle stages. Therefore, employee education needs to be accompanied by selection of managers with appropriate skills and attitudes.

Eliminating Employee Resistance

It is not uncommon that some employees resist the implementation of product lifecycle management because it requires that they must learn new concepts and skills. Employees who have succeeded previously in their organizations by mastering traditional concepts and skills may resent having to perform under new rules. They may fear that they cannot perform as well under the new rules as they did under the old. Such resentment and fear is normal, and can be lessened in many ways like one-on-one dialogues with those concerned employee, educating those employees who have no experience with product lifecycle concepts, or developing some specific policies to help employees cope with the impact of product lifecycle management (Wognum, Fisscher & Weenink, 2002).

PLM Standardization

In order for the product-related information to be exchanged, shared, or communicated across company borders and between dispersed systems in a heterogeneous environment, PLM systems need to be developed such that semantics originating from various life-cycle disciplines can be integrated in one information model. A core information model is needed to allow various business processes to exchange or integrate information independent of the type of business rules that governs a particular piece of information. Such a core information model should then be used to derive models for implementation.

Within ISO 10303 (STEP), a number of information models have already been standardized with this in mind. Hence, the core information model for PLM applications would benefit from referencing various parts of the STEP standard, or simply be developed on top of existing STEP standards. The core information model can represent the conceptual business domain model and downstream implementation models can change the logical structure (for a better fit into computer system artefacts such as database, APIs etc.), but not the semantics. The obvious reason for this need is simply because the information entities in the STEP information models are already networked and suited for file-based data exchange. The data needed to acquire the full description of a certain business entity (e.g. a Part and its Part versions) are associated via relationship entities, which results in a networked set of instances. It is not easy to directly navigate these business entities. An implementation model can be derived via transformation of the core information model into, for example, an XML Schema definition. Such an implementation model defines a logical structure of the conceptual information model that adds attributes in order to support easier navigation. A suitable implementation model for example could be an XML Schema that is used as a part of a Web Service Description Language (WSDL) (2007) API. A WSDL is platform neutral and can be implemented by any systems that implement the W3C standards such as Simple Object Access Protocol (SOAP) (2007) and WSDL. The derived implementation model can be used for exposing the API for new systems. More useful and important is that it can be used as an API wrapping up existing legacy systems.

There have been a number of standards from different professional engineering, manufacturing and quality societies, such as EIA-649 National Consensus Standard for Configuration Management, GEIA-859 Consensus Standard for Data Management, and US 12207 Software Life Cycle Processes. ISO 10303-239 (PLCS) (2005) is the only international standard that specifies an information model that defines what information can be exchanged and represented to support a product through life. The basic data structures that are exchanged are defined by EXPRESS Entities (ISO 10303-11, 1994). For example in PLCS there are entities defining Parts, versions of parts (Part_versions) and people (Person). Each entity may have attributes that provide further information about the thing being represented by an entity. For example, a person has a first name and last name. These are attributes of a Person.

PLCS encourages interoperability across enterprises and systems through integrated information models, as part of the ISO 10303 STEP standard. AP239 provides an extension to the capabilities of AP203 (Configuration Controlled Design) (ISO 10303-203, 1994) and AP214 (Automotive Design Process) (ISO 10303-214, 1994) and hence the Product Data Management Schema and Modules, to address the requirements for Configuration Management over the complete product life. AP239 also addresses the information requirements needed to define and deliver lifecycle support for complex assets. This includes specifications of,

- Identification and composition of a product design from a support viewpoint (as an extension of the PDM Modules);
- Definition of documents and their applicability to products and support activities (as an extension of the PDM Modules);
- Identification and composition of realized products;
- Configuration management activities over the complete lifecycle;
- Properties, states and behaviour of products;
- Activities required to sustain product function;
- Resources needed to perform such activities;
- Planning and scheduling of such activities;
- Capture of feedback on the performance of such activities, including the resources used;
- Capture of feedback on the usage and condition of a realized product;
- Definition of the support environment in terms of support equipment, people, organizations, skills, experience and facilities; and
- Definition of classes of product, activities, states, people, organizations and resources.

PLCS is considered as a key enabler for process improvements and transformation in several manufacturing and service-focused industries such as aerospace & defence, automotive, machinery, and telecommunications. It enables a number of functionalities,

- Activity Management – the functionality to request, define, justify, approve, schedule and capture feedback on activities and related resources;

- Product Definition – the functionality to define product requirements and their configuration, including relationships between parts and assemblies in multiple product structures;
- Operational Feedback – the functionality that describes and captures feedback on product properties, operating states, behaviour and usage; and
- Support Solution and Environment – the functionality to define and maintain the necessary support solution for a product in a specified environment including the opportunity to provide support, tasks, facilities, special tools and equipment, and personnel knowledge and skills required.

In developing PLCS, a modular architecture was used to construct a single integrated information model. The basic building blocks of the integrated information model are referred to as modules. A Data EXchange Specification (DEX) (DEXLib, 2007) is a subset of the overall PLCS information model, comprising of one or more capabilities, which in turn link to data modules. DEXs support a specific business process or purpose and can be related to existing information. The use of DEXs can facilitate modular implementation of AP 239 (ISO 10303-239, 2007).

PLCS is developed based on the functionality defined by other standards relevant to product support. These include ASD S1000D, ASD Spec 2000M, United States Military Specification 1388, United Kingdom Defence Standard 00-60, etc. It is also worth noting that ISO 10303-233 (2007) is another good candidate to further complement the standardized PLM information model landscape, since AP239 is based on the same information constructs used by the AP233.

Share-A-Space: PLM in Practice

Share-A-space is a business process neutral environment where organizations can work together throughout a product's life. It provides an environment where virtual organizations and teams can drive change and configuration management across the lifecycle processes, and organizational boundaries (CIMdata, 2007). Share-A-space™ is designed to operate across extended, widely distributed and heterogeneous enterprises, in support of accessing to large blocks of product-related information that are developed and used at different locations. This includes finding and gaining access to the right information about a product or project at any stage in its lifecycle, while ensuring that business rules applicable to both the data and users are defined and enforced.

The system is based on the broadly accepted standard for PDM information STEP AP203 (ISO 10303-203, 1994), AP214 (ISO 10303-214, 1994), PDM Schema (PDM Implementers Forum, 2002) as well as the PLCS standard, ISO10303-239 (ISO 10303-239, 2005), so that it can be quickly accessed without worrying about system dependent data models and applications. This approach allows for the separation of data and its structure from the applications that create and use it. As a result, applications can be changed without affecting other parties' ability to access the data. Share-A-space™ complements some of the existing engineering and product-related solutions such as CAD, CAM, CAE, PDM, ERP, Integrated Logistics Support (ILS) and Technical Document Management.

Core Features

Fundamentally, Share-A-space™ provides data consolidation on an extended enterprise level. This enables incremental changes to product data to be quickly captured from authoring systems, integrated into the shared total product definition and published, thereby supporting multiple views throughout a product's entire lifecycle. In addition, Share-A-space™ is a data sharing "hub" that provides a lower-cost alternative to costly maintenance of direct interfaces between multiple enterprise systems (e.g., CAD, PDM, ERP, SCM, etc.). Some of the key design features include,

- An Oracle database based on the ISO10303-214 and 239 standards, enabling a rich and neutral information repository;
- A model driven software design, enabling fast and information model consistent development;
- An independent data consolidation engine for advanced information access;
- Support for multiple data exchange formats based on either STEP technology or straight text-based formats.

Some of the main functionality features are,

- Context dependant identification, allowing for multiple, yet unique identifiers;
- Context dependant part structure, handling allowing for view separation of structures;
- Context dependant associations of properties, documents, parts, etc., for managing complex information constructs, and
- Information ownership driven access rights control

Architecture

Share-A-space's architecture takes advantage of XML and a set of Web-based technologies for data communication. STEP EXPRESS models are used to define the database. In a typical configuration, the Oracle database is run on a Linux, UNIX, or MS Windows® server with the application server run on a separate MS Windows® machine. The application server is of the layered architecture. Examples of layers include Business Logic Layer and Presentation Layer, leveraging the .NET™ Framework. The Business Logic Layer manages the core business rules of the application, while the Presentation Layer manages user interaction rules. The combination of these rules governs the behaviour of the application.

On the client side there is only the requirement for a Web browser such as MS Internet Explorer or Firefox. This is because the application layer leverages Active Server Pages (ASP.NET) that publishes pure HTML.

The Web Service layer of the architecture is the most commonly used integration mechanism. This mechanism allows for XML data transfer from and to any Web-enabled system. The Web Service layer currently supports the OASIS PLCS PLM Web Services based on ISO10303-239 and the OMG PLM Services based on ISO10303-214. The Web Service layer can either be used as an API allowing for remote control of Share-A-space™ or as a traditional Service Oriented Architecture (SOA) component. When used as an API, specialized clients, analysis tools, and interfaces can be built on top of it. When used as a SOA component, the Web Services together with its event engine can be used to orchestrate information driven change processes across the SOA environment (CIMdata, 2007).

LOOKING FORWARD TO "GRAND" INTEGRATION

Previous generations of engineering systems have had cleaner boundaries between them, such as CAD/CAM, CNC, PDM, PLM, ERP, finance and payroll, where boundaries between today's products are fuzzy, overlapping and inter-organisational. Some vendors offer a full suite of products covering "all" needs nicely linked together, while others focus on a specific business need and provide a "best-of-breed" system, leaving it to customers to debate the benefits of each. It is clear that there is a need to integrate different engineering systems that are in use in a company, as well as those shared with other organisations. This type of ultimate and "sweeping" integration may be termed as grand integration. While the need for such grand-scale integration is clear, this section makes no attempt to describe how to realise it. Instead, it discusses the four common techniques one may use and/or encounter for such system integration.

These four common techniques have been discussed by Ferman (1999) in his article, each representing a level of complexity and functionality created to solve differing business needs. Figure 16.7 shows these techniques in terms of business waste and flexibility. The waste axis describes integration efficiency and overall process cost. High waste means an integration method adds overhead (including headcount), errors and information-transfer delays. The flexibility axis refers to ability to accommodate change, either in systems being connected, or such organizational changes as acquisitions, product transfers or adding new facilities.

Figure 16.7. Integration techniques

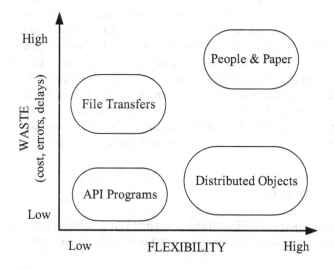

People-Paper Technique

When discussing system integration, users often dismiss the People and Paper technique, yet the majority of such integration at most manufacturing companies is done with people using paper, meetings and manual data entry and re-entry. Slow, error-prone, expensive but flexible, still it reflects the reality of limited resources for building automated integrations. The People-Paper technique was the only means prior to the CAD era. Its inefficiency was magnified and compounded by the situation in which both CAD and paper-based data co-existed when CAD first entered the business.

File-Transfer Technique

File Transfer techniques automate extracting, storing, and loading data via files. This greatly reduces errors, yet keeps generation and utilization systems isolated from each other. Most file-based information transfers are not real-time, therefore both systems (one sends and the other receives) have copies of transferred data that need to be kept synchronized. File transfer connectivity is relatively easy for organizations in the People and Paper connectivity generation to understand and accept. It usually involves minimal changes to business processes, just the automation of the data entry and transfer steps, often justified by cost reduction. Although most transfer file formats are tailored to an organization or to a vendor's product, a few standard formats exist, and they are covered mostly in Chapters II and XI. They include for example, STEP AP203, STEP AP214, STEP AP 224 and STEP AP 338.

API Programs

API integration uses custom code, i.e. API functions or libraries, to program an interface between systems. Programs are designed to understand both systems' data structures. They often remove the need for redundant data by allowing real-time access to the other system. API integrations have tighter functional integration and fast response time because they are tuned to business needs and business rules. These programs often run continuously, waiting for requests instead of a person or a timer to start them. By using the systems' published APIs, the system can enforce its internal business rules and security consistently. Many of today's systems allow complex business logic to be triggered in real time based on system transactions. APIs work in this scenario because they do not bypass system transactions. Major drawbacks to using API integration are their complexity and vendor-specific nature, making each connection a major effort from people with very specific skills.

One can simplify API integration by accessing a system's underlying database directly, using the database vendor's commands. By bypassing the system's APIs and transactions, this method reverts toward the file transfer technique. Direct database commands provide fast and flexible access to system data, but pose the danger of corrupting the system in the process.

Distributed Objects

Many system developers have adopted object-oriented programming languages and design techniques. Object technology allows breaking down large complex systems into smaller, well-defined modules that are very stable, and very autonomous. In fact, companies should consider distributed object technology for integration as their need for stable, autonomous systems grows. Distributed objects provide a means for dynamically changing the server's clients use without them realizing it.

There are a number of architectures supporting distributed objects, such as CORBA® (Common Object Broker Architecture), COM+ and DCOM, EJB (Enterprise Java Beans), RMI (Remote Method Invocation), the open-source project Dinopolis, and Web Services technologies such as Web services building blocks – SOAP, UDDI (Universal Description, Discovery and Integration), and WSDL. CORBA® and DCOM seem to be the two main architectures in applications. Unfortunately, DCOM does not run on the UNIX platforms. Many companies are running legacy systems on older platforms that do not support COR-BA® or DCOM. Interfacing them into a more standard computing platform and then using CORBA® (or DCOM) on the standard computing platform lets other CORBA® systems see the interface without knowing it as a legacy system. This technique can simplify an eventual migration from the legacy system without disrupting its integration.

CORBA®, as well as many other distributed object technologies, handles integration matters in a specific way. The main portion of CORBA® applying to integration standards is defining a common set of business objects. These common business objects offer a chance to make plug-and-play work at the enterprise-level, as long as the organization follows the same standards for their applications and business object components. What makes the integration interfaces work is the common definition of basic business objects, and the ability to add extensions to basic definitions without changing the original definition. CORBA® consists of multiple servers and multiple clients with a common set of definitions utilizing a 'broker' as matchmaker. Each server registers the services it can provide with the broker when it starts up. Each client asks the broker for the best server for each of its requests. By using the broker, the clients and servers are independent from each other.

Yet, CORBA® by itself is just a protocol to extend object technology across multiple systems. CORBA® does not provide a high-enough level of commonality to support plug-and-play systems. We need a set of classes (collectively called framework) that provide a set of compatible definitions. Usable systems are built on top of a framework by using framework classes. Implementation logic can then be added by sub-classing the framework's classes and coding the implementation logic to the sub-classes. Higher-level user applications use the framework class definitions without knowledge of the implementation sub-classes. The framework isolates high-level applications from the implementation classes. Isolation allows the applications to run with any implementation of the framework.

Most frameworks are used within an application on a single computer. These applications are usually pre-built as a single application, mainly for internal flexibility and maintainability. Some frameworks use Dynamic Linked Libraries (DLLs) to allow the implementation to be changed without physically re-linking the applications using it. DLL frameworks are still limited to a single computer, whereas CORBA®-based frameworks can work over a network of computers and allow substituting implementations on the fly (Ferman, 1999).

It is envisaged that in the long run, the interfaces among the CAD, CAPP, CAM, CNC, PDM, PLM, ERP and other enterprises solutions should be interchangeable to an international standard. The differences between these vendors should be what is on the inside. A useful feature of futuristic business systems is plug-and-play across the board of both hardware and software.

CONCLUSION

PDM systems integrate and manage all applications, information, and processes that define a product, from design to manufacture, and to end-user support. In other words, PDM systems are used to control information, files, documents, and work processes required to design, build, support, distribute, and maintain products. Typical product-related information includes geometry, engineering drawings, project plans, part files, assembly diagrams, product specifications, numerical control machine-tool programs, analysis results, correspondence, bills of material, engineering change orders, and many more.

It is evident that PDM becomes more adaptive and flexible if running on the Web infrastructure. Both PDM and Web, if integrated properly, will enhance each other's capabilities and performance. Some major benefits of applying Web-technology to PDM infrastructure include, (a) better user-friendliness; (b) greater accessibility and applicability; (c) more effective linking to the supply chain and (d) easier formation between geographically diverse organisations.

Some drawbacks that a Web-based PDM system is now facing include, not-large-enough bandwidth of the current Internet for CAD file transferring, the likelihood of making mistakes during data transferring, and ever-growing concerns over the security issues as the information flow between a company and its supply chain. These drawbacks inevitably offer some serious challenges to Web-based PDM systems for years to come.

STEP PDM Schema, together with other APs (e.g. AP203, AP214 and AP232), provides a standardised "toolset" for implementing PDM. This way, all stages of a product development process can be modelled and consolidated on a single data structure. By extending PDM to include VPDM and ERP, manufacturing processes can be managed by ERP systems in the production engine to become an integrated part of the design process, and manufacturing processes can be understood before design is released.

In the modern economy where no company can create a product entirely by itself, this type of globalization has led to the Extended Enterprise in which many organizations carry out the activities related to the entire lifecycle of a product. For all of these organizations to work together, PLM provides a paradigm in which all the activities related to a product and its related data and knowledge can be managed in an integrated way across the lifecycle from customer need to recycling and disposal.

Unlike PDM, PLM is much more than a technology or software product. PLM should be considered as a strategic business approach which empowers the business. Once implemented, it provides benefits with a positive impact on an enterprise's top and bottom lines. More importantly it is a catalyst for change within a business -- an opportunity to improve processes and organizational relationships to create an innovative, measurably improved business.

The effort of achieving single information model for PLM has led to the birth of ISO 10303-239, which also gives PLM a much needed standardized platform. One of the applications of ISO 10303-239 is Share-A-space™. Share-A-space™ provides a STEP-based (AP214, PDM schema (AP203, 210, 212), AP239 and AP233) information integration, consolidation and sharing solution. It has been designed to support secure asynchronous collaboration and data consolidation in an extended enterprise environment. With PLCS (.i.e. ISO 10303-239) as its key enabler, it has been designed to support the management of product related data throughout a product's complete lifecycle -- from requirements to in-service support. There are some common techniques suggested for building a grand integration system, such as People-paper, File-transfer, API programming and Distributed objects techniques.

REFERENCES

Bruce, M., Leverick, F., & Littler, D. (1995). Complexities of Collaborative Product Development, *Technovation*, *15*, 535-552.

Chu, X., & Fan, Y. (1999). Product Data Management Based on Web Technology, *Integrated Manufacturing Systems*, (10), 84-88.

CIMdata Report. (2002). *Product Lifecycle Management*. 3909 Research Park Drive, Ann Arbor, Michigan 48108, USA: CIMdata, Inc.

CIMdata Report. (2007). *Eurostep's Share-A-space™ Product Lifecycle Collaboration through Information Integration*, 3909 Research Park Drive, Ann Arbor, Michigan 48108, USA: CIMdata, Inc.

Clarke, J. (2002). Managing your products from cradle to grave. *Manufacturing Computer Solutions*, *8*, 22-23.

DEXLib, (2007). Retrieved January 30, 2008, from http://www.plcs-resources.org/dexlib/index.html. Eurostep Group.

Edwards, K. L. (2002). Towards more strategic product design for manufacture and assembly: priorities for concurrent engineering. *Material & Design*, *23*, 651-656.

Ferman, J. E., (1999, October). Strategies for successful ERP connections. *Manufacturing Engineering*, *123*(4), 48-57.

Grieves, M. (2005). *Product Lifecycle Management: Driving the Next Generation of Lean Thinking*. New York, USA: McGraw-Hill

Hameri, A., & Nihtila, J. (1998). Product Data Management: Exploratory Study on State-of-the-Art in One-of-a-Kind Industry. *Computers in Industry*, *35*, 195-206.

ISO 10303-11. (1994). *Industrial automation systems and integration – Product data representation and exchange – Part 11: Description methods: The EXPRESS language reference manual*. Geneva, Switzerland: International Organisation for Standardisation (ISO).

ISO 10303-203. (1994). *Industrial automation systems and integration – Product data representation and exchange – Part 203: Application protocol: Configuration controlled 3D designs of mechanical parts and assemblies*. Geneva, Switzerland: International Organisation for Standardisation (ISO).

ISO 10303-21. (1994). *Industrial automation systems and integration – Product data representation and exchange – Part 21: Implementation methods: Clear text encoding of the exchange structure*. Geneva, Switzerland: International Organisation for Standardisation (ISO).

ISO 10303-214. (1994). *Industrial automation systems and integration – Product data representation and exchange – Part 214: Application protocol: Core data for automotive mechanical design processes.* Geneva, Switzerland: International Organisation for Standardisation (ISO).

ISO 10303-239. (2005). *Industrial automation systems and integration -- Product data representation and exchange -- Part 239: Application protocol: Product life cycle support.* Geneva, Switzerland: International Organisation for Standardisation (ISO).

ISO/CD 10303-233. (2007). *Industrial automation systems and integration -- Product data representation and exchange -- Part 233: Systems engineering data representation.* Geneva, Switzerland: International Organisation for Standardisation (ISO).

Kovacs, Z., & Goff, J. (1998). Support for Product Data from Design to Production, *Computer Integrated Manufacturing Systems, 11*, 285-290.

Littler, D., Leverick, F., & Bruce, M. (1995). Factors Affecting the Process of Collaborative Product Development: A Study of UK Manufacturers of Information and Communication Technology Products. *Journal of Product Innovation Management, 12*, 16-32.

Liu, D. T., & Xu, X. (2001). A Review of Web-based Product Data Management Systems. *Computers in Industry, 44*, 251-262.

PDM Implementers Forum. (2002). *Usage Guide for the STEP PDM Schema,* V1.2, Release 4.3. January 2002.

Peltonen, H., Pitkanen, O., & Sulonen, R. (1996). Process-Based View of Product Data Management. *Computers in Industry, 31*, 195-203.

PTC Report. (2002). *Product Lifecycle Management for Product First Manufacturing Companies,* USA: Parametric Technology Cooperation (PTC).

Rosén, J. (2006). Federated through-life support, enabling online integration of systems within the PLM domain. In *Proceedings of 1st Nordic Conference on Product Lifecycle Management - NordPLM'06,* Göteborg, January 25-26 2006.

Saaksvuori, A., & Immonen, A. (2005). *Product Lifecycle Management.* London, UK: Springer.

SOAP. (2007). *Simple Object Access* Protocol. Version 1.2 Part 1: Messaging Framework (Second Edition). W3C Recommendation on 27 April 2007, Retrieved January 30, 2008, from http://www.w3.org/TR/soap12-part1/

Stark, J. (2004). *Product Lifecycle Management 21st Century Paradigm for Product Realisation.* UK: Springer.

Susman, G. I. (1998). *Product Life Cycle Management, Management Accounting Practices Handbook.* Canada: The society of Management Accountants of Canada.

Wognum, P. M., Fisscher, O. A. M., & Weenink, S. A. J. (2002). Balanced Relationships: Management of Client-Supplier Relationships in Product Development. *Technovation, 22*, 341-351.

WSDL. (2007). *Web Services Description Language. Version 2.0 Part 1: Core Language,* W3C Recommendation on 26 June 2007. Retrieved January 30 2008, from http://www.w3.org/TR/wsdl20/

Xie, H. (2002). Tracking of Design Changes for Collaborative Product Development, In *Proceedings of the fifth International Conference on Computer Supported Cooperative Work in Design,* pp 204-209.

Xu, X., Chen, L. Q., & Xie, S. (2003). New Paradigm for Manufacturing Industry in 21st Century. *Proceedings of the Third International Conference on Electronic Commerce Engineering (ICeCE2003) – Digital Enterprises and Non-traditional Industrialization,* 24-27 October 2003, Hangzhou, Zhejiang, P.R. China. pp 740-746.

Chapter XVII
Key Enabling Technologies

ABSTRACT

While computers have proven to be instrumental in the advancement of product design and manufacturing processes, the role that various technologies have played over the years can never be over-estimated. Because of the intimate involvement of computers in the product development chain, technologies that have severed as enablers are in many cases all software-oriented. There are a number of issues that a technology needs to address in better support of CAD, CAPP, CAM, CNC, PDM, PLM, and so forth. Knowledge acquisition and utilization is one of the top priorities and very often the first step of actions. Intelligent reasoning and optimization is another important task. More often than not, the optimization problems have multi-objectives and multi-constraints that are highly non-linear, discrete, and sometimes fuzzy.

Among the technologies that have been developed in the recent past are knowledge-based (expert) system, artificial neural network (ANN), genetic algorithm (GA), agent-based technology, fuzzy logic, Petri Nets, and ant colony optimisation. An expert system is a computer system which includes a well-organized body of knowledge in a bounded domain, and is able to simulate the problem solving skill of a human expert in a particular field. Neural networks are the techniques that can work by simulating the human neuron function, and using the weights distributed among their neurons to perform implicit inference. The genetic algorithms mimic the process of natural evolution by combining the survival of the fittest among solution structures with a structured, yet randomized, information exchange. Agent-based technology utilizes agents as intelligent entities capable of independently regulating, reasoning and decision-making to carry out actions and to achieve a specific goal or a set of goals. This chapter discusses these four technologies together with some applications of these technologies. Also briefly mentioned are the fuzzy logic, Petri Nets, and ant colony optimization methods. The objective is not to give a detailed account for each of these technologies. Instead, the intention is to introduce the technologies that are relevant to and suitable for applications such as CAD, CAPP, CAM, CNC, PDM, and PLM, as well as their integrations. This chapter can also be considered as a focal place for those who are interested in the technologies to further explore, as a collection of over 130 research publications have been cited and are all listed in the reference list at the back.

KNOWLEDGE-BASED SYSTEMS

In the domain of product design, process planning and manufacturing, multiple types of human expertise and knowledge are needed for various decision-making processes. This explains why knowledge-based systems are among the most researched technologies, and in many cases have proven to be effective systems.

Expert Systems Technology

Expert system (otherwise known as knowledge-based system) is an important branch of artificial intelligence (AI). Expert systems provide a natural, yet powerful and flexible means for obtaining solutions to a variety of manufacturing problems that often cannot be dealt with by other more orthodox methods. One study reported an investment of over $100 million in artificial intelligence research by large American manufacturing companies. Some of them have achieved impressive results (Dornan, 1987). Among the companies that benefited the most are Digital Equipment Corporation's XCON, Boeing and Lockheed Georgia Corporation's GenPlan. It is of the view of many that expert systems can make a significant contribution to improving process and production planning (Kusiak & Chen, 1988, Badiru, 1992, Jayaraman & Srivastava, 1996, Zhang & Chen, 1999).

Welbank (1983) defines an expert system as a program that has a wide base of knowledge in a restricted domain, and uses complex inferential reasoning to perform tasks, as human expert usually does. In other words, an expert system is a computer system containing a well-organised body of knowledge, which emulates expert problem solving skills in a bounded domain of expertise. The system is able to achieve expert levels of problem solving performance, which would normally be achieved by a skilled human when confronted with significant problems in the domain. As illustrated in Figure 17.1, an expert system consists of three main components, the knowledge base, inference engine and user interface.

Knowledge base is the heart of the system. It contains the knowledge needed for solving problems in a specific domain. Knowledge may be in the form of facts, heuristics (e.g. experiences, opinions, judgments, predictions, algorithms) and relationships usually gleaned from the mind of experts in the relevant domain. Knowledge may be represented using a variety of representation techniques (e.g. semantic nets, frames, predicate logic) (Jackson, 1986, Ignizio, 1991, Mital & Anand, 1994), but the most commonly used technique is "if-then" rules, also known as production rules. These rules are often represented in a tabulated form. The inference engine is employed during a consultation session to examine the status of the knowledge base, handle the content of the knowledge base and

Figure 17.1. Expert system's architecture

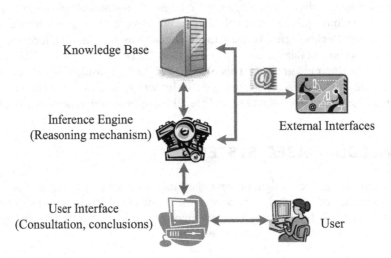

Knowledge Base

Inference Engine
(Reasoning mechanism)

External Interfaces

User Interface
(Consultation, conclusions)

User

determine the order in which inferences are made. It may use various inference methods. The user interface part enables interaction of the system with the user. It mainly includes screen displays, a consultation/ advice dialogue and an explanation component. In addition, expert systems provide interfaces for communication with external programs such as databases and spreadsheets.

Expert Systems Development Approaches

To successfully develop an expert system, one needs a well-planned course of actions, as shown in Figure 17.2. It is important that a systematic approach is adopted from the stage of identifying the problem domain, through to the construction of the knowledge base and eventually to the implementation and validation of the system (Metaxiotis, Askounis & Psarras, 2002).

There are mainly two streams of development approaches (Huntington, 1985, Townsend, 1986, Baker, 1988),

- *Computer programming languages.* They can be either conventional (e.g. C++, Pascal®, etc.) or AI languages (e.g. PROLOG®, LISP®, etc.). Using these languages, the system designer has a great deal of freedom in choice of knowledge representation techniques and control strategies. However, use of these languages requires a high degree of expertise and skill.
- *Expert system shells.* They attempt to combine the flexibility of AI languages with the cost-effectiveness and provide more general development facilities. There are a number of commercial shells available in the market with varying features (Nexpert Object, XpertRule, KnowledgePro, CLIPS®, ReSolver, EXSYS, VP-Expert®, ACQUIRE, etc.). Most of them provide a rule-based knowledge representation mechanism.

Figure 17.2 Expert system development approach

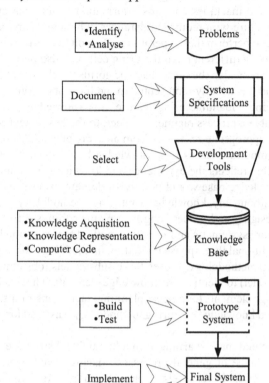

Knowledge in Product Design and Manufacturing

Knowledge acquisition is a key step in the development of an expert system, regardless of the domain. To certain extent, the success of an expert system depends on how much and what knowledge it uses, how qualitative the knowledge is, and how the knowledge is represented. Design and manufacturing knowledge in its natural form is hard to be captured and recorded directly in a knowledge database. Thus, there is a need to study the best way of representing this knowledge. The knowledge should be structured in a way that allows for easier reasoning.

Various forms of knowledge used in product design and manufacturing relate to the objects (e.g. entities in the manufacturing environment) and connections between them. They include the knowledge of part design, manufacturing operations, tools, machines, and the relationships between these entities. Part description is the essential knowledge which is needed as the input to process planning. Generally, the part description should be complete and unambiguous.

The part design knowledge consists of information about the geometrical, topological, tolerance, material and quantity attributes of the part. This knowledge may be represented in pure geometric forms as discussed in Chapters I and II, or in form of features as discussed in Chapters IV-VII. Other information, such as part material, tolerances, surface finish, etc., can be retrieved from a product design database. The knowledge about manufacturing operations, tools, and machines contains information about what operations to use to machine a certain feature with required tolerances, which tools are most appropriate, and on which machine to perform these operations. Data on the particular arrangement of machines and tools among different manufacturing cells are also part of this knowledge. This knowledge is hierarchical in the sense that it performs the classification of operations, machines and tools and it is usually represented in the form of options. Since there is no unique way of producing a manufacturing feature, this knowledge should be organized in a proper way to enable a process planner to select, to the best extent possible, the best methods and the most appropriate resources from an array of available options.

One of the most important issues in a knowledge-based system is the construction of a knowledge base that reflects the experience and knowledge of domain experts. One way of creating a knowledge base would be to visit domain experts and gather rules by interviewing them without any knowledge capturing methodology. Serious problems may arise as every designer and process engineer/planner thinks differently. Therefore, there is a need for a more systematic and scientific method for capturing knowledge. Park (2003) employed a traditional three-phase modelling methodology for the development of a knowledge capturing methodology. It uses three sub-models (object model, functional model and dynamic model) to identify the knowledge elements. These sub-models helped to derive four knowledge elements for process planning: facts, constraints, way of thinking and rules. The proposed knowledge capturing methodology was used for process planning of machining holes.

Knowledge represented may be arranged in a hierarchical structure. At higher levels of the hierarchy, the choice of general processes, machines and operation sequencing may be specified while at the lower levels machining parameters, fixturing methods, and tool path generation for the given instance of the part design, with numerical values for dimensions, tolerances and other attributes, may be specified. Some of these tasks depend on the completion of others, while others may be performed in parallel. There can be two different knowledge representation schemes to represent facts and rules. The first scheme is semantic network for representation of various entities and relations among them. A semantic network represents knowledge as a graph, with nodes corresponding to facts or concepts and arcs to relations or associations between concepts (Luger & Subblefield, 1989). The second scheme is a rule-based method. Examples of such rules are (Chang, Wysk & Wang, 1991),

- *If* surface roughness is between 63 and 32 μin,
  then the required operation for hole making is reaming.
- *If* flat surface roughness is 8 μin,
  then surface finish can be obtained by grinding, polishing or lapping, but rarely by milling.
- *If* the diameter of the hole is less than 10mm and greater than 0.2mm and diametric tolerance is greater than 0.1mm,
  then use drilling,
  else-if tolerance is less than 0.1mm,
  then use drilling and reaming; and so on.

Applications of Expert Systems

Expert systems have advantages over the traditional computer systems, since they organise knowledge in rules and control strategy, which allow users to modify a program with ease, and to organise knowledge in such a way that they can reason intelligently. Hence, expert systems are able to deal with far more complicated problems (Jiang, Lau, Chan & Jiang, 1999). Also, the systems can be designed so that they accumulate knowledge as time passes, in the form of separate facts, production rules, objects, etc. The inference mechanism of an expert system makes it possible to perform operations on the knowledge base of analysed elements (Grabowik & Knosala 2003).

Brown (2000) discussed the importance of a manufacturing database in support of digital manufacturing. The knowledge is gathered from the initial concept design phase of both product and production processes, detailed design and validation, manufacturing activities on the shop-floor and monitoring of the shop-floor performance. The manufacturing database serves as a knowledge repository that is shared by all enterprise members via a Web-based portal so that they have the right information at the right time to support their decisions. In the research by Sormaz and Khoshnevis (1997), a knowledge representation scheme was proposed to recognize both geometric and feature-based representation of a part. The system connects the feature and process knowledge with the part geometric model, and uses the object-oriented approach for the presentation of machining knowledge. The system is also able to generate alternative process plans. The integration of these features within a single system has resulted in an adaptable prototype system that fared better than some existing systems at the time. In a more recent research, Jia, Zhang, Xu and Huang (2003) described an object-oriented process knowledge representation and process knowledge acquisition. They adopted an object-oriented technology for building the process information model. The process decision knowledge and decision procedure control knowledge are represented by rules. Around the same time, Grabowik and Knosala (2003) presented a method representing the knowledge about the body construction and technology in an expert system, which aids the process of selecting the appropriate machining technology. Their representation is in the form of object sets. Jiang, Lau, Chan and Jiang (1999) created an automatic process planning system (APPS) for the quick generation of manufacturing process plans directly from CAD drawings. The APPS is able to assist the machinist to determine an optimal process plan for a prismatic component in the shortest possible time. The expert system methodology is used to generate appropriate process plans. It uses various items of knowledge, including machine limitations, tooling availability and other process-related manufacturing information.

Pham and Gologlu (2001) designed a hybrid CAPP system, ProPlanner, to facilitate concurrent product development. The system adapted the hybrid knowledge representation scheme, and objects were used to store domain-related declarative knowledge and production rules used to modify procedural knowledge, allowing modification and re-use. ProPlanner is restricted to prismatic parts with 2.5-dimensional features. Parts are also assumed to be machined from a near net form, and only simple geometric tolerance (straightness and parallelism) is implemented. Gologlu (2004) extended the ProPlanner system, by using an efficient heuristic algorithm (in the system operation sequencing module) for finding near-optimal operation sequences from all available process plans in a machining set-up. In the adopted approach, a four-level hierarchy was used: feature-level, machining scheme-level, operation-level and tool-level. This enables the problem of operation sequencing to be systematically addressed. In order to improve communication within design groups, concurrent integration of more knowledge during the design process is necessary. As a result, all the product life cycle issues are addressed in time, and in relation with other disciplines. In integrated design, design iterations are reduced because constraints from different disciplines are taken into account as soon as possible. This means that conflicting constraints can be identified and solved earlier than in a non-integrated design approach. Roucoules, Salomons and Paris (2003) have also attempted to address the above issue. The approach is based on two phases: the initial design and the detailed design phase. For the initial design phase, the structural technology is chosen according to the product main functions, aiming to define minimal functional data that are used as a starting point for other knowledge integration in the detailed design phase. In the detailed design phase, other people that are actively involved in the product development process evaluate the product with their own point of view and their own tools.

Liu, Duan, Lei and Wang (1999) used the analytic hierarchy process (AHP) - a mathematical decision modelling tool - to solve complicated process planning problems by decomposition, determination and synthesis. AHP can deal with universal modelling of process planning decision-making, which is difficult to describe quantitatively, by integrating quantitative analysis with qualitative analysis. More flexibility can be had if AHP is used for development. It enables users to consider many conditions during the process of decision-making, construct effective decision models, meet requirements of their enterprises and build judgment matrices.

Carpenter and Maropoulos (2000) developed a decision support system for milling operations called OPTIMUM. The system features a combination of rigorous mathematical modelling of the machining process and more flexible rule-based and statistical methods. Unlike a traditional CAPP system, the machinability assessor in OPTIMUM allows the generation of conservative initial cutting data from incomplete or fuzzy input data. As the system is implemented according to the theory of data driven design, the performance of the machinability assessor can be upgraded by adding more company specific historical cutting data to the main data tables. Similarly, Kim and Suh (1998) proposed a methodology for incorporating a combination of mathematical programming and the expert system to produce an optimal operation sequence to minimise the non-cutting time. The mathematical method performs grouping and sequencing simultaneously, and the expert system pre-processes the procedure by eliminating infeasible solution sets and clustering the operations according to the tool commonalities. The system performs local process planning for each machining feature of the part, and analyses the relationships among operations to generate a global process plan.

Kryssanov, Kleshchev, Fukuda and Konishi (1998) proposed a formal method to construct expert systems. Using the proposed methodology, they described a general class of declarative logical models for modelling the domain knowledge, and generalised the models to include analogues of the classical knowledge representation models. Jiang, Baines and Zockel (1997) developed an optimisation scheme for milling operations when machining prismatic components. It includes the sequencing of processes and has the capability of selecting the cutting tools. The procedure enables the component coding scheme to be integrated with a proposed expert system methodology for the selection of machining processes, the selection of machining sequence and the selection of cutting tools. Jain, Mehta, and Pandey (1998) developed a knowledge-based, interactive CAPP system for symmetrical turned parts. The developed strategy is for cut planning to optimise the selection of process parameters for rough turning operations, based on the minimum production time criterion.

Selection of cutting tools and machining conditions is a complex task. The objectives are to select the best tool holders and inserts from available cutting tool stock, and to determine the optimum cutting conditions. Arezoo, Ridgway and Al-Ahmari (2000) developed a knowledge-based system called EXCATS (expert computer-aided cutting tool selection), for the selection of tool holder, insert and cutting conditions, such as feed, speed and depth of cut. The system can be applied to an automated manufacturing system. It demonstrates the key role of a knowledge-based system in achieving maximum flexibility in the process planning automation and development of fully integrated computer integrated manufacturing systems. The rule-based knowledge base can be adapted to different working environments. The logic of the tool selection criteria is based upon a series of rules, which can be easily changed by users to meet specific needs. The utilisation of the machine tool power is optimised within the constraints imposed by the properties of the workpiece materials, tools and tool materials. Zhao, Ridgway and Al-Ahmari (2002) further extended the work by integrating the EXCATS with a CAD system, for the selection of cutting tools and conditions for turning operations. This system is capable of processing CAD data and automatically generates the component representation file for EXCATS.

Expert systems are also used in job-shop scheduling. Zhang and Chen (1999b) reported the development of a knowledge-based scheduling system for low-volume/high-variety manufacturing. Their system provides a practical facility for job scheduling which takes into account the influence of factors such as machine setup times, cell changes, replacement machines and load balancing among machines, and has been used in practical shop-floor scheduling in manufacturing factories of Japan and China as an experimental system. The scheduling results yield better machine utilization and less down-time. It proved that the knowledge-based paradigm works well in the case of complex job-scheduling for low-volume/high-variety manufacturing. Li, Li, Li and Hu (2000) proposed a production rescheduling expert simulation system. In their research, four sources of typical disturbances in production are identified. They are incorrect work, machine breakdowns, rush orders, and rework due to quality problems. The system integrated many techniques and methods, including simulation technique, artificial neural network, expert knowledge and dispatching rules. A more recent job scheduling expert system is proposed by Soyuer, Kocamaz and Kazancoglu (2007). They developed a methodology that consisted of two parts, the first is that all solution alternatives are considered to achieve greater rapidity, and secondly that the solutions are subject to elimination through the criteria that are based on the circumstances of real life conditions. The advantages of the methodology is that it is not limited to a certain sector and can be extended and applied to any sector dealing with scheduling problems, and the algorithm presented can be used as the basis for scheduling software designers and for professionals who work on the scheduling problem.

Kumar and Midha (2006) proposed an expert system-based approach for analysing a company's strategic PDM requirements. The proposed expert system incorporates the Quality Function Deployment (QFD) methodology along with a fuzzy inference system to generate a requirement specification for a PDM system. The fusion of the three techniques within a single framework helps provide an intelligent, robust and powerful framework for PDM requirement analysis. In the PDM-based system for manufacturing evaluation and analysis in the early design stages, Sharma and Gao (2002) embedded an expert system to resolve the abstract data usually associated with the early design stages. The system allows early measurement of design in terms of time, manufacturing cost and resources. STEP AP224 is used to model the product data.

ARTIFICIAL NEURAL NETWORK METHODS

Although expert system applications have been found in many areas of design and manufacturing, it has its intrinsic weaknesses. The system has total reliance on consultation with human experts for knowledge acquisition, thus is unable to automatically modify knowledge to suit the dynamic design and manufacturing environment. The information provided must be complete for it to work properly if at all. It tends to have a low degree of fault tolerance in the inference procedure (Ming, Mak & Yan, 1999). Neural network-based methods have been found useful in overcoming these problems.

Artificial neural networks, or simply neural networks, belong to a format of models that are based on the learning-by-example paradigm. The inference method in neural networks is performed by assigning the input data to the neural networks, and, then, running the neural networks by using the stored weights distributed among their neurons. The results of the outputs from neural networks can thus be directly generated.

Introduction to Neural Nets

A neural network is effectively an interconnected network of a large number of processing elements, called *neurons* or *nodes*. A neuron receives input stimuli from other neurons if they are connected to it and/or the external world. A neuron can have several inputs, but has only one output. This output, however, can be routed to the inputs of several other neurons (Figure 17.3). Each neuron has certain constant parameters associated with it. These are its *threshold, transfer function* and the *weights* associated with its inputs. Each neuron performs a very simple arithmetic operation, i.e. it computes the weighted sum of its inputs, subtracts its threshold from the sum, and passes the result through its transfer function. The *output* of the neuron is the result obtained from this function. The output of a neuron is, therefore, a mathematical function of its inputs, and can be expressed as,

$$y = f(\sum_{l=1}^{n} w_l x_l - \theta), \qquad l = 1, 2, \dots n \qquad (17.1)$$

where, y – output of the neuron;
n – number of inputs;
w – weight associated with input l;
x_l – value of input l;
θ – threshold.

Some commonly used transfer functions are *hardlimiter, threshold* and *sigmoid* nonlinearities. Neural-net models are specified by the *net topology, node characteristtcs* and *traimng* or *learmng rules*. The function of a neural-net model is determined by these parameters. The net topology, or the architecture of the net, determines the inputs of each node. The node characteristics (threshold, transfer function and weights) determine the

Figure 17.3. Neural network concept

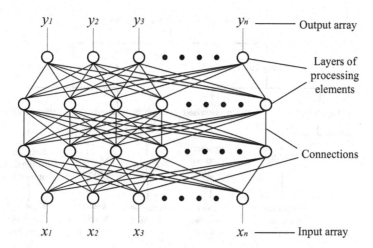

output of the node. The training or learning rules determine how the network will react when an unknown input is presented to it (Prabhakar & Henderson, 1992).

Figure 17.4 shows taxonomy of six important neural nets used for classification of static input patterns (Lippmann, 1987). Nets can have either binary or continuous valued inputs. Binary inputs take on one of two possible values, while continuous-valued inputs can take on more than two values. Both types can be supervised or unsupervised during training. During supervised training, the net is given the correct class along with the training pattern. The net produces an output based on its current weights, and compares it with the correct output. If there is a difference, the weights are changed as a function of the difference between the outputs. During unsupervised training, no information concerning the correct class is provided to the net. The net constructs an internal model that captures regularities in input training patterns. In other words, the net forms its own exemplars (during training) by clustering input patterns which are similar to each other within a specified tolerance. The algorithms listed at the bottom of Figure 17.4 are those classical algorithms which either perform the same or a similar function as the neural net.

ANN has been used in different feature technologies and process planning systems (Yue, Ding, Ahmet, Painter & Walters, 2002). The follow text is arranged according to the four aspects of ANN, network topology, input representation, output format and training or learning method.

ANN Used in Feature Technologies

Network Topology

There are three main ANN architectures: feed-forward, recurrent and competitive networks (Gurney, 1997). Feed-forward model is the most commonly used in feature technologies. It is a layered network, either fully interconnected from layer to layer or with hidden units. The typical topology can be defined by an input layer of neurons that receive binary or continuously valued input signals, an output layer with a corresponding number of neurons,

Figure 17.4. Taxonomy of neural nets that can be used as classifiers

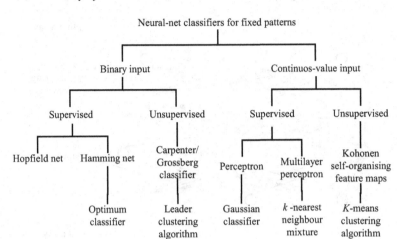

and a number of hidden layers that are highly interconnected (Nezis & Vosniakos, 1997). At present, three feed-forward architectures have been reported for feature recognition purposes.

Prabhakar and Henderson (1992) developed a five-layer, perceptron quasi-neural network system called PRENET. The system has five layers which respectively consist of N nodes, N groups of M nodes, N nodes with a threshold non-linearity, M nodes corresponding to the M conditions for a feature, and one node, where N is the number of faces in the test part and M the number of conditions required for the feature.

A three-layer feed-forward neural network has an input, a hidden and an output layer. Neurons on the hidden and output layers are defined from the neurons on the previous layer, the weights and a processing algorithm. For example, in Chuang's system (Chuang, Wang, & Wu, 1999), the lth neuron on the current layer, N_l can be calculated as:

$$N_l = \sum_{k=1}^{n} u_k w_{kl}$$

(17.2)

where u_k – kth neuron on the previous layer;

w_{kl} – weight.

The weight represents the strength of the relationship between the kth neuron on the previous layer and the lth neuron on the current layer.

Korosec, Balic and Kopac (2005) used the three-layer feed-forward architecture to build the so-called manufacturability evaluation function. The purpose is to identify and recognize the degree of difficulty of machining. It enabled simultaneous evaluation of features complexity in a CAD model and manufacturing capability in an environment description model. The number of neurons in the input layer is equal to the number of machining parameters used to assess surface features.

A four-layer, feed-forward neural network uses an input, a hidden, an output, and a threshold layer which is added to the network as the training is completed. The threshold layer performs the function of activating the neurons of the output layer by a threshold, e.g. 0.5. In Nezis and Vosniakos' work (1997), there are twenty neurons in the input layer, each representing an element of the input vector, and eight output neurons, each corresponding to a feature class. There are also eight neurons in the threshold layer, corresponding to the output layer neurons. Ten neurons are assigned to the hidden layer by experimentation. All elements of the hidden and output layers are connected with a bias element that can be considered as an activation threshold.

Input Representation

Neural nets typically, although not necessarily, receive a set of integer values as input. The problem then is how to convert a solid model to a format suitable to be used as neural net input in a convenient and efficient way. Peters (1992) proposed an ordered triplet (C_i, A_i, L_i) to represent each edge of a connected loop of a 2D feature, where C_i, A_i, and L_i are the curvature, interior angle and arc length of the ith element respectively. In this case, an encoded feature vector of the triplet (C_i, A_i, L_i) for a given profile is used as the input. Later, Chen and Lee (1998) developed an improved encoded feature vector, in which the representation of each edge is expanded from an ordered 3-tuple to an ordered 7-tuple. A face adjacency matrix is a 2D array of integer vectors converted from a solid model. Each integer vector represents a face and its relationship to another face, i.e. adjacency or common edge. The length of an integer vector depends on the number of parameters considered for the recognition of a feature. In Prabhakar and Henderson's work (1992), the vector has eight integers indicating characteristics such as edge type, face type, face angle type, number of loops, etc. Hwang (1991) used an eight-element face score vector to represent the relationship between the main face of a feature and its neighbouring faces.

An attributed adjacency matrix may also be used as input. An attributed adjacency matrix (Nezis &Vosniakos, 1997 and Gu, Zhang & Nee, 1995) described the geometry and topology of a feature pattern based on the attributed adjacency graph (Joshi & Chang, 1988). With this method, AAG is broken into sub-graphs which are converted into adjacency matrix using a heuristic method. Each matrix is then converted into a representation vector by interrogating a set of 12 questions about the adjacency matrix layout and the number of faces in the sub-graph. In the end, a binary vector is formed combining the 12 positive answers and the other 8 elements corresponding to the number of external faces linked to the sub-graph.

Zulkifli and Meeran (1999) presented an input matrix based on a cross-sectional method. The B-rep solid model is searched through cross-sectional layers and converted into 2D feature patterns, which are then translated into a matrix appropriate to the network. Four input matrices correspond to four feature classes: simple primitive, circular, slanting, and non-orthogonal primitive features.

Output Format

The output of an ANN is usually a nodal value in form of a vector. Many systems represent the neurons such that they correspond to different feature classes. In Chen and Lee's work (1998) for example, the six neurons on the output layer represent six feature classes: rectangle, slot, trapezoid, parallelogram, v-slot and triangle. Nezis and Vosniakos' system (1997) provides eight output neurons corresponding to eight feature classes. Other researchers have used neurons to represent the information of a recognised feature. Hwang (1991) uses six neurons as the output, representing the class, name, confidence factor, main-face name, list of associated faces of the feature found, and total execution time respectively. A matrix file has been used as the output containing the code for each recognised feature and its machining directions (Zulkifli & Meeran, 1999).

Training Method

The training process may be supervised or unsupervised. During supervised training, the correct class corresponding to the training pattern is given. The net produces an output based on its current weights, and compares it with the correct output. If there is a difference, the weights are adjusted according to a learning algorithm based on the output difference. Most ANN-based feature recognition work employs supervised training with a back propagation algorithm (Nezis & Vosniakos, 1997, Chen & Lee, 1998, Zulkifli & Meeran, 1999).

During back propagation, a given input called the training input is mapped to a specified target output. A training process usually undergoes six stages:

(1)　Wight initialization;
(2)　Presenting the training vectors/matrices to the network;
(3)　Comparison between the actual and desired outputs;
(4)　Calculation of the network's error, i.e. the difference between its output and target;
(5)　Backward propagation of the error to the hidden neurons; and
(6)　Adjustment of the weights.

After a number of iterations, the output will converge towards the target. The delta rule, also known as the Widrow-Hoff learning rule can be used to modify the weights (Nezis & Vosniakos, 1997, Chen & Lee, 1998).

ANN Used for Process Planning

ANN has assured itself as a powerful tool for process planning due to its specific nature and suited functionalities. Hence, this section is warranted.

Network Topology

While Feed-Forward network is the most commonly used architecture, some other ANN architectures have also been used, e.g. Hopfield network, Brain-State-in-a-Box (BSB) and MAXNET. With a Feed-Forward network, the appropriate structure is identified through several experiments during the learning process. The structure with the minimum errors and the fastest learning rate is chosen. Gu, Zhang and Nee (1997) employed a three layer feed-forward network with a 5-neuron hidden layer for manufacturing evaluation. Santochi and Dini (1996) proved in their experiment that a three-layer feed-forward network with a suitable number of neurons for each layer is the best architecture for selecting technological parameters for a cutting tool using the hyperbolic tangent sigmoid function. Ding, Yue, Ahmet and Jackson (2005) presented an optimisation strategy for process sequencing based on multi-objective fitness: minimum manufacturing cost, shortest manufacturing time and best satisfaction of manufacturing sequence rules. They used a three-layer feed-forward network to allocate the relative weights for the three main evaluating factors for process sequencing, and applied an analytical hierarchical process to evaluate the satisfaction degree of the manufacturing sequence rules for process sequencing.

Park, Park, Rho and Kim (1996) developed a 4-layer neural network to modify cutting condition based on several tests. Their network has a 15-neuron input layer, two 15-neuron hidden layers and a single-neuron output layer. Although four-layer feed-forward networks are more versatile than three-layer feed-forward networks, they train more slowly due to the attenuation of errors through the non-linearity (Principe, Euliano & Lefebvre, 2000). Le Tumelin, Garro and Charpentier (1995) proposed a 5-layer feed-forward network to determine appropriate sequence of operations for machining holes. Yahia, Fnaiech, Abid and Sassi (2002) presented a Feed-Forward network system. The sequence of manufacturing operations is based on the attributes of the features in a component. The process plan is generated by integration with CAD.

The Hopfield network is a single layer recurrent network that uses threshold process elements and an interconnect symmetric matrix. The dynamics of the Hopfield network can be described by the state of an energy function which eventually gets to a minimum point. Therefore, optimal operation sequencing can be expected with the continuous download trend of a global energy function. Shan, Nee and Poo (1992) adapted the Hopfield network to the operation sequencing problem.

Brain-state-in-a-box is a discrete-time recurrent network with a continuous state. The output values of a BSB consist of interconnected neurons. They depend on the learnt patterns, the initial values of given patterns and the recall coefficients. Sakakura and Inasaki (1992) used a BSB network in a CAPP system. The number of neurons assigned for the depth of cut, feed and surface roughness is 5, 5 and 9 respectively. The initial values are given by a feed-forward network run at the same time. The BSB repeats until the output value of each neuron converges to a certain value.

Maxnet is a competitive network in which only one neuron will have a non-zero output when the competition is completed. The network consists of interconnected neurons and symmetric weights. There is no training algorithm for Maxnet and the weights are fixed. Maxnet is suitable for situations where more information is needed than can be incorporated. Knapp and Wang (1992) used a Maxnet to force a decision between the competing operation alternatives. In their work, a sequence of operations for machining each feature of a part is generated independently by the Maxnet.

Input Representation

The input representation for neural network-based CAPP involves the conversion of design data into a proper input format. The input information to be considered relates to the activities involved in process planning, such as selecting manufacturing operations, determining setups, specifying appropriate tools and so on. It is important that each piece of the input information for a neural network be uniquely represented in a proper format and also in numerical forms.

Osakada and Yang (1991) converted the cross-sectional shape data of the product into standardised image data for the input. They use 12 "colours" to represent 12 outer or inner geometric primitives, such as cylinder and cone. Half of the product shapes are converted into a 16×16 "colour" data image. These 256 units are regarded as the input to the neural network.

Devireddy and Ghosh (1999) used an eight-unit input vector specifying the feature type (e.g. hole, step, taper, thread), and its attributes, e.g. diameter, length, tolerance, surface finish, etc. Le Tumelin, Garro and Charpentier (1995) designed a 12-unit vector describing the geometric and technological characteristics of a hole.

Amaitik and Kilic (2007) developed an intelligent process planning system for prismatic parts using STEP features, STFeatCAPP. The input vector of the neural network includes machining part characteristics and machining operation characteristics, and the output vector of the neural network contains recommended specifications of the machine tool to be used to perform the task.

Output Representation

Output vectors in an ordered binary form have been widely used. The output vector consists of a number of neurons, each with a value (i.e. 0 or 1) showing whether the corresponding item (e.g. machining operation, tool and so on) belongs to the process plan or not. The output vector in the first stage consists of eight neurons representing respectively drilling, reaming, boring, turning, taper, turning, grooving, grinding and precision. If the value of a neuron is "1", the corresponding operation is needed for the feature; otherwise, the value is "0". For instance, a hole requires the drilling operation, so the first neuron is assigned the value "1". The sequence of the vector represents the sequence of the operations, e.g. reaming is usually performed after drilling. Li, Mills, Moruzzi and Rowe (1994) used a 4-neuron vector corresponding to the abrasive type, grade, grit size and bond, whereas Le Tumelin, Garro and Charpentier (1995) designed a 23-neuron vector.

An output vector may also contain special values. Santochi and Dini (1996) developed a system for selecting the eight technological parameters of a cutting tool. For example, to select a normal clearance angle α_n, the number of output neurons is 5 which represent 48, 58, 68, 78, 88 respectively. The neuron with the value "1" represents the optimal value and "0.5" a second choice. There are also works whereby output matrix (Shan, Nee & Poo, 1992) and one-unit output (Mei, Zhang & Oldham, 1995) are used to represent the final results.

Training Method

In CAPP applications, the training method usually employs either an unsupervised learning algorithm or back propagation. A logical AND/OR operation-based unsupervised learning approach has been used by Chen and LeClair (1993). Features are clustered based on the approach direction and tool type. A process plan is then generated using the Episodal Associative Memory (EAM) approach. The AND operation was applied to solve multiple approach directions for some features. In the meantime, the OR rule is used to update the weight so that the probability of common tools can be increased.

A back-propagation algorithm is a form of supervised learning. The algorithm consists of two basic steps, initialisation of weights and repetition of training until the error is acceptably low. Back-propagation methods have proven highly successful in CAPP applications (Osakada & Yang, 1991 and Mei, Zhang & Oldham, 1995). Out of many back-propagation methods, there are three popular ones, the Delta Rule (Sakakura & Inasaki, 1992), Levemberg-Marquardt Approximation (Santochi & Dini, 1996) and Batch Training (Fausett, 1994, Devireddy & Ghosh, 1999) methods.

GENETIC ALGORITHM

Genetic algorithm is an intelligent search method requiring domain-specific knowledge to solve a problem. It has been successfully applied to various optimisation problems since the mid-1960s. Genetic algorithms belong to the category of *post-collation optimization approach*. By mimicking the evolutionary process of nature, such algorithms have been employed as global search and optimization techniques for various scientific and engineering problems. The essential principle of genetic algorithms is based on the natural selection rules of the "survival of the fittest" option. The algorithms operate by creating new and better solutions to problems through extracting and combining the best features across generations of possible solutions, and result in an incremental convergence on optimal or near-optimal solutions (Goldberg, 1989, Shi & Chen, 1992, McInerney & Dhawan, 1993, Donne, Tilley & Richards, 1995, Michalewicz, 1996, Deb, 1999, 2001).

The working principle of genetic algorithms is rather different from that of the most of the classical optimization techniques. Some of the distinguishing characteristics are (Singh, Jain & Jain, 2003),

- Work with the coding of a parameter set, not the parameters themselves;
- Search from a population of points, rather than a single point;
- Use payoff (objective function) information, but not derivative or other auxiliary knowledge;
- Use probabilistic transition rules, not deterministic rules.

Listed below are the general steps to be followed when implementing a genetic algorithm for optimization problems. Depending on the type and complexity of the problem, these steps may vary.

- Step 1. Coding of variables or representation of the solution(s);
- Step 2. Selection of the population size, crossover probability, mutation probability, genetic operators, number of generations, etc.;
- Step 3. Mapping of objective functions into appropriate fitness functions;
- Step 4. Evaluation of each string to obtain fitness;
- Step 5. Application of genetic operators:
  - Reproduction on the population.
  - Crossover on a random pair of strings, with specified probability of crossover p_c.
  - Mutation of random bit, with specified probability of mutation p_m.
- Step 6. Repeat Steps 4 and 5 for the given number of generations.

Implementation Procedure of Genetic Algorithm

There is no shortage of literature explaining the algorithm. Singh, Jain and Jain (2003) in their paper gave a rather succinct description of the implementation procedure that one can follow. Discerning readers are referred to Goldberg (1989)'s book on the technology.

Coding of Strings

The individual decision variables, δ, are coded in a string (chromosome) structure; each string represents a set of discrete points in the continuous space domain. Binary coded strings having 1's and 0's are commonly used. The length of each string is determined according to the desired solution accuracy. The range and the precision of the nth decision variable are controlled by mapping of the decoded unsigned integer, linearly from $[0, 2^{l2}]$ to a specified interval $[\delta_n^{min}, \delta_n^{max}]$. The value and precision of the variable δ_n through this mapping is represented by the following equations,

$$\delta = \delta_n^{min} + \frac{\delta_n^{max} - \delta_n^{min}}{2^{l_n} - 1} DV(s_n) \tag{17.3}$$

$$\pi_n = \frac{\delta_n^{max} - \delta_n^{min}}{2^{l_n} - 1} \tag{17.4}$$

where l_n – length of the string used for coding the nth decision variable,

$DV(s_n)$ – decoded value of string s_n.

In an optimization problem involving n variables, a string (chromosome) is represented by simply concatenating the n individual variable coding (substrings). The population structure of the optimization problem consists of a number of such strings and is represented as,

$$
\begin{aligned}
S_1 &= (s_{11}, s_{12}, s_{13}, \ldots, s_{1n}) \\
S_2 &= (s_{21}, s_{22}, s_{23}, \ldots, s_{2n}) \\
&\ldots \ldots \ldots \ldots \ldots \ldots \ldots \ldots \ldots \\
&\ldots \ldots \ldots \ldots \ldots \ldots \ldots \ldots \ldots \\
S_P &= (s_{P1}, s_{P2}, s_{P3}, \ldots, s_{Pn})
\end{aligned}
\tag{17.5}
$$

where P – population size.

Fitness Function

GAs do not work with objective functions as in a traditional optimization method. This is due to two reasons. GAs handle only the maximization problems, as the strings identified as "most fit" get more chances to reproduce children than those which are "less fit" during the reproduction operation. A function that is partially positive and partially negative is not suitable for application of GAs. Therefore, to handle minimization problems, as in the case of machining time, the objective function is suitably transformed to another function, called the fitness function. For such an objective function $h(\delta)$, the fitness function $\hat{h}(\delta)$ may take the form of,

$$\hat{h}(\delta) = b - h(\delta)$$

$$\hat{h}(\delta) = \frac{b}{h(\delta) + c}$$

(17.6)

where b, c – appropriately selected constants.

Genetic Operators

Genetic operators are used to simulate the phenomena of natural genetics so as to yield better results in successive generations. Reproduction, crossover and mutation are the most commonly used genetic operators. An algorithm involving these operators is called simple genetic algorithm (SGA).

Reproduction is normally the first operation applied on the population. Reproduction selects good strings in the population and forms a mating pool for subsequent operation. Several schemes of reproduction have been proposed over the decades. The most commonly used reproduction scheme is the roulette wheel selection scheme, where a string is selected for the mating pool with a probability proportional to its fitness. Thus, the qth string in the population is selected with a probability proportional to its fitness, i.e. the probability:

$$\Pr ob\Big|_q = \frac{fitness_q}{\sum_{p=1}^{P} fitness_p}$$

(17.7)

In reproduction, good strings in the population are probabilistically assigned a larger number of copies for the mating pool. The scheme may seem to be simple and straight forward; it suffers from two drawbacks, premature convergence at early generations and significant diversity within the population at later generations during progress of the algorithm. To solve this problem, the original fitness is modified using the linear fitness scaling (Goldberg, 1989). Figure 17.5 illustrates such a process in which one crossover point is generated randomly. Two parents (represented as $\{x_1, x_2, x_3, x_4, x_5\}$ and $\{y_1, y_2, y_3, y_4, y_5\}$) exchange their genes and generate two children (represented as $\{x_1, x_2, y_3, y_4, y_5\}$ and $\{y_1, y_2, x_3, x_4, x_5\}$).

Crossover is carried out on a pair of randomly selected strings from the mating pool. The operation is responsible for the search of new strings in the search space. The new strings are obtained by exchanging information between the strings in a pair. Many crossover schemes have been proposed in the literature (Lin, Ko, Wang, Tien & You, 2006, Dallaali & Premaratne, 2004, Venkatachalam, 1994). Single-point crossover is the most common, where a crossing site is selected randomly along the strings for each pair to perform crossover operation; all the bits on the right side of the crossing site are exchanged between the strings of the pair. The two strings resulting from the crossover may be superior or inferior to the participating strings, but the inferior ones will not survive too long and will die out in

Figure 17.5. Reproduction in Genetic Algorithm

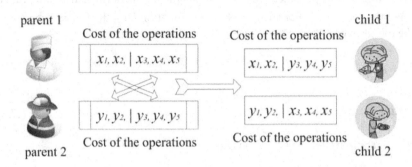

the subsequent generations during reproduction. All the strings do not undergo crossover; the strings for the operation are selected with specified crossover probability, p_c.

Next is the *mutation* operator, which is used for searching for new points in the search space, but sparingly. It is to create a point in the neighbourhood of the current point, thereby applying local search around the current solution. The bitwise mutation is performed bit by bit, changing 1 to 0, and vice versa, with specified mutation probability, p_m. As in case of crossover, the new strings obtained after mutation may also be superior or inferior to the original strings, but the inferior ones will have a shorter life-span. The crossover and mutation operators can be further explained by Figure 17.6.

Applications of Genetic Algorithm

A study made by Grefenstette (1986) indicated that genetic algorithms are effective for both selecting suitable optimization procedures and identifying the optimal parameters of genetic algorithms for a given set of numerical optimization problems. Since then, genetic algorithms have been used in various problems of process planning and manufacturing, be it at the macro-level or micro-level. Some researchers have tried to combine genetic algorithms with some other methods, yielding more favourable results.

Genetic Algorithms for Macro Process Planning

To support production scheduling, process plans with alternative routes and sequences must be generated to suit the changes in the workshop. The main advantage the genetic algorithm

Figure 17.6. Crossover and mutation operation

110	**1010**		**110**	0101	1100101	1101101
011	0101	→	011	**1010**	0111010	→	0011010
					1000110	1010110
Pair of strings			Pair of strings		Strings		Strings
Before crossover			After crossover		Before mutation		After mutation

approach has over conventional CAPP approaches is that selection of machines, tool, TAD's for each operation and the sequence among the operations are considered concurrently. Therefore, the resulting process plan successfully retains the entire solution space. This makes it possible to find a globally optimal process plan for a part.

Zhang, Zhang and Nee (1997) presented a computer-aided process planning model for machined parts to be made in a job shop manufacturing environment. It is able to deal with process planning problems by a concurrent manner in generating the entire solution space via considering the multiple decision-making activities, i.e., operation selection, machine selection, setup selection, cutting tool selection, and operations sequencing, simultaneously. Genetic algorithms were selected due to their flexible representation scheme, the ability to achieve a near-optimal process plan through specially designed crossover and mutation operators. Similar work done by Rocha, Ramos and Vale (1999), can generate the sequence of operations and select the machine and tools that minimise some parameters, such as machining time. Both of these GA approaches to process planning allow the users to define and modify the manufacturing environment, and since all available machines and tools are considered, the whole solution space is considered, allowing globally optimal solutions to be found. In Dereli and Filiz's (1999) work, a reward/penalty matrix called REPMAX for each setup was determined based on the selected criterion, such as safety or minimum tool change, and the objective of optimisation was to gain the least total penalty or largest total reward. Qiao, Wang and Wang (2000) proposed a GA-based operation sequencing method that provides a great potential for finding good machining operation sequences approaching the optimum. A fitness function is developed in the application of a genetic algorithm to operation sequencing, for considering multiple process planning rules simultaneously and flexibly in machining operations sequencing for prismatic parts. The value of the fitness function is a criterion to evaluate the degree of satisfaction of a searched operation sequence to generate a feasible operation sequence and, eventually, a near-optimal solution. Bo, Huan and Yu (2006) reconstructed GAs based on the analysis of various constraints in process route sequencing, including the establishment of coding strategy, evaluation operators and fitness function, to meet the requirement of sequencing work. The mentioned constraints are used as the control strategy for GAs in the searching process to direct the calculation of GAs, and to find the optimal result that can satisfy the constraints.

In the work of generating operation sequences with GA, by Dutta and Yip-Hoi (1996) and Usher and Bowden (1996), the search strategies of their GA methods were based on a defined feature precedence graph (FPG), which was used in coding operation sequences. The size of the solution space in operation sequencing can be reduced with the FPG. Since the nature of a FPG is that it represents the machining sequence of features according to process planning rules considered, it is useful for those turned parts containing an explicit and fixed relationship between feature orders and process planning rules. For prismatic parts, it is difficult to define such FPGs as there is no explicit and fixed relationship between feature orders and process planning rules.

Moon, Li and Gen (1998) proposed an evolutionary approach based on genetic algorithm, to solve the sequencing problem by simultaneously considering the operation flexibility, realistic shop factors and transportation time of an AGV (automatically guided vehicle) system. It was formulated as a bi-criteria mathematical model with minimising the total processing and transportation time, and the load variation between machines. From the numerical examples, the approach is found to be effective in offering a set of satisfactory solutions within a satisfactory CPU time, which is essential in a multiple objective environment, to enable the decision maker to determine the best solution. Therefore, the approach can be effectively used to solve the complex and large size process sequencing problem within a CAPP system. Li, Fuh, Zhang and Nee (2005) presented a genetic algorithm to search for the optimal process plan for a single manufacturing system as well as distributed manufacturing systems according to the prescribed criteria such as minimising processing time. The algorithm adopted a crossover operator described by Reddy, Shunmugam and Narendran (1999). The developed technique is comparative or better in the case of a single manufacturing system or factory.

Genetic Algorithms for Micro Process Planning

Reddy, Shunmugam and Narendran (1999) proposed a quick identification of optimal or near optimal operation sequences in a dynamic planning environment. They identified the feasible sequences based on a FPG and used minimum production cost as the objective function, which was calculated from a precedence cost matrix. The precedence cost matrix was generated for any pair of features based on the relative costs corresponding to the number of tasks that are needed to be performed in each category of attributes such as machining parameter change, tool change, setup change, machine change and the type of constraint one feature has with the others.

Optimal machining datum selection and tolerance allocation can greatly reduce the manufacturing cost and simplify the machining process. In Li, Bai, Zhang and Wang's (2000) research, machining datum selection is taken into consideration in the process of finding optimal machining tolerances. A mixed-discrete nonlinear optimisation model is formulated and genetic algorithms are applied to find the global optimal solution. The tolerance chart method is incorporated in the optimisation procedure and a simple and efficient dimension chain constructing method is employed. A dynamic tolerance chart constraints checking scheme is developed and implemented in the optimisation procedure. The tracing of optimisation procedure and the analysis of the result indicate that the proposed methodology is capable and robust in finding the optimal machining datum and tolerances. The topic of tolerance allocation was also researched by Ming and Mak (2001). They constructed two mathematical models to represent the behaviour of the tolerance allocation problem and the manufacturing operation selection problem, where a number of alternative sets of sequenced manufacturing operations were generated for each feature. They used genetic algorithm to solve the optimal tolerance allocation problem, and by using the results from the tolerance allocation procedure, a Hopfield neural network was used to select the optimal sets of manufacturing operation for all the features of the part. The advantage of their approach is that it is an efficient approach to obtain the optimal tolerances for alternative sets of manufacturing operations to machine features in a part, and has the ability to generate optimal sets of manufacturing operations by considering not only the manufacturing cost in terms of the tolerances, but also the dissimilarities in the manufacturing resource requirement among the selected sets of manufacturing operations. Singh, Jain and Jain (2003) reported on an integrated approach for simultaneous selection of design and manufacturing tolerances based on the minimisation of the total manufacturing cost, to overcome the drawbacks of the more conventional approach in tolerance design, such as more time consumption and sub-optimality. Unlike the conventional approach in which CAD and CAPP are performed in a sequential manner, the system uses genetic algorithms and the penalty function approach with proper normalization of the penalty terms to handle both design and manufacturing constraints. Shunmugam, Mahesh and Reddy (2002) used an object oriented feature modeller for the representation of part with all the manufacturing features and their technological information. An intelligent search strategy generated initial feasible sequences from the feature precedence relation based on precedence and geometric tolerance constraints. Then these sequences are optimised using GA with multiple criteria concerning datum/reference feature, feature adjacency and feature preference that represents setup change, tool changes and preferred shop-floor practices.

The criteria for selecting a set of optimum machining parameters depend on either the maximum production rate (i.e. minimum production time), or the maximum profit rate. In the work of Shunmugam, Reddy and Narendran (2000) where face-milling operations are considered, the machining parameters such as number of passes, depth of cut in each pass, speed and feed were obtained using a genetic algorithm. The goal is to yield a minimum total production cost while considering technological constraints such as allowable speed and feed, dimensional accuracy, surface finish, tool wear and machine tool capabilities. From experiments, the method proposed always yields production cost values less than or equal to the values obtained by other methods, and the authors conclude that the module developed can be well-integrated with the CAPP package to select the machining parameters once the operation is identified.

Genetic Algorithms in PDM

Yao, Xiong, Fan and Fan (2004) integrated Design Structure Matrix (DSM), genetic algorithm and expert system techniques to analyze and improve the product development process managed by PDM systems. Based on DSM representation, GA orders the sequence of activities in process with guidance provided through the export system to get a reasonable and optimal sequence.

Luo, Wang, Tang and Tu (2006) developed an optimizing model for task scheduling problem in PDM, in order to minimize the duration of the project, number of split and total interrupted time of tasks. In this model, a hybrid genetic algorithm based on greedy approach is used. The priority rule is applied in the coding scheme of the chromosome and the greedy criterion is adopted in decoding rule to process assembled task units. Neighbourhood search approach is integrated into mutation operator of the individual to improve the mutation efficiency.

When events such as rushed orders or machine breakdown occur during the production process in a job shop, the delivery date of order may be delayed. To solve this problem, Zou and Li (2006) built an events-oriented job shop scheduling model integrated with an enterprise information system. This enterprise information system combines systems such as CAPP, PDM and ERP. A genetic algorithm and a hybrid allocation-based method are used in scheduling.

AGENT-BASED TECHNOLOGY

Hewitt (1997) introduced the concept of agent technology using his distributed artificial intelligence "Actor model", where an Actor is a computational agent that has a mail address and behaviour. Actors communicate by message-passing and carry out their actions concurrently. In recent years, agent technology has been widely used in different branches of engineering, including design and manufacturing.

Basics of Agents

Despite the ubiquitous use of the phrase "agent-based" in many fields, there are perhaps as many definitions as the applications of agent technology. This may be explained by the versatility and robustness of the technology. From this point of view, it is worth listing some of the definitions. Wooldridge and Jennings (1995) once defined agents as having individual internal states and goals. They act in such a manner as to meet its goals on behalf of its user. A key element of their autonomy is their proactiveness, i.e. their ability to "take the initiative" rather than acting simply in response to their environment. Another definition from the same authors says that "an agent is a computer system situated in some environment, and that is capable of autonomous action in this environment in order to meet its design objectives (Jennings & Wooldridge, 1998). From the software and hardware point of view, Nwana (1996) defined an agent as an entity that resides in environments where it interprets data that reflect events in the environment and executes commands that produce effects in the environment. Some of the definitions are more relevant to engineering applications. Westkamper, Ritter and Schaefier (1999) considered an agent as an autonomous and interactive unit in complex systems with the aim of process optimization and stabilization, intelligence, and the ability of co-operation and co-ordination. Chan, Zhang and Li (2003) defined an agent as an intelligent entity (a real or a virtual entity) capable of independently regulating, reasoning, and decision-making to carry out some actions according to its abilities, status, resources, knowledge, and information about outsides in order to achieve a specific goal or a set of goals.

Regardless what area an agent is used, it always has the following three basic parts: (1) knowledge base, containing the data and domain knowledge necessary for an agent to carry out all its activities; (2) coordination unit, controlling interactions with other agents, including intercommunications, negotiations, coordination, and cooperation; and (3) problem solver, charging independently learning, planning, reasoning, and decision-making to execute corresponding activities to accomplish tasks.

There are different types of agents being used, depending on an agent's behaviour, its functionality, mobility and structure (Figure 17.7). In terms of its behaviour, an agent can be classified as a reactive agent, deliberative agent, or hybrid agent which is a combination of reactive agent and deliberative agent. This is the most commonly used classification approach of agents. Deliberative agents have domain knowledge and the planning capability necessary to undertake a sequence of actions with the intent of moving towards or achieving a specific goal. Reactive agents respond in an event-action-mode, by simply retrieving pre-set behaviours similar to reflexes without maintaining any internal state. They respond solely to external stimuli and the information available from their sensing of the environment. A combination of these two types of agents can be used to overcome the weaknesses of each of them (Zhang & Xie, 2007).

When agents are used in the manufacturing environment, they are often referred to as logical (software) or physical (hardware) agents. When a machine tool is treated as a task agent responsible for accepting or refusing tasks in a scheduling system, it is a logical

Figure 17.7. Different types of agents

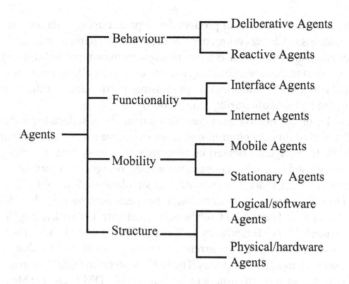

agent. If a machine tool is part of the integrated resources, it can be defined as a physical agent. Therefore, in many cases, logical agents and physical agents co-exist and cooperate with each other.

For agents to be effectively employed in an engineering problem, a number of agents need to "work" in a coherent way. This gives rise to a multi-agent system (MAS). An MAS can be defined as a loosely coupled computer system structured by a group of inter-connected autonomous agents across a computer network (e.g., LAN, intranet or internet, etc.). Each of the agents in an MAS is independent of other agents in functions and logical relationships, and has the capabilities of planning, reasoning, decision making, learning, and executing activities by itself. However, as its knowledge, information, resources and skills are limited, it may unavoidably conflict with other agents in subtasks, plans, decisions and behaviour. Because of this, these agents have to communicate, negotiate, coordinate, and cooperate with one another to share their knowledge, information, resources and skills, resolving their conflicts and reaching compromised or optimal global solutions.

Applications of Agent Technology

Agent-based applications provide a new way of viewing problems and designing solutions. Agent-based architectures are robust and dynamic; they can quickly react to unexpected events, and adapt to changing conditions. They are inherently distributed and scaleable: more agents and more computers can be added as necessary to increase the performance or the capacity of a system. These unique features of agent technology make it suitable for developing adaptive, dynamic, distributed and collaborative design and manufacturing systems. An agent-based architecture can lead to a distributed problem-solving paradigm in that complex design and manufacturing problems can be broken down into small and manageable sub-problems to be solved by individual agents.

Applications of Agent Technology in Engineering Design

Parker (2000) described the risks of product development using collaborative mode. The main risks include loss of direct control over the product development process, lack of transparency, incomplete information disclosure, ambiguous roles/responsibilities specification and allocation. Agent technologies can help to reduce risks of collaborations for concurrent, distributed and collaborative information processing, particularly for the concurrent and distributed design and manufacturing (Tang, 2004).

Agent-based approaches have been dominant during the past decade for the implementation of collaborative product environments. An extensive review can be found in (Shen & Wang, 2002). In an agent-oriented collaborative design system, intelligent software agents are mostly used to enable cooperation among designers, to provide wrappers to integrate legacy software tools, or to allow better simulations (Hao, Shen, Zhang, Park & Lee, 2006). The use of agents in product design has been demonstrated by a large number of R&D projects. PACT (Palo Alto Collaborative Testbed) (Cutkosky, Engelmore, Fikes, Genesereth, Gruber, Mark, Tenenbaum & Weber, 1993) is one of the earliest successful projects in this area. PACT is a concurrent engineering infrastructure that encompasses multiple sites, subsystems, and disciplines. The PACT systems include NVisage, a distributed knowledge-based integration environment for design tools; DME (Device Modelling Environment), a model formulation and simulation environment; Next-Cut, a mechanical design and process planning system; and Designworld, a digital electronics design, simulation, assembly, and testing system. SHARE (Toye, Cutkosky, Tenenbaum & Glicksman, 1993) was concerned with developing open, heterogeneous, network-oriented environments for concurrent engineering, particularly for design information and data capturing and sharing through asynchronous communication. Co-Designer (Hague & Taleb-Bendiab, 1998) was a system that can support localized design agents in the generation and management of conceptual design variants. A-Design (Campbell, Cagan & Kotovsky, 1999) presented a new design generation methodology, which combines aspects of multi-objective optimization, multi-agent systems, and automated design synthesis. It provides designers with a new search strategy for the conceptual stages of product design, which incorporates agent collaboration with an adaptive selection of designs.

Huang (2004) presented an agent-based system to support modular product collaborative design. Mitkas, Symeonidis, Kehagias and Athanasiadis (2003) discussed how software agent technology can be used to control a large number of concurrent engineering tasks and present a multi-agent development framework for constructing multi-agent systems. Liu, Tang and Frazer (2004) proposed a multi-agent collaborative design system for dynamically creating and managing design tasks in a distributed and dynamic design environment. Jia, Ong, Fuh, Zhang and Nee (2004) presented an adaptive and upgradeable agent-based system for coordinated product development and manufacturing. The system consists of a central managing agent and several other functional agents such as the manufacturability evaluation agent, process-planning agent, and scheduling agent.

In more specific domains, Tang (2004) developed a multi-agent-based system to integrate die-maker's activities into customer product development process within a distributed, collaborative and concurrent environment. Zha (2002) developed a knowledge intensive, multi-agent framework for concurrent design and assembly planning.

Multi-agent systems provide a cooperative environment for the sharing of design information, data, and knowledge among distributed design team members. However, this data sharing mechanism could only be easily achieved by using the Web technology. This is why most of the above-mentioned agent-based systems are Internet and Web-based.

Applications of Agent Technology in Manufacturing

Agent-based and Web-based technologies have also been adopted by the manufacturing industry. Areas of successful implementations include shop-floor automation, product data management, manufacturing execution systems, enterprise resource planning, customer management, supply chain management, and even B2B e-commerce (Renner, 2002).

Balasubramanian and Norrie (1996) proposed one of the earliest architectures for a multi-agent manufacturing system (Figure 17.8). It is an open architecture in which other agents can be added to address issues such as assembly and recycling. It involves four main components: inventory agent, design agent, design feature agent, and shop-floor control agent.

The design feature agent contains information regarding products' specifications. The design agent receives a list of production requests, the list of production resources (e.g. cutting tools and grippers) and a list of components (e.g. machine tools, robots, pick-up, etc.). The shop-floor control agent screens any unnecessary messages and maintains the virtual grouping of the shop-floor resources. The inventory agent helps collect information regarding the available manufacturing tools and machines.

When agent-based technology is used for manufacturing, three main approaches have been taken, cooperative, blackboard architecture and integrated approach (Zhang & Xie, 2007). The cooperative approach intends to solve process planning and manufacturing problems by effective cooperation and negotiation of intelligent agents. CoCAPP (Cooperative

Figure 17.8. A multi-agent architecture for manufacturing systems

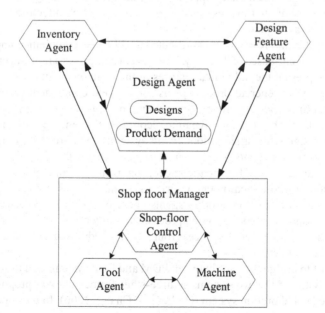

CAPP) (Zhao & Wu, 1999) was developed to meet five major requirements of a distributed CAPP system, autonomy, flexibility, interoperability, modularity, and scalability. The Co-CAPP system deals with process planning problems by distributing them to some special process planning agents. All the process planning agents coordinate and cooperate with each other via a commonly shared language with the expectation of reaching agreements when conflicts occur. These agents have their own tasks to perform, which are notified by a blackboard agent. Utpal (1999) introduced a cooperative distributed problem-solving (CDPS) framework to solve CAPP problems stemmed from a rigid hierarchical structure of tasks. The framework decomposes a problem into sub-problems and distribute them among a network of problem-solvers (defined as agents), which cooperate with each other to work out the best solutions for the problem.

Blackboard architectures solve the problems of sequential architectures by providing flexible control methods. In an agent-based system, the blackboard is used by agents to write messages or post partial results as well as obtain information. One of such systems was developed by Lander, Staley and Corkill (1996), in which agent-based blackboards are used to manage agent interactions. The CoCAPP system discussed earlier is also a blackboard architecture system. The blackboard agent (B-agent) in this system has a registered list of all participating agents and their functions. B-agent provides a coordination mechanism for all the participating agents. When there is a problem, the B-agent notifies all the registered process planning agents for action, so that these process planning agents can perform specified process planning tasks.

Agent-based systems adopting an integrated approach tend to integrate different product development activities such as design, process planning, manufacturing, and scheduling. Agent-based technology provides a natural way for such integration. Wang and Shen (2003) presented a distributed process planning methodology by integrating machining feature-based planning, function block-based control, and agent-based distributed decision-making. The proposed methodology is suitable for dynamic, reconfigurable and distributed manufacturing environments. An agent-based approach was adopted for intelligent decision-making involved in the distributed process planning. A two-level architecture for supervisory planning and operation planning was adopted.

Newman, Allen and Rosso (2005) presented a STEP-NC compliant computational environment using agent-based technology. The system comprises a multi-agent framework, where agents represent the individual features of the component and work independently and cooperatively to generate process plans for discrete component manufacture. Lim and Zhang (2000) introduced an agent-based dynamic process planning and scheduling system (APPSS), which is used for dynamic reconfiguration and optimization of resource utilization in a manufacturing shop-floor. In this system, agents are classified into execution agents and information agents. Execution agents are responsible for carrying out procedures and making decisions. Information agents on the other hand, play an important role in the operation of multi-agent manufacturing systems. They serve as data brokers and provide necessary information to other agents upon requests. Gu, Balasubramanian and Norrie (1997) proposed a bidding-based process planning and scheduling system. This is a multi-agent system in which the process routes and schedules of a part are accomplished through the contract net bids.

In the effort to bridge the gaps between PDM and ERP systems and to support the collaboration activities of the two systems, a three-stage framework was proposed to develop the agent-based collaboration system (Ou-Yang & Chang, 2006). In the concept stage, the modelling tools such as virtual address descriptor and extended event process chain were used to capture collaboration requirements between PDM and ERP. In the design stage, a UML-based analysing method was used to develop the agent-based system. Also, an agent development tool ZEUS (Nwana, Ndumu, Lee & Collis, 1999) was used to generate agent code.

In order to model the constantly evolving design process and the rationales resulted from collaboration, a collaborative PDM system based on agent technology was proposed by Wang and Tang (2005). The system extends traditional PDM and a constraint-based collaborative design process model. These are intended to facilitate the management and coordination of collaborative product design process and knowledge management. In the conceptual PLM system architecture developed by Li, Liu, Feng and Wang, (2005), a J2EE (2008) standards-based and multi-agents based information system infrastructure is used in order to achieve the collaborative product development.

OTHER TECHNOLOGIES

There are also other technologies used to solve design and manufacturing problems. Some of them are related to the previously discussed technologies; many are used in conjunction with other method(s) to yield better performance. The following text summarises fuzzy logic, Petri Nets and ant colony optimization technologies, and some of the application cases.

Fuzzy Logic

Fuzzy logic finds its use in design and manufacturing with little surprise. Much of the decision-making in design and manufacturing takes place in an environment in which not only goals but also constraints are fuzzy. Human knowledge also plays a key part in the decision-making. Fuzzy logic theory can effectively carry out the transformation of the human knowledge to mathematical formulae, and provide a scientific foundation for working with imprecise data. The Fuzzy design system described in Chapter VII is such an example.

Recently, Lin, Lai and Yeh (2007) developed a fuzzy logic approach to determining the best combination of mobile phone form elements for matching a given product image. A new experimental process was conducted to objectively generate a set of fuzzy rules with the most influential form elements. The fuzzy rules generated outperform neural network models in predicting the product images of a mobile phone with a given set of form elements.

Wong, Chan and Lau (2003) described a fuzzy approach for solving the process selection and sequencing problem under uncertainty. The proposed approach comprises a two-stage process for machining process selection and sequencing, the intra-feature planning and inter-feature planning stage. A genetic algorithm with fuzzy numbers and fuzzy arithmetic was developed to solve a global sequencing problem. Beg and Shunmugam (2003) proposed a methodology for two modules of inspection planning: the selection of the most stable part orientation and the sequencing of probe orientations. In their research, fuzzy decision-making has been applied to carry out the selection of part orientation and sequence of probe orientations.

Petri Nets

Petri Nets (PNs) have the ability to represent and analyse concurrency and synchronization phenomena in an easy way, like concurrent evolutions, where various processes that evolve simultaneously are partially independent (Li, Yu & Lara-Rosano, 2000). Design and manufacturing activities are such type of processes. PNs have an inherent quality in representing logic in intuitive and visual way. Furthermore, PN approach can be easily combined with other techniques and theories such as object-oriented programming, fuzzy theory, neural networks, etc.

Chen and Siddique (2006) described a Petri-net process model that captures the dependency relationships of design decision making and information exchanges among multiple design problems in a distributed environment. The Model of Distributed Design (MDD) allows quantitative representation of a collaborative design process in which designers from multiple disciplines can effectively work together. The MDD is developed based on the Petri-net graph, which allows various performance analyses to be performed to evaluate and improve a collaborative design process.

Huang (2006) developed an intelligent methodology for integration of design and assembly planning processes, including product design, assembly evaluation, redesign, assembly process planning and etc. A unified class of knowledge-based Petri nets was defined through the introduction of two new extensions of Petri nets, i.e. knowledge-based Petri nets and fuzzy knowledge-based Petri nets. Kasirolvalad, Motlagh and Shadmani (2004) presented an AND/OR net approach for planning CNC machining operations, and showed that Petri nets could be used to model all CNC machining operations in a graphical manner.

Dou, Zhang, Li and Zhang (2001) argued that how to exert the enable effort in PDM system is the key factor to guarantee the quality and effect of integrating the information, functions and processes. How to control and estimate the developments in enabled process was researched by giving a concrete instance and constructing the emulation model with the enable process based on the Petri network. The compound binary graph based on the activities in process's Petri network provided an instructional formwork for scientific and logical global decision-making from the point of view of virtual realism.

Ant Colony Optimization

Ant colony optimization (ACO) algorithms are multi-agent systems in which the behaviour of each ant is inspired by the foraging behaviour of real ants to solve the optimization problem.

Huo, Li, Teng and Sun (2005) proposed a human-computer cooperative ant colony/genetic algorithm (HCAGA) to assist satellite module layout design. Artificial individuals are integrated with algorithm individuals by the unified code form and are operated in the individuals' population. Viana, Kotinda, Rade and Steffen (2006) presented a system that can deal with the optimal tuning of a vibrating blade dynamic vibration absorber by using ACO.

Tiwari, Dashora, Kumar and Shankar (2006) developed a system to resolve the machining process plan selection problem. The algorithm has a diversified search space and gives the optimal/suboptimal outcomes among various alternative routings. The effectiveness of the algorithm lies in its considerably shorter execution time. The primary advantage of using ACO is that it stabilizes the solution with considerably less computational effort and time without any deterioration in the quality.

CONCLUSION

Expert systems are generally perceived to be useful in product design, process planning, scheduling and PDM, and are therefore the most commonly used technology in the domain. Expert systems have advantages over the traditional computer systems, since they organise knowledge in rules and can use control strategy to mimic the way an expert solves a problem. However, an expert system's total reliance on consultation with human experts for knowledge acquisition makes the system a rigid one. It is not easy to automatically modify knowledge to suit the dynamic design and manufacturing environment. Neural network can tolerate slight errors from input and most important of all, it has the ability to derive rules or knowledge through training with examples and can allow exceptions and irregularities in the knowledge/rule base. Neural network enables parallel consideration of multiple constraints. However, the neural networks based inference method cannot express the inference procedure and results in an explicit manner. There is lack of systematic and efficient methods to identify an appropriate training set for a specific application.

The power of genetic algorithms comes from the fact that the technique is robust and can deal successfully with a wide range of difficult problems. Genetic algorithms are not guaranteed to find the global optimum solution to a problem, but they are generally good at finding "acceptably good" solutions to problems "acceptably quickly". A problem with genetic algorithms is that the genes from a few comparatively highly fit (but not optimal) individuals may rapidly come to dominate the population, causing it to converge on a local maximum. Both genetic algorithms and neural nets are adaptive and robust. They can learn and deal with highly nonlinear models and noisy data. They do not need gradient information or smooth functions. In both cases their flexibility is a drawback, since they have to be carefully structured and coded and are fairly application-specific.

Agent-based approaches offer many advantages for distributed product design and manufacturing, i.e. modularity, reconfigurability, scalability, upgradeability, and robustness. At the moment, agent-based systems are focused on the fundamental research to enhance the rationality or intelligence of software agents, and the development of more efficient and effective coordination and negotiation mechanisms. Fuzzy logic, Petri Nets and ant colony optimisation methods have all found their applications in design and manufacturing. The fact that all of the above-mentioned technologies have strength and weaknesses, means that combining one with another is likely to offer a better solution. This is certainly true with some effective combinations of the technologies, i.e. genetic algorithm combined with fuzzy logic, fuzzy logic combined with Petri net to give raise to a more effective fuzzy Petri net, and integration of fuzzy logic rules, artificial neural networks, agent-based technology and expert system.

REFERENCES

Amaitik, S. M., & Kilic, S. E. (2005). STEP-based feature modeller for computer-aided process planning. *International Journal of Production Research*, *43*(15), 3087-3101.

Arezoo, B., Ridgway, K., & Al-Ahmari, A. M. A. (2000). Selection of cutting tools and conditions of machining operations using an expert system. *Computers in Industry, 42*(1), 43-58.

Badiru, A. B. (1992). *Expert Systems Applications in Engineering and Manufacturing.* Englewood Cliffs. NJ. USA: PrenticeHall.

Baker, S. (1988). Nexpert object: mainstreaming AI applications. *IEEE Expert.* Winter. p. 82.

Balasubramanian, S., & Norrie, D. H. (1996). A multi-agent architecture for concurrent design, process planning, routing, and scheduling. *Concurrent Engineering Research and Applications, 4*(1), 7-16

Beg, J., & Shunmugam, M. S. (2003). Application of fuzzy logic in the selection of part orientation and probe orientation sequencing for prismatic parts. *International Journal of Production Research, 41*(12), 2799-2815.

Bo, Z. W., Hua, L. Z., & Yu, Z.G, (2006). Optimization of process route by Genetic Algorithms. *Robotics and Computer-Integrated Manufacturing, 22*(2), 180-188.

Brown, R. G. (2000). Driving Digital Manufacturing to reality. In *Proceedings of Winter Simulation Conference*, Orlando, FL,USA.

Campbell, M. I., Cagan, J., & Kotovsky, K. (1999). A-Design: An agent-based approach to conceptual design in a dynamic environment. *Research in Engineering Design, 11*, 172–192.

Carpenter, I. D., & Maropoulos, P. G. (2000). Flexible tool selection decision support system for milling operations. *Journal of Materials Processing Technology, 107*(1-3), 143-152.

Chan, F. T. S., Zhang, J., & Li, P. (2003). Agent- and CORBA®-based application integration platform for an agile manufacturing environment. *International Journal of Advanced Manufacturing Technology, 21*(6), 460-468.

Chang, T. -C., Wysk, R. A., & Wang, H. -P. (1991). *Computer-Aided Manufacturing* (Prentice Hall, Englewood Cliffs, NJ).

Chen, C. L. P., & LeClair, S. R. (1993), Unsupervised neural learning algorithm for setup generation in process planning. In *Proceedings of International Conference on Artificial Neural Networks in Engineering*, (pp. 663-8).

Chen, Y. H., & Lee, H. M. (1998), A neural network system for 2D feature recognition. *International Journal of Computer Integrated Manufacturing, 11*(2), 111-7.

Chen, Z., & Siddique, Z. (2006). A model of collaborative design decision making using timed Petri-net. In *Proceedings of the ASME Design Engineering Technical Conference.*

Chuang, J. H., Wang, P. H., & Wu, M. C. (1999), Automatic classification of block-shaped parts based on their 2D projections. *Computers & Industrial Engineering, 36*(3), 697-718.

Cutkosky, M. R., Engelmore, R. S., Fikes, R. E., Genesereth, M. R., Gruber, T. R., Mark, W. S., Tenenbaum, J. M., & Weber, J. C. (1993). PACT: An Experiment in Integrating Concurrent Engineering Systems, *IEEE Computer Archive, 26*(1), 28-37.

Dallaali, M. A., & Premaratne, M. (2004). Controlled content crossover: A new crossover scheme and its application to optical network component allocation problem. *Lecture Notes in Computer Science (including subseries Lecture Notes in Artificial Intelligence and Lecture Notes in Bioinformatics), 3103*, 387-389.

Deb, K. (1999). *An introduction to genetic algorithms*. Sadhana, 24, 293-315.

Deb, K. (2001). *Multi-objective Optimization Using Evolutionary Programming*. London, UK: Wiley.

Dereli, T., & Filiz, I. H. (1999). Optimisation of process planning functions by genetic algorithms. *Computers and Industrial Engineering, 36*(2), 281-308.

Devireddy, C. R., & Ghosh, K. (1999), Feature-based modelling and neural networks-based CAPP for integrated manufacturing. *International Journal of Computer Integrated Manufacturing, 12*(1), 61-74.

Ding, L., Yue, Y., Ahmet, K., & Jackson, M. (2005). Global optimization of a feature-based process sequence using GA and ANN techniques. *International Journal of Production Research, 43*(15), 3247-3272.

Donne, M. S., Tilley, D.G., & Richards, W. (1995). The use of multi-objective parallel genetic algorithms to aid fluid power system design. *Proceedings of IMechE, 209*, 53- 61.

Dornan, B. (1987). A status report: artificial intelligence. *Production*, (pp. 46-50).

Dou, W.-C., Zhang, F.-Y., Li, D.-B., & Zhang, S.-Q. (2001). Study of enable technology in product data management. *Computer Integrated Manufacturing Systems, 7*(8), 49-53.

Du, P., & Huang, N.-K. (1990). *Principles of Computer-Aided Process Planning,* Beijing: Beijing University of Aeronautics & Astronauts Press.

Dutta, D., & Yip-Hoi, D. (1996). A genetic algorithm application for sequencing operations in process planning for parallel machining. *IIE transactions, 28*, 55- 68.

Fausett, L. (1994). *Fundamentals of Neural Networks: Architectures, Algorithms and Applications*. Prentice Hall International, Inc.

Goldberg, D. E. (1989). *Genetic Algorithms in Search, Optimization and Machine L earning*. Reading, MA: Addison-Wesley.

Gologlu, C. (2004). A constraint-based operation sequencing for a knowledge-based process planning. *Journal of Intelligent Manufacturing, 15*(4), 463-470.

Grabowik, C., & Knosala, R. (2003). The method of knowledge representation for a CAPP system. *Journal of Materials Processing Technology, 133*(1-2), 90-98.

Greenstette, J. J. (1986). Optimization of control parameters for genetic algorithms. *IEEE Transactions on Systems, Man, and Cybernetics, 16*(1), 122- 128.

Gu, P., Balasubramanian S., & Norrie, D. H. (1997). Bidding-based process planning and scheduling in a multi-agent system. *Computers & Industrial Engineering*, (2), 477–496

Gu, Z., Zhang, Y. F., & Nee, A. Y. C. (1995), Generic form feature recognition and operation selection using connectionist modelling, *Journal of Intelligent Manufacturing*, 6(4), 263-73.

Gurney, K. (1997), *An Introduction to Neural Networks*. USA: UCL Press.

Hague, M. J., & Taleb-Bendiab, A. (1998). Tool for management of concurrent conceptual engineering design, *Concurrent Engineering: Research and Applications*, 6(2), 111–129.

Hao, Q., Shen, W., Zhang, Z., Park, S-W., & Lee, J-K. (2006). Agent-based collaborative product design engineering: An industrial case study. *Computers in Industry*, 57, 26–38.

Hewitt, C. (1997). Viewing control structures as patterns of passing messages. *Artificial Intelligence*, 8, 323–364.

Huang, C. C. (2004). A multi-agent approach to collaborative design of modular products. *Concurrent Engineering: Research and Applications*, 2(1), 39-47.

Huang, G. Y. (2006). Analysis of artificial intelligence based Petri net approach to intelligent integration of design. In *Proceedings of the 2006 International Conference on Machine Learning and Cybernetics*, Dalian, P. R. China.

Huntington. D. (1985). *EXSYS expert systems development package*. Albuquerque. NM: EXSYS Manual.

Huo, J., Li, G., Teng, H., & Sun, Z. (2005). Human-computer cooperative ant colony/genetic algorithm for satellite module layout design. *Chinese Journal of Mechanical Engineering*, 41(3), 112-116.

Hwang, J.-L. (1991), *Applying the perceptron to 3-D feature recognition*, PhD Thesis Arizona State University, USA.

Ignizio. J. P. (1991). *Introduction to Expert Systems*. New York. NY: McGraw-Hill.

J2EE. (2008). *Java 2 Platform, Enterprise Edition*. Sun Microsystems, Inc. Retrieved 30 January, 2008, from http://java.sun.com/j2ee/overview.html

Jackson. P. (1986). *Introduction to Expert Systems*. Wokingham: Addison-Wesley.

Jain, P. K., Mehta, N. K., & Pandey, P. C. (1998). Automatic cut planning in an operative process planning system. *Proceedings of IMechE, Part B: Journal of Engineering Manufacture, 212*(2), 129-140.

Jayaraman, V., & Srivastava. R. (1996). Expert systems in production and operations management. *International Journal of Operations & Production Management*, 16(12), 27-44.

Jennings, N. R., & Wooldridge, M. J. (1998). Applications of intelligent agents. In N. R. Jennings and M. J. Wooldridge, (Ed.). *Agent Technology: Foundations, Applications, and Markets*, pp. 3–28, Berlin: Springer.

Jia, H. Z., Ong, S. K., Fuh, J. Y. H., Zhang, Y. F., & Nee, A. Y. C. (2004). An adaptive and upgradable agent-based system for coordinated product development and manufacture. *Robotics and Computer-Integrated Manufacturing, 20*, 79-90.

Jia, X., Zhang, Z., Xu, J., & Huang, N. (2003). The research on representation and processing of process knowledge based on object-oriented modelling. In *Proceedings of 2003 International Conference on International Conference on Machine Learning and Cybernetics, 2*, pp. 657-660

Jiang, B., Baines, K., & Zockel, M. (1997). A new coding scheme for the optimisation of milling operations for utilisation by a generative expert C.A.P.P. system. *Journal of Materials Processing Technology, 63*(1-3), 163-168.

Jiang, B., Lau, H. Chan, F. T. S., & Jiang, H. (1999). An automatic process planning system for the quick generation of manufacturing process plans directly from CAD drawings. *Journal of Materials Processing Technology, 87*(1-3), 97-106.

Joshi, S., & Chang, T.-C. (1998), Graph-based heuristics for recognition of machined features from a 3D solid model. *Computer-Aided Design*, 20(2), 58-66.

Kasirolvalad, Z., Motlagh, M. R. J., & Shadmani, M.A. (2004). An intelligent modular modelling approach for quality control of CNC machines product using adaptive fuzzy Petri nets. In *Proceedings of 2004 8th International Conference on Control, Automation, Robotics and Vision (ICARCV)*, Kunming, P. R. China.

Kim, I. T., & Suh, H. W. (1998). Optimal operation grouping and sequencing technique for multistage machining systems. *International Journal of Production Research, 36*(8), 2061-2081.

Knapp, G. D., & Wang, H. P. (1992), Acquiring, storing and utilising process planning knowledge using neural networks. *Journal of Intelligent Manufacturing, 3*(5), 333-44.

Korosec, M., Balic, J., & Kopac, J. (2005). Neural network based manufacturability evaluation of free form machining. *International Journal of Machine Tools and Manufacture, 45*(1), 13-20.

Kryssanov, V. V., Kleshchev, A. S., Fukuda, Y., & Konishi, K. (1998). Building a logical model in the machining domain for CAPP expert systems. *International Journal of Production Research, 36*(4), 1075-1089.

Kumar, R., & Midha, P. S. (2003). An objective approach for identifying the strategic components of a PDM system. *Industrial Management and Data Systems, 104*(1-2), 56-67.

Kumar, R., & Midha, P. S. (2006). An intelligent web-based expert system for analysing a company's strategic PDM requirements. *International Journal of Product Lifecycle Management, 1*(3), 230-248.

Kusiak. A., & Chen. M. (1988). Expert systems for planning and scheduling manufacturing systems. *European Journal of Operational Research, 34*(2), 113-30.

Lander, S. E., Staley, S. M., & Corkill, D. D. (1996). Designing integrated engineering environment: blackboard-based integration of design and analysis tools. *Concurrent Engineering: Research and Applications, 4*(1), 59–72

Le Tumelin, C., Garro, O., & Charpentier, P. (1995), Generating process plans using neural networks. In *Proceedings of 2nd International Workshop on Learning in Intelligent Manufacturing Systems*, Budapest, Hungry.

Li, H., Li, Z., Li, L. X., & Hu, B. (2000). A production rescheduling expert simulation system. *European Journal of Operational Research, 124*(2), 283-293.

Li, H.-Y., Liu, X., Feng, G.-Q., & Wang, C.-E. (2005). A web-based PLM system research and implementation in a collaborative product development environment. In *Proceedings - ICEBE 2005: IEEE International Conference on e-Business Engineering*, 2005, art. no. 1552945, pp. 549-552.

Li, L., Fuh, J. Y. H., Zhang, Y. F., & Nee, A. Y. C. (2005). Application of genetic algorithm to computer-aided process planning in distributed manufacturing environments. *Robotics and Computer-Integrated Manufacturing, 21*(6), 568-578.

Li, W., Bai, G., Zhang, C., & Wang, B. (2000). Optimization of machining datum selection and machining tolerance allocation with genetic algorithms. *International Journal of Production Research, 38*(6), 1407-1424.

Li, X., Yu, W., & Lara-Rosano, F. (2000). Dynamic knowledge inference and learning under adaptive fuzzy Petri net framework. *IEEE Transactions on Systems, Man and Cybernetics Part C: Applications and Reviews, 30*(4), 442-450.

Li, Y., Mills, B., Moruzzi, J. L., & Rowe, W. B. (1994), Grinding wheel selection using a neural network, In *Proceedings of the 10th National Manufacturing Research Conference*, Loughborough, UK. pp. 597-601.

Lim, M., & Zhang, Z. (2000). APPSS – An agent-based dynamic process planning and scheduling system. In *Proceedings of the IFAC Workshop*, pp 51–56

Lin, P. C., Ko, P. C., Wang, H. C., Tien, Y. J., & You, J. A. (2006). An evolutionary weight encoding scheme and crossover methodology in portfolio assets allocation. In *Proceedings of the 9th Joint Conference on Information Sciences, JCIS 2006*, art. no. CIEF-159.

Lin, Y.-C., Lai, H.-H., & Yeh, C.-H. (2007). Consumer-oriented product form design based on fuzzy logic: A case study of mobile phones. *International Journal of Industrial Ergonomics, 37*(6), 531-543

Lippmann, R. P. (1987). Introduction to Computing With Neural Nets. *IEEE ASSP magazine, 4*(2), 4-22.

Liu, D., Duan, G., Lei, N., & Wang, J.-S. (1999). Analytic hierarchy process based decision modelling in CAPP development tools. *International Journal of Advanced Manufacturing Technology, 15*(1), 26-31.

Liu, H., Tang, M., & Frazer, J. H. (2004). Supporting dynamic management in a multi-agent collaborative design system. *Advances in Engineering Software, 35*, 493-502.

Luger, G. F., & Stubblefield, W. A. (1989). *Artificial Intelligence and the Design of Expert Systems,* Menlo Park, CA: Benjamin/Cummings.

Luo, X., Wang, D., Tang, J., & Tu, Y. (2006). Research of task scheduling problem in product data management. In *Proceedings of the World Congress on Intelligent Control and Automation (WCICA)*, 2, art. no. 1714446, pp. 7018-7022.

Mcinerney, M., & Dhawan, A. P. (1993). Use of genetic algorithm with back propagation in training of feed-forward neural networks. In *Proceedings of IEEE International Conference on Neural Networks*, San Francisco, pp. 203 - 208.

Mei, J., Zhang, H. C., & Oldham, W. J. B. (1995), A neural network approach for datum selection in computer-aided process planning. *Computers in Industry, 27*(1), 53-64.

Metaxiotis, K., Askounis, D., & Psarras, J. (2002). Expert systems in production planning and scheduling: A state-of-the-art survey. *Journal of Intelligent Manufacturing, 13*(4), 253-260.

Michalewicz, Z. (1996). *Genetic Algorithms þ Data Structure ¼ Evolution Programs.* Berlin: Springer.

Ming, X. G., & Mak, K. L. (2001). Intelligent approaches to tolerance allocation and manufacturing operations selection in process planning. *Journal of Materials Processing Technology, 117*(1-2), 75-83.

Mital. A., & Anand. S. (1994). *Handbook of Expert Systems.* London: Chapman & Hall.

Mitkas, P. A., Symeonidis, A. L., Kehagias, D., & Athanasiadis, I. (2003). Application of data mining and intelligent agent technologies to concurrent engineering. In *Proceedings of the 10th ISPE International Conference on Concurrent Engineering Research and Application*, Enhanced Interoperable Systems, pp. 11-18.

Moon, C., Li, Y-Z, & Gen, M. (1998). Evolutionary algorithm for flexible process sequencing with multiple objectives. In *Proceedings of the IEEE Conference on Evolutionary Computation, ICEC*, pp. 27-32

Newman, S. T., Allen, R. D., & Rosso Jr., R. S. U. (2003). CADCAM solutions for STEP-compliant CNC manufacture. *International Journal of Computer Integrated Manufacturing*, 16, 590–597.

Nezis, K., & Vosniakos, G. (1997), Recognising 2.5D shape features using a neural network and heuristics. *Computer-Aided Design, 29*(7), 523-39.

Nwana, H. S. (1996). Software Agents: An Overview. *Knowledge Engineering Review, 11*(3), 1–40.

Nwana, H., Ndumu, D., Lee, L., & Collis, J. (1999). ZEUS: a tool-kit for building distributed multi-agent systems. *Journal of Applied Artificial Intelligence, 13*,187–208.

Osakada, K., & Yang, G. B. (1991), Neural networks for process planning of cold forging. *Annals of the CIRP, 40*(1), 243-46.

Ou-Yang, C., & Chang, M. J. (2006). Developing an agent-based PDM/ERP collaboration system. *International Journal of Advanced Manufacturing Technology, 30* (3-4), 369-384.

Park, M. W., Park, B. T., Rho, Y. M., & Kim, S. K. (2000), Incremental supervised learning of cutting conditions using the Fuzzy ARTMAP neural network, *Annals of the CIRP*, 49(1), 375-8.

Park, S. C. (2003). Knowledge capturing methodology in process planning. CAD *Computer-Aided Design, 35*(12), 1109-1117.

Parker, H. (2000) Interfirm collaboration and the new product development process. *Industrial Management and Data Systems, 100*(6), 255-60.

Peters, T. J. (1992), Encoding mechanical design features for recognition via neural nets. *Research in Engineering Design, 4*(2), 67-74.

Pham, D. T., & Gologlu, C. (2001). A computer aided process planning system for concurrent engineering. In *Proceedings of the Institution of Mechanical Engineers, Part B: Journal of Engineering Manufacture, 215*(8), 1117-1131.

Prabhakar, S., & Henderson, M. R. (1992), Automatic form-feature recognition using neural network- based techniques on B-rep of solid models. *Computer-Aided Design, 24*(7), 381-93.

Principe, J. C., Euliano, N. R., & Lefebvre, W. C. (2000), *Neural and adaptive system: Fundamentals through Simulations*, Wiley.

Qiao, L.,Wang, X. Y., & Wang, S.-C. (2000). A GA-based approach to machining operation sequencing for prismatic parts. *International Journal of Production Research, 38*(14), 3283-3303.

Reddy, B. S. V., Shunmugam, M. S., & Narendran, T. T. (1999). Operation sequencing in CAPP using genetic algorithms, *International Journal of Production Research, 37* (5), 1063-1074.

Renner, K. (2002, June). The future of real time—Web-based services will enable realtime manufacturing ecosystems, *MSI Magazine*.

Rocha, J., Ramos, C., & Vale, Z. (1999). Process planning using a genetic algorithm approach. In *Proceedings of the IEEE International Symposium on Assembly and Task Planning*, pp. 338-343.

Roucoules, L., Salomons, O., & Paris, H. (2003). Process planning as an integration of knowledge in the detailed design phase. *International Journal of Computer Integrated Manufacturing, 16*(1), 25-37.

Sakakura, M., & Inasaki, I. (1992), A neural network approach to the Decision-making process for grinding operations. *Annals of the CIRP, 41*(1), 353-6.

Santochi, M., & Dini, G. (1996), Use of neural networks in automated selection of technological parameters of cutting tools. *Computer Integrated Manufacturing Systems, 9*(3), 137-48.

Shan, X. H., Nee, A. Y. C., & Poo, A. N. (1992), Integrated application of expert systems and neural networks for machining operation sequencing, *Neural Networks in Manufacturing and Robotics. ASME, 57,* 117-26 PED.

Sharma, R., & Gao, J. X. (2002). A Progressive design and manufacturing evaluation system incorporating STEP AP224. *Computers in Industry, 47* (2), 155-167.

Shen, W., & Wang, L. (2002). Web-based and agent-based approaches for collaborative product design: an overview. *International Journal of Computer Applications in Technology, 16*(2–3), 103–112.

Shi, H.-M., & Chen, J.-H. (1992). Principles of genetic algorithms and their use in mechanical engineering. *Chinese Mechanical Engineering, 3*(3), 18-31.

Shunmugam, M. S., Mahesh, P., & Reddy, B. S. V. (2002). A method of preliminary planning for rotational components with C-axis features using genetic algorithm. *Computers in Industry, 48*(3), 199-217.

Shunmugam, M. S., Reddy, B. S. V., & Narendran, T. T. (2000). Selection of optimal conditions in multi-pass face-milling using a genetic algorithm. *International Journal of Machine Tools and Manufacture, 40*(3), 401-414.

Singh, P. K., Jain, P. K., & Jain, S. C. (2003). Simultaneous optimal selection of design and manufacturing tolerances with different stack-up conditions using genetic algorithms. *International Journal of Production Research, 41*(11), 2411-2429.

Sormaz, D. N., & Khoshnevis, B. (1997). Process planning knowledge representation using an object-oriented data model. *International Journal of Computer Integrated Manufacturing, 10*(1-4), 92-104.

Soyuer, H., Kocamaz, M., & Kazancoglu, Y. (2007). Scheduling jobs through multiple parallel channels using an expert system. *Production Planning and Control, 18*(1), 35-43.

Tang, D. (2004). An agent-based collaborative design system to facilitate active die-maker involvement in stamping part design. *Computers in Industry, 54,* 253-71.

Tiwari, M. K., Dashora, Y., Kumar, S., & Shankar, R. (2006). Ant colony optimization to select the best process plan in an automated manufacturing environment. *IMechE Proc. 220 Part B: J. Engineering Manufacture.* pp 1457-1472.

Townsend. C. (1986). Mastering Expert Systems with Turbo Prolog. Sams. Indianapolis. IN.

Toye, G., Cutkosky, M. R., Leifer, L., Tenenbaum, J., & Glicksman, J. (1993). SHARE: a methodology and environment for collaborative product development, In *Proceedings of Second Workshop on Enabling Technologies: Infrastructure for Collaborative Enterprises,* pp. 33–47.

Usher, J. M., & Bowden, R. O. (1996). The application of genetic algorithms to operation sequencing for use in computer-aided process planning. *Computers and Industrial Engineering, 30*(4), 999-1013.

Utpal, B. (1999). A cooperative problem solving framework for computer-aided process planning. In *Proceeding of 32nd Hawaii International Conference on System Sciences.*

Venkatachalam, A. R. (1994). Analysis of an embedded crossover scheme on a GA-hard problem. *Computers and Operations Research, 22*(1), 149-157.

Viana, F. A. C., Kotinda, G. I., Rade, D. A., & Steffen Jr., V. (2006). Can ants design mechanical engineering systems? In *Proceeding of 2006 IEEE Congress on Evolutionary Computation, CEC 2006*, art. no. 1688397, pp. 831-837.

Wang, J. X., & Tang, M. X. (2005). Knowledge representation in an agent-based collaborative product design environment. In *Proceedings of the 9th International Conference on Computer Supported Cooperative Work in Design*, 1, pp. 423-428.

Wang, L. H., & Shen, W. (2003). DPP: An agent-based approach for distributed process planning. *Journal of Intelligent Manufacturing, 14*, 429–439

Welbank. M. (1983). *A review of knowledge acquisition techniques for expert systems.* Ipswich: British Telecommunications Research Laboratories Technical Report.

Westkamper, E., Ritter, A., & Schaefier, C. (1999). Asimov-holonic multi-agent system for AGVs, In *Proceedings of the 2nd International Workshop on Intelligent Manufacturing Systems.*

Wooldridge, M., & Jennings, N. (1995). Intelligent agents: theory and practice. *The Knowledge Engineering Review, 10*, 115–152.

Yahia, B. N., Fnaiech, F., Abid, S., & Sassi, H. B. (2002). Manufacturing process planning application using artificial neural networks. In *Proceedings of the IEEE International Conference on Systems, Man and Cybernetics*, Yasmine Hammamet, USA.

Yao, Y., Xiong, G., Fan, W., & Fan, X. (2004). Product development process intelligent analysis and improvement. In *Proceedings of IEEE International Conference on Networking, Sensing and Control, 1*, 412-417.

Yue, Y., Ding, L., Ahmet, K, Painter, J., & Walters, M. (2002). Study of neural network techniques for computer integrated manufacturing. *Engineering Computations (Swansea, Wales) 19*(1-2), 136-157.

Zha, X. F. (2002) A knowledge intensive multi-agent framework for cooperative/collaborative design modelling and decision support of assemblies, *Knowledge-Based Systems, 15*, 493-506.

Zhang, F., Zhang, Y. F., & Nee, A. Y. C. (1997). Using genetic algorithms in process planning for job shop machining. *IEEE Transactions on Evolutionary Computation, 1*(4), 278-289.

Zhang, W. J., & Xie, S. Q. (2007). Agent technology for collaborative process planning: A review. *International Journal of Advanced Manufacturing Technology, 32*(3-4), 315-325.

Zhang. Y., & Chen. H. (1999). A knowledge-based dynamic job-scheduling in low-volume/high-variety manufacturing. *Artificial Intelligence in Engineering, 13*(3), 241-9.

Zhao, F. L., & Wu, S. Y. (1999). A cooperative framework for process planning. *International Journal of Computer Integrated Manufacturing, 12*(2), 168–178

Zhao, Y., Ridgway, K., & Al-Ahmari, A. M. A. (2002). Integration of CAD and a cutting tool selection system. *Computers and Industrial Engineering,* 42(1), 17-34.

Zou, Z., & Li, C. (2006). Integrated and events-oriented job shop scheduling. *International Journal of Advanced Manufacturing Technology, 29*(5), 551-556.

Zulkifli, A. H., & Meeran, S. (1999), Feature patterns in recognising non-interacting and interacting primitive, circular and slanting features using a neural network, *International Journal of Production Research, 37*(13), 3063-100.

Index